Contemporary Capitalism
and Mental Health

For Teasie and Lily-Rose

Contemporary Capitalism and Mental Health

Rhythms of Everyday Life

Conor Heaney

EDINBURGH
University Press

Edinburgh University Press is one of the leading university presses in the UK. We publish academic books and journals in our selected subject areas across the humanities and social sciences, combining cutting-edge scholarship with high editorial and production values to produce academic works of lasting importance. For more information visit our website: edinburghuniversitypress.com

Edinburgh University Press Ltd
13 Infirmary Street
Edinburgh EH1 1LT

First published in hardback by Edinburgh University Press 2024

Typeset in 11/13pt Bembo
by Cheshire Typesetting Ltd, Cuddington, Cheshire

A CIP record for this book is available from the British Library

ISBN 978 1 3995 2993 8 (hardback)
ISBN 978 1 3995 2994 5 (paperback)
ISBN 978 1 3995 2995 2 (webready PDF)
ISBN 978 1 3995 2996 9 (epub)

Contents

Preface

In *Contemporary Capitalism and Mental Health: Rhythms of Everyday Life*, Conor Heaney enhances ecosophical thinking by exploring its rhythms, and he has created the kind of approach that is both new and valuable for philosophers interested in the writings of Félix Guattari and Henri Lefebvre, whose conceptual innovations intersect in rhythmic ecology. Indeed, the combination of Guattarian ecosophy and Lefebvrean rhythmanalysis is a fount of inspiration. This book poses, however, a futural, virtual ecology in which the conditions for the creation of unprecedented formations of subjectivity are at stake.

The flexibility of rhythm is tantamount. It can be diagrammed and rediagrammed. Since diagrams are participatory, the kind of rhythms they lay down are neither universal nor static, but invite experimentation with, and transformation of, the world. We might call this approach ecosophical rhythmanalysis. But if we sought to diagram the rhythmic timescapes of our everyday lives, the task would be challenging, for the experience of heterogenesis, in the Guattarian sense of creative enrichment against the stultifications of homogenesis, is polyrhythmic. It is not a matter of exposing and re-presenting existing rhythms, but of making and bringing new rhythms in the plural into the world. The revolutionary critique of the everyday is a key moment here because the relation between desire and rhythm produces capitalist subjects and milieus. The rhythms of alienation in everyday life are abundant, and it is with great urgency that Heaney seeks out disalienating rhythms in a world seemingly saturated with refrain-controls and anxiety machines!

A particularly salient distinction at play throughout this book is between arrhythmia and hyperrhythmia. Arrhythmia tends towards stasis (this makes it perfectly capitalistic and homogenetic because it closes the future by attempting to manage everything) and hyperrhythmia tends towards chaos. When rhythm seeks security it decelerates chaos, while still remaining open to the future. This subtraction suggests that in tending towards chaos hyperrhythmia accelerates towards it.

What is called a salient distinction is, as Heaney specifies, more about tendencies: in the case of arrhythmia, a tight, closed-off, silent mono-rhythm that really goes nowhere. And as for hyperrhythmia, a noisy, radically open leaning into the future. Rhythm is a mixture of stability and instabilty, closedness and openness.

A rhythmanalytical critique of rhythmic subjection (producing specific types of normative subjects, i.e., depressed and anxious, and tuning all rhythms to set channels) and machinic enslavement in everyday life is valuable for exposing the question of existential refrains and their control by capital, how this works homogenetically, and what can be done about it. The subjection/enslavement relation is recoded through rhythmic processes in terms of the productions of subjectivity. Here, debt plays a major role in subjection, and asignifying semiosis emerges in enslavement as an automated-control-modulation of components (below, above and besides subjectivity, the deterritorialised bits). Heaney calls this rhythmic containment: repayment of debt, confession of inadequacy, neutralising distraction-attention ecology.

A rhythmanlaysis of desire's flows is accomplished through the lenses of the syntheses, exposing pulse patterns that steady the connections; arrestive and redirective recordings; interplays of connection, recording and the emerging subject.

Heaney is at his most inventive in the idea of scaping. Mindscaping is an inventive exploration of the mental inspired by a Guattarian approach to the overlapping three ecologies. The rhythmanalysis of tendencies is a method for sculpting concepts that qualify as a rev-olutionary practice of immanent critique. What is revolutionary is unpredictable: high-risk creativity. Aesthetic interventionism plays a significant role in recasting sensibilities in a disruptive manner by injecting new pluridirectional rhythms, and carving new openings, into dominant conditions.

In the happiness–depression ecology, the knots of depression are tight and hard to loosen beyond unsatisfactory adaptations. Sculpting a milieu therapeutics in a caring milieu, engaging role experimentation, singu-larisation, role rotation, open listening, can be built within a long-term perspective.

It is important to note that rhythmic method does not pre-exist fully formed and is thus simply applied to problems of scaping. On the contrary, scaping is a creative practice of immanent critique that only emerges through the activity of critique itself. This makes it a species of processual epistemology: contextually aware, mobile, pure (resistant to transcendence), explorimentally constructive, rhizomatic mapping.

In the distraction-attention ecology, the subjugating and enslaving features of the digiverse – social media platforms, search engines, etc. – move towards the question of the future's foreclosure. How, then, to re-sculpt processually in the long term? Processes of reversal such as disentangling the knotted capitalist homogenesis and memory, of short-termism and interruptive imagineering, are invoked. Evolutive adaption to the milieu through indifference is rejected for the transformation of the milieu by creative adoption.

Using the subjection-enslavement relation, the profound indebtedness of the mental environment is explored in depth and then contrasted with new sustainable modes of exchange. In the debt-credit ecology, one's sense of debt is continuously expanding, rhythmically subjugating the capitalist ego, temporally colonising and subordinating one to indebtedness, foreclosing the future for debtors and opening the future for creditors. Exiting from capitalism requires a de-subjection of the credit-debt relation as everyday life is thoroughly debtified, and the possibilities of sculpting alternatives are heavily curtailed. Minor experiments are introduced from copyfarleft piratage through tactical hacker fictions to striking and decolonising debt, schizopraxic collaborative enhancements and common investments; these molecular pinpricks unfurl affirmative counter-actualising processes of singularisation. Yet these openings do not preclude the reassertion of the (im)balance sheet of debt-credit.

Throughout this book there are startling glimpses of the many anti-capitalist facets of schizoanalysis, in the cracks where the rhythms allow for the gathering of strength, and patience, for the long road of processual revolution, where new caring milieus can be co-operatively sculpted, from the middle.

Contemporary Capitalism and Mental Health: Rhythms of Everyday Life is concerned with mental ecology. This brave book announces that the social and environmental ecologies will require separate volumes. What better prospect for a trilogy than the model of Guattari's tri-ecological vision in *The Three Ecologies*! Such works to be composed would provide both for the writer and readership concretised rhythms of everyday practices of philosophical engagement and reflection in the existential territories of our scholarly pursuits, the machinic phyla our outputs traverse, and the universes of ideas in which we travel together, sometimes as allies, and other times as adversaries.

Gary Genosko

Acknowledgements

This project, and its attempted experimental vein, is a result of the encouragement and support of more people than I could exhaustively list here, and to whom I have accumulated incalculable debts. First and foremost I would like to thank Iain MacKenzie, who provided both creative encouragement and a critical eye with an unmatched pedagogical flair and care. I view this text as the product of an extended conversation with Iain over the past nine years, and I was especially privileged that he agreed to co-author the postscript in this form. Charles Devellennes also needs to be thanked, as his generous readings and suggestions improved and sharpened this work in innumerable places. I would also like to extend my deepest gratitude to Gary Genosko and Connal Parsley, not just for their close reading and challenging questions regarding this work – which were hugely formative, invigorating and enriching – but also in how they have continued to offer continual support and guidance in the succeeding years. Without question, this book would not have reached this stage without them.

Those who have had to put up with me and my obsessive work patterns over the years of this project's fruition (and since) have had their patience tested. My appreciation of my parents and sister for their lifetime of support both goes without saying but also must be said; and of Kamila, with whom I have shared and will share many joys. Nor can I omit thanking Alfie.

This project was written across interactions with numerous people and in a litany of places. Conor Crummey, Hollie Mackenzie, Ben Cook, Joel Lazarus, Erzsébet Strausz, Lucas Van Milders, Jonjo Brady, Ben Turner, Rob Nagel and Jack Bridgewater supported the work and completion of this project more than they realise. A special mention, too, must go to Vinylhead in Ramsgate, who in the later stages of this project offered community, friendship, and an office on many weekends and weekdays. The entire team at EUP of course must be thanked – but I have to especially acknowledge the work of Geraldine Lyons, whose thorough copy-editing ensured that numerous slips were caught before publication. The research for this book was supported by a 50th Anniversary Scholarship at the University of Kent.

Part I

Rhythmic Ecology: An Introduction to Scaping

Introduction: Rhythm, the Map, and the Territory

The territory is not primary in relation to the qualitative mark; it is the mark that makes the territory. Functions in a territory are not primary; they presuppose a territory-producing expressiveness. In this sense, the territory, and the functions performed within it, are products of territorialization. Territorialization is an act of rhythm that has become expressive. (Deleuze and Guattari, 2013a: 367)

In the beginning is not the word. The word comes from what is expected. One writes initially through a wave of music, a ground-swell that comes from the background noise, from the whole body, maybe, and maybe from the depths of the world or through the front door, or from our latest loves, carrying its complicated rhythm, its simple beat, its melodic line, a sweet wafting, a broken fall. One cannot grip one's pen but this thing, which does not yet have a word, takes off. In the beginning is the song. (Serres, 1995: 138)

My approach to method is rhythmic. A method lays down, or maps, a rhythm. Broadly defined, for introductory purposes, a rhythm implies a temporality, or series, of iterations, repetitions, swerves, and returns. A method maps a rhythm with its assemblage of conceptual instruments. Sometimes, a method semantically defines the epistemological and onto-logical parameters and scope of analysis. More constructively, and more interestingly, a method can be a rhythmic risk, a *fiat*, or a creation. This constructive *fiat* is not an attempt at representation, but this does not make it epistemologically arbitrary. Rather, it is *aesthetically interventionist*. It is an invention-intervention of a new rhythm; sampling and remixing between and through the experiences of the past and towards expe-riences yet to come: rhythm connects. Rhythms imply relative levels of consistency and metastabilisation, but they are punctuated by holes, gaps, fissures, and cracks. Rhythms are not rigid: they can be – and are always – remixed. The creative philosopher is the disc jockey or turn-tablist of methods: through her instruments, she creates concepts and institutes a pre-conceptual plane upon which these concepts operate. She also occupies a point of view, a diagrammatic position or territory across this plane. In other words, she lays down a conceptual rhythm and composes relative levels of insistence (accentuating and emphasising certain tempos and tones and omitting others) upon a pre-conceptual plane generated by this conceptual creation. This is the triple task of method: 'Laying out, inventing, and creating constitute the philosophical trinity – diagrammatic, personalistic, and intensive features' (Deleuze and Guattari, 2013b: 77). This triple task is *immanently effectuated*. This is another way of saying the *development* of this rhythmic method is itself a *process of application*: the method is already in processual development in its explication. Creation.

Who listens to these rhythms, inventions, and creations? That cannot be predetermined in advance. Nonetheless, it will not be a universal rhythm; universality requires homogenising syntheses, while rhythm moves through flows of (relative) homogenous stabilisations and heterogeneous disruptions. Universal concepts are *arrhythmic* concepts. Indeed, as Félix Guattari argues, gestures towards universality are gestures which *foreclose* imagination and creation (1984: 36), and by extension, foreclose heterogeneity and movement, foreclosing rhythm. In addition, universal conceptual gestures omit the very diagrammatic positionality that brings those concepts to life. We cannot *measure* philosophy. This is why Guattari, with Gilles Deleuze, claims that *taste* is a regulator of invention and reception in conceptual creation: 'Taste is this power, this being-potential of the concept: it is certainly not for 'rational or reasonable' reasons [i.e. universal] that a particular concept is created or a particular component chosen' (ibid.: 78, our addition).[1]

Roland Bleiker (2001) discusses the distinction between *mimetic* and *aesthetic* methods in political theory. Whilst the former attempts to 'map the real' – statically represent or depict the real in all its reality – aesthetic methods occur in the dynamic gap *between* the real and its map. For Bleiker, academic disciplines, by nature, discipline the possibilities of mapping: disciplines define the 'methods, techniques, and instruments that are considered proper for the pursuit of knowledge' (2001: 524). Disciplines define the inside (what is proper) and outside (what is improper) of proper academic practice and exchange. *Disciplines set limits as to what kinds of rhythms are possible.* If composition is about inventing new rhythms, then disciplinary boundaries serve to condemn participants to repeating old rhythms, blocking new refrains, preventing the creation of new concepts. While this *contraction* around stable elements can often catalyse new ontological and epistemological vectors in disciplinary settings, their hardened codification can ultimately sediment and close off new vectors of potentiality. Arrhythmia. Contraction is pharmacological.

Alfred Korzybski most famously highlighted this 'map/territory' distinction: 'A map *is not* the territory it represents, but, if correct, it has a *similar structure* to the territory, which accounts for its usefulness' (1994: 58). Korzybski's is an experimental injunction: test the usefulness of your maps! Only in such testing will we know the *utility* of theory. The bare instrumentality of technics (the world as picture). Experimentation does not enable access to the territory *as such*, it can only be an indicator of the utility of the conceptual instruments that have been created. We can add a triple proviso to Korzybski here. First, is there not an unnecessarily strong ontological border assumed as existing between the map and the territory ('but, if [the map is] *correct . . .*'), as if the map and the territory could not interpenetrate and affect each other? Does he not rigidify and reify not only 'the territory' *as such*, but its inaccessibility and impenetrability? The territory has a rhythm, he seems to say, and all we can do is test the coalescence of our maps with this rhythm. Second, is his thinking perhaps too spatial ('[the map] has a *similar structure . . .*'), and not rhythmic enough? Korzybski treats maps as *static depictions* of *static reality*. Our rhythmic approach injects time, and therefore movement, into the practice of mapping. Rhythm, as we will develop in Chapter 1, can function diagrammatically and transversally; immanent mapping: the diagram as a 'germ of order or rhythm' (Deleuze, 2016: 72). Third, does Korzybski's invocation of the notion of the 'usefulness' (or *utility*) of maps as being bound up with 'correctness' not foreclose the possibility that usefulness could be related instead to other elements? Seeing as 'correctness' is an epistemological category, does Korzybski not discount that, perhaps, the usefulness of maps could be related to ontological, political, or temporal elements such as 'importance', 'problematicity', 'creativity', or 'extemporaneousness'? Our triple proviso in relation to Korzybski therefore pertains to (1) the relation between mapping and the map, which we situate as one of ecological entanglement; (2) spatialised modes of thinking which arise with the notion of 'mapping,' and in which we seek to inject time (process, rhythm); and (3) judgements or evaluations of this or that map, which we seek to broaden beyond notions of truthfulness or similarity tied to utility, towards other categories of judgement.

We will say more on the ontological, political, and temporal elements in the next chapter, but it suffices here to note that a rhythmic approach to method sees no obvious reason to presuppose an 'uncrossable border' between map and territory, such an approach striking us as too spatialised. To put this more precisely, the map (which lays down a certain rhythm) *immanently participates in the territory* in part due to its rhythmicity. If the map *immanently participates in the territory*, and the map can present us with avenues for experimentation, then, with regards to methods and concepts, the questions then become: *What does this particular rhythm allow us to do? How, if at all, does it alter our experience? How, if at all, does it enable us to transform the territory through immanent experimentation?* These questions point towards the *experimental functionality* and *ontological effects* of a method, and, therefore, not to its *static* and *spatialised epistemic depictionality*.

The questions are not ones of putative (and static) representational mimesis (or lack thereof), but rather ones of (active) experimentation and transformation. They are questions of immanent participation '*of*' or '*through*' the map '*in*' the territory. The map is not immanent *to* the territory, such a gesture would position the territory as an ontological domain transcendent to the map. Rather, the map and the territory immanently co-exist and interact. Nor is the map an 'epistemic result'; it does not push us in the direction of epistemological closure. Rather, the map is an experimental creation and is itself a practical injunction to experiment. In this way, the knowledge 'gained' from map-experimentation is not that of fixed, static, knowledge that 'is' (*à la mimetic/representative maps*). Taken ontologically and epistemologically seriously, the map asks us to experiment with and transform the world along new vectors and rhythms. The map, through its immanent participatory function (diagrammatism), can open the territory to a new future, rather than closing the territory to the confines of the past and present through gestures of static mimetic representation. Its results are not to be measured through the fixity of its knowledge-claims (epistemological assessment) but through how and in what sense it *throws the dice of thought* and performs an opening of the present (ontological effectuation). *Throwing the dice of thought* performs a double embrace: an embrace of *constructivism* and an embrace of *chance*. This will be explored in greater detail in Chapter 2, where we will develop and bend the notion of constructivism towards that of *sculpture*, 'Every thought is a Fiat, expressing a throw of the dice: constructivism [. . .] [E]very concept is a combination that did not exist before' (Deleuze and Guattari, 2013b: 75). To sum:

[1] A method lays down, or conceptually maps, a rhythm.
[2] The methodological *fiat* is *aesthetically interventionist*.
[3] The map is not the territory, but the map immanently participates in the territory. Maps, then, might help us rhythmically experiment with and transform the territory.
[4] With regards conceptual map-rhythms, they can be approached for how they embed or totalise the rhythms of the present, or how they attempt to transform them.

[5] The triple task of a rhythmic philosophical method is diagrammatic, personalistic, and intensive. The rhythmanalyst lays down a conceptual rhythm and composes relative levels of insistence (accentuating and emphasising certain tempos and tones and omitting others) upon a pre-conceptual plane *generated by* this conceptual creation.

Note

1. The invocation of *taste* here is the invocation solely of a *necessarily aesthetic dimension to thought and to conceptual determinations*, rather than a gesture towards notions of 'good' and 'bad' taste. Taste is a qualitative and aesthetic dimension of thought. In his book on Kant's oeuvre, and which centralised the role of the third Critique (the *Critique of Judgement* (2000)), Deleuze (2008) argues that, in Kant's formulation of the application of aesthetic judgement, he 'allows' for a 'free-play' of the faculties in which elements of taste are crucial. More precisely, Deleuze noted that in Kant's formulation of aesthetic judgement, there is a '*free and indeterminate accord* between faculties. This agreement defines a properly aesthetic common sense (taste)' (2008: 41).

1

Rhythm and Desire

[H]abit is not an external necessity of constraint, but a necessity of attraction and desire [. . .] Between habit and instinct, between habit and nature, the difference is merely one of degree, and this difference can always be lessened and reduced. Like effort between action and passion, habit is the dividing line, or the middle term, between will and nature; but it is a moving middle term, a dividing line that is always moving, and which advances by an imperceptible progress from one extremity and another. Habit is thus, so to speak, the infinitesimal *differential*, or, the dynamic *fluxion* from Will to Nature [. . .] Consequently, habit can be considered as a method. (Ravaisson, 2008: 57–59)

Desire, of which so much has been said (in psychic terms), is both work and the product of work. Yet it has a rhythm; it *is* a rhythm. (Lefebvre, 2015: 35)

Music dispatches molecular flows. Of course, as Messiaen says, music is not the privilege of human beings: the universe, the cosmos, is made of refrains; the question in music is that of a power of deterritorialization permeating nature, animals, the elements, and deserts as much as human beings. The question is more what is not musical in human beings, and what already is musical in nature. (Deleuze and Guattari, 2013a: 360)

We should be more precise as to what it is that constitutes *rhythm* and what the ontological implications might be through our attempt at a rhythmic method. In other words, we need a rhythmic ontology to accompany our rhythmic method. This chapter will therefore discuss Deleuze's development of the three passive syntheses of time in Chapter 2 of *Difference and Repetition*, connecting these with the three syntheses of desire which Deleuze and Guattari develop in *Anti-Oedipus*. We will situate this within our own attempt at a rhythmic ontology through introducing the revolutionary element in connection with futurity, and by articulating and defining two rhythmic tendencies (*arrhythmia* and *hyperrhythmia*) which will be used as analytical categories in Part II of this book. These are the tasks of this initial chapter, which will allow us the conceptual space to develop the method of *scaping* with more substance in Chapter 2, and make better sense of our comments in the introduction.

a. The first synthesis of the living present | the connective synthesis of production

A rhythm, at least as initially noted in the Introduction, implies a temporality, or series, of iterative repetitions: a series of interrupted but normalising periodicities. So put, the notion of rhythm is bound up with the notion of *repetition*. Our discussion of rhythm will first, therefore, require an exploration of the notion of repetition. In *Difference and Repetition*, Deleuze seeks to conceptualise repetition 'for itself', which is to say, conceptualise repetition in such a manner that is not reducible to the empirical instances that are repeated. In order to do this, his discussion of repetition first addresses the question of what it is that is required in order for there to be an instance of 'repetition' at all. The transcendental question of repetition: *what makes repetition possible?*

His answer is deceptively simple: *contraction*. Or more precisely, the *habit of contraction*. For there to be a repetition at all – say, the repetition of an empirical instance P following empirical instance Q (a P-Q conjugation or coupling), a 'tick-tock' succeeded by an empirically independent 'tick-tock', or the type of iterative repetitions that we connected with rhythm in the preface – necessitates a third element in addition to those isolated empirical instances. This third element, or process, is contraction. Contraction is the *passive* and *habitual* process by which the independent instances of P and Q are *synthesised*, are ontologically coupled, and through which the expectation that Q will follow P in the future is founded (contraction as the foundation of *expectation* or *protention*). So, in the movement of repetition there is an interplay of past, present, and future. Contraction 'contracts the past' by retaining preceding instants in the present (retention) and 'contracts the future' through the mechanism of expectation, adding a directional and purposive element to the present (protention); the past and the future are both contained in the present under the first passive synthesis. This is the first synthesis of time, the synthesis of the living present.

Of course, this is an argument indebted to David Hume. For Hume, famously, *expectation* is generated through habitually experienced

conjunctions; expectation is produced not through processes of ration-
alisation or abstraction but, for Hume at least, 'by an act of the mind,
by some instinct or mechanical tendency [. . .] [which] may be independent of all the laboured deductions of the understanding' (Hume,
2007: 40, our addition). Likewise, for Henri Bergson, our living navigation of the world, and the 'know-how' we practise is 'like a habit we
have contracted' (Bergson, 2014: 88) and is not the product of intellec-
tualisation. Jerrold J. Abrams, here discussing Charles Sanders Pierce's
famous transcendental semiotics (which Guattari independently developed on), captures this point well: 'beliefs are modes of action that *propel*
future behavior. As these modes are reinforced through repetition and
selection, they settle down into our physiology and psychology; and
ultimately become *enduring* habits (i.e., they become 'fixed')' (Abrams,
2004: 631). Deleuze terms this machinic habit which both produces
and is a practice of this 'know-how' the *first passive synthesis.* The contraction of the past and future produces the mechanism of expectation.
Importantly, this also means that *contraction is externally related to the*
terms it contracts. By this we mean that, for example, the P-Q *relation*
(their synthesis) is generated independently of the terms 'themselves',
or simply that (as Deleuze notes in his early book on Hume, *Empiricism*
and Subjectivity): 'Relations are external to their terms. This means that
ideas do not account for the nature of the operations that we perform
on them, and especially of the relations that we establish among them'
(1991: 101).

Bergson likewise affirmed the externality of relations to their terms:
'A relation is nothing outside of the intellect that relates' (2014: 198).
One of the upshots of the externality of relations to their terms pertains
to how it enables one to approach change, movement, and relation –
three terms which rhythm encompasses – in a manner that does not
reduce the relation to a determination, and therefore does not reduce
change to a negation of determination. If the terms of a relation are
given in advance, then the encounter of the relation often slides into a
structured realisation (the actualisation of the possible), belying change.
Brian Massumi argues that the externality of relations to their terms
enables the conceptualisation of change and movement to go beyond the
negation of determination (deviation, rupture, subversion) and towards
one which attends to what is produced through the coming-together of
terms in relation which are 'coderivatives of an immanent relation [. . .]
as differential emergences from a shared realm of relationality' (2002: 71).

To return to the question of contraction again: Deleuze argues,
developing on Hume and Bergson, therefore, that *passive contraction is*
a transcendental condition of repetition, and that contraction can therefore

be situated as the 'foundation' of time. Rhythm, too, can be situated in this temporal analytic. Passive contraction is the synthesisation of independent empirical instances ontologically fused into a 'flux', 'flow', or a 'living present'. Bergson calls this the experience of *duration:* a flux or flow of continuous transition. The ontology, and experience, of the *song* seems inseparable from passive contraction and this experience of flow: the song is ontologically demarcated through the synthesisation of independent, different, but interlocking temporal periodicities which *contract* into a distinct temporal object (melodic repetition, tempo, progression, and so on) (Deleuze, 2014: 94).[1] Nicolas Abraham connects this flux or flow to the rhythmising of consciousness and the processual creativity of conscious experience as such:

> Consciousness is entirely synthesis. A synthesis that is constantly forming, unforming, renewing itself [. . .] The present *retains* the past – a past that is not rigidly fixed, but capable of being recreated in a future synthesis – and *extends* toward a future in order to deliver this past to it. (Abraham, 1995: 56)

> It is clear that rhythmization, just like the apprehension of a melody, includes an act radically different from a simple encounter with the rhythm-object – an essentially creative act that, synthesizing the successive emergences, sights a phenomenon irreducible to either the mere perception of these emergences or their mechanical production: it is precisely this phenomenon that we call *rhythm*. (Ibid: 73)

However, is it fair to use the term *rhythm* when speaking of a continuity? Are rhythms not only present when there are gaps in terms, rather than continuities? Here, we are already beginning to introduce Gaston Bachelard's central criticisms of Bergsonian continuity in his *Dialectic of Duration*, which seeks, as the title suggests, to conceptualise the experience of duration not in terms of continuity, but in terms of dialectics. The text also contains a foundational contribution to rhythmanalysis, with its final chapter devoted to the theme, and which develops on the work of L. Pinheiro dos Santos, *Ritmanálise*. Introducing Bachelard's criticisms here will allow us to refine our approach to time, and our use of the term *rhythm*, before returning more closely to the first passive synthesis. More specifically, Bachelard argues that the experience of time is constituted *not* by a continuity or flow, but rather by fundamental *discontinuities* between 'willed' or 'active' time and 'lived' or 'inactive' time – the time of action and the time of inaction - perceptual-temporal experience itself becomes subject to dialectic of Being and Non-Being, respectively. Bachelard argues that it is through the dialectic of continuity (Being) and discontinuity (Non-Being) that rhythm emerges, and further that this 'rhythm of action and inaction therefore seems to us inseparable from all knowledge of time. Between two useful, fruitful events the dialectic of the useless must be in play' (Bachelard, 2016: 44). Temporal experience is the subject of a fundamental and strict hierarchy (ibid.: 63, 81) between active ('anagenic') and inactive ('catagenic') durations.

For example, consider the example of our 'know-how' of the world we mentioned above (which for Bergson is a contracted habit, and for Bachelard useless and inactive time): such know-how is marked by flows and arrests, ceaseless beginnings and ends, wherein we are constantly confronted with changing conditions which arrest our inattentive and inactive experience towards the incitation of reflection and the creation of *new* ideas and actions. *Skilled* know-how (in, for example, the instrumentalist) is only possible *through* interruption, reflection, and decision, which is also to say through *discontinuity*. As he notes, 'reflection imposes an interval of inaction and then an opposite conclusion. The action takes place through the contradiction' (ibid.: 74). Further, *expectation*, which we conceptualised above through habit and contraction, is for Bachelard an experience of negativity, of a void, paving the way for a potential movement of active thought (ibid.: 51). There are, thus, three key criticisms that Bachelard raises which will be important for us to consider, as he poses some key challenges to the conceptualisation of rhythm we are developing. First, for Bachelard, time is not at all about continuity, but about intervals, interregnums, and heterogeneity; the appearance of continuity emerges only as a result of a fundamental and, in a sense, *ceaseless and continuous rhythm of continuity and discontinuity* (ibid.: 86, 54). Second, that such discontinuities provide the dialectical condition for the emergence of 'higher' psychic activity and the production of the new as such (ibid.: 37, 71). Third, that therefore the type of habitual activity discussed in the first passive synthesis is of a 'lower' psychic order: 'Our everyday knowledge of temporal phenomena is produced by an unconscious, lazy kind of stroboscopy' (ibid.: 67). Discontinuity rather than continuity; hierarchy of psychic activity rather than immanence of psychic activity.

On the first criticism, it is of note that Deleuze's reading of Bergson interprets duration in terms of a fundamental heterogeneity, and that heterogeneity is *precisely* what is continuous in duration, not homogeneity. Duration, in Deleuze's Bergson, consists in time's ceaseless qualitative differentiation from itself (Deleuze, 1988a: 31); duration as a movement of differentiation. Taking the example of (impatiently) waiting for sugar dissolving in a glass, Deleuze notes how such impatience reveals 'other durations that beat to other rhythms, that differ in kind from mine', that is, that the sugar 'has a duration, a rhythm of duration', which, in its dissolution, 'shows how this sugar differs in kind not only from other things, but first and foremost from itself' (ibid.: 32). Eleni Ikoniadou's work, on this note, attempts to grapple with the disjuncts between human perceptions and digital rhythms, and suggests that digitality (like the sugar) confronts us with other levels of temporality (perceived passing, atomic temporality, computational temporality, etc.). Polyrhythmia:

> Rhythm is not understood as a quality or an asset belonging exclusively to an object or an entity, a sound or music (i.e., measured time), a digital or analog process, or a human being. Rather, it points to a temporal dynamism that traverses every event beyond human intentions and chronologies, and which largely remains invisible, imperceptible, hidden in analog duration. Time, as it were, *vibrates*; beneath solid structures, organized spaces, specific spatiotemporal dimensions, peoples, and events. (Ikoniadou, 2012: 272; also see Ikoniadou, 2014a: 154)

The *gap* of discontinuity is not an experience of Non-Being so much as an experience of the acceleration and decelerations of rhythms, rhythms of our own and different from our own, and of the rhythmic timescapes slower and faster than our own; that is, a continuous experience of *heterogenetic polyrhythmia*. The experience of duration is not a homogenous continuity, on this we agree with both Bachelard and Deleuze. However, the heterogeneity of time is unduly narrowed by Bachelard through its dialectical to-and-fro between Being and Non-Being. Deleuze goes further in search of heterogeneous time: 'duration divides up and does so constantly: That is why it is a *multiplicity*' (Deleuze, 1988a: 42). In other words, if, as Bachelard claims, time is marked by heterogeneity and discontinuity, then why restrict it to an oppositional form? Theorising duration in terms of a 'fundamental duality' (Bachelard, 2016: 40) is not to theorise time heterogeneously. Massumi highlights how the combination of continuity and discontinuity points us towards rhythm rather than dialectical opposition:

> The true duality is not between the subject and object [. . .] The true duality is between continuity and discontinuity (trans-situation and context). This is not a metaphysical opposition. It is a processual rhythm, in and of the world, expressing an ontological tension between manipulable objectivity and

elusively ongoing qualitative activity (*becoming*). Much useless theoretical fretting could be avoided by deflecting issues customar-
ily approached by critiquing or deconstructing the subject–object
'divide' onto pragmatic inquiry into modes of continuity and discontinuity. These also are in embrace [. . .] Continuity embraces
discontinuity as walking includes falling. (Massumi, 2002: 217)

We can develop these comments while also moving on to the notion
of hierarchy, that is, Bachelard's division between higher and lower psychic activity. Bachelard consistently notes forms of inactive and passive
thought (and, as we noted above, this includes *expectation*) as indicative
of the necessary 'negativism' (Bachelard, 2016: 50) in our experience
of time, which is nothing but a 'rhythm of *yes*'s and *no*'s' (ibid.: 33). For
Deleuze, however, Bergson's great advance was to think *difference-in-kind*
without reducing it to the negative figures of limitation or opposition.
Bachelard, no doubt, is correct to emphasise that the experience of time
is not quite one of ceaseless and uninterrupted continuity, and that it
is marked by discontinuities, breakdowns, (at times) continuities, and
accelerations; that is, by various interlocking rhythmic variations or heterogenetic polyrhythms. However, reducing such rhythmic heterogeneity to an oppositional form is but Bachelard's *imposition* of the abstract
dialectical framework *onto* his theory of time.[2] The 'gaps' between repetitions, between continuities and discontinuities, or between rhythms,
are no empty voids: they teem with virtual potentiality and are abuzz
with movements other than our own. Ikoniadou makes this precise point
by situating rhythmic approaches as being *of* this gap:

> Rhythm is a middle force that occupies the distance between
> events, hinting that there is no empty space or void waiting to be
> filled by human perception. It resides between actualized sense
> perception and the abstract virtual sphere that encompasses it [. . .]
> In this in-between milieu, perception is revealed as only a part of
> the assemblage and as affective rather than subjective. (Ikoniadou,
> 2014b: 13, 37, 73)

Or Massumi: 'Empirical grounding – the entropy, closure, and stability
of formed perception – is provisional, but a beat in a rhythm. Its solidity is continually moved, removed, and refreshed by iterations of force'
(Massumi, 2002: 160).

That the experience of time is marked by continuities, discontinuities, contractions, relaxations, accelerations, and so forth, can be easily
accepted without thereby adducing that these rhythms are in any sense

indicative of an overall oppositional structure of temporal experience.[3] This oppositional framework also lies at the heart of Bachelard's strict hierarchy of psychic activity. As such, our claim here is that we can accept and radicalise Bachelard's call for a heterogenisation of the approach to time, but in order to do so this must go beyond a dialectics of opposition and negation, and by extension beyond the psychic hierarchy it implies in his conceptualisation. Rather these interlocking processes are always enmeshed, in which phenomenology itself is partially dislodged in favour of ever-enmeshed modes of movement. With these qualifications and developments, our future uses of Bachelard will be clearer. Let us now return to our development of the first passive synthesis of time.

Recall that the passive synthesis of time is about the *habit of contraction* and the *production of expectation*, and is a response to the question of what constitutes the transcendental condition of repetition. We need not, and indeed Deleuze does not (and this is where he departs from both Hume and Bergson, and indeed, we can add, also Bachelard), limit the scope of the passive synthesis of the living present to the *perceptual experience* of the living present. Deleuze's claim is that the passive synthesis is ontologically prior to such perceptual experience, and that both Bergson and Hume do a disservice to the passive synthesis of the living present by stopping at this level of human perceptual experience (Deleuze, 2014: 96). Deleuze additionally identifies this passive synthesis as operating at the organic level: 'Every organism, in its perceptual elements, but also in its viscera, is a sum of contractions, of retentions and expectations' (ibid.: 96).[4] The living present of contractions, retentions, and expectations constitute the very habits through which life is lived. John Protevi and Massumi, usefully for our purposes, find such habits and rhythms across disparate modes, scales, and speeds of existence:

> There are thousands of rhythmic periods that compose the organic being of humans: from the long periods of childhood, puberty, adulthood, and menopause to monthly hormonal cycles to daily cycles (circadian rhythms) to heart beats and breathing cycles, all the way down to neural firing patterns. Everything has a period of repetition, everything is a habit, and each one of these repetitions forms of living present that synthesizes the retention of the past and the anticipation of the future. (Protevi, 2013: 161)

> Habit lies at the hinge of nature and these divergent process lines of culture. Habits are socially or culturally contracted. But they reside in the matter of the body, in the muscles, nerves, and skin, where they operate autonomously. Although they are contracted in

social/cultural context, they must be considered self-active auton-omies: spontaneous self-organizations that operate on a level with movements of matter. But, in that case, can't the self-organizations of matter described by chaos theory also be considered habits? Aren't they inhumanely contracted habits of matter? (Massumi, 2002: 236–237)

Life as lived becomes, on this reading, inseparable from a durative rhyth-mic negotiation and experience of heterogenetic polyrhythmia (even within the milieu that is the embrained body of the human, itself a beat-ing polyrhythmia). The rhythmic-habitual practice of the passive syn-thesis achieves 'connections between successive moments [and] produces a centre around which chaotic elements may become stabilised, the beginnings of order may crystallise, and from which the growing assem-blage may be given a direction' (Turetsky, 2004: 144, our addition). Such rhythms are processes of organisation, in other words, and it is through such rhythms, their contractions, retentions, and continual repetitions that patterns of practice can sediment, lock, or freeze. The heterogeneity can become subject to (an always unstable) taming. Habits, this is to say, can sediment or contract at different levels of tendential intensity. With a low intensity implying a loose or *liquid* habit, newly acquired or not yet necessary for the security of the milieu; a high intensity implying a tight and rigid habit, continuously repeated, felt as necessary for the security of the milieu; and between these a realm of *viscous* habits, which are settled but can be rhythmically negotiated with and through. These different intensities of acquisition and reliance upon particular habits we term differential levels of *rhythmic contraction*. Such contraction is, as we already hinted, both retentional and protentional. Rhythmic contrac-tion is made possible by the inhabited *milieu*, in which there is a co-constitution of a milieu and its diverse rhythmics; 'From chaos, *Milieus* and *Rhythms* are born' (Deleuze and Guattari, 2013a: 364).

We can intersect and develop our discussion of the first synthesis of time with a later distinction that Deleuze and Guattari will introduce, in *A Thousand Plateaus*, between 'pulse' and 'rhythm'. This is a distinction which revolves around levels of contraction, ontological security (and the attached attempt to constitute a *milieu*), and onto-communicative openness. For Deleuze and Guattari, a series of iterative repetitions can constitute a *milieu* which is both *territorialising* and, by extension, generates a (*deterritorialising*) *border* (the milieu as 'a combination of geo-graphical and historico-cultural determinations' (Stiegler, 1998: 55)). Milieus can be of different scales – the level of the human body, of society, planetary, galactic, etc. Milieus, as noted above, exhibit levels of rhythmic contraction, closure, and stability. The territorial element of iterative repetitions is the extensive element of the milieu, or which is made possible by the milieu (habits or patterns of practice), whereas its border is its intensive element. We stated this in another way above in relation to academic disciplines: iterative repetitions over time define the inside (what is proper (the milieu)) and outside (what is improper (what is beyond the milieu)) to that milieu's ontological habits or practice. Let us call this territorial-extensive element of patterns of practice – the constitution of a milieu – *pulsive*. Pulsive flows establish ontological security through connections as well as the contraction and delimitation of iterative or periodic repetitions. Or more precisely: *pulse functions to code rhythmic parameters of ontological security*. The milieu has a pulse: the milieu vibrates to its rhythmics. A pulse is a relatively frozen or relatively contracted pattern of practice. Indeed, expectation is one such relatively frozen pattern of practice; 'coding and codification are forms of event self-referentiality – the folding back of the event onto itself, towards its repetition' (Massumi, 2002: 83). In the terms of the first synthesis of time, let us say that *habits are constitutive of an ontological milieu* – 'a centre around which chaotic elements become stabilised' – and the pulsive element, here, pertains to the *level* or *intensity* of contraction and closure the milieu exhibits. The milieu's border is thereby – through certain rhythmic parameters of ontological security flowing from its pulsive element – *securitised*. As Georges Canguilhem notes (here comparatively discussing the work of Jean-Baptiste Lamarck), 'The milieu provokes the organism to orient its becoming by itself' (Canguilhem, 2008: 115). The milieu provokes *choices* under extant conditions (Stiegler, 1998: 45; Leroi-Gourhan, 1943: 13). Importantly, however, such orientation is rendered *possible* by the milieu: the milieu and its constitutive rhythms as a condition of orientation.

In the case of human milieus, it is without doubt that one of the central *conditions* and *effects* of orientation within the milieu (which we will discuss further in Chapter 3) are *technics*, taken broadly as encompassing *technical objects* and the human relationship with the inorganic as such. As Stiegler notes:

> The zootechnological relation of the human to matter is a particular case of the relation of the living to its milieu, the former passing through organized inert matter – the technical object. The singularity of the relation lies in the fact that the inert, although organized, matter *qua* the technical object itself evolves in its organization: it is therefore no longer merely inert matter, but neither is it living matter. *It is organized inorganic matter that*

transforms itself in time as living matter transforms itself in its interaction with the milieu. In addition, it becomes the interface through which the human *qua* living matter enters into relation with the milieu. (Stiegler, 1998: 49)

We will have much more to say on the question of technics. For now, however, what we wish to emphasise is that, within human milieus, the place of technics is decidedly *ambiguous:* they 'exist' within the milieu, they form an indissociable part of the milieu in which the embrained body is *thrown*, and it is in part through technics that s/he *orients* herself; technics as a condition for orientation. However, as 'organized inert matter', technics are themselves *effects* of human interaction; they therefore also emerge as an *effect of orientation:* one creates technical objects, and therefore, *one can transform the conditions of orientation (retention and protention) in the milieu* (Stiegler, 1998: 57; Hui, 2016a: 221–222).

Let us now be clearer on how we are here conceptualising this *pulsive* element. It is here where the notion of *desire* enters, too. Transversally, this notion of *pulse* can be attached to another set of claims and arguments developed by Deleuze and Guattari in their earlier work *Anti-Oedipus*. Early in this text, they centralise the question of the relationship 'between drives (*pulsions*) and symptoms' (Deleuze and Guattari, 1983a: 23). Or, in other words, the relationship between the *pulsive* (or *conative*) movement of desire and 'what is desired' (or the objects of desire), and psychic mechanisms and effects which can be produced when this pertains, for example, to the human. For Deleuze and Guattari, famously, this is a question of various *processes of production*; psychic production, economic production, and so on, in an economy or ecology of desire oozing with the 'qualitative flows of the libido' (ibid.: 66). Such production processes, no doubt, produce desiring subjects and desired objects, but what is absolutely crucial and central for Deleuze and Guattari's conceptualisation of desire and its operation are those processes themselves, which relies for them upon another set of *passive syntheses* of desire or of the unconscious. Consider the following:

If desire produces, its product is real. If desire is productive, it can be productive only in the real world and can produce only reality. Desire is the set of *passive syntheses* that engineer partial objects, flows, and bodies, and that function as units of production. The real is the end product, the result of the passive syntheses of desire as autoproduction of the unconscious. Desire does not lack anything; it does not lack its object. It is, rather, the *subject* that is missing in desire, or desire that lacks a fixed subject; there is no fixed subject unless there is repression. (Ibid.: 26)

Subjectless and objectless, this plenitudinous and Spinozist conceptualisation of desire is rather about the *production* of the subject, the object, the social, and so forth, and is inseparable from an examination of the mechanisms by which desire's pulsive movements become subject to capture, contraction, and sedimentation by certain regimes: the production of milieus and the possibilities of orientation within and between milieus. That is, the process through which what they call *desiring-machines* become subject to *codification* (ibid.: 33), a term we have already introduced, with the pulsive element of desire coding certain rhythmic parameters of ontological security. As such, mechanisms of contraction, retentions, and expectations become themselves likewise coded. Desiring-machines are those pulsive or conative engines of desire in their vast factory of the unconscious engaged in connective labour. Deleuze and Guattari term the first synthesis of desire *the connective synthesis of production*, which is here being explicated alongside the *first synthesis of the living present*. The connective synthesis of production pertains to the flows of desire, or the production of production, through which desiring-machines connect or concatenate with each other, that is, with other partial objects, continuously and ceaselessly, but in fragmentary or partial ways, creating new flows and pulsive directionalities thereby ('Desiring-machines work only when they break down, and by continually breaking down' (ibid.: 8)).[5]

This first synthesis of desire, in other words, relates the ceaseless combinatory activity of desiring-machines, how they connect, combine, and mutate, and the effects of this pulsive production process. As such, where and how one partial object and desiring-machine ends (through libidinous flows and their interruption), and another begins, is always bound up with local conditions and local contexts, local milieus, resulting in what can be described as an open and pulsive monadology (Leibniz, 1991) or *transmonadology* (Guattari, 2006: 115) of desire:

> Every 'object' presupposes the continuity of a flow; every flow, the fragmentation of the object. Doubtless each organ-machine interprets the entire world from the perspective of its own flux, from the point of view of the energy that flows from it: the eye interprets everything – speaking, understanding, shitting, fucking – in terms of seeing. But a connection with another machine is always established, along a transverse path, so that one machine interrupts the current of the other or 'sees' its own current interrupted. (Deleuze and Guattari, 1983a: 6)

Desiring-machines connect and combine their flows with other desiring-machines, contracting and sedimenting certain *pulsive patterns*. The manner in which this pulsive element can itself become subject to capture will be rendered more explicit once we move onto the next section. For now, however, we will conclude this section with some further observations on the *connective synthesis of production*. First, it is important to underline the oft-repeated point that this conceptualisation of desire is explicitly machinic, functionalist, materialist, and decidedly non-idealist. The key questions, for Deleuze and Guattari, pertains to *how desiring-machines function* – and further, how they come to function under certain regimes, within certain milieus – not what desire *means* nor what it *represents*. As such, their development of this first, and the further two syntheses of desire which we will visit in the next two sections, is concerned with isolating and determining how desire is disciplined and coded on psychic and social levels (*'social production is purely and simply desiring-production itself under certain conditions'* (ibid.: 29)), and whether or not these coding processes deploy what they term *legitimate* (immanent) or *illegitimate* (transcendent) uses of these syntheses (ibid.: 109), terminology we will follow for explicative purposes. For Deleuze and Guattari, broadly speaking, syntheses can be described as operating immanently or non-immanently. This should not be taken, of course, as a dualism, and it is more fitting to think of this distinction in terms of syntheses 'tending' to operate immanently or non-immanently. How does the *connective synthesis of production* function immanently, for Deleuze and Guattari? As was already hinted at, the pulsive flow of desire is one of connections, concatenations, interruptions, new connections, new concatenations, and so on, bound up with the connectability of partial objects, local contexts, and local milieus. This is what Deleuze and Guattari call a 'partial and nonspecific use' (ibid.: 110) of the connective synthesis of production, and which they contrast with a 'global and specific use' (ibid.: 70).

In the latter, transcendent use of the connective synthesis of production, desire, and its pulsive movements are explicated in terms not of partial objects and their connections, but rather in terms of abstract persons and their pairings (alliance). The pre-constituted egoic subject is situated, in the illegitimate and transcendent use of the connective synthesis of production, as *the* desire-*er* or locus of desire who, for example, desires familial reproduction and will therefore, depending on the overall conditions of social production, have certain illegitimate (incestuous) and legitimate (non-incestuous) objects of desire (ibid.: 71). Desire is still, here, about connections, but instead is about the connections of persons rather than its pulsive subjectless flows. Further, on this schema, desire is inseparable from a *lack* which the ego intuits as the object-cause of desire (the lack of an appropriate sexual partner) and which must be 'fulfilled'. For Deleuze and Guattari, this is a transcendent use of the connective synthesis of production insofar as it (idealistically) projects onto the positive, partial, and pulsive movement of molecular desire an image of the abstract and pre-constituted egoic person in a context of libidinous lack. Not only, in other words, is the subject of desire pre-constituted, but these desires themselves are pre-constituted. Lack and fulfilment, rather than production.

But what, more precisely, does this analytics of desire have to do with our comments on rhythm and the first synthesis of the passing present? Recall what we noted earlier: pulsive flows establish ontological security through connections as well as the contraction and delimitation of iterative or periodic repetition: *pulse functions to code rhythmic parameters of ontological security*, to which we can now add, *pulse codes the flows of desire*. The capturing of desire constitutes the capture of time and vice versa; or, more precisely, they are only ever captured together. The coding of desire's pulsive moments is also to code what patterns of practice are launched into, repeated, or avoided. As we noted above with Canguilhem, 'The milieu provokes the organism to orient its becoming by itself' (Canguilhem, 2008: 115); as such, under certain conditions, the milieu *provokes* desire to orient its becoming, i.e., those connections and concatenations it enacts, in accord with those rhythmic parameters of ontological security which have been coded. When we use this term *pulse*, or the related term *pulsive flows*, we are here discussing the rhythmic flows (and arrests) of desire through time. Desire operates temporally, its processes are heterogeneous and variable, yet nonetheless rhythmic insofar as its processes of production are marked by connections, interruptions, repetitions, and experiments, in the production of a heterogenetic polyrhythmia of desiring-machines. In addition, injecting rhythm into desire further helps us temporally conceptualise desire without *lack*, but while still recognising that desire's pulsations are constituted, to repeat, by connections and interruptions, by variable ebbs and flows, accelerations and decelerations, by interlocking and mutating rhythms. That is, by a heterogeneity. On this, Bachelard was astute: 'there is a fundamental heterogeneity at the very heart of lived, active, creative duration, and [. . .] in order to know or use time well, we must activate the rhythm of creation and destruction, of work and repose' (Bachelard, 2016: 21).

So, a rhythmanalysis of desire enables us to situate the ways in which repetitions and the contraction and codification of habits permeate our everyday lives and developmental movements. For example, Alexander Freer considers how such rhythmic movements psychoanalytically function to transform 'a stream of unmediated difference into a comprehensible form' (2015: 554). It is the production of a sensed continuity and security amidst impermanence (or rather it *makes sense* of such impermanence), and to this we can attach that an *attunement* to the risings and fallings of 'external' experience and the movements between satiated and unsatiated desires works as a *coping mechanism*:

> [R]hythm-making is an activity that grants order and stability to fluctuating stimuli, and thus constitutes a form of sense-making. Because some measure of sense is vital for our mentally healthy experience of the world, it might also be considered as a form of coping. If the perception of rhythm requires activity, it also depends upon a substrate: something moving repetitively, be it the dancer's body, the drum's skin, or the vocal chords. (Ibid.: 556)

We are thus conjoining the first synthesis of the passing present with the connective synthesis of desire, insofar as the contractive, retentive, and expectation-generating movement of the first passive synthesis is one marked by the pulsive movements of desire achieving connections, stabilisations, interruptions, repose, and repetitions. Habit, contractions, and expectations are all produced. The coding of desire's pulsive flows, and thereby patterns of practice, helps to ensure the *security* of the milieu: security entails the mobilisation of time and desire. We will now move onto the second synthesis of memory and the disjunctive synthesis of recording, where this combined reading of the syntheses of time and desire will gain more clarity.

b. The second synthesis of memory | the disjunctive synthesis of recording

Let us now turn to the second synthesis of time: the synthesis of *memory*. Turetsky's neat explanation here will help us begin: 'While the first synthesis establishes time in the present through habit, the second grounds time in the past as a condition of memory' (2004: 147). The passive synthesis of the living present raises the key question as to how the present can pass at all, or what precisely it might mean to say the present passes: how can the living and continuous flux of the present pass at all? What element enables the present to 'pass' if what is experienced is continuous flow or duration? Once again, Deleuze's answer is deceptively simple: *memory*. For the present to move, memory is an essential ontological element; memory 'constitutes the being of the past (that which causes the present to pass)' (Deleuze, 2014: 105). Memory situates the past *as past* (which means that memory takes place in the present) establishing the possibility of passage and functioning as the condition for active reflection and representation. While Deleuze calls the first synthesis the 'foundation' of time, the second synthesis is its 'ground'. The passive synthesis of memory operates through the constitution of the past *as past* and the present as *that which will pass* and functions to produce memory. It therefore envelops 'the former and the present present' as 'two asymmetrical elements of this past as such' (ibid.: 106).[6] The point we will focus on is the following: whilst the passive synthesis of the living present *contracts* distinct empirical elements into a flux or continuous present, the passive synthesis of memory positions the present as 'the most contracted degree of an entire past' (ibid.: 108).[7] The present present, under the second passive synthesis, is the *maximal contraction* of the entire past: the present present contains the entire past 'within' it. Bergson's useful metaphor for this is that of the cone: the cone here as a metaphor for the 'whole' of the past co-existing with itself at various levels of contraction and relaxation, with the tip of the cone, the present, as the *maximal contraction* of the entirety of the past in the present (ibid.: 108; Turetsky, 2004: 148). Bergson notes this with helpful clarity:

> Memory, as we have tried to prove, is not a faculty of putting away recollections in a drawer, or of inscribing them in a register. There is no register, no drawer; there is not even, properly speaking, a faculty, for a faculty works intermittently, when it will or when it can, whilst the piling up of the past upon the past goes on without relaxation. In reality, the past is preserved by itself, automatically. In its entirety, probably, it follows us at every instant; all that we have felt, thought and willed from our earliest infancy is there, leaning over the present which is about to join it, pressing against the portals of consciousness that would fain leave it outside. (Bergson, 2014: 12; also see Bergson, 2011: 196–197)

Since memory occurs in the present, this means the past is continually reconstituted in the present, (differentially) actualising different elements of the 'cone' of the past, to continue the metaphor. Though this is not to rigidify the 'cone' as such: quite the contrary. As Turetsky highlights, the past-as-cone 'is a virtual multiplicity which is also dynamic; it is continuously becoming actual, becoming present' (2004: 148). By this, we mean here that memory occurs in the present, and differentially actualises the past in the present, altering the virtual structure of the past as such. The past becomes an active element in the present ('continuously becoming') under the second passive synthesis, not a static or fixed past which 'is'.

A milieu of ontological security is one in which the pulsive flows of desire exhibit a level of contraction and sedimentation. The securitisation of the milieu involves freezing or arresting the activity of desire, or in a more minimal sense *containing* the pulsive flows of desire by subjecting it to a certain code or minimal rhythmic pattern. In other words, a milieu, insofar as it is ontologically secure, will thereby attempt to 'freeze' the virtual structure of the past; a key element of ontological security is, therefore, its relationship to and governance of *memory*, often established through *inscribing* 'what is remembered' as fixed (an attempt to establish *ontological equilibrium*). Inscription is a retentional process. This constitution of a historical-territorial milieu, obeying its *pulse*, freezes or delimit patterns of practice (high intensity rhythmic contraction) through the governance of memory and the attendant *transmission* of memory into the future: a process of *securitisation* and *reproduction of the milieu*. The process of *inscription*, as such, emerges as one of *retention*, and as a condition of *transmission* of memory (retention-protention). The governance of repetition (governance of the retention-transmission process) that is, is a process of protentional securitisation of the milieu. Guattari describes the constitution of 'hegemonic' territorial subjectivities as one in which the governance of repetition is inscribed in and between bodies and the earth through a rhythmics which establishes, and continually re-establishes (and thereby protentionally securitises), the memory of the milieu:

> [C]ollective territorialised subjectivity is hegemonic: it folds one Universe of value into another in a general movement of folding over on itself. It gives rhythm to times and spaces at the pleasure of its interior tempo, its ritual refrains [. . .] Space and time are thus never neutral receptacles; they must be accomplished, engendered by the productions of subjectivity involving chants, dances, stories about ancestors and gods . . . (Guattari, 2006: 103)

Explicating further on the questions of inscription and transmission will allow us to revisit the question of desire and move onto its second synthesis which Deleuze and Guattari develop in *Anti-Oedipus*: the disjunctive synthesis of recording. Recording is another term for inscription and, indeed, also connects to how we have been discussing terms such as 'coding' and, to an extent, 'contraction'. Recording is the process through which particular practices, habits, desires, become *inscribed* in the functioning of, say, a subject within a milieu. Coding is therefore a practice of inscription or recording, enabling the repetition of that which has been recorded. Recall how the connective synthesis of production functioned. The pulsive flows of desire, there, are made of connections, concatenations, interruptions, new connections, new concatenations, and so on, bound up with the connectability of partial objects, local contexts, and local milieus. These continuous processes of connection are *inclusive* (non-restrictive, affirmative), which is also to say that desire functions under the connective synthesis of production partially, locally, and non-oppositionally.

However, as we already noted, *contractions* and *codes* do emerge, and further, that the pulsive flows of desire do *halt* or are *arrested*; and it is here where the second synthesis of desire, the disjunctive synthesis of recording, is crucial; disjunctive syntheses reciprocate the connective syntheses, they capture connective syntheses and produce new connective syntheses (Massumi, 1992: 49–51). The arrest of flows, what is recorded, is always a singular response to the milieu in question, not reducible to the milieu but not detachable from it. This arrest of desire – through which the pulsive flows of desire are blocked, redirected, and put in reserve, channelled instead into 'anti-productive' *recording* processes which, as the term indicates, *record* desire's pulsive connections rather than continuing the production of production (Deleuze and Guattari, 1983a: 8; Holland, 1999: 28; Freud, 1961) – is the function of the disjunctive synthesis of recording, inserting these codes into new feedback loops of the first synthesis. The connective synthesis of production flowed through organs (partial objects) and their connections. As such, Deleuze and Guattari's famous term for the site of this recording process is the *body without organs*, that 'unproductive' and 'sterile [. . .] body without an image' (Deleuze and Guattari, 1983a: 8) which is a continuous agent of breakdown, blockage, disjunction, and dis-organ-isation. The disjunctive synthesis of recording therefore pertains *both* to (1) the arrest of continuous processes of production (the production of production), which is necessary for (2) the *recording* of those partial object connections of desire. The disjunctive synthesis therefore is also, crucially, itself a type of production: the production of *recording* or *inscription*. *What* is dis-organ-ised and blocked are those continuous pulsive, productive, and connective flows of desire. There is, then, a to-and-fro between production (connective syntheses) and anti-production (disjunctive syntheses), which Eugene Holland describes in terms of 'alternating rhythms of attraction and repulsion between the organ–machines and the body-without-organs' (1999: 31). Such a disorganisation and blockage of desire's inclusive and nonrestrictive flows is effectuated, for example, through psychic processes of *memory* and *repetition* (ibid.: 29), but also through a multiplicity of systems of signification, codes, and writing (Deleuze and Guattari, 1983a: 39):

> The connective synthesis of the statistical accumulation of parti-
> cles and their folding and condensation into rock was a 'produc-
> tion of production,' the creation of an individual as if from scratch.
> The end of this two-part connective synthesis of the beginning of
> a new synthesis, this time a 'production of recording': once the
> particles and their geologic pasts have been registered in a stable
> formation, more regulated perceptions and more elaborate cap-
> tures become possible: the deposit is quarried. It is inscribed in
> the balance books, recorded in the economy of capital. (Massumi,
> 1992: 49)

Again, *pace* Bachelard, this rhythm of production and anti-production is
not at all an oppositional dialectic, insofar as anti-production is itself a
process of production, namely, the production of inscription or recording. Already, the *contraction* of habit constitutes an effect of the disjunctive
synthesis's recording processes. The process of *recording* is thus a process
through which memory can become *inscribed* into the flows of desire,
enabling repetition and the contraction of habit. *Recording, therefore* – to
reiterate – *emerges as a condition for retention and transmission.* Modes of
recording are diverse, but we will now continue with one of our key
examples from earlier, namely, that of technics. As memory, technics
are *records* or *imprints* of recording processes; the 'organization of inert
matter' as a process of recording, of the production of memory. Technics,
as a condition of orientation in the milieu, constitutes for embrained
bodies material traces of *the past* of the milieu prior to their existence,
but within their milieu, and therefore as a past which is their own: 'there
is no already-there, and therefore no relation to time, without artificial
memory supports' (Stiegler, 1998: 159). Technics, as organised inorganic
matter, is the 'pursuit of life by means other than life' (ibid.: 17; also
see Haworth, 2016). Rather than simply reduced to non-productivism
or non-being, the movement of 'anti-production' in the syntheses of
desire constitutes the *production of recording*, for us the production of
technics, material traces, the sedimentation of memory. Without the
'anti-production' which the production of memory through technics
is, in other words, the human grouping's capabilities to remember and
transmit the past would be delimited to the realm of organic memory.

It is important to note that our relationship to technics becomes
inscribed, through feedback, into the habitual syntheses already discussed; this is what Gilbert Simondon calls the technical object's status of
a 'minority' in relation to the human, where the 'technical object is first
and foremost an object of utility, necessary for everyday life, belonging
to the heart of the environment where the human individual's growth

and training takes place [. . .] Technical knowledge is implicit, non-reflective, and habitual' (Simondon, 2017: 103).[8]

The sense in which this synthesis is *disjunctive* is precisely insofar as it functions through disconnections, dis-organ-isation, and interruption of the connective synthesis of production – each *recording* of an organ-connection achieved by the connective synthesis of production is therefore *itself* indicative of an arrest of desire's pulsive-connective flows and a redirection of libidinal energy (or else no recording would occur) – but it also this process which allows patterns and *retentional systems* to emerge: 'Machines attach themselves to the body without organs as so many points of disjunction, between which an entire network of new syntheses is now woven, making the surface off into co-ordinates, like a grid' (Deleuze and Guattari, 1983a: 12). This is, again, to note how the process of recording functions as a condition for transmission. We noted in section 1a that the manner in which desire's *pulsive flows* can sediment and contract, and indeed, become subject to capture, would be rendered more explicit in this section. Recall that the transcendent (non-immanent) use of the connective synthesis of production figures desire in terms of lack, but also through the pre-constituted egoic subject with pre-constituted desires. For Deleuze and Guattari, such illegitimate or exclusive uses of the connective synthesis flows first of all *from* illegitimate uses of the disjunctive synthesis of recording which then *react* on the synthesis of production and profoundly alter its connections: a feedback process between the syntheses (ibid.: 70–71). To be more specific, when the disjunctive synthesis of recording becomes coded within certain *exclusive* or *restrictive* disjunctions ('either/or') this in turn affects the connective synthesis of production, freezing or contracting its paths of connection; and it is through the *freezing* of this inscription process that the continual *transmission* of these exclusive disjunctions function ('Exclusive usage spreads like a cancer. It is not only reactive but imperialist by nature' (Massumi, 1992: 57)). This, to give their central example, is in part how the nuclear family codes desire within an Oedipal inscription and ensures the continual reproduction of its psycho-social repression (Deleuze and Guattari, 1983a: 71, 76), the inscription serves *both* as the condition for the constitution of 'complete' objects of desire and their attendant prohibition. Oedipal inscription *produces* (complete) objects of desire (which are also egoic co-ordinates or abstract persons: 'daddy-mommy-me') at the same time that it forbids them; which is also to say that the 'personal material for transgression does not exist prior to the prohibition, any more than does the form of persons' (ibid.: 71). This *displacement* of desire – a displacement insofar as it, for Deleuze and Guattari, *illegitimately* alters the function of the connective synthesis and its ceaseless connections of partial objects – is what is rendered possible by the Oedipal inscription; its *recording* process enables the transmission of psycho-social repression: 'Thus the parental or familial use of the synthesis of recording extends into a conjugal use, or an alliance use, of the connective syntheses of production' (ibid.).

These *exclusive* or *restrictive* (or, indeed, parental or familial) uses of the disjunctive synthesis of recording constitute *illegitimate* or *transcendent* uses of the disjunctive synthesis of recording. For our purposes, what is crucial is not necessarily the determination of 'legitimate' and 'illegitimate' deployments of the connective synthesis, but rather to open up the virtual field of libidinal possibilities through this critique of their exclusive deployments. Nonetheless, the distinction maps onto that of 'inclusive' or 'exclusive', whereby 'A synthesis is inclusive when it multiplies' (Massumi, 1992: 56) and 'A synthesis is exclusive when it subtracts' (ibid.: 57). Deleuze and Guattari describe the *immanent* use of this synthesis as one which is 'affirmative, nonrestrictive, inclusive' (1983a: 76). Such a use of the disjunctive synthesis of recording *still* proceeds through disjunctions, disconnections, and so forth, but one which *does not exclude 'the other' through disjunction* ('Either . . . or . . . or . . .'). Such a use of the disjunctive synthesis would be which is *constitutively open* in which difference is continuously affirmed. In *The Logic of Sense*, Deleuze developed an earlier version of the disjunctive synthesis and its affirmative uses, which is worth quoting at length:

> We speak [. . .] of an operation according to which two things or two determinations are affirmed *through* their difference [. . .] We are rather faced with a positive distance of different elements: no longer to identify two contraries with the same, but to affirm their distance as that which relates one to the other insofar as they are 'different.' [. . .] this divergence is affirmed in such a way that the *either . . . or* itself becomes a pure affirmation. Instead of a certain number of predicates being excluded from a thing in virtue of the identity of its concept, each 'thing' opens itself up to the infinity of predicates through which it passes, as it loses its center, that is, its identity as concept or as self. (Deleuze, 2004a: 197–199)

Such a use of the disjunctive synthesis of recording would, therefore, constitute quite a different relationship between the milieu and its memory, and between the milieu and desire. We will not discuss these in detail in this chapter. For now, we will briefly turn to some examples to support what we have developed so far on the importance of memory and transmission to a rhythmanalysis of milieus.

i. Social rhythms: ethno-national memorialisation, performativity, entrainment

A group of examples that we can point to is that of ritualistic public or national ceremonies or commemorations, many of which are performatively re-enacted annually. In Northern Ireland, for example, the 'Ulster-Protestant' community annually enacts certain symbolic, historical, and socio-political rituals. Collectives march along certain routes moved by metres generated in part by the musical instruments marching bands use. While we will not go into details or the specifics of these rituals, such ceremonies lend themselves easily to our rhythmic approach. These annual rituals are *retentive* rituals that are crucial in the *transmission* of memory, and to the *security* of the Ulster-Protestant community. Reconstituted through the iterative repetition of selected retentive components (garments, routes, songs, etc.), such activities are the participating Ulster-Protestant community's attempt to *repeat* (a repetition of the same), but also *transmit the desire for repetition*, and so, attain or (re)constitute ontological security (to continually constitute that territory as an Ulster-Protestant *milieu*).[9] Such marching habits contract the past insofar as they incorporate in their practice the historical element of their previous iterations: it is a practice which contracts the past, a *memorialising* practice, which participates in the present in such a way as to recall and attempt to repeat and contract rhythmic elements from the past, involving the 'selection and actualisation of rhythmic motifs' (Turetsky, 2004: 150). These marches attempt to freeze the virtual structure of the past – that is, govern memory – through *inscribing* specific meanings to symbols, narratives, and historical events. Such marching practices also contract the future insofar as they both generate the expectation of future iterations *and* function to *transmit* the desire to repeat through reacting on the connective synthesis of production. Recall that the process of *recording* is a process through which memory can become *inscribed* into the flows of desire, enabling repetition and the contraction of habit. The rhythmic parameters of ontological security in this case are the reconstitution and resignification of those historical elements these marches memorialise and the means and capabilities of future pulsed repetitions. (This amounts to saying the same thing as that any *disruptions* to such future contractive repetitions may potentially push the Ulster-Protestant assemblage to a region of ontological insecurity.) As André Leroi-Gourhan notes:

> Individuals at birth are faced with a body of traditions that belong to their ethnic group; a dialogue takes place, from childhood,

between the individual and the social organism. Tradition is as biologically indispensable to the human species as genetic conditioning is to insect societies: Ethnic survival relies on routine, the dialogue taking place produces a balance between routine and progress, routine symbolizing the capital required for the group's survival and progress the input of individual innovations toward a better survival. (1993: 228–229; Stiegler, 1998: 172)

Another indicative example of this that we will only gesture towards is Judith Butler's famous claim that *gender* is 'an identity instituted through a *stylized repetition of acts*' (1988: 519; 2006: 190). In the terms we are using, we can say that Butler's performative theory of gender ontology is one in which gender emerges as an ontological effect of a series of iterative repetitions. Gendered patterns of practice – which, for Butler, amounts to the same thing as the production of 'gender' – obey certain pulses or codes: the pulse of gender performativity functions to set rhythmic parameters of the ontological security of the grid of gender. Interpreted rhythmically, performativity – whether Butler's gender performativity, John Austin's speech-act theory (taking the specific example of the marriage ceremony), or Jacques Derrida's performative interpretation of the US Declaration of Independence – is about repetitive patterns (some continuously repeated, others constituted by exceptional moments which are then memorialised repetitively) of practice which, in their very practice, serve to territorialise and constitute a putatively ontologically secure milieu (gender identity, the marriage relationship, the legitimacy of the US state) (Austin, 1976; Derrida, 1974). Security is thereby bound up with, and indissociable from, previous, present, and future repetitions of the same; that is, continuous processes of securitisation.

The examples just given point us towards research on *human entrainment* or *rhythmic entrainment*. Research on entrainment traverses political theory, history, military studies, music theory, and neuroscience, taking examples such as the military drill as collective, intercorporeal, pulsed practices which, through continuous practice, serve to constitute ontologically secure milieus and which enable unified collective practice (McNeill, 1995; Kelso, 1995; Protevi, 2013). Entrainment is *pulsed* or *metric* group movement (Bispham, 2006: 128) which plays a role in the affective-bodily-mental regulation of groups; the regulation of the pulsive flows of desire and producing the possibility of relative temporal and affective *synchronisation* or *attunement* as well as the spread of affective contagion (Bösel, 2014; Trost, 2014). With proper entrainment, music can play a role in 'military arousal' (Bispham, 2006: 130). Protevi, for example, cites the pulsed marching practice of the Spartans before battle as a practice that rhythmically generated an affectively charged and intimidating spectacle which became absolutely essential to their warfare practices (2013: 90; Lazenby, 1985). Protevi quotes from Plutarch's famous invocation of the sight of the Spartans as:

> equally grand and terrifying when they marched in step with the rhythm of the flute, without any gap in their line of battle, and with no confusion in their souls, but calmly and cheerfully moving with the strains of their hymn into the deadly fight. Neither fear nor excessive fury is likely to possess men so disposed, but rather a firm purpose full of hope and courage. (Plutarch, 1914: 276–277)

Turetsky likewise describes entrainment as the 'tendency for an oscillating body to synchronise or lock into phase with other oscillating bodies' (2004: 145). Entrainment, in other words, performs a 'rhythmic contraction' (ibid.: 146) (the example Turetsky uses is that of the haka dance).

For Guattari, the nexus produced through the concatenation of human groupings, territories, and rhythmics (and the relationship this nexus establishes to the cosmos) is constitutive of the ever-partial production of subjectivity: different modes of subjectivation constituted by different 'rhythmics' (Guattari, 2006: 15):

> In archaic societies, it is through rhythms, chants, dances, masks, marks on the body, ground and totems, on ritual occasions and with mythical references, that other kinds of collective existential Territories are circumscribed. (Guattari, 2006: 15)

Let us now move onto our second example.

ii. Biorhythms: metabolism, genome, light

Another example that we can gesture towards is in the domain of biology: that of evolutionary development and metabolic processes, and the rhythmicity of embodied organic life. Beginning with the latter, we can situate the embodied everyday life of the human as in an ongoing processual and rhythmic entanglement with its milieu; the human body, as Yi Chen (2018: 34) notes, is a 'site of rhythm which is constituted by a myriad of materialities that are not restricted to the body'. Brian Goodwin's theoretical biology centralised rhythm to biology, noting:

> [O]rganisms are essentially rhythmic systems accounting for the universality of biological clocks. But I was interested in the spectrum

of frequencies showing that control systems oscillate, they have rhythms, the whole organism is an integrated dynamic system that works on many different frequencies. This results in the notion of homeodynamics instead of homeostasis. Instead of having physiological variables that are constant, you have variables that are rhythmic: your temperature, concentrations of substances in your blood, your heartbeat, your respiration, circadian rhythms, menstrual cycles – what is now known as chronobiology. (Goodwin, 1996: 97–98)

The body as a beating polyrhythmic nexus. Protevi identifies the practice of organisms as rhythmic-metabolic; metabolic processes are necessarily rhythmic and necessarily contain a 'memory' or a contraction of the past in these rhythmic practices. He argues that 'the essential temporal structure of any metabolism is the rhythmic production of a living present synthesizing retentions and protentions, conserved conditions and expected needs' (2013: 156). Take, further, the genome. The genome 'contains' the past: how it functions is bound up with an inscribed historicity, with its 'memory' (recall that, under the second synthesis, the present present is the *maximal contraction* of the past). In recent work in this field (West-Eberhard, 2003), for example, there has been a growing emphasis upon the notion of 'developmental plasticity'. The basic point to emphasise here is the following one: not only do genomes exhibit 'memory' – their rhythmic patterns of practice exhibit such memory through the interactions between inscriptions, retentions, and transmissions – but, in addition, evolutionary developments and mutations appear to occur non-deterministically through genomic and epigenetic factors (to name only two) in such a way that an organism's *future* developmental vectors are not only not predictable, but also such developments differentially actualise the 'memory' of that organism. Or, to put this differently, that disjunctive inscriptions need not *lock* the future of the organism into certain frozen patterns; the relationship between milieu and memory can be more open, fluid, and open to unforeseen transformations in the operation of the connective synthesis. This is to make the double point that the genome contains a 'memory' – it passively contracts its entire past in its present functioning, i.e., its rhythmic patterns of practice – and that its developmental trajectories differentially actualise this past, pushing its development in new, unforeseeable directions. Protevi goes as far as to claim that 'the genome is something akin to a musical score from which musicians draw and recombine bits and pieces while leaving a track of their actions, thus in effect rewriting the score in the very playing of it' (2013: 197; West-Eberhard, 2003: 63). Unexpressed genetic variation is thus positioned *not* as a set of pre-constituted 'possible' variations awaiting the proper conditions for their 'realisation', but instead as a process of differential actualisation which alters the virtual structure of the past in its very actualisation (Protevi, 2013: 198). Indeed, this third example already points us in the direction of the future, in the onto-logical direction of the (deterritorial) border, so to speak, to which we now turn, after a brief mention of the vital importance of *light* to the consideration of the biorhythmic.

Organic life in our cosmic locality is a downstream emanation of the Sun; and it is the Sun that has been the principal anchor around which human circadian rhythms have historically been synchronised to our planetary light/dark cycle, via intrinsically photosensitive retinal ganglion cells in the eye. The invention of *artificial* light has constituted a recent, contingent, and major daily disturbance to this ancient cycle, and in relation to which our organic sum of retentions and protentions tend to be disturbed; this is what some researchers refer to as *social jetlag* or *circadian misalignment*, whenever 'internal' organic-temporal cues are misaligned to 'external' social-temporal cues (as with, for example, shift work) (for example, see Caliandro et al., 2021).

c. The third synthesis of the future | the conjunctive synthesis of consumption-consummation

> Nature is more and better than a plan in course of realization. A plan is a term assigned to a labor: it closes the future whose form it indicates. Before the evolution of life, on the contrary, the portals of the future remain wide open. It is a creation that goes on for ever in virtue of an initial movement. (Bergson, 2014: 66)

Let us move on to the third synthesis: the synthesis of the future. Conceptualising time as 'the most radical form of change' (Deleuze, 2014: 116), the third synthesis develops on this insight of the past as a differential virtual structure. Since the present, as a contraction of habits, involves (which we know from the second synthesis) the con-stant rhythmic negotiation not with a past that 'is', but with a past that is virtual and differentially actualised through rhythmic negotiation, the future too becomes open and undetermined. Under the third synthesis, Deleuze positions the present as a state of permanent *caesura* (a break or interruption). The present contains within it the constant potential of confronting the intensive deterritorial border which can incite rhythmic transformation. If the second synthesis constitutes the 'ground' of time, the third synthesis offers us 'groundlessness, a universal ungrounding which turns upon itself and causes only the yet-to-come to return' (ibid.: 118). In other words, the third synthesis radically opens the past, present, and, thus, future. This is where Deleuze will re-conceptualise Nietzsche's notion of *the eternal return* under the third synthesis as the *eternal return of difference* (ibid.: 117). Turetsky highlights this with clarity:

> To produce something new an assemblage must become capable of dislodging the agency of habit, changing and disrupting its cycle. Moreover, what is created must become something other than a mere repetition of the same assemblage subordinated to the condition of memory. For something new to emerge, then, it must happen in a present belonging to the third synthesis [. . .] This becoming constitutes the event in which the assemblage becomes capable of changing, when it comes into its power of acting. This moment is precarious, always in danger of collapsing into incoherence or falling back into its past, into the same old forms [. . .] Relative to past forms, the synthesis creates [. . .] a difference which is extreme and excessive. (Turetsky, 2004: 153–154)

The third synthesis fits with our three examples from the previous section (that of collective practices of memorialisation constituting a rhythmic milieu and territorial assemblage of ethno-national identity; performativity which constitutes a rhythmic milieu of gender identity with ontological security; the genome's rhythmic negotiation with its immediate environment and the potential for rhythmic disruption to push it in unpredictable directions). If a milieu is threatened by ontological insecurity – i.e., if pulsive flows of desire are pushed towards the deterritorialising border (a disruption of the code) – an opportunity for *rhythmic transformation* or *risk* presents itself. Whether such an opportunity is taken or not cannot be predicted in advance, but the central point here is that rhythmic transformations can serve to establish *new* contractions, expectations, inscriptions, retentions, transmissions, and milieus, through this confrontation with the deterritorialising border (or not, as the case may be).[10] Deleuze and Guattari underline this:

> Every milieu is vibratory, in other words, a block of spacetime constituted by the periodic repetition of the component [. . .] Every milieu is coded, a code being defined by periodic repetition; but each code is in a perpetual state of transcoding or transduction. Transcoding or transduction is the manner in which one milieu serves as the basis for another, or conversely is established atop another milieu, dissipates in it or is constituted in it. The notion of the milieu is not unitary: not only does the living thing continually pass from one

milieu to another, but the milieus pass into one another; they are essentially communication. The milieus are open to chaos, which threatens them with exhaustion or intrusion. *Rhythm is the milieus' answer to chaos.* (2013a: 364, our emphasis)

Or again:

Since the associated milieu always confronts a milieu of exterior-ity with which the animal is engaged and in which it takes nec-essary risks, a *line of flight* must be preserved to enable the animal to regain its associated milieu when danger appears [i.e., re-attain ontological security] [. . .] A second kind of line of flight arises when the associated milieu is rocked by blows from the exte-rior, forcing the animal to abandon it and strike up an association with new portions of exteriority, this time leaning on its interior milieus like fragile crutches. (Ibid.: 63, our addition)

On this note, let us now return to the question of desire. Given the rhythmic interplay of the forces of production (connective synthe-sis) and anti-production or recording (disjunctive synthesis) (see Zepke, 2009: 208), the third synthesis of desire – the conjunctive synthe-sis of consumption-consummation – is focused on what *emerges* from this interplay of the production of production and the production of record-ing. What emerges is bound up with that very rhythmic interplay, and as such the effects are variable and heterogenous. We can, however, isolate various tendencies. As the term for this synthesis indicates, there is a pro-cess of consummation in the function of desire in this synthesis, which, on the part of, say, the human subject, involves a retrospective and habit-uated identification with the pulsive flows of desire and their operations in the connective and disjunctive syntheses. Or, in short, what occurs in this synthesis is the retrospective identification of the subject with the impersonal flows of desire and the particular relations that pertain between connective and disjunctive syntheses in that case; or, more pre-cisely, with what has been *recorded* or *inscribed* on the body without organs (Deleuze and Guattari, 1983a: 84–85). *How* the conjunctive synthesis of consumption-consummation functions therefore, to reiterate, will depend on the rhythmic interplay between production and anti-production, and those intensities which have been recorded on the body without organs. All of the syntheses interact in a vast process of production:

For the real truth of the matter – the glaring, sober truth that resides in delirium – is that there is no such thing as relatively independent spheres or circuits: production is immediately con-sumption and a recording process (*enregistrement*), without any sort of mediation, and the recording process and consumption directly determine production, though they do so within the production process itself. Hence everything is production: *production of pro-ductions*, of actions and of passions; *productions of recording processes*, of distributions and of co-ordinates that serve as points of ref-erence; *productions of consumptions*, of sensual pleasures, of anxi-eties, and of pain. Everything is production, since the recording processes are immediately consumed, immediately consummated, and these consumptions are directly reproduced. This is the first meaning of process as we use the term: incorporating recording and consumption within production itself, thus making them the productions of one and the same process. (Ibid.: 4)

What is recorded on the body without organs constitutes that which the emerging subject identifies herself with: 'individuations are produced only within fields of forces expressly defined by intensive vibrations [on the body without organs]' (Deleuze and Guattari, 1983a: 85, our addi-tion) or 'The subject as product claims as its own the very process that constitutes it as subject' (Holland, 1999: 34). More simply, this could be the described as the process – a process sedimented through habit – through which we come to identify ourselves with what we habitually think, desire, and do.

For Deleuze and Guattari, the 'first things' to be recorded, or dis-tributed, on the body without organs are 'races, cultures, and their gods' (1983a: 85); what is recorded on the body without organs is therefore a question of memory, that intensive field of virtuality, which functions as a sort of *historical a priori* (Foucault, 2002). The subject, therefore, emerges in the conjunctive synthesis of consumption-consummation as a *derivative* (or a *subtraction* (n-1) (Deleuze and Guattari, 2013a: 5)) from the body without organs and the intensities distributed and recorded upon it; the emergence of the subject is always a question of desire and rhythm, of the milieu and history, not simply of the family (or it is only a question of the family *insofar* as the Oedipal-nuclear family emerges from the history of the milieu, a habit we have contracted from history). As Christian Borch notes, here developing Gabriel Tarde's contributions to rhythmanalysis:

[T]he individual does not exist prior to the rhythms but, on the contrary, is produced by them and their momentarily stabilized junctions, and since the subjectification of the individual therefore changes as the rhythms and their junctions change, rhythmanalysis not merely a perspective on imitations per se, but equally a tool to demonstrate a society's dominant ways of promoting subject positions. (Borch, 2005: 94–95)

Recall in section 1b where we noted that recording on the body without organs functions as a condition for retention and transmission, and, when bound up with illegitimate (exclusive/restrictive) uses of the disjunctive synthesis, this produced a *feedback* whereby the pulsive flows of desire constitutive of the connective synthesis become themselves displaced and coded. The conjunctive synthesis, here, involves the emergent subject's identification of herself *with* those illegitimate uses of the connective and disjunctive syntheses, confusing not only the process (the pulsive flows of desire) with its effect (the subject), but also applying transcendent uses of the connective and disjunctive syntheses: 'the subject is produced as a mere residuum alongside the desiring–machines [. . .] he confuses himself with this third productive machine and with the residual reconciliation that it brings about' (Deleuze and Guattari, 1983a: 17). A key further insight that the conjunctive synthesis offers us is that *such* identifications emerge only through a retrospective identification of the subject with intensities on the body without organs, that is, they emerge from the production of the socio-historical field (Massumi, 1992: 70).[11]

So, as in the connective and disjunctive syntheses of desire, there are for Deleuze and Guattari legitimate (immanent) and illegitimate (transcendent) uses of the conjunctive synthesis. They specify two illegitimate uses. First: a *segregative use* of the conjunctive synthesis. The segregative use of the conjunctive synthesis occurs when desire invests in certain modes of group integration pertaining in the *milieu*, that is, from the available socio-historical field or the intensities distributed and inscribed on the body without organs and through technics. There are a variety of intensities thusly distributed: classes, races, sexes, genders, nationalities, religions, and so forth. This use of the conjunctive synthesis is termed *segregative* precisely insofar as the subject's retrospective self-identification with an aggregate of intensities distributed on the body without organs is executed in a segregative, exclusive, and hierarchical fashion. This pertains to, as they put it, 'the feeling of "indeed being one of us," of being part of a superior race threatened by enemies from the outside' (1983a: 103). This is the first illegitimate use of the conjunctive synthesis. Second: what they call 'a constellation of biunivocal relations' (ibid.: 100), that is, a series, constellation, or *ensemble* of *one-to-one* correspondences *between* social relations or the subject's relation to the social *and* familial figures. Such aggregates of biunivocal relations constitute a vast reductionism that crushes socio-historical complexity and effaces the extent to which the field of social possibilities of identification (such as that of the family) is itself a contingent and narrow historical product; through this second illegitimate use of the conjunctive synthesis,

> the collective agents will be interpreted as derivatives of, or substitutes for, parental figures, in a system of equivalence that rediscovers everywhere the father, the mother, and the ego [. . .] Whence the magical formula that characterizes biunivocalisation – the flattening of the polyvocal real in favor of a symbolic relationship between two articulations: so *that* is what *this* meant. (Ibid.: 101)

This second illegitimate use of the conjunctive synthesis is of particular relevance to psychoanalysis; but more generally, Deleuze and Guattari's central point on this is how the socio-economic relations of capitalism have produced such restrictive grids of identification, largely due to the nuclear family's centrality to the 'segregative reproduction of subjectivity' (Holland, 1999: 39).

How might the conjunctive synthesis function immanently, if not functioning segregatively or biunivocally? An immanent use of the conjunctive synthesis will relate to the intensity and fixity of libidinal investments emerging from the rhythmic interplay between production and anti-production. Deleuze and Guattari call the immanent stylistics of libidinal investment *nomadic* and *polyvocal*. Processual, continually processual, the subject that emerges from the immanent use of the conjunctive synthesis is 'born of each state in the series, is continually reborn of following state that determines him at a given moment, consuming-consummating all these states that cause him to be born and reborn' (1983a: 20).

How, importantly, can we link these uses of the conjunctive synthesis to the *future?* To the third synthesis of time? Bound up with the rhythmic interplay of production and anti-production, the subject(s) emerging from the conjunctive synthesis may have unconscious libidinal investments that are segregative and biunivocal, or nomadic and polyvocal; not in an oppositional sense, but rather one of tendencies, with 'paranoiac-segregative and schizonomadic' (ibid.: 105) functioning as two *poles*. These poles are indissociable from a relationship to the future. How so? The segregative pole, constituted by the seemingly fixed egoic subject (fixed race, class, nationality, etc.), protective of the ontological security proffered by such fixity; paranoia is directed towards all objects that may threaten such apparent ontological fixity, closure, and repetitive stability. It is no coincidence in this sense that Deleuze and Guattari argue that such unconscious libidinal investments are of a fascist or reactionary type (ibid.: 105). The schizonomadic pole, however, is constituted by a radical openness, continuous movement, or permanent process. Not that the schizonomadic pole is not marked by the sort of retrospective conjunctive identifications with intensities on the body without organs, but its operation is both fluid and rhythmic, constituted continuously by arrivals and departures (ibid.: 131). This is why Deleuze and Guattari argue that such unconscious libidinal investments are of a revolutionary type, with the potential to cut across all those inscribed intensities on the body without organs (races, classes, and so forth), dismantling paranoi-ac-segregative blockages, always carving out new lines of flight, *piercing* into the future and transforming the present:

> [The] schizorevolutionary type or pole [follows] the *lines of escape* of desire; breaches the wall and causes flows to move; assem-blages its machines and its groups-in-fusion in the enclaves or at the periphery [. . .] [T]he revolutionary knows that escape is revolutionary – *withdrawal, freaks* – provided one sweeps away the social cover on leaving, or causes a piece of the system to get lost in the shuffle. (Ibid.: 277, our addition)

It is through these two poles, paranoiac-segregative and schizonomadic or revolutionary, and the relation to futurity, that the distinction between *arrhythmia* and *hyperrhythmia* becomes important to explicate. Let us now turn to the final substantive section of this chapter in order to do this.

d. Arrhythmia ← → hyperrhythmia

There are two rhythmic tendencies in relation to the future that we can extract from these two 'poles' theorised by Deleuze and Guattari and which pertain to the relationship between the organism, the milieu, and rhythm (comprising past-present-future). Insofar as every 'milieu is coded, a code being defined by periodic repetition' (Deleuze and Guattari, 2013a: 364), the *limit-case* of such a rhythmic tendency towards such periodic repetition – an obsessive and repetitive practice bound up with the continual constitution of ontological security and closure in relation to past, present, and future – is one in which desire has been *captured*, subjected to illegitimate uses of the connective, disjunc-tive, and conjunctive syntheses. Periodic repetition is pulsive repetition within a milieu: it is not just time but desire that has been captured; indeed, as we already noted, the capture of desire is indissociable from the capture of time. This *limit-case* of periodic-pulsive repetition we will call *arrhythmia*. We will call *arrhythmic* those pulsive flows of desire which are *captured*, exhibiting the *minimum of rhythm* or the *maximum of rhythmic contraction* in their functioning (repetition with a *minimum* of difference, or *metre*). *Arrhythmic*, in the terms we are developing, therefore is not to be conflated with the *absence* of rhythm, but rather its metric minimum, its freezing, its resistance to multiplications of rhythm (eurhythmia, polyrhythmia). Paul Virilio makes a similar claim when he argues that 'Our societies have become arrhythmic. Or they only know one rhythm: constant acceleration. Until the crash and systemic failure' (Virilio, 2012: 27). Henri Lefebvre theorises the arrhythmic in terms of a *disturbance* which can become pathological (Lefebvre, 2015: 30); that is, as a sort of *dysrhythmia*, or condition for dysrhythmia (as if the arrhythmic could not *itself* become normalised and function according to its own minimal patterns and processes of securitisation). Instead, whilst we do not at all deny the potential constricting *effects* of arrhythmia − indeed, this will be a key argument in Part II when we mindscape the mental environment − we do not theorise the arrhythmic *in the terms of* pathology. Such a theorisation would imply the existence of a *rhythmic norm*, a sort of pre-constituted desirable harmonic arrangement of rhythms knowable in advance. As such, Lefebvre's arrhythmic does not coalesce with ours. Such a pre-constituted rhythmic norm can be called *eurhythmia*, which Chen defines as a 'harmonious relationship between assemblages' (2018: 5); for example, in the co-ordination of breath, heartbeat, and blood flow (ibid.: 75), the body can be said to be in a (metastable) eurhythmic 'state'; or when the integration of different rhythmic assemblages (embodied, technological, transport, institutional, etc.) enables the sustenance of order or function (ibid.: 157). Chen acknowledges that eurhythmia is constituted by differential relations, dependent on singular complexities and contextual materialities (ibid.: 5), and building on this, we would resist any simplistic biomedicalisation of rhythm which neatly pathologised the arrhythmic. As Canguilhem notes, the division between the normal and the pathological is notoriously problematic and ambiguous, and, further, the theorisation of the pathological itself often implies the normal as designative of 'an ideal, a positive principle of evaluation, in the sense of a prototype or a perfect form' (Canguilhem, 2008: 122). Canguilhem also clearly highlighted (1991: 200–201) how given the human's relationship to technics, that 'in order to discern what is normal or pathological for the body itself, one must look beyond the body', which for us underlines how any account of the *norm* should never remain at the level of the body, *as if* it could be separated from its milieu. The norm also has its coloniality: Frantz Fanon's *damné* are 'placed in a permanent state of exception as it stands for the negative of the norm, the very place from which the norm is created' (Sanín-Restrepo, 2016: 174).

With these provisos, for us, *arrhythmia* pertains to the overdetermination of the pulsive flows of desire, which become resistant to change and caught in a metric pattern of repetition with a minimum of difference, the 'measured repetition of equal pulses' (Bogue, 2004: 103). Arrhythmia closes the future. The segregative-paranoic pole is, no doubt, *arrhythmic*, monorhythmic (e.g., Virilio's 'constant acceleration'), resistant to qualitative transformation, desiring the future in terms of the continual repetition of the same. Indeed, in these terms, excessive order is *arrhythmic*, not eurhythmic. Abraham highlights this well in his attempt to develop a phenomenological rhythmics:

> [A]n absolutely monotonous *drumming*, is a succession that *does not advance:* the same cycle is constantly repeated, and duration – the very environment of conscious acts – marches in place. Clearly, this is not free and creative rhythmizing consciousness, but a *fascinated* consciousness, subjected to an inevitable, horizonless future. A gradual increase of volume accompanied by a shortening of the intervals can carry this fascination as far as the total abdication of freedom, to the point of the abolition of consciousness, to catalepsy or ecstasy. (Abraham, 1995: 84)

This notion of eurhythmia provides for some the possibility of a judgement of health or normality; as a notion, it names those assemblages (or integrated numbers of assemblages) which appear to 'function properly' or to produce a sense of 'order'. This effaces the extent to which the ordered and the metric do not dovetail with the rhythmic and, as we will argue later in this section, the metric and the rhythmic must be distinguished. Ordered and perpetually functioning eurhythmia runs the risk of what Deleuze calls the error of reformism and technocracy and the error of totalitarianism. It is Deleuze who here points us towards what we are developing as the entanglement of the rhythmic with the revolutionary (we will discuss this in more detail in the following chapter). It is the social reformer, technocrat, or totalitarian who knows, designates, and regulates the eurhythmic (the normal) and the dysrhythmic (the pathological):

> It is not at all the case that revolutions are determined by technical progress. Rather, they are made possible by this gap between two series, which solicits realignments of the economic and political totality in relation to the parts of the technical progress. There are

therefore two errors which in truth are one and the same: the error of reformism or technocracy, which aspires to promote or impose partial arrangements of social relations *according to the rhythm of technical achievements*; and the error of totalitarianism, which aspires to constitute a totalization of the signifiable and the known, *according to the rhythm of the social totality existing at a given moment*. The technocrat is the natural friend of the dictator – computers and dictatorship; but the revolutionary lives in the gap which separates technical progress from social totality, and inscribes there his dream of *permanent revolution*. This dream, therefore, is itself action, reality, and an effective menace to all established order; it renders possible what it dreams about. (Deleuze, 2004a: 59, our emphases)

Before turning to *hyperrhythmia*, and to be clearer on our usage of the term, we will first discuss the broad functioning of 'rhythm' between these poles of *arrhythmia* and *hyperrhythmia*, away from ascriptions of eurhythmia. If *arrhythmia* constitutes a *minimum* of rhythm, and a resistance to the multiplications of rhythm, where is rhythm in the pulsive flows of desire? For Deleuze and Guattari, *rhythms* serve a transformational function *between* coded pulses (hence their term *transcoding*) or between milieus. For there to be transformation, there must be rhythm, insofar as rhythm operates *through* open relations between 'heterogeneous space-times' (Deleuze and Guattari, 2013a: 365) (that is, between different milieus).[12] Rhythm is the *intensive* element that can produce a transformation in the extensive elements of a pulse; *rhythm operates on the border*. So, whereas *arrhythmia* is the periodic repetition of pre-defined extensive spacetime elements which serves to securitise the territorialised milieu, rhythm is the transformative or *differential* element which deterritorialises: it is the affirmative response to the confrontation with ontological insecurity (the border). Ilya Prigogine and Isabelle Stengers make the same point using the language of 'equilibrium' and 'non-equilibrium' (or dissipative) ontological structures. Structures (assemblages) which appear to be operating near equilibrium conditions are structures which behave *repetitively*. What might such equilibrium conditions be? In short: ontological closure (a frozen virtual structure of the past and future), security, and relatively frozen rhythmic parameters. Structures that appear to be operating in what they call 'far-from-equilibrium' conditions, however, generate new reactions and relations in what they explicitly call a 'rhythmical fashion', where a rhythmical fashion is identified (precisely as in Deleuze and Guattari) with open relations with external milieus and with a degree of *ontological openness* (Prigogine and Stengers, 1984: 13–14). At the same time, rhythm's intensive-transformational function still nonetheless *holds together:* rhythm is both an index of *transformation* and *stability*, *duration* and sustainable concretisation. This is why rhythm is not simply a leap into chaos, and why it is precisely an *answer* to chaos. What matters in the creation of new milieus, new worlds, new ways of life, is the 'mutant rhythmic impetus of temporalization able to hold together the heterogenous components of a new existential edifice' (Guattari, 2006: 20).

Now, let us add our second limit tendency: *hyperrhythmia.* To reiterate, these are distinct – not oppositional – *tendencies* of rhythm. If *arrhythmia* is constituted by the periodic, metric, and compulsive repetition of the same (repetition with a minimum of difference) bound up with ontological security and closure, then *hyperrhythmia* can be positively and inversely defined as *chaotic.* This is not to say that hyperrhythm *is* chaos, but rather to make the smaller definitional claim that *hyperrhythm tends towards chaos.* A radical ontological openness is what marks hyperrhythmic chaos; milieus cannot withstand hyperrhythmia, insofar as such a relation is destructive to the possibility of any secure milieu, any home: 'milieus are open to chaos, which threatens them with exhaustion or intrusion. *Rhythm is the milieus' answer to chaos'* (Deleuze and Guattari, 2013a: 364, our emphasis). Desire is not captured, coded, or blocked in the case of hyperrhythmia; its pulsive flows are not restricted, not blocked, and are in a process of continuous self-differentiation. The schizonomadic pole is *hyperrhythmic* in its openness, its relationship to the future is one of groundlessness. Rhythm is an *answer* to chaos precisely in the sense that it generates *some* stable parameters of ontological security, some habits, some contractions, some relationship to the past, present, and future; rhythm not only is necessary to the construction and securitisation of milieus, however partial, but is also that which allows milieus to connect and transform. Rhythms are 'between' repetition and difference – between the maintenance of ontological security, the new, risky, line of flight, and open abandonment of security; between, this is to say, arrhythmia and hyperrhythmic chaos: 'What chaos and rhythm have in common is in the in-between – between two milieus, rhythm-chaos or the chaosmos' (ibid.: 364). Hyperrhythmia neither repeats nor contracts, or only does so minimally. Just as *arrhythmia* is constituted by repetition with a minimum of difference and rigid contractions of the flows of desire, *hyperrhythmia* is constituted by the *minimum* of repetition, the *maximum* of difference, its repetitions and contractions are *porous*, permeable, and filled with (virtual or plenitudinous) *lacunae.* Hyperrhythmia can, in this sense, be positively defined as *noise*, the multiplicity of multiplicities, the virtual, the heterogeneous procession of process, that *chaos* from which rhythm is produced as a metastable, or unstable, temporary order. Michel Serres:

> Background noise, stable and unstable, does without sense, it is the non-sense of sense or the absence of sense, because it is going, locally, every which way: everything flies. Everything is going from everywhere in every direction and refracting everywhere. (Serres, 1995: 63)

Order subtracts from the noise, introduces a redundancy, repetition, or feedback loop; or more precisely, we designate as ordered that which is not noise, we designate as ordered that which exhibits redundancy and repetition ('Cognition is subtraction of the noise received and of the noise made by the subject' (ibid.: 61)). Language: the (always already musical) subtraction, extraction, or creation of rhythm and repetition from the noisy murmurings and cries of the species (ibid.: 70). Reflection: a looping rhythm of thought escaping the noise of directionless (noisy) thought. Hyperrhythmia tends towards the *minimum* of redundancy or repetition, and arrhythmia towards the 'maximum limits of redundancy, totally ordered' (ibid.: 117). The noise and the chaos, the noisy chaos, or the chaos of noise (although, of course, noise is not at all an acoustic phenomenon, it is not loudness, nor can it simply be reduced to an error in transmission (cybernetics) (Malaspina, 2014: 52)) is positively and constitutively open, and is the multiple from which codes (closures) are created; it is not *non-repetitive*, it is *open* to repetition, not eliminating the possibility of repetition (Serres, 1995: 117). In this sense, we cannot at all reduce noise, chaos, or hyperrhythmia as *secondary* to the signal, order, or information, for one cannot have the latter without a murmuring of the former. Serres calls this minimum redundancy, the minimal repetition, or the minimal order from the background of noise the *echo*. As such, while there can be said to be (in an ambiguous sense) an inverse relation between *noise* and *redundancy* – less noise as equalling more redundancy, more clarity and closure in the message transmitted, more information (Malaspina, 2014: 54) – this would be to prioritise order over disorder, it would be to subject disorder, chaos, noise, or hyperrhythmia to *closure*, as simply the negative of the ordered, and as *in principle* eradicable *if only* we could eliminate noise, *as if* we could escape chaos. Deleuze and Guattari note how, in language, the relation between the statement and the act is a 'relation of *redundancy*' (2013a: 92): language involves the redundant-repetitive transmission of order words (common sense). This redundancy of language is its (never complete) tendency to *tend* towards a paranoiac flight from that through which it is constituted, namely, noise:

'The most general schema of information science posits in principle an ideal state of maximum information and makes redundancy merely a limitative condition serving to decrease this theoretical maximum in order to prevent it from being drowned out in noise' (ibid.: 92). The flight which sees us flee away from ambiguity, chaos, noise, and change is the paranoiac dream of stasis, absence of process, and elimination of doubt (final methodological and epistemological closure). No rhythm or time is allowed into this paranoiac dream in which philosophy is but a functionary of truth moving along a straight methodological path. To open to the noise is to open to the future, insofar as to open to noise is to escape from excess repetition, closure, and redundancy; time as a multiplicity, the third synthesis of time and its groundlessness ('Nothing divides and multiples the individual so much as its own relation to the future' (Massumi, 2015b: 9)). Serres again:

> Chaos is open, it gapes wide, it is not a closed system. In order to code, one has to close, in order to class, one has to define, or shut off with a boundary. Chaos is patent. It is not a system, it is multiplicity. It is multiple, unexpected [. . .] Chaos is nebulous. It does not flow out with a point or a direction, or following some rule, or abiding by some law. Look how much trouble we have thinking or seeing it. The whole of reason protests – I mean logically. Our whole classified rationality, all the coding, habits and methods, lead us to speak in externals or negotiations: outlaw and nonsense. But I say positive chaos. (Serres, 1995: 98)

Rhythm takes hold of, negotiates with, and temporarily manages this noise or chaos without becoming subsumed in its extremities:

> [C]haosmosis does not oscillate mechanically between zero and infinity, being and nothingness, order and disorder: it rebounds and irrupts on states of things, bodies and the autopoietic nuclei it uses as a support for deterritorialisation; it is relative chaotisation in the confrontation with heterogeneous states of complexity. (Guattari, 2006: 112)

While the milieu could not subsist if it were to tend towards hyper-rhythmia, this does not at all indicate that the milieu is the opposite of chaos. Chaos, rather, 'is the milieu of all milieus' (Deleuze and Guattari, 2013a: 364), and it is through rhythm that milieus can pierce chaos and create connections, inscriptions, and stability *between* milieus. That is, it is through rhythm that *new* milieus can be created. Rhythm pierces into the future while retaining a level of security, a 'stabilisation, localisation and rhythmisation of decelerating chaosmic stases and strata' (Guattari, 2006: 111). Rhythm closes off from chaos, though remains open to it: rhythm is a mixture (a remix). *Arrhythmia* is that attempt to close off from chaos and noise, the dream of silence or methodological closure.

Let us take some musical examples. First, that of improvisational jazz. We noted above, in relation to the first synthesis of time, that the song is ontologically demarcated through the synthesisation of independent, different, but interlocking temporal periodicities (melody, tempo, progression, and so on). The ontology of the song is inseparable from the type of rhythmic contraction its experience effectuates; and indeed, usually, the borders – those rhythmic parameters of ontological security – it contracts, book-ending it. Improvisational jazz is an open confrontation with the ontology of the song. As Eugene Holland notes, 'improvisational jazz repudiates "reproducing" [the same] in favour of following or indeed creating [. . .] jazz bands intentionally depart from what is already known in order to improvise and create something new' (2004: 26, our addition). Improvisational jazz creates the new, and becomes rhythmic, by confronting the present as a site of permanent caesura, as an opening, as in Deleuze's third synthesis of time. This point is what permits Deleuze and Guattari to make the following ethico-political claim about the distinction between rhythm and metre:

> Meter, whether regular or not, assumes a coded form whose unit of measurement may vary, but in a noncommunicating milieu, whereas rhythm is the Unequal or the Incommensurable that is always undergoing transcoding. Meter is dogmatic, but rhythm is critical; it ties together critical moments, or ties itself together in passing from one milieu to another. (2013a: 365)

It is not initially clear, however, whether jazz, and its improvisational extensions, would fit within the schema of meter and rhythm that Deleuze and Guattari develop. They lean heavily on the work of Olivier Messiaen, for whom the notion of rhythm was so central to his studies and works on rhythm as well as his compositions. Messiaen argues that 'nothing is less rhythmic than the military march', a point which Deleuze and Guattari repeat (Messiaen, 1994: 68; Deleuze and Guattari, 2013a: 365). For Messiaen, 'rhythmic music is music that scorns repetition, squareness, and equal divisions, and that is inspired by the movements of nature, movements of free and unequal durations' (Messiaen, 1994: 67).[13] Insofar as jazz still operates upon a background of equal note-values, Messiaen argues, even its creative, experimental, and improvisational elements of syncopation still do not escape the *arrhythmic* metric repetition which serves as its foundation (ibid.: 68). However, it is through developing on this point that we must differentiate our approach from Deleuze, Guattari, and Messiaen; namely, on this vaguely moralistic distinction between metre and rhythm. This is for two reasons. First, it is not at all clear why rhythmic music must 'scorn' repetition, and in effect, Messiaen's claim here, in our terms, is that only that which tends towards the hyperrhythmic qualifies as rhythmic music ('movements of free and unequal durations'). We have suggested, to the contrary, that rhythm *requires* an element of repetition – contraction – and by extension that even if hyperrhythmic music would *tend* towards chaos, it would still itself harbour (however minimal) repetitions. This would not at all render Messiaen's music non-rhythmic; the point is rather the reverse, that Messiaen – and Deleuze and Guattari in this particular case – risk excluding too much when they divorce the repetitive from the rhythmic. It is here where Deleuze and Guattari appear to *dialecticise* the relationship between metre and rhythm; as if metre was only the negative of rhythm.[14]

Second, developing on this issue, Steve Goodman notes how the process of syncopation atop a seemingly repetitive and arrhythmic beat is vital to 'Afro-diasporic rhythmic pragmatics' (Goodman, 2012: 116; also see Chernoff, 1981), and that such rhythmic work cannot be reduced to the sort of dogmatic metrics which Deleuze and Guattari, through Messiaen, claim. In the same vein, Jean-Godefroy Bidima argues that Deleuze's musical foci do not take into account the minor traditions that, for example, existed in France at that time. He cites *Zouk* music which grew in popularity in the early 1980s in France, and which, according to Bidima, 'deterritorialises the French language through the revision of vocabulary and syntax' through the collective rhythmic articulation of Caribbean identity in France (Bidima, 2004: 189).[15] A similar rhythmic-linguistic deterritorialisation is likewise practised in its own sense by hip-hop (one need only listen to Big L's *Ebonics*); atop of minimal, looping 808 drums (i.e., the *Roland TR-808* drum machine), those minimal beats foundational to hip-hop have helped to, and continue to help, transform the soundscape of contemporary music (to take just one example). Both jazz and hip-hop actualise this element of syncopation in distinct ways, in a manner – *pace* Messiaen – which does not at all reduce such music to a negative of rhythm. Erik Davis, here discussing the polyrhythmic syncopating experiments of what he calls the 'Black Electronic' (in which he includes dub, jungle, and hip-hop, and which is a term he develops from Paul Gilroy's (1993) work on the *Black Atlantic*), notes the following:

The game is to push the beats to the edge of bifurcation without allowing them to settle into a singular basin of attraction. For listeners that means remaining constantly open to productive chaos: to the disorienting surprise of beats struck earlier than expected, or to the little voids that open up when beats are unpredictably dropped out – an experience Chernoff brilliantly likens to missing a step on a staircase. (Davis, 1996; also see Goodman, 2012: 116)

We resist this (vaguely moralised and dialecticised) distinction between rhythm and metre, therefore, for the reasons already outlined, and also insofar as such a distinction would allow us only to situate the 'truly' rhythmic as that which 'scorns' repetition. Recall what we noted at the beginning of the previous section on the operation at the border of a milieu as both a threat to its ontological security and an opportunity for rhythmic transformation. Pushing beats to the 'edge of bifurcation' and, through an affirmative confrontation with this border or edge, new connections, inscriptions, and transmissions can be produced. Upon a repetitive beat, the new can emerge. No difference without repetition, no repetition without difference. Davis's claims here will also further help us develop and refine our approach to arrhythmia, rhythm, and hyper-rhythmia. Rhythms, to reiterate, are 'between' repetition and difference – between the maintenance of ontological security and a new, risky, line of flight, between the 'already known' and the 'new' – and *arrhythmic* music secures itself in the safety of the repetition of the same, of the maintenance of security, of the already known. Messiaen, Deleuze, and Guattari underplay and underestimate the extent to which syncopation and other forms of temporal experimentation atop repetitive or looping beats can themselves inject *rhythm* into what they seem to charge with *arrhythmia*. Syncopation constitutes the permanent possibility of a *rhythmic risk*, of the carving out of a new line of flight which can transform the milieu through that very carving. Even the arrhythmic military march, this is to say, contains the possibility of *rhythmic* syncopation, of a self-differentiation, of a rhythmic transformation of the movements, directionalities, and functions of those bodies and their collective equipment (Guattari, 2016: 11–14). The gathering of bodies is always both political and rhythmic: from the pedestrian everyday, to the spectacular and symbolic (rituals, ceremonies), to the seemingly chaotic (the state of emergency, the riot).

Arrhythmia as minimal metric repetition, as a pattern a key function of which is to retain ontological security within its narrow parameters of variation into the future (Protevi, 2013: 88; Bispham, 2006: 131), and which *resists* rhythmic multiplication and transformation in order to retain this *ontological closure*. Rhythmic syncopation can function as a transformational movement whereby the element of rhythm is injected into metric repetition, and whereby the minimal elements of a repetitive or looping beat can function as a rhythmic differentiator, opening a sonic motif onto a heterogenetic soundscape which is anything but *arrhythmic*. Discussing Jamaican dancehall music, Goodman discusses the hyperactive and ever-transforming methods of 'riff replication and mutation' (2012: 161), or how 'whole sonic microcultures [breed] out of one core loop' which are to be found in, for example, the *Greensleeves Rhythm Album* series (ibid., our addition). Even though these beats may oftentimes be minimal, repetitive, and looping – all the ingredients for Messiaen's arrhythmic – it is difficult to imagine another sonic movement itself so marked by movement, change, and rhythm. For Bergson, immersion in 'pure duration' is to immerse oneself at the ontological border of the milieu, wherein the actant in question concentrates 'itself in a point, or rather a sharp edge, pressed against the future and cutting into it unceasingly' (2014: 118); the heterogenetic movements of Jamaican dancehall are a clear case of such ceaseless cutting and transformation, a rhythmic Bergsonian sculpturing rasp, or what Stiegler calls the transformations between thought and practice towards new decisions and selections that are 'slices *into* becoming, [which carve] *into* [becoming] in order to carve *out* a future, that is, a protention that is *desirable*' (Stiegler, 2017a: 136, our additions). To inject a new rhythm into the pulsive flows of desire amounts to an attempt at *ontological destabilisation*, but it is also a constructive or *sculptural* gesture towards the future, potentially pushing the milieu's pulse towards its deterritorialising border, hence why we can call such a movement a *rhythmic risk*: *to attempt a rhythmic risk amounts to an attempt to 'cut into' the future and sculpt it anew.*

e. Chapter 1 reprise

[6] *Passive contraction is a transcendental condition of repetition.*
[7] Habits can sediment or contract at different levels of tendential intensity. With a low intensity implying a loose or *liquid* habit, newly acquired or not yet necessary for the security of the milieu; a high intensity implying a tight and rigid habit, continuously repeated, felt as necessary for the security of the milieu; and between these a realm of *viscous* habits, which are settled but can be rhythmically negotiated with and through. These are different intensities of *rhythmic contraction*.
[8] A series of iterative repetitions constitutes an ontological *milieu* which is both *territorialising* and, by extension, generates a *deterritorialising border*. The milieu necessarily exhibits a level of rhythmic contraction; all of which is a process of *securitisation*.

[9] Desiring-machines connect and combine their pulsive flows with other desiring-machines, contracting and sedimenting certain *pulsive patterns.*

[10] Pulsive flows establish ontological security through connections as well as the contraction and delimitation of iterative or periodic repetition: *pulse functions to code rhythmic parameters of ontological security*; and, further, *pulse codes the flows of desire.* The coding of desire's pulsive moments is also to code what patterns of practice are launched into, repeated, or avoided.

[11] When we use this term *pulse*, or the related term *pulsive flows*, we are here discussing the rhythmic flows (and arrests) of desire. Desire operates temporally, its processes are heterogeneous and variable, yet nonetheless rhythmic insofar as its processes of production are marked by connections, interruptions, repetitions, and experiments, in the production of a heterogenetic polyrhythmia of desiring-machines.

[12] Conjoining the first synthesis of the passing present with the connective synthesis of desire involves examining the contractive, retentive, and expectation-generating movement of the first passive synthesis as processes marked by the pulsive movements of desire achieving connections, stabilisations, interruptions, repose, and repetitions. Habit, contractions, and expectations are all produced. The coding of desire's pulsive flows, and thereby patterns of practice, helps to ensure the *security* of the milieu.

[13] The passive synthesis of memory operates through the constitution of the past *as past* and the present as *that which will pass* and become accessible to memory in the future.

[14] The present present, under the second passive synthesis, is the *maximal contraction* of the entire past: the present present contains the entire past 'within' it.

[15] Memory occurs in the present, and differentially actualises the past in the present, altering the virtual structure of the past as such. The past becomes an active element in the present ('continuously becoming') under the second passive synthesis, not a static or fixed past which 'is'.

[16] Recording is the process through which particular practices, habits, desires, become *inscribed* in the functioning of, say, a subject within a milieu. Coding is therefore a practice of inscription or recording, enabling the repetition of that which has been recorded.

[17] The process of *recording* is thus a process through which memory can become *inscribed* into the flows of desire, enabling repetition and the contraction of habit. *Recording, therefore* – to reiterate – *emerges as a condition for retention and transmission.*

[18] When the disjunctive synthesis of recording becomes coded within certain *exclusive* or *restrictive* disjunctions, this in turn affects the

connective synthesis of production, freezing or contracting its paths of connection. It is through the *freezing* of inscription that the continual *transmission* of these exclusive disjunctions function.

[19] Whereas the second synthesis *grounds* time in memory, the third synthesis offers us *groundlessness*. In other words, the third synthesis radically opens the past, present, and thus, future.

[20] The conjunctive synthesis is concerned with the *emergence* of the subject, who identifies herself with the impersonal flows of desire and the particular relations that pertain between connective and disjunctive syntheses in that case; or, more precisely, with what has been *recorded* or *inscribed* on the body without organs.

[21] Bound up with the rhythmic interplay of production and anti-production, the subject(s) emerging from the conjunctive synthesis may have unconscious libidinal investments that are segregative and biunivocal, or nomadic and polyvocal. These poles are indissociable from a relationship to the future. The segregative pole, constituted by the seemingly fixed egoic subject, protective of the ontological security proffered by such fixity; paranoia is directed towards all objects that may threaten such apparent ontological fixity, closure, and repetitive stability. The schizonomadic pole is constituted by a radical openness, continuous movement, or permanent process. These poles also transversally connect to two *rhythmic tendencies*: arrhythmia and hyperrhythmia.

[22] We will call *arrhythmic* those pulsive flows of desire which are *captured*, exhibiting the *minimum of rhythm* or the *maximum of rhythmic contraction* in their functioning (repetition with a *minimum* of difference, or *metre*). Arrhythmia freezes the virtual structure of the past, delimits patterns of practice in the present, and so *forecloses* the future. *Arrhythmic* therefore is not to be conflated with the *absence* of rhythm, but rather its metric minimum, its freezing, its resistance to multiplications of rhythm (eurhythmia, polyrhythmia).

[23] If *arrhythmia* is constituted by the periodic, metric, and compulsive repetition of the same (repetition with a minimum of difference) bound up with ontological security and closure, then *hyperrhythmia* can be positively and inversely defined as *chaotic*. This is not to say that hyperrhythm *is* chaos, but rather that *hyperrhythm tends towards chaos*. A radical ontological openness is what marks hyperrhythmic chaos; milieus cannot withstand hyperrhythmia, insofar as such a relation is destructive to the possibility of any secure milieu, any home. The schizonomadic pole is *hyperrhythmic* in its openness, its relationship to the future is one of groundlessness. Hyperrhythmia neither repeats nor contracts, or only does so minimally; *hyperrhythmia* is constituted by the *minimum* of repetition, the *maximum* of difference, its repetitions and contractions are

porous, permeable, and filled with *lacunae*; desire ceaselessly, which is to say hyperrhythmically, making connections.

[24] Rhythm is an *answer* to chaos precisely in the sense that it generates *some* stable parameters of ontological security, some habits, some contractions, some relationship to the past, present, and future; rhythm not only is necessary to the construction and securitisation of milieus, however partial, but is also that which allows milieus to connect and transform. Rhythm is the *intensive* element that can produce a transformation; *it operates on the border*. Rhythms are 'between' repetition and difference – between the maintenance of ontological security, the new, risky, line of flight, and open abandonment of security; between arrhythmia and hyperrhythmic chaos. Rhythm pierces into the future while retaining a level of security.

[25] To inject a new rhythm into the pulsive flows of desire amounts to an attempt at *ontological destabilisation*, but it is also a constructive or *sculptural* gesture towards the future, *to attempt a rhythmic risk amounts to an attempt to 'cut into' the future and sculpt it anew.*

Notes

1. Although not discussing this issue, Jaron Lanier captures this point precisely: 'Music is no longer a nutrient to be supplied, but something more mystical, a forge of meaning and identity: *the realization of flow in life*' (2013: 20, our emphasis).

2. As Deleuze notes, 'The heart of Bergson's project is to think differences in kind independently of all forms of negation: There are differences in being and yet nothing negative. Negation always involves abstract concepts that are much too general' (1988a: 46). It is also of note that Bachelard criticises Bergson on precisely these grounds throughout *Dialectic of Duration*, i.e., of an imposition of a framework *onto* the experience of time in his reading of Bergson's theory of continuity.

3. Interestingly, recent research in empirical psychology has, too, contributed to this discussion. Commenting on the work of Ap Dijksterhuis (2004), Nicholas Carr notes how this research indicates that 'breaks' in attention – the site of Bachelardian non-being – can often be sites of unconscious thought and problem-solving which, when a problem is clearly performed, often 'out perform' sustained 'conscious' problem-solving (Carr, 2010: 119). The 'break' is therefore a virtual multiplicity, not a void: a site teeming with different movements of thought.

4. This is not a *reductive* gesture by Deleuze, precisely because the patterns of contraction, retention, and expectation are not themselves homogeneous. Quite to the contrary, these patterns are intensely heterogeneous: 'The duration of an organism's present, or of its various presents, will vary

according to the natural contractile range of its contemplative souls' (2014: 101). It is, however, a *naturalist* gesture.

5. Bachelard made the same point, although filtered through his dialectical framework, when he noted that 'A function cannot be permanent; it has to be succeeded by a period of non-functioning since energy diminishes as soon as it is expended' (2016: 32).

6. In the original French, this distinction corresponds to that between *la synthèse passive de l'habitude* (which constitutes *le présent vivant*) and *la synthèse passive de la memoire* (which constitutes *le passé pur*): 'Alors que la synthèse passive de l'habitude constitue le présent vivant dans le temps, et fait du passé et du futur les deux éléments asymétriques de ce présent, la synthèse passive de la mémoire constitue le passé pur dans le temps, et fait de l'ancien présent et de l'actuel (donc du présent dans la reproduction et du futur dans la réflexion) les deux éléments asymétriques de ce passé comme tel' (Deleuze, 1968: 110).

7. In this second chapter of *Difference and Repetition*, Deleuze explores with Bergson some paradoxes of time in the development of his ontology of time. Although these are beyond the scope of this chapter to explore, they are important aspects of his development of a non-representationalist account of memory, and of the role of the virtual in the present. For a more detailed exploration of this, see Al-Saji (2004).

8. Proviso: while our focus will consistently be on the human-technical relationship, this is not at all a manoeuvre which reinstates anthropocentrism through the guise of a techno-ontology or which restricts *technics* to *anthropos*. Discussing this question, Keith Ansell Pearson has forcefully argued how such a techno-ontology 'overlooks the simple fact that the genesis of the human is not only a technogenesis but equally, and more importantly, a *bio-technogenesis*' (1997: 182). Indeed, the conceptualisation of desire as *machinic* in Deleuze and Guattari is a move which always already institutes the machinic and technical alongside and entangled with the biological and organic, an imbrication of the organic and inorganic analysed through 'differential rhythms and affective intensities' (ibid.: 183). Neither the human nor the organic monopolises the technical: 'Deleuze and Guattari's most radical gesture is to suggest that there has never been purely "biological" evolution, since "evolution" is technics, nothing but technics [. . .] In nature there is invention (technics)' (ibid.: 183–191).

9. For an interesting Louis Althusser-inspired discussion of Ulster-Protestant identity, see Finlayson (1996).

10. Indeed, cannot *Gender Trouble* be read as Butler's attempt to incite feminism to confront this deterritorialising border affirmatively? In any case, this is how we can read her claim that: 'it may be time to entertain a radical critique that seeks to free feminist theory from the necessity of having to construct a single or abiding ground which is invariably contested by those identity positions or anti-identity positions that it invariably excludes' (2006: 7).

11. No doubt, Deleuze and Guattari's claims on this point vibrate to a similar rhythm to the Foucault of *The Order of Things*, who famously argued on the historicity of the modern subject (Foucault, 2002: 330–374).

12. It should be noted that the sense in which Deleuze and Guattari use the term 'communication' here is distinct from the sense in which they use it in their later work *What is Philosophy?* (which we will discuss in the next chapter). For the purposes of this chapter, and to avoid confusion in the next, we here use the term 'open relations' (transduction or transcoding) to highlight inter-milieu transcoding or transduction *rather than* communication.

13. In Émile Benveniste's *Problems in General Linguistics* there is a famous discussion of the development of the notion, idea, or concept of *rhythm* tracing its etymology and use through Latin and ultimately to ancient Greek. In this chapter, Benveniste refutes the claim that the term can be traced to anything resembling the movement of the waves and their flow. The key point Benveniste underlines is the following: that in these ancient atomists, rhythm (ῥυθμός) was primarily related to *form*, *shape*, or *schema*, and reliably referred to the distinctive and proportioned form, figure, or arrangement of things (1971: 285), and further, that one of Plato's central innovations was to impose upon rhythm an idea of numerical regulation and measure: 'We may then speak of the "rhythm" of the dance, of a step, of a song, of a speech, of work, of everything which presupposes a continuous activity broken by meter into alternating intervals. The notion of rhythm is established' (ibid.: 287). This is discussed further in Heaney (2023: 37–41) and extensively detailed in Michon (2018: 15–80). We thus see in Deleuze and Guattari, with the help of Messiaen, a resistance to this entanglement of rhythm and form through rhythm's subordination to the metric or the quantitative. Deleuze and Guattari seek to dissociate rhythm from measure, metre, or the metric, identifying rhythmic movements in non-metric or smooth spacetimes, what they call 'nonmetric aggregates' (2013a: 424). Rhythm then becomes *qualitative* (smooth) as much as it can be *quantitative* (striated).

14. This is not always the case in Deleuze and Guattari, of course. Their conceptualisation of the *refrain*, which we will discuss in Chapter 3, section b, centralises securitising and non-dialectical repetition.

15. At the risk of being unfair to Guattari, when discussing jazz he did highlight its genealogical emergence (highlighting jazz as an assemblage of subjectivation with territorial components) which creates 'rhythms, forms, colours and intensities of dance' (2006: 94), and even highlighted the emergence of hip-hop as a potential new molecular war machine harbouring the potential for being an essential instrument of 'subjective resingularisation [which] can generate other ways of perceiving the world' (ibid.: 97, our addition).

2

Scaping: Revolutionary Rhythmanalysis

Our survival on this planet is not only threatened by environmental damage but by a degeneration in the fabric of social solidarity and in the modes of psychical life, which must literally be re-invented. The refoundation of politics will have to pass through the aesthetic and analytical dimensions implied in the three ecologies – the environment, the socius and the psyche [. . .] We cannot conceive of a collective recomposition of the socius, correlative to a resingularisation of subjectivity, without a new way of conceiving political and economic democracies that respect cultural differences – without multiple molecular revolutions. (Guattari, 2006: 20–21)

This chapter will build upon the rhythmic ontology, and combined reading of rhythm and desire, conducted in the previous chapter, introducing the central methodological *fiat* or *rhythmic risk* of this book: *scaping*. Scaping is a *rhythmanalytical* practice. Scaping's rhythms are experimentalist and concerned with the transformational *sculpting* of the milieu; which is also to say that scaping seeks to become a *revolutionary rhythmanalytical* practice. To scape implies an inventive and constructive composition of the co-ordinates of the present in order to help generate potential holes, gaps, fissures, or cracks in extant dominating pulses, pushing them to their deterritorial border or region of ontological insecurity (*extemporaneous counter-actualisation*) and in the pursuance of an emergent sculpting process of the new or of the creation of new milieus, which is to say, new worlds (*rhythmic dramatisation*). Recall that rhythm partakes in the space *between* repetition and difference, that rhythmic practice exists in the space *between* coded pulsations and their relationship to ontological (in)security: scaping attempts to pierce this gap with affirmation and sculpture. Or, to repeat from Chapter 1: to inject a new rhythm into the pulsive flows of desire amounts to an attempt at *ontological destabilisation*, a constructive or *sculptural* movement towards the future, *to attempt a rhythmic risk amounts to an attempt to 'cut into' the future and sculpt it anew.*

To say that scaping is a *composition* of the co-ordinates of the present, rather than a *search*, is therefore to elude any representationalist charge that such co-ordinates pre-exist their creation. It is also to signal agreement with Bleiker's claim that the formal elements of political analysis, i.e., method and rhythm, signal 'colour choices, brushstrokes, angles, framing', and as such is an 'inherently political exercise' (2001: 513). There is nothing apolitical about scaping. Nor anything which seeks to 'capture' or 'depict' inert objects of analysis; rhythmanalytical practice, as Lefebvre notes, 'transforms *everything* into presences, including the *present*', that is, 'the act of rhythmanalysis integrates these things [i.e. objects of analysis] in a dramatic becoming, in an ensemble full of meaning, transforming them no longer into diverse things, but to presences' (Lefebvre, 2015: 33, our addition). When we discuss the rhythms of everyday life, or of the production of subjectivity in contemporary capitalistic milieus as they pertain to the attention-distraction, happiness-depression, and debt-credit ecologies, it is never to lock bodies upon a fixed grid in the socio-mental environment. The movement of the brain-body is one of a heterogeneous dynamic metastable unity that we call the rhythms of everyday life. This means that the 'emphasis is on process before signification or coding' (Massumi, 2002: 7). To isolate *tendential* positionalities in the mental environment is to sense the ever-moving rhythmic feedback loops and habits which are constitutive of our milieus. A co-ordinate, in our sense, is not an extensive, fixed, and static co-ordinate, but an *intensive* co-ordinate of movement or a moving co-ordinate; a co-ordinate in the sense of a *co-ordination* of an ensemble of processes, patterns, and libidinal habits. Further, this *composition* (not identification, not discovery, not revealing, not uncovering, not disclosing) of co-ordinates, as an attempt at a revolutionary conceptual gesture, *cannot proceed eschatologically*. Recall that rhythm, when revolutionary, opens the virtual structure of the past, attempts transduction or transcoding with patterns of practice other than its own, and so, *opens the future*. Eschatological theory, on the contrary, envelops history and the present within a closed, finalist, and homogeneous teleological frame: eschatology is arrhythmic, and *encloses* the possibilities of the present through the imposition of a compensatory and homogenising future (temporal unidirectionality), as Deleuze notes in relation to good sense: 'Good sense is by nature eschatological, the prophet of a final compensation and homogenization' (Deleuze, 2014: 296; also see Deleuze, 2004a: 88). *Scaping is not concerned with developing a conceptually frozen ecology, but rather with the genesis of immanent revolutionary vectors on the borders of the present.* It is in this precise sense that scaping constitutes a *rhythmic* method: 'rhythm is critical; it ties together critical moments, or ties itself together in passing from one milieu to another. (Deleuze and Guattari, 2013a: 365, our alteration).

Recall the triple task of method: 'Laying out, inventing, and creating constitute the philosophical trinity – diagrammatic, personalistic, and intensive features' (Deleuze and Guattari, 2013b: 77). This triple task will be elucidated in this chapter as it pertains to our method of *scaping*. Scaping will be elucidated as an immanent, naturalist, ecological, decolonial, and revolutionary creative conceptual practice; as a mode of *immanent critique* which functions through a *mobile* or *rhythmic perspectivism*. This mobile perspectivism attempts a creative injection of new rhythms into the present; a movement we will term *aesthetic interventionism*. Making sense of these claims, and this terminology, is the express purpose of this chapter. In section 2a, the relationship between scaping and immanent critique will be discussed. Immanent critique will be distinguished from criticality, and instead associated with conceptual movements of creativity which attempt to practise epistemologically open and honest conceptual creation. In doing so, it will also practise a resistance to non-immanence (e.g., supernaturalist or transcendent explanations or arguments 'beyond the reach of critique'). This resistance to non-immanence flows into a commitment to naturalism (section 2b) and is animated by what we will call *mobile perspectivism*. This mobile perspectivism recognises and folds into its practice its own changeability (mobile) and contingency (perspectivism) in its *necessarily limited practice of knowing*.

In this book we will pursue one *ecological entry-point* – a mental ecology – although we will pursue others in future research (social and environmental ecologies). Scaping's mode of conceptual sculpting will proceed through what we call *aesthetic interventionism* (section 2c), a notion developed from the insight indicated in the Introduction that scaping immanently participates in the territory and does not ontologically divorce itself from it. This chapter will conclude with a development on why and how we can situate scaping as concerned with the genesis of immanent revolutionary vectors on the borders of the present (section 2d). The processual reading of the notion of 'revolution' that will be offered acquires momentum from the insights on the third synthesis of the future we discussed in the previous chapter; but also through the problem of how to *decolonise* critique and practices of knowing more generally. We will now turn to the task of explicating and defending these conceptual instruments.

a. Scaping as immanent critique

Critique is not criticism. Critique is creative and constructive; criticism is communicative. While this distinction may appear initially scant, it will become methodologically crucial. Criticism, as communicative, operates through the 'to-and-fro of opinions about that which is assumed as given' (MacKenzie, 2004: xvii); in other words, communication takes place upon a pre-constituted, pre-assumed, and pre-justified plane (a plane of 'given' elements). That which is given is precisely that which is pre-constituted, pre-assumed, and pre-justified. What might such given elements be? MacKenzie (ibid.: 27) helpfully points us towards three. The first element of givenness is *the object of thought*. Assuming a shared – which is to say identical or self-same – world prior to the activity of conceptualisation, for example, situates this world as in some sense *beyond* or *transcendent* to conceptualisation as such. This renders the *object of thought* as transcendent, given, and inert. The second element of givenness is *the mode of critical activity*. Assuming the proper mode of critical activity prior to the practice of critical activity as such situates the concept of critical activity beyond the reach of the critical activity. This renders the *activity of thought* as transcendent and given. The third mode of givenness is *the agent of critique*. Assuming a self-same agent of critical activity homogenises the agent of critique as a-social, a-temporal, a-historical, and so on: beyond the reach of critical activity. Indeed, is such a homogenising of the subject not precisely what John Rawls (1999) conducts through his famous development of the 'original position' in *A Theory of Justice*? The subject of the original position is a pure generality: devoid of historical, social, political, and economic determinations (through the 'veil of ignorance') but endowed with Rawlsian rationality in its decision-making (choosing the best worst outcome or 'maximin' social arrangement) (Kymlicka, 2002). This renders the *subject of thought* as transcendent and given. Levi Bryant, here discussing Deleuze but applicable for our purposes, usefully summarises the 'inadequacy' of methods which fall prey to any of these triple dangers of non-immanence:

> If method shows itself to be inadequate, it is because it (1) presupposes an affinity with the truth or good will on the part of the thinker [i.e., rendering the *subject of thought* as transcendent], (2) presupposes the nature of what it sets out to know or understand [i.e., rendering the *activity of the thought* as transcendent] and (3) supposes a strict difference between the knowing subject and the object known [i.e., rendering the *object of thought* as transcendent]. It presupposes that it *can* know, what it is to know, and that what it knows is independent of its own subjective peculiarities and such. (Bryant, 2008: 76, our additions)

So, the triple danger of non-immanence is to render the (1) *object of thought*; (2) *activity of thought*; and/or (3) *subject of thought* as transcendent *to* conceptualisation. If any or all of these elements are assumed, we can properly call the mode of critical activity as 'non-immanent' (or 'impure', to use MacKenzie's term).

These given elements, to varying degrees in different conceptual practices, are precisely what enable theorists of communicative inter-subjectivity to posit *consensus* as the teleological end-point of communication: consensus is rendered possible precisely insofar as the to-and-fro of opinions takes place upon some shared justificatory plane assumed in advance. This shared plane of the given is the *non-immanent ground* upon which communication proceeds. Let us be more precise on why such an installation is non-immanent. It is non-immanent precisely because this shared plane *installs a domain beyond the reach of communication*. This domain we can properly call *transcendent* (or *supernatural*). The installation of an ontological domain beyond the reach of intersubjective communication is the installation of a domain that transcends the communicative interplay as such. This transcendent justificatory framework, the given, is that which the participants in communication *must not criticise* and subordinate themselves to in order for the communicative interplay to reach a point of consensus (we see here the decidedly moral nature of the demands placed upon participants in communication). MacKenzie calls the installation of such a transcendent domain as a movement that can only found *impure* critique; it can only do so precisely because this installation places a realm *beyond* critique, and so, communicative interplay 'fails the first test of critique, namely that it should be comprehensive' (MacKenzie, 2004: xvii). Hence why we can call communicative interplay *criticism* rather than critique. Installing an ontological realm beyond the reach of communication (the plane of given elements) is to place communication as immanent *to* this realm, rendering this realm transcendent or non-immanent. So, in this example, the plane of given elements is that which cannot be communicated about. When x is immanent *to* y, in other words, we are not in fact speaking of immanence but rather of the transcendence of y with regards to x: the minimal condition of immanence being that what is immanent is immanent to *itself* (Beistegui, 2010: 14).

We can point to some examples on this beyond this notion of communication. Karl Marx can be positioned as attempting to forward a type of immanent critique which analyses 'objective material and social conditions' in order to unlock the 'immanent potential of Communism' in the objective movement of history.[1] A naïve reading of this, which we relate to highlight one danger of non-immanence, relates to its potential inscription of the movement of history with eschatological-teleological purposiveness – such purposiveness potentially harbouring transcendence whenever class politics is positioned as immanent *to* history (or similarly when the notion of class becomes *ahistorical* rather than something subject to historical production). At the risk of generalising, and of being unfair to Marx on this point, it is important to note that these aspects in Marx himself are rare, they are flirted with, and are evidence of a potentially idealist Hegelian residue in his works (Sayers, 1990: 165–167; 1991: 90; 1997: 547–548). The point here is *not* to offer a grand and over-reaching claim on Marx's thought as such, but to point towards a residue that exists in portions of it which are vital to resist if immanence is claimed.[2] Moving on, and further: Kant's project was an attempt to generate an immanent critique of reason and assess it with regards to its legitimate and illegitimate uses. For an immanent critique of reason to remain immanent only to itself, what is demanded is an immanent critique of reason *by* reason; as Deleuze notes, here describing Kantian method: 'An immanent Critique – reason as the judge of reason – is the essential principle of the so-called transcendental method' (2008: 3). Similarly, in *Anti-Oedipus*, as we saw in the previous chapter, Deleuze and Guattari attempt to generate an immanent critique of desire and assess it with regards to its legitimate and illegitimate uses. For an immanent critique of desire to remain immanent only to itself, what is demanded is an immanent critique of desire *by* desire (Beistegui, 2010: 118). Scaping will attempt an immanent critique of rhythms *through* a rhythmic method.

The implications of such a non-immanent (transcendent or supernatural) grounding of criticism are to condemn *in advance* the communicative interplay to impurity and incompleteness. For critique to achieve *immanence* or *purity* it will proceed without justificatory recourses to standards beyond the critique as such; that is, it will attempt to avoid supernaturalism and dogmatism (in the Kantian sense).[3] Crucially, this means that the creations developed by any attempt at immanent critique are themselves open to critique. More precisely, we can position immanent critique as a triple response to the triple danger of non-immanence (the transcendentalisation of the object of thought, activity of thought, and subject of thought). Recall from the previous chapter: 'Laying out, inventing, and creating constitute the philosophical trinity – diagrammatic, personalistic, and intensive features' (Deleuze and Guattari, 2013b: 77). This triple response is as follows: *immanent critique proceeds through conceptual creation which institutes a plane of immanence which is activated by rhythmic characters.* Here, Marc Rölli, describing Deleuze's approach to immanence in his *transcendental empiricism*, notes the following, which highlights key elements that an immanent method must seek to pass through:

> [P]hilosophical concepts *as such* always imply a plane on which they distribute themselves and which 'registers' their relations, even when specific assignments of concepts reflexively reproduce their immanent conditions on an 'ideological' level, thereby losing sight of their genealogical affiliations. Deleuze is particularly anxious that concepts be made to display in their construction as much as possible their immanent position, that is, that they do not distort, eliminate or transcend their genetic relation to the non-conceptual problems they answer. (Rölli, 2016: 210)

We will here be using the term *rhythmic characters* instead of the much more often used *conceptual personae*, to immanently animate and display the construction of scaping as a practice of *revolutionary rhythmanalysis.* At the beginning of their translation of Deleuze and Guattari's *What is Philosophy?*, Hugh Tomlinson and Graham Burchill connect the notion of *conceptual personae* (*personnages conceptuel*) with that of *rhythmic characters* (*personnages rythmiques*), which Deleuze and Guattari devote space to in *A Thousand Plateaus*, developing on the work of composer Messiaen, who we briefly discussed in the previous chapter. Consider the following:

> [T]erritorial motifs from [sic] [form] *rhythmic faces or characters,* and [. . .] territorial counterpoints form *melodic landscapes.* There is a rhythmic character when we find that we no longer have the simple situation of a rhythm associated with a character, subject, or impulse. The rhythm itself is now the character in its entirety; as such, it may remain constant, or it may be augmented or diminished by the addition or subtraction of sounds or always increasing or decreasing durations, and by an amplification or elimination bringing death or resuscitation, appearance or disappearance. Similarly, the melodic landscape is no longer a melody associated with a landscape; the melody itself is a sonorous landscape in counterpoint to a virtual landscape. (Deleuze and Guattari, 2013a: 370, our addition)

'The melody itself is a sonorous landscape in counterpoint to a virtual landscape.' In *What is Philosophy?* Deleuze and Guattari argue that philosophical practice, as immanent critique, proceeds through conceptual creation that institutes a plane of immanence that is activated by conceptual personae. In the quote from *A Thousand Plateaus* above, conceptual creation is the territorial motif, the plane of immanence which is instituted is the melodic landscape, the conceptual persona is the rhythmic character. The rhythmic character constitutes a *perspective* or *point of view*. As MacKenzie notes:

> When a concept is created it institutes a plane of immanence, but since no concept can encompass THE plane of immanence, philosophy always simultaneously invents a 'point of view' which 'brings to life' the concept and the plane [. . .] The conceptual persona, in other words, constitutes the impersonal field as a 'perspective' which then 'activates' or 'insists upon' the creation of concepts. (MacKenzie, 2004: 35)

The rhythmic character activates the concept and the plane through laying down rhythms (conceptual (or other types of) practice). This institution of a plane of immanence or melodic landscapes is a ground, but a ground in movement, a rhythmic ground open to intensification, prolongation, habituation, and dissipation, to name some examples. As Massumi notes:

> The ground is full of movement, as full as the air is with weather, just at different rhythm [sic] from most perceptible movements occurring with it (flight of the arrow). Any geologist will tell you that the ground is anything but stable. It is a dynamic unity of continual folding, uplift, and subsidence. (Massumi, 2002: 10)

As such, Deleuze and Guattari noted above, the rhythmic character is a perspective, but this perspective is by no means necessarily static (the rhythm 'may be augmented or diminished by the addition or subtraction of sounds or always increasing or decreasing durations'). The perspective is *mobile*, in movement. Hence why scaping employs a *mobile perspectivism*. The perspective or point of view constitutes and ignites the relation between the concept created and plane instituted by the concept. Concepts are rhythmic in part through their connective power, and how they produce *new* repetitions in thought and affect: the unpredictability of the remix. Massumi, again, helps us conceptualise this:

> A concept is defined less by its semantic content than by the regularities of connection that have been established between it and other concepts: its rhythm of arrival and departure in the flow of thought and language; when and how it tends it relay into another concept [. . .] You can think of it as the rhythm without the regularity, or a readiness to arrive and relay in certain ways. Rhythm,

relay, arrival and departure. These are relations of motion and rest: affect. (Massumi, 2002: 20)

It will be useful, here, to add some further comments on our usage of this term *mobile perspectivism*. In James Williams's *A Process Philosophy of Signs*, he notes how a process philosophy approach to signs cannot, for example, render objects of analysis as in any sense inert, but rather as processes with variable degrees of stabilisation (apparent fixity) and destabilisation (apparent chaos) (Williams, 2016: 13); stability therefore emerges as relative, as an *effect* of tendencies and processes (ibid.: 62). Signs invite a multiplicity of analyses bound up with the extent to which signs are theorised as processes, inert objects, tools of communication, or something else entirely. Indeed, as we met in the previous chapter, through Canguilhem, the question of the *norm* enters here, too; insofar as attaching *fixity* or *necessity* to particular selections, signs, and interpretations is to retroactively impose a code upon processes: 'A norm, rule or code is always an imposition over process' (ibid.: 102). Against such processes of normalisation, which seek closure in the fixity of the sign, processes of signification are, for Williams, indissociable from those movements which *transform* signs, transform thought, and transform milieus, as, that is, processes of 'speculative, experimental and critical intervention' (ibid.: 128). The focus on process, or likewise on tendencies as a particular modality of process, is therefore also a focus on the rhythmic interplay between continuities and discontinuities, on what Stiegler calls in his key example of the evolution of technics as the 'successive displacement' of 'limits' (Stiegler, 1998: 33) or what we have been calling the milieu's rhythmic parameters of ontological security.

Our *rhythmanalytic mobile perspectivism*, and notion of critique, emerges from these insights as what we can call a type of *process epistemology*. We use this term in two senses: (1) insofar as it takes rhythms, tendencies, and processes (or what Lefebvre terms *presences*) as (mobile) 'objects' of analysis or selection. This is a difficult task, not least because, as Stiegler notes, tendencies and *facts* are not at all to be conflated: tendencies generate a multiplicity and diversity of *effects* he calls *facts*; the task of a processual-tendential analysis will be to examine both while resisting their conflation (Stiegler, 1998: 47) in the interplay of the global and the local over time historically, contemporaneously, and protentionally. This is a distinction Stiegler draws from Leroi-Gourhan, whose differentiates between technical *tendencies* (which he positions as necessary) and *facts* (which he positions as accidental). Yuk Hui, on this distinction, provides the example of the invention of the wheel as a technical *tendency*, the fact of whether or not a wheel has spokes is a 'matter of technical fact' (Hui, 2016b: 8). Or, to provide another example, while the invention of the hammer may be positioned as a technical tendency, different solutions to the emergent problem of the handle emerge. The different solutions of this problem are matters of technical fact, relating to the milieu in which the problem emerged. Simondon suggests the options of whether a handle is fitted with glue, shell, rush, or silk and how it bears an ecological relation to what wood is used to construct the tool (hard, medium, or soft woods and the climate in which trees grow) (Simondon, 2012).

In other words, our rhythmanalysis of tendencies seeks to offer a level of conceptual explanation of our historical and contemporary conditions, in particular milieus and the relations between milieus and of the rhythms permeating the mental environment, but also while focusing upon *where these tendencies are taking us*. For example: *what futures are possible under conditions of contemporary capitalism's stranglehold upon the rhythms of everyday life in the mental environment?* This question will be confronted in Part II. Further, a second aspect of this notion of *process epistemology* is its reflexive or *epistemologically open* element, that is, (2) insofar as our rhythmanalytical approach is open to its own changeability, *open* to critique rather than beyond its reach, and as the task of critique is always one to be *repeated* (always differently), then the analyses, and practices of knowledge we embody, can never remain static. *As* a process of individuation, the very explication of this *mobile perspectivism* is itself enveloped in a movement of differentiation:

> *Individuation is mobile*, strangely supple, fortuitous and endowed with fringes and margins; all because the intensities which contribute to it communicate with each other, envelop other intensities and are in turned enveloped. The individual is far from indivisible, never ceasing to divide and change its nature. (Deleuze, 2014: 335)

There is a rhythmic interplay between (1) and (2), and while we will not discuss it in extensive detail here, a key point worth emphasising is that our process of revolutionary rhythmanalysis conducts political-strategic modes of selection, naming, and creation. Indeed, as Williams notes, such selection in any process philosophy of signs is always a 'prompt and a critical move' (Williams, 2016: 128); and insofar as selection always occurs relative and contingent to a milieu, it is in this sense that all such sign selections harbour politicality ('selection is only every against a background' (Williams, 2016: 132; also see Deleuze and Guattari, 1983a: 163)). Having said this, insofar as such selection is always relative to a milieu – and further, that the milieu always *provokes* certain selections in order to tighten the bond between rhythm and desire in the hardening of the milieu's rhythmic parameters of ontological security – pursuing processes of selection and decision which may become *revolutionary* is no simple task. On this, Williams is keen to highlight that the 'concept of selection is independent from a selecting subject' (Williams, 2016: 158). But perhaps more pertinently, as Guattari notes, such a task harbours *dangers*: only too often has the revolutionary dissolved into the reactionary, the paranoiac, the dogmatic, the exploitative, and so forth:

> Ecological praxes strive to scout out the potential vectors of subjectification and singularization at each partial existential locus. They generally seek something that runs counter to the 'normal' order of things, a counter-repetition, an intensive given which invokes other intensities to form existential configurations [. . .] However, as experiments in the suspension of meaning they are risky, as there is the possibility of a violent deterritorialization which would destroy the assemblage of subjectification [. . .] A more gentle deterritorialization, however, might enable the assemblages to evolve in a *processual fashion*. (Guattari, 2014: 30, our emphasis)

The task of scaping, therefore, is to construct a conceptual apparatus worthy of the task of such creation. In *The Logic of Sense*, Deleuze places the task of becoming 'worthy of what happens to us' (2004a: 170) as enveloping the task of ethics (and by extension politics insofar as the spreading of *ressentiment* is the task of tyranny; the spreading of *ressentiment* constituting an *unworthiness* of that which happens to us) and a task which is indissociably temporal: to be worthy of what happens to us is, in part, to participate in one's own becoming, divisibility, and transformation. To not lapse into weakness, breakdown, and *ressentiment* are further elements incorporated into such a task of becoming-worthy (ibid.: 171–174). In order to attempt this, *scaping* seeks to acknowledge and fold it into its own practice this inevitable politicality of any selection, and use it as an impetus to further develop its *process epistemology*, while seeking always to not submit to the dangers of *ressentiment*, whether they be of a cynical-resignatory form (it is always *my* fault) or paranoiac-blaming form (it is always the *other's* fault). We are concerned only with particular selections and co-ordinate compositions; however, we will in future research revisit this problem in order to conduct this rhythmic process of reflexivity.

To gather some of these elements on process, tendency, and perspectivism together: scaping, as a rhythmanalytical practice, extracts from these comments that our mobile perspectivism is about the creation-ignition of new selections, their creative explication through *co-ordinate composition* – intensive co-ordinates, in the sense of a co-ordination of processes – towards the creation of new milieus. Such selections themselves, to reiterate, are processes – and are of an intense difficulty, and are potentially dangerous, insofar as they seek to be of the order of a *counter-repetition* (what we will call, later in this chapter, an *extemporaneous counter-actualisation*), contingent and relative to the conditions of selection (Williams, 2016: 79). And although we do not use this term extensively, William calls this process *speculative:* 'A speculative philosophy is itself an essay in certain selections and a critical exercise in their presuppositions, repercussions and critical positions. To speculate is to create new signs' (ibid.: 27). Such a speculative-creative process of sign creation can disrupt the existing milieu, insofar as milieus exhibit normalised patterns of sign selection forming a crucial part of their rhythmic parameters of ontological security, closure, or sense of belonging (ibid.: 49). The creation of new selections, new signs, new modes of understanding: all of these facets are geared in the practice of *scaping* towards the creative sculpting of *new milieus.*

Returning to the question of scaping's relationship to immanence again. Let us say more succinctly how scaping's triple response to the triple danger of non-immanence functions. Instead of rendering the *object of thought* as transcendent, scaping proceeds through the *composition* of co-ordinates. In so doing, it makes no claims to static representational mimesis: its mode of conceptual sculpting is rhythmic-processual and *aesthetically interventionist*. In addition, by treating the map as an immanent participation 'in' and 'through' the territory, no ontological boundary is supernaturally (non-immanently) inserted between the subject and object of thought. Instead of rendering the *activity of thought* as transcendent, scaping attempts to proceed through immanent (or *pure*) critique, which is creative or constructivist, constructing the idea of a rhythmic method in the critique itself and not placing this method 'outside' of the activity of thought as a given justificatory framework; in other words, scaping *rhythmically* 'problematizes its own conditionality' (MacKenzie, 2004: 48). Finally, instead of rendering the *subject of thought* as transcendent, scaping employs a *mobile perspectivism*.[4] Scaping's process epistemology recognises and folds into its practice its own changeability (mobile) and contingency (perspectivism): 'Pure critique is always aware of its context and always ready to be on the move' (ibid.: 52; Deleuze and Guattari, 2013a: 243–270).

There are, however, two notions of methodological importance which have silently animated our discussion of scaping as immanent critique thus far: the spectres of *naturalism* and *ecology*. We have so far identified non-immanence with transcendence and supernaturalism, so we will now situate scaping's relationship to naturalism and ecology.

b. Scaping as naturalist ecology

What does it mean to claim that scaping's practice is that of a naturalist ecology? Broadly speaking, scaping-as-naturalism is bound up with its commitment to immanence, and scaping-as-ecology is bound up with its mobile perspectivism and pragmatism.

Put bluntly, scaping can, we hope, be situated in the lineage of the type of naturalism which resists ontological and epistemological recourses to *transcendence* or *supernaturalism*. Such a resistance flows from scaping's commitment to immanence: recourses to transcendence or supernaturalism install non-immanence into conceptual practice and install an ontological domain which conceptual practice is divorced from. In this sense, scaping's approach to naturalism has nothing to do with normatively prioritising 'nature' and assuming a pre-given 'nature/culture' binary. It problematises the nature/culture binary as such, opening up these categories to the activity of critique and to their permanent rhythmic entanglement. It also problematises any putative 'human/machine' binary insofar as such a binary often installs a transcendent humanism or essentialist anthropology in the relationship between the human and the technical, and foregoes their own respective evolutionary entanglements and embedded relations.

Since scaping seeks immanence, it cannot ontologically divorce itself from the milieu in which it participates: 'pure critique is a task for thought in the world rather than an interpretation by thought of the world' (MacKenzie, 2004: xxiv). This brings us back to the issue of the 'map/territory' distinction we mentioned in the introduction. Gregory Bateson (who himself is drawing on Korzybski's 'map/territory' division) describes 'conceptual mapping' as a practice of mapping the constitutive *difference* of the territory. What occurs in the practice of mapping? Bateson is clear on this:

> What gets onto the map, in fact, is *difference*, be it a difference in altitude, a difference in vegetation, a difference in population structure, difference in surface, or whatever. *Differences are the things that get onto a map.* (Bateson, 2000: 457, second emphasis ours)

All mappings are mappings of difference (such as, precisely, rhythmic differences, mappings of tendencies and facts): in the terms of scaping, conceptual mappings involve the *composition* or *sculpting* of difference. Likewise in language, Bateson will note that linguistic exchange, like mapping, cannot communicate the objects themselves. Rather, 'language bears to the objects which it denotes a relationship comparable to that which a map bears to a territory' (ibid.: 180). For Bateson it goes further: conscious perception itself is positioned as a practice of mapping (always 'flawed'), a process through which informational differences figure onto how we perceive objects and the world. Stiegler likewise affirms such a claim when arguing, this time against Leroi–Gourhan, that there can be no such thing as a purely 'technical language', that is, a language which *only* expresses the pure contextual singularities of the specific territory. All *signs* are symbolic:

> Now a sign that is not a signal is a symbol designating a general-
> ity, a conceptual class, always already an 'abstraction,' and not a
> unique and singular referent – for in that case there would have
> to be as many signs as there are realities to designate; we would
> have an infinity of signs. And there would simply no longer be
> this general and abstract economy in which language consists and
> which allows it to name, in an indefinite combination of a finite
> ensemble of signs, an infinite reality. All language, being essen-
> tially finite and able nevertheless to account for an a priori indef-
> inite and *quasi*-infinite reality, is necessarily and immediately the
> implementation of a process of abstraction and generalization. A
> 'concrete language' is therefore a contradictory concept. (Stiegler,
> 1998: 166)

As such, all conceptual mapping participates in such a *quasi*-infinity, and, as such, partakes in part in a *creative movement*: conceptual mappings are experiments with symbols and signs, they do not technically depict and capture; 'information processing will always remain a derived, secondary function of language' (Massumi, 1992: 41). Alfred North Whitehead, similarly, centralises a processual and affective symbolism as the nest within which he situates language (as but one form of symbolic activ-ity). Symbolic activity, and our 'vast system of inherited symbolism' (1985: 73) – words, phrases, etc. – being always individual and collective (transindividual), indicating meaning, yes, but also always carrying 'with them an enveloping suggestiveness and an emotional efficacy' (ibid.: 67) which forms a crucial component in 'how a society bends its individual members to function in conformity with its needs' (ibid.: 73). In other words, Whitehead immediately centralises the *political* nature of symbolic activity and the transformations in our modes of symbolic exchange:

It is the first step in sociological wisdom, to recognize that the major advances in civilization are processes which all but wreck the societies in which they occur: – like unto an arrow in the hand of a child. The art of free society consists first in the maintenance of the symbolic code; and secondly in the fearlessness of revision, to secure that the code serves those purposes which satisfy an enlightened reason. Those societies which cannot combine reverence to their symbols with freedom of revision, must ultimately decay either from anarchy, or from the slow atrophy of a life stifled by useless shadows. (Ibid.: 88)

Although we will not explore this in any further detail here, it is important to note that Whitehead defined such a 'progressive' combination with *rhythm* itself.[5] An injection of creativity into not just symbolic activity, but vitality as such:

The Way of Rhythm pervades all life, and indeed all physical existence. This common principle of Rhythm is one of the reasons for believing that the root principles of life are, in some lowly form, exemplified in all types of physical existence. In the Way of Rhythm a round of experiences, forming a determinate sequence of contrasts attainable within a definite method, are codified so that the end of the one such cycle is the proper antecedent stage for the beginning of another such cycle [. . .] Thus the Rhythm of life is not merely to be sought in simple cyclical recurrence. The cycle element is driven into the foundation, and variations of cycles, and of cycles of cycles, are elaborated. (Whitehead, 1929: 16–17)

This rhythmic and processual symbolic openness dovetails with what Deleuze calls the productive indeterminacy or conceptual inexhaustibility of the Idea (which we will return to later in this chapter), or what Massumi defined as a type of *pragmatics* that 'opens language to the vagaries of "context," indexing grammar to relations of power and patterns of social change' (Massumi, 1992: 42) In *A Thousand Plateaus*, Guattari and Deleuze distinguish between mapping in the sense of 'tracing' (which we identify with static representational mimesis) and in the 'rhizomatic' sense (2013a: 12). Like scaping, rhizomatic mapping is not about representational tracing, but about experimental construction: 'the rhizome pertains to a map that must be produced, constructed, a map that is always detachable, connectable, reversible, modifiable, and has multiple entryways and exits and its own lines of flight' (ibid.: 22).

Scaping's naturalism is bound up with its situatedness 'within the territory'. Its compositional mapping is a practice which is 'in' the world, not 'of' (or 'outside') the world. In other words, scaping's resistance to ontological and epistemological recourses to transcendence is not itself a movement of transcendence or even negativity, precisely because this resistance flows from its commitment to, and affirmation of, immanence. As we have already noted, recourses to transcendence install a domain beyond the reach of critique as such (placing a domain 'outside' the composed conceptual map); scaping's commitment to naturalism is a commitment to the *total* scope of critique. Scaping is still a mobile perspectivism, however, so it does not *totalise* its conceptual creations, which is the same thing as saying that it does not ascribe *ontological* or *epistemological closure* to its conceptual creations (such is its process epistemology). As such, *if the scope of critique is to be total, critique must be non-totalising in its creations, always opening up the possibility for future movements of critique (composition, sculpture).*

If we resist ontological recourses to transcendence, then we by definition resist ontological closure, staticity, or fixity. In other words, immanence pushes us towards an open ontology of becoming rather than a closed ontology of being. Such an open ontology of becoming was already strongly gestured towards in the previous chapter in relation to Deleuze's third synthesis of time: recall that the third synthesis of time radically opens the past, present, and, thus, future. Such ontological openness was already well articulated by Deleuze and Spinoza:

> Nature is not collective, but rather distributive, to the extent that the laws of Nature distribute parts which cannot be totalized. Nature is not attributive, but rather conjunctive: it expresses itself through 'and,' and not through 'is.' (Deleuze, 2004a: 304)

> Nature has no end set before it, [and all] final causes are nothing but human fictions. (Spinoza, 1996: 27, our addition)

The resistance to totalisation and to eschatology ('final causes') likewise flows from a commitment to immanent naturalism. This is the finalism that Bergson famously rallies against in *Creative Evolution*, against interpretations of evolution which submit it to a pre-defined movement.

Further, if we resist epistemological recourses to transcendence, then we by definition resist the staticity, closure, or fixity of our 'knowledge-claims' and practices of knowing.[6] In this sense, such a naturalism consists in a thorough departure from Kant, whose transcendent model of recognition situates morality in the form of an ontologically hierarchic law (Connolly, 2008: 303) grounded in a certain 'apodictic' (dogmatic, transcendent, supernaturalist, non-immanent, impure) epistemological foundation: transcendental consciousness.[7] Scaping will be an attempt to develop a novel naturalism through its rhythmic method. Where does the notion of *ecology* fit in here, however? What does it add to our situating of scaping as both immanent and naturalist, if anything? We will devote the rest of this section to this question.

Broadly speaking, *ecology* denotes the study of the relations and interdependent interactions between organisms and their environments. It is the complex (and multi-disciplinary, even *beyond* disciplinary) study of relational networks between human and non-human animals, food chains, habitats, energy, geography, molecular processes, cognition, behaviour, weather, technology, media, and technical objects generally, etc., to the determination and analyses of relations and milieus. Bateson divides traditional ecology into two 'faces', whose distinction lies in different approaches to the 'boundedness' of the units of study. One face (which he identifies as bioenergetic ecology) considers ontological units (a coral reef, a city, an individual), i.e., the objects of analysis, as *bounded*, and these boundaries function as onto-ecological *frontiers* at which we can determine the *difference* between that unit and its environment. The other face (which he identifies as entropic ecology) does not so much deal with bounded ontological units, but rather with relationships, pathways, and the transformative interplay between different 'units'. These units are not simply *enclosed*, but rather *disclose differences through pathways* (Bateson, 2000: 466–467). Bateson will lean firmly to, and indeed go further than, the latter. For Bateson's (alternative and third) 'cybernetic' approach to ecology: 'The mental world – the mind – the world of information processing – is not limited by the skin' (ibid.: 460):

> The cybernetic epistemology which I have offered you would suggest a new approach. The individual mind is immanent but not only in the body. It is immanent also in pathways and messages outside the body; and there is a larger Mind of which the individual mind is only a sub-system. This larger Mind is comparable to God and is still immanent in the total interconnected social system and planetary ecology. (Ibid.: 467)

For Bateson, the individual mind is neither an *enclosed* unit nor a *disclosing* unit, but more radically, mind is expanded or extended outward *as also being* those cybernetic circuits and informational flows that it is interinvolved with.[8] The supposed independence of subject and object is, and even the concepts of subject and object as such are, for Bateson, indicative of a pathological epistemology (Shaw, 2015: 155), insofar as not only do such approaches belie ecological connectedness, but they also threaten the human and the planet's continued existence. Bateson's cybernetic ecology or cybernetic naturalism is not actor-network theory, although like actor-network theory (Latour, 1991), it ontologically collapses the human/non-human distinction and positions analytical focus on inter-locking ontological processes and rhythms (Harman, 2014: 18), and Bateson's combination of naturalism with cybernetics also dissolves the human/machine distinction.

It will be useful, here, to say a little more on cybernetics, both in order to render clearer Bateson's self-description of his position in terms of a cybernetic epistemology, but also in order to sharpen scaping's differen-tiation from cybernetics. Scaping is a rhythmic ecology, not a cybernetic ecology. The early cybernetic approach, which grew especially through post-Second World War development of technologies developed during wartime (for example, the Turing machine) through to our contempo-rary digital moment (Goodman, 2012: 32; also see Kittler, 1999; and Geoghegan, 2023), was an interdisciplinary approach devoted to techni-cal objects, particularly automata, and the function and communication in and between technical objects within, at least initially, closed systems (such as the elements of transmission and feedback that occur within and define the functioning of cybernetic computer systems) and the possi-bilities of efficient control of these systems. Norbert Wiener's (1961) famous *Cybernetics: Or Control and Communication in the Animal and the Machine*, published originally in 1948, is a key foundational text in the academic study of cybernetics. As Goodman notes, and as even the title of Wiener's text indicates, cybernetics often extends beyond simply the technical object, blending a study of the technical and the human anal-ogously, relying upon an *informational ontology*, whereby 'human thought and perception could be conceived of in terms of information pro-cessing' (Goodman, 2012: 55). As the study of *relations*, systems, feed-back, and control, the history of cybernetics and ecological study are entangled. Indeed, see the first quote from Bateson above, where the 'mental world' is identified as the 'world of information processing'. The 'object' of cybernetic analysis did undergo modifications in its develop-ment, with early cybernetics focusing more explicitly on *closed* systems with feedback loops, and second-order cybernetic thinkers like Bateson would transform this object and incorporate into his cybernetic epis-temology an awareness of the observer's active role in systems thinking as such (Burton, 2017: 256); second-order cybernetics attempts to fold into its practice the insight that 'an observer observes a world that not only operates circularly, but to which he himself belongs, and he knows it' (Esposito, 2017: 288) and a degree of systemic openness. However, what is shared by a broad spectrum of cybernetic thinkers is some sort of *informational ontology.*[9] As Andrew Iliadis notes, the mathematical theory of communication that grounded particularly early cybernetic informational ontology functions within closed systems of negative and positive feedback loops (again, recall Bateson's quote above, where he describes his cybernetic epistemology as forwarding an ontology of sub-systems of informational flow immanent to an entire system he calls God – another extension of cybernetic ontology beyond the technical which analogises the human and the technical). This mathematical theory of communication was originally developed by Claude Shannon in a 1948 paper in which he famously notes the following on the opening page:

> The fundamental problem of communication is that of reproducing at one point either exactly or approximately a message selected at another point. Frequently the messages have *meaning*; that is they refer to or are correlated according to some system with certain physical or conceptual entities. These semantic aspects of communication are irrelevant to the engineering problem. The significant aspect is that the actual message is one *selected from a set* of possible messages. The system must be designed to operate for each possible selection, not just the one which will actually be chosen since this is unknown at the time of design. (Shannon, 1998: 31)[10]

It is important to note, here, that neither Shannon nor indeed early cybernetic theory explicitly *reduced* communication to information; however, it did treat such informational flow as a *condition* of any semantic content, what Iliadis describes as an informational *undergridding* of semantics and meaning; and, further, that different '*types* of information mattered to the cyberneticists, as any careful reading of their work will show, and this little acknowledged fact flies in the face of contemporary, dehumanizing critiques of that tradition' (Iliadis, 2013). (We have already distinguished our approach from this, when we noted with Stiegler above that language's immediate conceptuality resists any potential 'purely technical' language.) Simondon develops and radicalises certain aspects of this informational ontology from cybernetics (he describes cybernetics as a potentially universal system of technical intelligibility (Simondon, 2009a: 17)), but does at times firmly differentiate himself from it, emphasising that what occurs in informational flow is not simply informational exchange or the exchange of data, but also the engagement and transformation of relational systems in various and relative states of metastabilisation and the production of new vectors of functioning within and between *open* systems through processes of individuation, transduction, and concretisation, for example within associated milieus (technical milieus and human-geographical milieus) (Simondon, 2017: 55).

A distinctive difference, therefore, between the cybernetic theory existing at the time Simondon was writing and Simondon is the shift of focus from closed systems to open ones, which pivoted Simondon's focus to the transformational relations *between* milieus: Simondon's is an 'open informational schema' (Iliadis, 2013) ('the greatest perfection [of machines] coincides with the greatest openness' (Simondon, 2017: 18, our addition; Simondon, 2015)), contra cybernetics, in which *indeterminacy* and *relations between systems* are crucial. In effect, one of the key charges Simondon brings to bear against the cybernetics with which he engaged is how it universalises the present, as if the objects of cybernetic theory had not emerged from a process of technical evolution and concretisation, and treats technical beings as if they were no different than organic, or what he calls living beings:[11]

> [T]echnology must deal with the universality of technical objects. In this sense, cybernetics is insufficient: it has the immense merit of being the first inductive study of technical objects, and of presenting itself as a study of the intermediate domain between the specialized sciences; but it has specialized its domain of investigation too narrowly, because it started from the study of a certain number of technical objects; it accepted as its point of departure that which technology must reject: a classification of technical objects according to criteria established according to genera and species. Automata are *not* a species: there are only technical objects, which in turn have a functional organization that results in various degrees of automatism [. . .] Instead of considering one class of technical beings, automata, one must follow the lines of concretization throughout a temporal evolution of technical objects. (Simondon, 2017: 51)

Cybernetics, then, lacks time, and the progressive evolution of technical objects according to what Simondon calls a 'rhythm of technical progress' of 'continuous and minor improvements' and 'discontinuous and major improvements' (Simondon, 2017: 40) is absolutely crucial to any study of technical objects. Such a temporal study obeys what he calls a 'law of serrated evolution' through a discernible 'rhythm of relaxation' through which the technical time of relaxation can help engender major improvements and the birth of new milieus insofar as it can 'synchronize other rhythms of development and appear to determine the entire

historical evolution' (ibid.: 68). In this sense, Simondon adds time and
rhythm in his self-differentiation from cybernetics.

So, building on our initial definition of ecology – denoting the study
of the relations and interdependent interactions between organisms and
their environments – and folding into our practice of scaping a concern for the *technical* in such a naturalist and immanent ecology, is to
bring us in the direction of a Simondonian ecology. Insofar as much of
Simondon's thought is primarily focused on the technical object, and
technics generally, it is also profoundly ecological insofar as not only
are relations primary to the study of technical objects 'themselves', but
also the relations between technical elements, individuals, and ensembles
have with the human-geographical milieu, which are the conditions of
possibility of *invention* of new milieus (combining technical, geograph-
ical, and human elements) (ibid.: 58). For Erich Hörl, one of the key
factors that unites various distinct approaches to ecological analysis is this
precise focus on *relationality* (and, relatedly, on *milieus*) which Simondon
emphasises. Insisting upon the primacy of relationality is, for Hörl, constitutive of the 'fundamental principle of general ecology' (Hörl, 2013:
122). The analyses of distinct ecological domains will always, that is, be
a question of the analysis of relations pertaining to that domain, in addition to their timescapes. Ecology, too, must also thereby open itself to
the *future* and to the *virtual*: such an opening being constitutive of scaping
as such. As Guattari notes:

> The contemporary world – tied up in its ecological, demographic
> and urban impasses – is incapable of absorbing, in a way that is
> compatible with the interests of humanity, the extraordinary tech-
> noscientific mutations which shake it. It is locked in a vertiginous
> race towards ruin or radical renewal. All the bearings – economic,
> social, political, moral, traditional – break down one after the
> other. It has become imperative to recast the axes of values, the
> fundamental finalities of human relations and productive activity.
> *An ecology of the virtual is thus just as pressing as ecologies of the vis-
> ible world* [. . .] *Virtual ecology will not simply attempt to preserve the
> endangered species of cultural life but equally to engender conditions for the
> creation and development of unprecedented formations of subjectivity that
> have never been seen and never felt.* (Guattari, 2006: 91)

The question then becomes that of which processes, tendencies, and
distributed facticities are significant to a particular domain, and the virtual potentialities of transformation 'therein'. Scaping, as a rhythmic
ecology open to the virtual, is therefore an opening to the creation

of new ecologies of value; as a modality of libidinal investment, value is 'active in the world, alive with appetition and self-transformation' (Massumi, 2017b: 356). But it is also always political. With Massumi, we agree that the '"object" of political ecology is the coming-together or belonging-together of processually unique and divergent forms of life' (2002: 255), which immediately centralises the possibility of care ('a *caring for* belonging as such' (ibid.: 255)) and opens onto the question of our *values* to come. Opening onto the question of value would not be to non-immanently instate a 'set' of values prior to ecological production, but rather, as Massumi notes, to open onto value insofar as values themselves reach no 'final resting point' (2017b: 356). Here, we must again emphasise the importance of the technical, of technics, to any such ecology, or techno-ecology, in the 'natural-technical continuum' (Hörl, 2013: 128), without, however, conflating them: the evolution of technical objects is not the same as the evolution of organic beings, but their historical relations of development are entangled. More specifically, under the conditions of the present, this is a question of the continual rhythmic processes of the digitalisation, informationalisation, and cyberneticisation of everyday life, which will we discuss more closely in the next chapter; that is, our contemporary imbrication with the technical. We therefore agree with Hörl that the 'concept of ecology itself is situated indisputably in processes of displacement, reformulation, and indeed revaluation' (ibid.: 126). There is a rhythmic interplay between tendential processes and how such processes produce new configurations of relationality as such, which, for Hörl, have produced new dangers: 'the all-encompassing cyberneticization and computerization of our form of life has brought with it a new form of closure, a new dogmatism, and a new form of bondage through mediation and processuality' (ibid.: 123). For now, the key point we wish to make here is that whilst scaping is not at all a cybernetics, we are here much closer to a Simondonian ecology, it nonetheless seeks to confront the question of cyberneticisation through the question of technics in our digital epoch: digital technology having become, and continuously becoming, absolutely central to relations pertaining in our contemporary *mental ecology*, or what Simondon calls the very ground of thought, the 'mental milieu' (Simondon, 2017: 62). This mental milieu is the precise object of our practice of *mindscaping* in Part II.

Through our rhythmic method, rhythmic ecology is situated as an immanent and naturalist analytical practice which focuses on the rhythmic relations between 'agents' broadly construed as pertaining to the 'ecological domain' and milieus in question ('human', 'social', and 'environmental', with the 'technical' transversing each). Positioning scaping as a type of ecology in this tradition enables it to pursue its method in different ecological domains.

Let us flesh out this notion of an 'ecological domain' in a little more detail. Guattari begins his *Three Ecologies* with a quote from Bateson. Indeed, according to Erick Heroux, Guattari's ecological project is firmly in the Batesonian lineage (2008: 182). Guattari's *Three Ecologies* is an indispensable springboard for scaping's ecological production. In this text, Guattari distinguishes between three different ecological domains: a mental ecology, a social ecology, and an environmental ecology. It should be noted from the outset that denoting specific *types* of ecology serves simply as a method to delimit relational-ecological analysis *rather than* an attempt to isolate this or that ecology as being *independent* from other ecological processes. There is no sense in which the 'mental' is taken as existing ontologically independent of the 'social' or the 'environmental'. Quite the contrary, whilst each ecology might have certain delimited properties, features, or temporalities, ecologies overlap (*transverse*). Ecological study can be positioned as the precise attempt to analyse these delimited properties and transversal points in conjunction through its creative conceptual practice. Different ecological domains are different assemblages that exhibit different rhythmic practices, different speeds and intensities, different levels of rhythmic contraction, and, so, are conceptually pursued separately.

Scaping does not take these three ecological 'domains' as given nor as independent from each other. Each ecology is a *problem*, and, as such, our forays into these ecologies will incorporate a problematisation of that ontological demarcation as such, as well as a creative move which offers a rhythmic and sculptural formulation of that ecological domain. These three *ecological entry ways* are different *modes* of scaping insofar as scaping practices a *mobile perspectivism*. Recall that Deleuze and Guattari's practice of rhizomatic mapping 'has multiple entryways and exits and its own lines of flight' (Deleuze and Guattari, 2013a: 22). Scaping folds a recognition of the constructedness of its perspectivism in its practice. *The analytical delimitation of three distinct ecologies is not a firm ontological demarcation but an application of scaping's mobile perspectivism*: 'One never commences; one never has a *tabula rasa*; one slips in, enters in the middle; one takes up or lays down rhythms' (Deleuze, 1988b: 123). As has been noted already, the task of Part II is concerned with a mental ecology, on scaping the mental environment, that is, *mindscaping*.

Having identified scaping-as-naturalism as bound up with a commitment to immanence, and scaping-as-ecology as bound up with its mobile perspectivism, we will now move onto the penultimate element we will discuss in this chapter: scaping as a practice of *aesthetic interventionism*.

c. Aesthetic interventionism: a rhythmic-sculptural refrain

We noted above that scaping attempts to creatively inject new rhythms into the present and, in so doing, functions as a type of *aesthetic interventionism*. Our claim in this section is the following: *scaping's aesthetic interventionism functions as an intervention into the aesthetic through extemporaneous counter-actualisation and rhythmic dramatisation: it is a rhythmic-sculptural refrain.*

i. Aesthetic interventionism

To begin to explicate this with some clarity, let us first pivot towards the notion of 'aesthetics' being deployed. We noted above – in connection with Deleuze's productive use of Kant's third *Critique*, as well as with Bleiker's notion of an *aesthetic method* – the necessarily aesthetic dimension of conceptual practice, though we did not develop with any clarity upon the notion of 'aesthetic'. Aesthetics, on our reading, encompasses much more than evaluations upon the objecticity of beauty, the ascription of beauty to objects, or the desire 'for' beauty (itself only an effect of the syntheses of time and desire). Aesthetics – derived from the Greek verb '*aisthesthai*', i.e., 'to perceive' – pertains to the domain of perception or the production of sensibility itself: the ontology of sensibility or what Deleuze calls the 'being of the sensible' (Deleuze, 2014: 184). Rather than *assuming* the realm of perceptibility – usually taken as the 'empirical' – as a set of diverse *given* elements, scaping employs an approach to this realm of perceptibility with (1) a concern for *genesis* (i.e., the *genesis* of the given *as* given); and, by extension, with (2) an injection of contingency and changeability, with a concern for how patterns are sedimented and how they might change.

On (1): this concern for *genesis* is drawn both from Deleuze's *transcendental empiricism*, and by extension from Simondon's own account of genesis in his account of the genesis of technicity, and animates itself through a focus on the *conditions of genesis of certain modes of perception or sensibility.* As Rölli notes, this question of *genesis*, for Deleuze, bears connections to Edmund Husserl's move from *static* to *genetic phenomenology*, that is, Husserl's move towards a *transcendental* phenomenology:

> Genetic phenomenology differentiates itself from a merely static one by making itself at home in a new problem area, namely one in which passivity is understood as constitutive 'substratum' for all occurrences of consciousness [. . .] What is statically present

as a resultant is seen in genetic reflection as *the product of passive syntheses.* (Rölli, 2016: 101, our emphasis)

This concern for *genesis* in relation to the aesthetic is geared, therefore, to keep us connected to those *passive syntheses of time and desire* which formed the basis of our previous chapter. Passive and active syntheses, too, for Husserl, formed a key part of his 'transcendental aesthetics', which he describes as a 'transcendental doctrine of sense' which 'wants to investigate, constitutively, precisely all the dramatization of aesthetic, perceptual apperception, and intuitive apperception in general' (Husserl, 2001: 444–445). The notion of aesthetics, and its connections to those passive syntheses of time and desire, should be taken therefore in this Husserlian sense, with the Deleuzian and Simondonian (2009b) concern for genesis. Take the following:

> The very notion of genesis, however, deserves to be made more precise: the word genesis is taken here in the sense [. . .] [of] the process of individuation in its generality. There is a genesis when the coming-into-being of a system of primitively oversaturated reality, rich in potential, greater than unity and harbouring an internal incompatibility, constitutes for this system the discovery of compatibility, a resolution through the advent of structure. *This structuration is the advent of an organization that is the basis of an equilibrium of metastability.* (Simondon, 2017: 168, our addition, our emphasis)

For Simondon, genesis occurs in the process of individuation when a set of interlocking processes produce a 'resolution' which is what he calls the 'advent of structure' or *structuration*. This, therefore, is a new moment in any process of individuation: the movement of genesis which founds a new 'equilibrium of metastability'. This is not at all far away from Rölli's comments on Deleuze above, where he noted that genetic phenomenology is concerned with the 'problem area' of what Simondon might have termed the coming-into-being of consciousness, with, that is, the genesis of a *metastable* aesthetic. In both cases, that is, the movement of genesis is a movement in a process of individuation through which a new 'stable point' is produced, a stable point which produces a new 'statically present' given for consciousness or a new 'equilibrium of metastability' between the organism and the milieu, as examples. For our purposes, the question of aesthetic genesis is therefore: How does this or that perception come to be taken as *given*, rather than something which has been *produced* under particular conditions and as a particular response?[12] That is, how such a process of genesis plays a role in the production of structurated and metastable conditions of perception and sensibility. Aesthetics (taken as the theory of what is sensed, the sensible) has, classically, founded itself upon what can be represented based on the given. Deleuze, rather, seeks – as did, in distinct ways, Husserl and Simondon – to enquire into the genesis of the sensible itself (Bryant, 2008: 9).

On (2): this injection of contingency and changeability situates the realm of 'intervention' as one of historical context rather than historical immutability. 'What modes of perception are dominant in a particular historical context?' becomes a crucial question insofar as the genesis of sensibility occurs in particular historico-empirical spacetimes. The focus on *genesis*, therefore, and how aesthetic regimes are produced and sedimented in vast and complex processes of individuation, flows into a focus on how it might be possible to *intervene* in such politico-aesthetic conditions and sculpt them anew. See how, for example, Franco 'Bifo' Berardi situates our approach to aesthetics as necessarily entwined with an analysis of contemporary global capitalism (he is here discussing Félix Guattari's notion of the 'aesthetic paradigm'):

> What is aesthetics? In contrast to the prevalent understanding of Western philosophy, aesthetics is not only the science of an object's beauty. Aesthetics is also (and this is what is of greatest interest) the science of sensibility, of perception, the science of the contact between epidermises, and thus the science of the projection of worlds by subjectivities in becoming. *There is no social question any more essential than this one, because cognitive capitalism is an affection of sensibility more than anything else.* (2008: 32, our emphasis)

We will not address the italicised element now, as this will be taken up in much greater detail in Part II. However, it does gesture towards the historical forces at play in the genesis and sedimentation of perception, the production of which, as we developed in the previous chapter, is indissociable from the capture of the operations of the syntheses of time and desire. With Deleuze, scaping emphatically *does not* take the sensible as a set of given elements receivable to the self-same faculty of perception; rather, 'sensibility is itself the result of *productive processes* that actually create or produce the qualities of sensibility' (Bryant, 2008: 9, our emphasis). Consider again the first synthesis of the living present we addressed in Chapter 1. The 'living present' of contractions, retentions, and expectations, we argued above, constitute the very habits through which life is lived. One of the upshots of the notion of 'aesthetic' which we are employing is to situate this experienced 'living present' as an *aesthetic product* or *effect*, that is, as a *mode of perception which is produced in determinate conditions and through certain production processes* (though the 'modes of perceptions' which are produced are not reducible to their conditions: relations remain external to their terms). As such, the 'aesthetic conditions' of a given context cannot be disassociated from the politics of these aesthetic conditions, nor from how desire becomes rhythmically sedimented into certain practices of retention and protention. Readers of Rancière would be correct to see resonances between this account and his notion on the centrality of certain 'aesthetic regimes' to 'political regimes'. For Rancière, 'aesthetic regimes' *distribute the sensible* in new ways; which is to say that an aesthetic regime organises forms of visibility, invisibility, speech, silence, perceptibility, imperceptibility, imaginability, and unimaginability (2004). In *The Future of the Image*, Rancière argues that, in the nineteenth century, the proliferation of the possibilities of popular culture made possible a new aesthetic regime:

> [A] major trade in collective imagery was created [. . .] that was devoted to a set of functions at once dispersed and complementary: giving members of a 'society' with uncertain reference-points the means of seeing and amusing themselves in the form of defined types; creating around market products a halo of words and images that made them desirable; assembling, thanks to mechanical presses and the new procedure of lithography, an encyclopaedia of the shared human inheritance: remote life-forms, works of art, popularized bodies of knowledge [. . .] It is a period that witnesses an unlimited proliferation of the vignettes and little tales in which a society learns to recognize itself. (2009: 16)

Stiegler, too, highlights the indissociability of aesthetics, desire, politics, and technics:

> Politics is the art of securing the unity of the state in its *desire* for a common future, in its in-dividuation, its singularity as becoming-one. Such a desire assumes a *common aesthetic ground:* being together is a feeling together. A political community is, therefore, a community of feeling. (Stiegler, 2014b: 2, second emphasis ours)

The developments Rancière highlights are too, no doubt, indissociable from movements in *technical* evolution; the development of modern printing techniques, mass production, and so on (namely, the Industrial Revolution), rendered possible the coalescing and sedimenting of a new aesthetic regime; such a movement of technical evolution has already been signalled as a key development in the growth of modern nation-states by Benedict Anderson in his *Imagined Communities* (2006). Three points can be added to Rancière's depiction here. First: famously, Rancière is critical and, indeed, dismissive of approaches which depict 'aesthetic regimes' as all-powerful determinants insofar as they implicitly depict and rely upon passive and obedient subjects of these regimes. Such an approach Rancière identifies in the lineage of Guy Debord's *Society of the Spectacle* (2002), wherein the aesthetic regime's distributed power and distributed agency inversely corresponds to the disempowerment and passivity of 'meek' subjects of that regime; 'a rather simplistic view of the poor morons of the society of the spectacle, bathing contentedly in a flood of media images' (Rancière, 2009: 28). Our notion of 'aesthetic regimes' or 'aesthetic conditions' refuses such a hardened and hierarchic approach insofar as it is interested in the *genesis* and potential *changeability* of aesthetic regimes, which we noted above. Indeed, *the entire notion of aesthetic interventionism acquires momentum through the insight that such regimes are by no means beyond the capabilities of those subject to those regimes to transform and sculpt anew.* Second, we do not occupy the same aesthetic regime which Rancière depicts here. Third, as Stiegler notes, and bringing us closer to the present, the 'technologies of *aisthēsis*' are key sites of political contestation – in what Stiegler calls our contemporary *aesthetic war* – through which the '*conscious and unconscious rhythms of bodies and souls*', that is, the 'rhythms of consciousness and life' are subject to control and modulation through, among other things, audiovisual and digital technologies (Stiegler, 2014b: 2), bringing us again to the question of the cyberneticisation of everyday life, which we will return to in greater detail in the next chapter. For now, we will move on to the notion of *extemporaneous counter-actualisation*, which develops in more detail the potential changeability of aesthetic regimes.

ii. Extemporaneous counter-actualisation

Extemporaneousness echoes the Greek term *phrónēsis*, a type of practical wisdom which indicates a sort of flair for timing: *a rhythmic flair*. An extemporaneous gesture is extemporaneous *in relation to* the aesthetic conditions or regime in which that gesture is actualised. The extemporaneous gesture is a gesture which effectuates a certain ontological intensification. This temporal notion is one we can signal towards through a conversation between Heidegger, Bergson, and Deleuze (and we will revisit some of the temporal themes of Chapter 1). For all three of these thinkers, the concept of time cannot be accounted for simply through a *quantitative* conceptualisation of time; that is, time is not reducible to *static*, extensive, divisible, reversible 'units'. That is, it cannot be thought in terms of metricised or metric time. Indeed, famously, it is Bergson's contention that such a conception of time submits time to *spatialisation*: extensivity, divisibility, reversibility, and quantifiability effectuate an ontological subordination of the concept of time to a certain way of viewing *space*. For Bergson, empirical sciences belie the 'direct experience' of the qualitative and continuous flux of duration which forms the prediscursive ground of extensive time (and which we met in Deleuze's first synthesis of the living present). Similarly, for Heidegger, time is not adequately captured by extensive or spatial descriptions. The experience of time, for Heidegger, is always one of futural projection. Heidegger's *Dasein* doesn't exist in the 'now', but rather, *Dasein* exists through its temporal projection into the future. *Dasein* is always 'ahead of oneself' in some way. No doubt, we cannot conflate Heidegger and Bergson, though there are clear resonances in their dissatisfaction with spatialised and scientistic conceptions of time (Bergson, 1910: 78–79; Heidegger, 2013: 235–341).

What does this have to do with extemporaneousness? Discussing this, James Gilbert-Walsh argues that philosophical practice can be positioned and gauged regarding the extent to which it *disrupts* extant dominating rhythms. In other words, extemporaneous philosophical practice disrupts the present: it injects a new rhythm into conceptual practice, it *disrupts* extant aesthetic conditions. Extemporaneous disruptions are situated and contingent. Which is also to say that *what* disrupts will always in part depend on the ontological parameters of the present: what can disrupt depends on what is being disrupted. (Or, to phrase this differently, what effects maps have on territories – since the map immanently participates in the territory – depends on what relationship the map creates with regard the territory.) Bergson and Heidegger both, he argues, attempted to effectuate such disruptions in problematising the dominant conceptual approaches to time. It is always *this* interruption, rather than interruption as such. Extemporaneous interruption is 'a precarious, interruptive *praxis* which must repeatedly begin anew, turning back upon its concrete discursive circumstances' (Gilbert-Walsh, 2010: 188). Or, as Deleuze might say, interruption is repeated, but what is repeated is always repeated *differently*. Indeed, this notion of extemporaneous philosophical practice dovetails with Deleuze's comments on the relationship between philosophy and time in *Nietzsche and Philosophy*:

> If philosophy's critical task is not actively taken up in every epoch philosophy dies [. . .] Stupidity and baseness are always those of our own time, of our contemporaries, our stupidity and our baseness. Unlike the atemporal concept of error, baseness is inseparable from

time, that is from this rapture of the present, from this present condition in which it is incarnated and in which it moves. This is why
philosophy has an essential relation to time: it is always against its
time, critique of the present world. The philosopher creates concepts that are neither eternal nor historical but untimely and not of
the present [. . .] philosophy [is] always untimely, untimely at every
epoch. (Deleuze, 2006: 107, our addition)

There are, however, open questions as to disruptive extemporaneous
practice: What kind of ontological modifications might such a practice
help effectuate? Are there transcendental conditions for 'successful' disruptions, as if such disruptions ontologically pre-exist their actualisation
as a formal possibility that we need only actualise? As we noted above,
scaping is about the *genesis* of immanent revolutionary vectors along
the contours of the present. The language of genesis was deliberate. As
Miguel de Beistegui (2010: 15) notes, utilising a language of 'possibility'
and 'actualisation' reintroduces a (transcendent or supernaturalist) logic
of resemblance into a theory of historical change (what we termed above
when discussing eschatology in terms of *temporal unidirectionality*).

Why is such language transcendent or supernaturalist, that is, non-
immanent? Insofar as such language implies disruptions ontologically
pre-exist as a formal possibility, it succumbs to finalism or eschatology
insofar as it would posit historical movements as being the actualisation
of some 'inner potential' of history: as if (transcendent) history has already
decided the ontological movement. Scaping is not about the (identitar-
ian) actualisation of history's inner potential, but about the (differential)
genesis of an alternative future. Extemporaneous interruption is a movement in line with the third synthesis of the future: it radically opens
the past, present, and future. It seeks to *transform* and *sculpt* the territory
along new vectors from the only place it can: in the middle, through
laying down new rhythms, attempting counter-actualisation and dramatisation. Such a transformation, however, is ontologically risky. Opening
the present is a precarious and tenuous task which can generate new
co-ordinates in the present. The effects of counter-actualisation cannot
be predetermined in advance, and hence, can generate dangers.

To *counter-actualise* is to attempt to rip open the extant hegemonic
rhythms of thought, life, and perception (Beistegui, 2010: 113–114):
*counter-actualisation is positioned here as an attempt to intervene into dominant
aesthetic conditions*, a departure from *habit* and *habitat* (Massumi, 1992: 95).
Forcefully developed by Deleuze in *The Logic of Sense*, counter-actualisation
is Deleuze's term for an ontological movement which disrupts the extant
'actual' through an intensive movement of virtualisation (on Deleuze's

virtual-intensive-actual ontology).[13] Counter-actualisation is a 'grasping' of the rapturous event (Deleuze, 2004a: 173) – opening up a zone of indeterminacy (Massumi, 1992: 99) – affirming its disjunction (an immanent use of the disjunctive synthesis) with the extant and hegemonic series (or rhythms) of the present (Deleuze, 2004a: 204). Somewhat poetically and certainly affirmatively, Deleuze notes:

> [The rupturous event] is as distinct from its actualization as from the causes which produce it, using to its advantage the eternal part of excess over these causes and the part which is left unaccomplished in its actualizations, skimming over its own field, making us its own offspring. And if it is indeed at the point where the actualization cannot accomplish or the cause produce that the entire event resides, it is at the same point also that it offers itself to counter-actualisation; it is here that our greatest freedom lies – the freedom by which we develop and lead the event to its completion and transmutation, and finally become masters of actualizations and causes. (Ibid.: 243, our addition)

Counter-actualisation is a virtualisation, not an actualisation. Counter-actualisation establishes the conditions under which a new actualisation can take place, though it is by no means an 'actualisation of the virtual'. Counter-actualisation is an intensive opening of the present, which is part of the movement towards generating a new future. Chris Colwell, for example, notes how Foucault's genealogies can be read as counter-actualisations. Foucault's genealogies did not seek to produce a new, static, mimetic, representationalist 'version' of history. Rather, they *counter-actualised* (or *problematised*) hegemonic approaches to it. Foucault's genealogies are not new representationalist histories, but movements of counter-actualisation. The task of Foucauldian genealogy is not the discovery of solutions, but the invention of new problems. As Colwell notes:

> [Counter-actualisation] is an attempt to return to the virtual structure of the event to pave the way for a new actualization. The problem is that, if I have Deleuze right, we cannot isolate and individuate the virtual components of events as discrete elements since to do so is to make them present, to make them actual. That is, identifying and isolating them is to serialize them and repeat them in such as to bring them to bear on the present. A project of this sort would be an actualization of the virtual which would defeat the purpose of returning to the virtual itself. Moreover, it would reduce genealogy to history by re-introducing representation at

the heart of genealogy. Such a project would presuppose that the virtual could be represented, that there are discrete, fixed events in history that contain the truth of the matter. (Colwell, 1997, our alteration)

The movement of counter-actualisation, as virtualisation, is described by Rölli as a *withdrawal* from the present, through which *past* and *future* are radically opened and experienced as *non-given* (Rölli, 2016: 152). This movement of opening is always untimely: 'in the temporal mode of counter-actualisation, where breaks in the continuum of hardened habits *open up*, where transitions between clear perceptions must be produced or where unanticipated problems pose themselves' (ibid.: 283). As untimely, counter-actualisation creates new problems to be solved; here, Deleuze highlights how this moment is where our 'greatest freedom' lies precisely insofar as it opens the past and future to the virtual: to the potential production of the new.[14]

Desire re-enters our discussion here insofar as the interruptive counter-repetitions constitutive of counter-actualisation involve the launch of a 'counterinvestment whereby revolutionary desire is plugged into the existing social field as a source of energy' (Deleuze and Guattari, 1983a: 30). This constitutes a withdrawal from or *suspension of* the molecular interlockings of rhythm and desire that pertain in the present (ibid.: 181) through an aesthetic-libidinal break transforming and opening the experience of the present:

> The actualization of revolutionary potential is explained less by the preconscious state of causality in which it is nonetheless included, *than by the efficacy of a libidinal break at a precise moment, a schiz whose sole cause is desire – which is to say the rupture with causality that forces a rewriting of history on a level with the real, and produces this strangely polyvocal moment when everything is possible.* (Ibid.: 378, our emphasis)

The movement of extemporaneous counter-actualisation, therefore, functions in what Deleuze and Guattari call the revolutionary pole of group fantasy, and through the potential 'power to experience institutions themselves as mortal, to destroy or change them according to the articulations of desire and the social field' (ibid.: 63). Or, to put this in slightly different terms, the movement of extemporaneous counter-actualisation constitutes an intensive *dislodging*, interruption, or *disruption* of habit – habit, which, in Félix Ravaisson's terms, functions as a 'infinitesimal *differential*' (2008: 59) between 'Will' and 'Nature', or between the

arrhythmic repetition of the same and the differential-intensive movement of rhythmic differentiation – *through which the spacetime is produced
for the creation of new habits, practices, milieus, or in short: new rhythms.*

Revolutionary practices emerge not through the actualisation of an
inevitability, nor a probability, but through a *grasping* and *becoming-worthy*
of those rupturous events that revolutions must be, a creative grasping which produces that excess 'when everything is possible', when
mental-social-environmental ecologies are experienced in line with
the third synthesis of the future: groundlessness. It is important, however, not to fetishise any apparent 'moment' when such a movement
has been effectuated. We have used the term 'movement' in part as a
rejection of the notion of the 'moment', as any reduction of the former
to latter risks reducing this *process* to particular isolated, static, spatialised, pre-constituted, and metricised temporal co-ordinates. The event
is processual not momentary; it is created, produced, generated, and is
not pre-constituted. Furthermore, foregoing process in favour of the
'moment' is *also* to forego the inclusion of rhythm into revolutionary
practice: our approach, instead, inserts into such practices the importance of the cumulative, generative, and rhythmic practices which may
be necessary in order to produce such a rhythmic-libidinal break, and
therefore into our conceptualisation of revolution (which we discuss
further in the following section).[15] Lefebvre was prescient on this:

> All becoming irregular [*dérèglement*] (or, if one wants, all *deregula-
> tion*, though this word has taken on an official sense) of rhythms
> produces antagonistic effects. It *throws out of order* and disrupts; it
> is symptomatic of a disruption that is generally profound, lesional
> and no longer functional. It can also produce a lacuna, a hole in
> time, to be filled in by an invention, a creation. That only happens,
> individually or socially, by passing through a *crisis*. Disruptions
> and crises always have origins in and effects on rhythms: those of
> institutions, of growth, of the population, of exchanges, of work,
> therefore those which make or *express* the complexity of present
> societies. (Lefebvre, 2015: 52–53)

So, we are here able to gather some of these threads between 'aesthetics' and 'extemporaneous counter-actualisation'. Taken broadly
and ontologically as concerned with the *conditions of genesis of sensibility*, conditions which are partly historico-empirical, the movement of
extemporaneous counter-actualisation is a situated mode of *aesthetic intervention* which intervenes and interrupts extant dominating aesthetic
regimes and rhythms of life, opening up the spacetime for the creative

elaboration of new rhythms, that is, new habits, new practices, and new milieus. *Aesthetic intervention temporally disrupts aesthetic conditions which pertain in a given context*: it is an aesthetico-temporal interruption. Rancière would term such a movement the beginnings of a *redistribution of the sensible* (1989: 22).

iii. Rhythmic dramatisation

Let us pivot to the notion of dramatisation. This term is another Deleuzian one. Didier Debaise, discussing the function of dramatisation in Deleuze's method, argues that to dramatise is to perform a sort of creative ontological exploration. To quote: 'dramatization makes no claim to establish once and for all their [concept's] coordinates [. . .] one might say that drama is discovered only insofar as it is first constructed or invented' (2016: 9–11, our addition). Dramatisation is taken here as a mode of *co-ordinate creation* or *composition*. In our practice of scaping, we will call it a *rhythmic-sculptural process*. The productive indeterminacy of concepts (given we are not aiming for static representational mimesis or epistemological closure) is seized upon by dramatisation as a process of *intensification* and of *actualisation*, unlike the movement of extemporaneous counter-actualisation, which is a process of *virtualisation*. As MacKenzie and Porter note (2011: 493): 'dramatization as method requires that we stage new relations within and between the concepts that animate politics in order to express the indeterminate yet endlessly provocative nature of the Idea of the political'.[16] Though dramatisation is by no means limited to conceptualisation. *Dramatisation injects new rhythms into the present.* Such an injection is a movement of creative actualisation. Deleuze argues that movements of actualisation 'may be called *differential rhythms* in view of their role in the actualisation of the Idea' (2014: 282, our emphasis). Injecting new rhythms into the present – *rhythmic dramatisation* – is a movement which partakes in the process of a new (differential) actualisation (Deleuze, 2004b: 100). Dramatisation is a movement of actualisation partaking in a process of individuation, and is approached in terms of *process*, rather than in terms of the putative end-point of any such process (Rölli, 2016: 273); Deleuze speaks of the movement of dramatisation in terms similar to that of the refrain (which we will discuss in more detail in Chapter 3), as a movement which partakes in the production of internal and external milieus, interiorisation-exteriorisation (qualitative and extensive (Deleuze, 2014: 321)) and thus as a type *bordering* practice:

> A living being is not only defined genetically, by the dynamisms which determine its internal milieu, but also ecologically, by the

external movements which preside over its distribution within an extensity [. . .] Everything is even more complicated when we consider that the internal space is itself made up of multiple spaces which must be locally integrated and connected, and that this connection, which may be achieved in many ways, pushes the object or living being to its own limits, all in contact with the exterior; and that this relation with the exterior, and with other things and living beings, implies in turn connections and global integrations which differ in kind from the preceding. Everywhere a staging [i.e., a *drama*] at several levels. (Ibid.: 281–282, our addition)[17]

Dramatisations are always processes of differentiation, each requiring 'the time of their actualisation' (ibid.: 284). Such processes of differentiation are explained by Deleuze in terms of *intensity*, or, more precisely, in terms of a *difference in intensity* (ibid.: 293), but it is more precise to define intensity *as* difference, 'in so far as [intensity] is the reason of the sensible. Every intensity is differential, by itself a difference' (ibid.: 294, our addition; also see Crockett, 2013: 48–53). Importantly, especially for our purposes, difference in intensity is identified by Deleuze as the sufficient reason of the *given*, as that by which the given is given, or that through which the *genesis* of the given – the aesthetic, the being of the sensible – is to be explained:

The reason of the sensible, the condition of that which appears, is not space and time but the Unequal in itself, *disparateness* as it determined and comprised in difference of intensity, in intensity as difference. (Deleuze, 2014: 294)

It is difference in intensity, not contrariety in quality, which constitutes the being 'of' the sensible [. . .] It is intensity or difference in intensity which constitutes the peculiar limit of sensible. (Ibid.: 310)

If, as Deleuze repeatedly emphasises, it is characteristic of the process of actualisation to *efface* its constitutive difference in extensity, the process of rhythmic dramatisation as we are articulating it nonetheless seeks to, as much as possible, *remain intensive*, making difference into a continual object of affirmation (ibid.: 307, 309). Rhythmic dramatisation is nothing other than a continuous, which is to say processual, affirmation of intensity and production of difference, a process of individuation remaining constitutively open in its actualisation. Rhythmic dramatisation must remain intensive, for it 'is intensity which *dramatises*' (ibid.: 321).

The notion of rhythm, here, allows for and envelops within its practice the ever-present possibility of the effacement of difference and intensity, but attempts to keep this spacetime for differentiation-intensification open through the attached permanent possibility of *repeating anew* the practice of rhythmic dramatisation made possible through new movements of counter-actualisation, that is, through the invention of new problems. This coupling of dramatisation and counter-actualisation is the coupling of two elements in the self-same conceptual-ontological movement or refrain: scaping attempts to rip open the extant hegemonic rhythms of thought and life (counter-actualisation) towards a creative ontological exploration which lays down new rhythms and invents co-ordinates – a sculptural process (dramatisation). *And which is a task to be repeated, differently.*

Above, we referred to aesthetic interventionism as a *rhythmic-sculptural refrain*. In addition to this, we have intermittently used the term 'sculpture' but have not yet accorded it the importance that it will come to have in our project of *scaping*. The notion of sculpture employed here is a notion drawn from a re-reading of Joseph Beuys's practice which he termed *social sculpture*. The notion and practice of *social sculpture* can, it is hoped, provide us with an assemblage of enunciation through which to partially explicate how it might be possible to make intensity and difference a *continual and processual object of affirmation in practice.* Further, our development of Beuys's notion of social sculpture is not of an exegetical nature. Scaping, to reiterate, is not about static representational mimesis, but experimental construction. As such, our account of Beuys's will coalesce with and depart from him at various junctures.

Social sculpture is an expanded concept of art which Beuys developed in order to blur distinctions between thought and life; between aesthetics, ethics, and politics; and between the 'process' of artistic invention and its 'object' or end-point.[18] Social sculpture operationalises this expanded concept of art practice through rendering artistic practices as having the immanent potential of experimenting with social practices and creating new social rhythms. Consider the following quote:

> My objects are to be seen as stimulants for the transformation of the idea of sculpture, or of art in general. They should provoke thoughts about what sculpture can be and how the concept of sculpting can be extended to the invisible materials used by everyone.
>
> THINKING FORMS – how we mold our thoughts or

SPOKEN FORMS – how we shape our thoughts into words or

SOCIAL SCULPTURE – how we mold and shape the world in which we live: SCULPTURE AS AN EVOLUTIONARY PROCESS; EVERYONE AS AN ARTIST.

That is why the nature of my sculpture is not fixed and finished. Processes continue in most of them: chemical reactions, fermentations, color changes, decay, drying up. Everything is in a STATE OF CHANGE. (Beuys, 1990: 19)

Social sculpture is also, for Beuys, an *ecological* approach, which seeks to attune itself to the relations we have with ourselves (mental ecology), with others (social ecology), and with 'nature' (environmental ecology) (note that Beuys was a founding member of the German Green Party in 1979):

The socio-ecological approach begins with 'Everyone is an Artist' [. . .] with a concept of freedom and creativity involving social totality, and establishing for the first time socio-ecological work whereby environmental damage is eliminated from the roots. (Beuys, quoted in Tisdall, 1979: 268–269)

Beuys's invocation of 'the invisible materials used by everyone' in the first quote above – i.e., thought, speech, and social relations – becomes a vital processual 'object' of social sculpture. This involves an expanded and ever-extending array of experimental practices of our relations with our own thoughts and bodies, and in being with others: intensive experiments and the production of difference. As such, social sculpture becomes an array of practices in which art refers not at all to institutions of art or the production of artistic objects of consumption, but rather expands to concern itself with the ecology of the milieu as such. Consider the following quote from Volker Harlan on Beuys's work:

The creative, forming process begins in our thought process: 'Thinking = Sculpture'; it begins to voice itself in our speaking: 'Speaking = Sculpture'; it is taken further into writing: '*Even when I write my name, I am drawing,*' and can manifest as a drawing, an object, an installation, an action, or a social process work. Indeed, Beuys stresses again and again that the genesis and making of an artwork is the most essential and important thing: it is, in itself, an '*Action.*' The object is simply the imprint, the trace of the creative activity. (Harlan, 2004: 1)

The art object is rendered as a trace *effect* of 'sculpture-as-social-action' (Risk, 2006: 140). Beuys continually centralises process, rhythm, and ecology when discussing his artistic practice. His is an aestheti-co-temporal practice which attempts a creative refiguring of how subjects, objects, art, and artistic processes are squeezed and filtered through dominant social, political, economic, and artistic institutions under contemporary capitalism. Such a creative refiguring harbours the potential, for Beuys, of alternative and new relationships to ourselves, to others, and to the non-human (Beuys, 2004: 22–23). *The invention of new rhythms are sculptural processes; rhythmic dramatisation is the aestheti-co-temporal sculpture of new habits, new processes, new modes of perception, new thoughts, new ways of being.* In short, social sculpture becomes indissociable from a carving into the future, an attempt to sculpt a new future (Beckmann, 2008: 97).

Traditional sculpture is not a central theme in Deleuze nor in Deleuze and Guattari (Risk, 2006: 141), or is only gestured towards tangentially. In *What is Philosophy?*, however, Deleuze and Guattari do note that painting, (traditional) sculpting, composition, and writing attempt to wrestle with sensations (affects and perceptions) and have the potential to unleash 'strange becomings' (2013b: 169) – i.e., have the potential to participate in new movements of intensification and dramatisation – through distinctive methods which redistribute the sensible in new, unforeseeable directions. Rhythmic dramatisation – positioned as a type of social sculpture through which *life rhythms* become indissociable from *sculpting the social* – cuts into and sculpts the future *processually*, in which it 'is always a question of freeing life wherever it is Imprisoned, or of tempting it into an uncertain combat' (ibid.: 171).

Two key questions emerge in our utilisation and development of Beuys's notion of social sculpture. The first relates to whether this notion fetishises and reifies 'the social'; and, relatedly, whether this notion onto-logically prioritises the social *at the expense* of 'the individual'. This will be addressed in more detail in Chapter 3 (in particular with the notion of a *singularising existential refrain*) and in Part II we will explore some specific examples of such practices, but for now it will suffice to add two caveats to ensure our later developments of these concepts are clearer. First, insofar as all artwork is generative of, or partakes in, the consti-tution of a milieu (milieus which always *provoke the organism to orient its becoming*), repetitively or rhythmically, our account of rhythmic-sculp-tural dramatisation is concerned with the *conditions* of how such orienta-tion can be practised. Those 'invisible materials' that orient and cement the milieu, and channel becomings within the milieu and the milieu's becoming (thought, speech, relations (e.g., institutions and economic organisations)), constitute the veritable *conditions* for not only all 'conventional' artwork but social existence within the milieu as such. To these 'invisible materials' we include time and change, that is, rhythm. Take, for example, Beuys's *Bureau for Direct Democracy*, at *documenta 5* in 1972, in which over the course of 100 days (the standard length of the *documenta* exhibitions), Beuys participated in discussions with anyone who wished to participate on direct democracy (and ideas on how to 'achieve' it), the relationship between art and politics, among other things, and on which records were taken.

All we will note on this particular experiment is how those 'invisible materials' of thought, speech, and relations – which were the very 'stuff' of the experiment for all participants (Beuys included) – all become subject to challenge and change over the course of its 100-day practice (Beuys and Schwarze, 1979: 244–249; Fitzpatrick, 2014: 126). Indeed, one of Beuys's central criticisms of, for example, minimal artworks was how they displayed an inertness, a closedness, in which the artwork, once completed, was resistant to change (Suquet, 1995: 150). Social sculpture's extended conception of art seeks to make those very conditions of artistic practice the object of change in the process, challenging us to experiment with and *transform* them in practices which reshuffle the co-ordinates of artistic-social practice through such experimentation. Second, those invisible materials (thought, speech, relations), and indeed what appears initially as the active agent of sculpture (the 'social' of *social sculpture*), are thereby themselves subject to transformation through the practice of social sculpture: those materials, as well as the social itself, never remain unchanged in the practice of social sculpture; thought, as sculpture, is *sculpted anew* in the practice of social sculpture (Lechte, 1997: 20) – an *intensive* process – the social is that which *emerges*, and always emerges *anew*, from the practice of sculpture, whether that be through individual practices (which always relate to the social in some particular way, i.e., all individual practices are transindividual) or collaborative ones (which always relate to and depend upon diverse individual engagement and practice, i.e., all collective practices are transindividual). (In many of his artworks, Beuys used fat as a medium, due to fat's transitional fluidity, the ease at which it could be moulded, and which helped to express softening, fluidity, and change: 'Beuys admired fat's easy transition between a melted, unformed, chaotic state and a cooled, specific form' (Adams, 1992: 29).) This dovetails with what Deleuze and Guattari describe in relation to the tasks of schizoanalysis: 'That is what the completion of the process is: not a promised pre-existing land, but a world created in the process of its tendency, its coming undone, its deterritorialization' (1983a: 322); and which Gary Genosko clarifies in terms of mutually supporting processes of theoretical development and organisational change organised towards 'self-positing trajectories and processes of singularization' (2018: 208). Social sculpture is psycho-social, simultaneously both singular and collective (Stiegler, 2015: 99). Two caveats, therefore, resisting any putative fetishisation of the social: rhythmic-sculptural dramatisation as concerned with the *conditions* of practice within the milieu, and with how whatever 'the social' is, or becomes, as only *emerging* (like the art object) as an *imprint* or *effect* of the practices which constitute social sculpture.

The second question raised by our development of this concept relates to the question of the *instigation* of social sculpture, and the related question of *authority* over the practice. While Beuys's social sculpture experiments were explicitly geared towards invigorating the discussion, debate, and practice of, for example, direct democracy, these experiments often faced criticism due to the centrality of Beuys in the instigation and practice of these experiments, as well as the authority he maintained throughout the practice. To take one example that Lünen highlights:

> On one of his several visits to Ireland (both Northern Ireland and the Republic of Ireland) in 1974, for example, he would meet with members of the Catholic community in a Belfast district, who were not pleased to be at the end of 'impenetrable language' and his 'elitism', and to be lectured about the benefits of education when their own parish priest was organizing educational sessions in the community center already [. . .] This is, alas, a contradiction seen in many Fluxus artists, as Frieling [2008: 41] remarks, who 'stage events' that 'were ultimately driven by the artist's persona (this was the inherent paradox of Beuys's collaborative and participatory practice)'. (Lünen, 2016: 35, our alteration)

This paradox is one that any 'participatory' experiment must confront, that is, the boundaries of participation and authority therein. Further, and to be fair to Beuys, there are different reports emerging from his experiments with social sculpture, as Beckmann points out:

> I heard [Beuys] give speeches in which he talked for more than two and a half hours in front of over 500 students; yet when he was finished, he continued the discussion for two more hours. Although the doors of the auditorium were all open, no one left early – an intensity I have never experienced anywhere else. (Beckmann, 2008: 96–97, our alteration)

The purposes of this discussion of Beuys are, to reiterate, not exegetical, nor are they concerned with 'deciding' on these questions in relation to Beuys himself.[19] This is, for us, besides the point in articulating our concept of rhythmic dramatisation. What, then, is at stake in developing on Beuys's concepts, works, and practices, in affirming every human being as an artist, in enlivening the process of social sculpture? Stiegler's own discussion of Beuys can sharpen this. He relates the affirmation of EVERYONE AS AN ARTIST to the parallel philosophical assertion, 'which implies that *everyone is a philosopher by right if not in fact,* which is to say *potentially if not in act*' (2015: 61). The *division* between, say, 'artists' and 'non-artists', or between 'philosophers' and 'non-philosophers' – though these are only two examples – in the contemporary distribution of the sensible is, for Stiegler, *precisely* the object of a combat (in today's aesthetic war) and evolutionary dissolution through social sculpture. Or, to put it differently, social sculpture in this sense is concerned with *total access to the (r)evolutionary transformation of the social*, constituting a vast *opening* of the future to its participatory transformation; this constitutive openness retaining the element of intensity. This is also a question of *access* to technics (Stiegler, 1998: 240–243; Simondon, 2017: 121), or what Simondon calls the creation of a new encyclopaedism, that is, the creation of open 'block[s] of available and open technical knowledge' through which a milieu 'govern[s] itself on its own' (Simondon, 2017: 111, our additions) and can continually produce difference itself. It is not simply that, through social sculpture, 'everyone is an artist' in the sense of an artist who produces artworks linked to artistic institutions. Rather, for us, it relates to revolutions in everyday life, and of about the *total access* to the participation in the work that is the creation of *new* milieus, *new* habits, and *new* practices, cutting into the future and sculpting it anew; all of which is to say the milieu's participation in its *own* singularisation, intensification, or differentiation:

> [N]o man [sic] is *ever* an artist *in act* – never except in intermittent ways, and turned towards an *everyone* which, being no one in particular, is all the more improbable, uncertain, adventurous and fortuitous: singular. *Otium* is self-moulding by way of self-discipline and self-practise [i.e., technics, techniques], it is a *self-production* as *self-other* through the techniques of individuation: it is a *poetics* to the precise extent that it is a *poiēsis*. But such a self-moulding only makes sense as a *social* sculpture. (Stiegler, 2015: 110, our addition)

Social sculpture, Stiegler goes on to note, is a 'struggle for the organization of the sensible' (ibid.: 110), that is, what we here are calling the *aesthetic:* it is in this sense that the work of social sculpture is ever-and-always a process of *aesthetic intervention.* Given this, and to return more closely to the topic of this section: practices of rhythmic dramatisation, as a rhythmic-sculptural refrain, are positioned as direct political practices and experiments; such a practice of social sculpture is instigated, generated, and produced in the milieu in question, and towards (r)evolutionary transformation. Rigid hierarchies are subject to constant transformation in the process of social sculpture. Indeed, to quote Beuys again, social sculpture is defined as 'how we mold and shape the world in which we live: SCULPTURE AS AN EVOLUTIONARY PROCESS; EVERYONE AS AN ARTIST', and in which he consistently emphasises the *processual nature* of sculptural practice: 'Everything is in a STATE OF CHANGE' (Beuys, 1990: 19). *Rigid, permanent,* or *stable* hierarchies, in this sense, are constitutive of a failed attempt at social sculpture: they have failed to keep the intensive element open. Effects (i.e., 'subjects' and 'objects') may be produced in this process (indeed, such effects are the to-be-expected moments through which intensity is effaced in extensity), but *rhythmic dramatisation* is more concerned with the rhythmic-processual element of such sculptural practice. At times, however, Beuys's ambitions for social sculpture blends into utopian-teleological, as if this process could be finished:

> This most modern art discipline – Social Sculpture/Social Architecture – will only reach fruition when every living person becomes a creator, a sculptor or architect of the social organism. Only then would the insistence on participation of the action art of FLUXUS and Happening be fulfilled; only then would democracy be fully realized. (Beuys, quoted in Tisdall, 1979: 268)

In this quote, Beuys appears to inscribe social sculpture with an element of finalism or teleology, removing the processual aspect which is absolutely crucial if the intensive or differential element is to remain open, itself a condition for social sculpture as a potentially revolutionary production. First, through positioning 'social sculpture' as a pre-constituted possible (it must be if it can 'reach fruition'). Second, through positing the possibility of the 'fulfilment' of 'FLUXUS' (i.e., becoming or transformation reaching an 'end-point'). Third, through the speculation on the 'realisation' of 'democracy' (as if 'democracy' were a pre-decided concept which needed only to be properly or correctly actualised) (also see Crowley, 2012: 51). If the rhythmic-sculptural refrain of aesthetic interventionism through which scaping attempts to operate were to insert elements of 'fruition', 'fulfilment', or 'realisation' into its practice, then, importantly, this would be to *tend towards arrhythmia*, running the risk of freezing the past, delimiting the present, and foreclosing the future; all of which would *foreclose* the intensive element and thereby *forego* dramatisation. As we noted in the previous chapter: rhythm, when critical, opens the virtual structure of the past, attempts transduction or transcoding with patterns of practice other than its own, and so, *opens the future*. While there may indeed be elements of partial closure or sedimentation in such processes, and indeed certain subjects and objects produced through such practices (as effects), *sedimentation or freezing of the process would be to submit to arrhythmia*. Scaping, as a form of *rhythmic ecology*, is, as we have already said, *about the genesis of immanent revolutionary vectors along the contours of the present*, and such a genesis is inseparable from intensity and the production of difference. Here, therefore, we attenuate our approach to social sculpture away from any such invocations of finalism; indeed, on this point of finalism Stiegler is correct to emphasise that such a search for completion effaces the extent to which all work, and for our purposes the sculptural work of rhythmic dramatisation, works '*with the incalculable* – that is, [works] with that infinity of the desirable which means that a process of individuation is constituted *through its unachievability*' (2010a: 47, our alteration), and, as such, our approach to social sculpture is 'intrinsically long-term' (Stiegler, 2010a: 86) and pitted against any such finalism, which, again, would thereby introduce *arrhythmic* temporalities into its practice. Simondon makes a similar point when he notes that 'coming-into-being is a series of spurts of structurations of a system, or of successive individuations of a system', and further:

> The relation of man to the world is not a simple adaptation, governed by a law of self-regulating finality that would find ever increasingly stable states of equilibrium; on the contrary, the evolution of this relation, in which technicity participates among other modes of being, manifests an ability to evolve that grows at each stage, discovering new forms and forces capable of making it evolve even more, rather than stabilizing it and making it tend toward more and more limited fluctuations; the very notion of finality, applied to this coming-into-being, appears inadequate, since *one can indeed find limited finalities within this coming-into-being* (search for food, defense against destructive forces), *but there is no unique and superior end that one could superimpose on all aspects of evolution in order to coordinate them and account for their origination through the search for an end that would be superior to all particular ends.* (Simondon, 2017: 169, our emphases)

Rhythmic dramatisation may encompass 'limited finalities' – these are those effects 'covering over' intensity which are to be expected – but as a process it is invariably one of constant projection, attuned to the future without subordinating its practice to some superior final cause. In this specific sense, it is fair to label rhythmic dramatisation *objectless*; that is, objectless in the same sense as we described desire in the previous chapter (when we noted that this conception of desire was about the *production* of the subject, the object, the social, and as inseparable from an examination of the mechanisms by which desire's pulsive movements become subject to capture, contraction, and sedimentation by certain regimes).

Our rhythmic-sculptural refrain of rhythmic dramatisation must, inevitably, pass through this relation to desire; for Deleuze and Guattari, the question of desire is the question of revolution: 'Desire does not "want" revolution, it is revolutionary in its own right' (1983a: 116). The work of rhythmic dramatisation is the work towards what Deleuze and Guattari call the *revolutionary investment* (ibid.: 341) which desire can make (following the distinction they make between *preconscious class interests* – which is defined by a regime of syntheses and thus 'refers to the selection of flows, to the detachment of codes, to the subjective remains or revenues' (ibid.: 344) – and *unconscious investments of desire* – which bear upon 'the degree of development of the forces or the energies on which these syntheses depend [. . .] upon the nature of the codes and the flows that condition them' (ibid.: 345)). Libidinal investment comes prior to interest, which is also to say that *revolutionary investment* does not necessarily coincide with revolutionary interest. As Aislinn O'Donnell notes, one of the key stakes of this distinction between libidinal-unconscious investments and preconscious interests, is that 'lifting the veils of false consciousness will not transform desire and will not enact revolutionary sentiments' – a transformation towards revolutionary investments requires instead both a politics of desire and a 'disruption at the level of affective life in order to create space for different ways of seeing, perceiving and thinking' (O'Donnell, 2017: 7–8).

For rhythmic dramatisation to be a process of revolutionary investment, then, it must constitute an affirmation of the immanent uses of the syntheses of desire, affirming intensity and the production of difference, *against* the overcoding of the pulsive flows of desire that pertain in the present, and which, we should reiterate, works with what Stiegler calls that *infinity* of desire, the incalculable, and unachievable. Rhythmic dramatisation, then, emerges for us as an affirmation of revolutionary investment: what Deleuze calls (as we shall see in the next section), invoking but not citing Marx, *permanent revolution* (Deleuze, 2004a: 59):

it is here where the affirmation of intensity and the production of difference dovetails with the notion of revolution we are developing. It also moves us towards what we discuss in the next chapter concerning our critique of the rhythms of everyday life. For now, the question of permanent revolution brings us to the connections between revolution, finalism, and process, to which we now turn in the final section of this chapter: what might it mean to conceptualise 'revolution' *without* the inscription of teleology, finalism, or prophecy?

d. Rhythm and revolutionary pluralism

The notion of 'revolution' is as essentially contested as a concept can come. Semantically, the term hovers between two extremes (respectively: transformational or rotational): one can (usually) *either* define a revolution as a complete overthrow and subsequent redesign of (usually) social relations; or, as a three-hundred and sixty-degree rotation, as a return to one's initial starting point (as in the revolution of one star around another star).

It is not unfair to note that this term is most obviously (historically and theoretically) associated with the Marxist tradition, and, by extension, with the revolutionary overthrow, transformation, and dissolution of state structures. As Adam Schaff (1973: 264–265) notes, Marxism usually operates on one of two definitions of revolution. In its first definition, revolution is situated as a *qualitative* transformation in state structures (a change in the social base and social super structure). A formal revolution. In its second definition, revolution is situated as a *quantitative* transformation in state structures (a rearrangement within extant socio-economic co-ordinates, also known as reformism). A social revolution. Whilst the former situates 'authentic' revolutionary praxis as that which seeks qualitative transformation imminently (with violence, if necessary), the latter instead situates 'realistic' revolutionary praxis as qualitative transformation *brought about* through continuous quantitative transformation (it is, then, a type of gradualism or evolution-towards-revolution).

As is clear, both of these Marxist definitions of revolution which Schaff notes situate themselves as transformational rather than rotational, and are primarily focused on the institutions of state and capital as the primary objects of revolution. They are focused on its qualitative transformation through different techniques of initial state centralisation and the rearrangement of capital ownership.[20] But who is, or are, the *subject(s)* or *agent(s)* of revolutionary knowledge and practice? Slavoj Žižek outlines three historical manifestations of the dialectical relations which pertain to putatively revolutionary practice and situates them with a Hegelian-Marxist ontological triad of Universal, Particular, and Singular.

On the first manifestation, which Žižek calls Marxist, the ontological hierarchy pertaining to revolutionary social transformation is one in which the Communist Party (the Singular) acts as an *ontological mediator* between History (the Universal, global movement) and the Proletariat (the Particular class with a privileged relationship to the Universal, the privileged agents of revolutionary practice). The Party, as ontological mediator, enables the formal conversion of the Proletariat from a class-in-itself to a class-for-itself (that is, from a position of shared exploitation to a position of shared class consciousness, solidarity, and revolutionary subjectivity). The Party's role, while ontologically significant, is short-lived; it is 'merely the operator of the actualization of this universal potential of the particular' (Žižek, 2000: 114). The Proletariat has the privileged relationship to the Universal, and the Party's role is to help fulfil and participate in the realisation of this relationship.

On the second manifestation, which Žižek calls Leninist, the ontological hierarchy pertaining to revolutionary social transformation is one in which the Party takes a more ontologically crucial and sustained role. The Proletariat, in this second manifestation, suffers an ontological demotion to the role of an ontological mediator between History and the Party. The Party's role becomes that of a benign educator or intellectual revolutionary vanguard; as, that is, the new privileged agents of revolutionary knowledge. The Party's role shifts from that of an ontologically necessary mediator to that of a necessary epistemological superior; here, the Party has a privileged (epistemological) relationship to the Universal when compared to the Proletariat (ibid.: 115) through and because of which the *Party* can intervene and alter objective social conditions.

On the third manifestation, which Žižek terms Stalinist, the ontological hierarchy pertaining to revolutionary social transformation is one in which, this time, History suffers an ontological demotion to that of a mediator between Proletariat and Party. How does this function? Žižek claims that Stalinist social ontology is one in which, with History divorced of its ontological importance, the onto-epistemological hierarchy (between Party and Proletariat) is even further hardened as the Party now stands in a position of hierarchy with respect to History; that is, the Party/Proletariat inegalitarianism is solidified to the extent that history is simply invoked to justify the former's exploitation of the latter (ibid.). We can see here how a putatively *transformational* revolutionary movement becomes *rotational* in the third manifestation: a return to, or rather a maintenance of, exploitation.

Žižek's comments here are partly historical and seek to track how Stalinism grew immanently from Leninism, and Leninism from Marxism. Let us focus on the question the *agency* with respect to revolutionary practice, and the process through which social transformation is conducted by a group seized or motivated by revolutionary subjectivity as the agents of revolutionary knowledge and practice. As Georg Lukács, early in his famous *History and Class Consciousness*, notes:

> Only when consciousness stands in such a relation to reality can theory and practice become united. But for this to happen the emergence of consciousness must become the *decisive step* which the historical process must take towards its proper end [. . .] The historical function of theory is to make this step a practical possibility. (Lukács, 1971: 2)

On this Marxist reading, the proletariat is positioned as requiring an 'entrance' into 'consciousness' mediated through 'theory' which enables the proletariat's *conversion* into a properly revolutionary class. No doubt, such a task is rendered more difficult given extant ideological conditions in which *ideas* form a key battleground, as another mode of class struggle, as the early Marx and Engels argued:

> The ideas of the ruling class are in every epoch the ruling ideas, i.e. the class which is the ruling *material* force of society is at the same time its ruling *intellectual* force. The class which has the means of material production at its disposal, consequently also controls the means of mental production, so that the ideas of those who lack the means of mental production are on the whole subject to it. (Marx and Engels, 2010: 59)

In the Lukács quote above, there is an invocation an 'inner potential' held by consciousness to move history in its 'proper' direction towards revolution, which, in this case at least, is 'actualised' through theory, and by the examples Žižek gave in the Leninist and Stalinist moments, through the intermediary of the Party. One aspect which is missing from such unidirectional accounts is the distinction between unconscious investments of desire and preconscious class interests, the effacement of which leads the equation of the lifting of 'false consciousness' with the acquisition of or conversion into a *revolutionary subjectivity*. What is missing, in other words, is desire, and the mechanisms of capture it can become subject to, independent of the 'objective interests' of a particular class. As Guattari notes, taking the example of the Leninist moment: the 'fundamental objective of taking political power at the level of the State, by the "avant-garde" of the proletariat, is considered by Marxist-Leninist to be the condition *sine qua non* of an autonomous coming into consciousness of itself by the working class' (2016: 64), and he goes on to note how the mechanisms of the state (such as bureaucratic structures) worked towards the (libidinic) integration of individuals into long-standing structures of power, highlighting this distinction between desire/the unconscious and class interests (ibid.: 13–14, 182).

Interestingly, Žižek notes how this invocation of 'inner potential' *itself* is the source of the dialectical logic which allows Stalinism to grow from Marxism. In *all three cases*, Žižek argues, there is no ontological space for what he calls the *act proper*:

> [T]he more we insist on how a revolutionary stance directly trans-lates the true 'inner nature' of the working class, the more we are compelled to exert external pressure on the 'empirical' work-ing class to actualize this inner potential [. . .] If class conscious-ness arises 'spontaneously,' as the actualization of inner potentials inscribed into the very objective situation of the working class, then there is no real act at all, just the purely formal conversa-tion from in–itself to for–itself [. . .] If the proper revolutionary class consciousness is to be 'imported' via the Party, then we have, on the one hand, 'neutral' intellectuals who gain the 'objective' insight into historical necessity (without engaged *intervention* into it). Then, their instrumental-manipulative use of the working class as a tool to actualize the necessity already written in the situation leaves no room for an *act* proper. (Žižek, 2000: 121–122)

In a clear sense, Žižek's point here is one we have already met. We noted above how utilising language of 'possibility' and 'actualisation' inscribes historical movement within a supernaturalist or transcendent movement in a non-immanent and non-naturalist fashion. Further, Žižek's notion of the 'act proper' is not dissimilar from conceptual themes we have already developed (though, we will distinguish our approach on this from Žižek's later in this section). For Žižek, the 'act proper' is an act which ruptures the present. In this way, he departs from those certain Marxist theories of revolution which are *onto-politically unidirectional*. By *onto-politically uni-directional*, we mean the sense in which on one reading of the Marxist revolutionary movement – whether this is theorised in terms of the rev-olutionary rearrangement of social relations or in terms of a subject's 'conversion' towards revolutionary subjectivity – is gauged towards the 'realisation' or 'actualisation' of the 'inner potential' of becoming-Marxist or a generalised becoming-communist. An act proper, in distinction, is an act which reshuffles the very co-ordinates of the initial context of decision-making (ibid.: 118); it is an act which is not reducible to its (in Marxist parlance) 'objective social co-ordinates'. An 'act proper' – for us: extemporaneous counter-actualisation and rhythmic dramatisation – is revolutionary here precisely insofar as it (a) reshuffles the co-ordinates of the possible through a redistribution of the sensible and (b) insofar as it does this, prevents the ontological movements of revolution from being rotational. Such rotationality is prevented *precisely* insofar as the 'new' which emerges through rhythmic dramatisation is not reducible to those 'aesthetic regimes' from which it emerged. Guattari expresses this thought with clarity:

> A revolution is something of the nature of a process, a change that makes it impossible to go back to the same point. This, incidentally, goes against the meaning of the term 'revolution' when used to refer to the movement of one star around another. *Revolution is, rather, a repetition that changes something, a repetition that brings about the irreversible.* A process that produces history, taking us away from a repetition of the same attitudes and the same significations. Therefore, by definition, a revolution cannot be programmed, because what is programmed is always the *déjà-là*. Revolutions, like history, always bring surprises. By nature, they are always unpredictable. That doesn't prevent one from working for revolution, as long as one understands *'working for revolution' as working for the unpredictable.* (Guattari, in Guattari and Rolnik, 2007: 258–259)

Such 'working for the unpredictable' coalesces with Stiegler's own comments on working on the incalculable we met at the end of the previous section; an essential aspect in any revolutionary process should it keep the intensive-differential element open. To inject new rhythms into the present is to change something, a process that brings about the irreversible; this is the sense of term 'revolution' which subsists in the practice of scaping. Hence its riskiness, and hence its creativity. Michael Gallope, discussing Deleuze's formulation of the relationship between affirmation, chance, and creativity, notes that through 'affirming both the risk and the creativity possible in every moment, we become attuned to the asynchronous rhythms that flow through the entire cosmos' (2017: 210). We do not need to subscribe to, or even explicate, Žižek's Lacanian-Marxist approach at this point in order to highlight how his gesture is important if we wish to keep the notion of revolution free from predictive ontological fixity (i.e., prophecy or eschatology). Revolutionary rhythms are ontologically pluridirectional and heterogenising. Revolutions are processual. Aesthetic interventionism attempts to effectuate revolutionary rhythms; scaping as heterogenesis. What this also means is that scaping's revolutionary directedness is not simply 'state-centric' or bound up with the rearrangement of material relations. State-centric approaches to revolution are fully programmatic and are onto-politically unidirectional: they are extensive reform programs and not revolutionary processes. As Guattari notes: '*revolution is either processual or it isn't revolution*. When the French Revolution stopped, signs were put up in all the town halls, and school children had to learn the declaration of human rights by heart: it was a revolution that no longer had a processual character' (Guattari, in Guattari and Rolnik, 2007: 260). Massumi:

> The end is for there to be no end, to turn collective existence into a repeatedly self-applied series of incorporeal transformations. This state of supermolecular hyperdifferentiation might be called 'permanent revolution,' *provided that it is understood that the revolution has many rhythms*, it can be instantaneous or spread over ages. (Massumi, 1992: 104, our emphasis)

In different terms: revolutions need not *climax*. What is crucial is the *maintenance of intensity*. It is of note that this pertains diagrammatically to the concept of *plateau*, which Deleuze and Guattari extracted from the work of Bateson. As Robert Shaw notes (and here note that *schismogenesis* was Bateson's term for processes which proceeded through a continual building of intensity and conflict up to a 'breaking point' or 'point of release', which he discussed in terms of socio-political conflict in the 1930s, sex, and mental health):

> Schismogenesis is avoided via a constant maintenance of plateaus of intensity in which neither normality nor neurosis, neither structure nor crisis, are the goal. Rather, the plateau of intensity is a goal-in-itself, a situation of constant evolution and becoming in which conflict does not build, but is expressed and released. Conflict and pleasure are thus maintained together, in complex 'rhizomes'. (Shaw, 2015: 157)

We noted at the top of this chapter that our discussion of revolution must pass through the question of how to *decolonise* critique, and, further, towards an opening of the concept of revolution through which revolutionary processes are decolonising processes. Here, we will begin by following Sara Motta's recent work on this issue. In a chapter entitled

'Decolonising Critique: From Prophetic Negation to Prefigurative
Affirmation', she critically engages with Žižek, charging elements of
his work and practice with that of exhibiting 'the Prophetic knowing-
subject of orthodox critique' (2016: 34). Crucially, some of her key
criticisms are placed against Žižek's notion of the 'act proper' which we
invoked above; and her criticisms are pertinent to our considerations of
both the activity *of* 'revolutionary critique' – which we seek to elaborate
a modality of through our attempt at *revolutionary rhythmanalysis* – and,
crucially, the relationship between the agent of revolutionary critique
and the agent of revolutionary practice. We have, thus far, resisted a
firm distinction between these two practices, as for us, scaping *immanently participates* in the territory, and to suggest an onto-epistemological
boundary between the agent of critique and the agent of praxis would
be to *supernaturalise* the agent of critique as somehow 'beyond' or 'above'
revolutionary praxis. Motta traces, among other things, such a logic of
non-immanence in Žižek's notion of the act proper. To be more precise, she traces a logic through which any act proper, for Žižek, necessitates a violent (negative) differentiation from the other, a negativism
through which 'authentic' political events must be 'impervious to any
call from the Other' (Žižek, 2001: 111, 175, quoted in Motta, 2016:
37). This negativism – a negation of all that 'is' – paves the way for the
universality that revolutionary politics must have, for Žižek, insofar as
the *shared* antagonism and negation of all that 'is' is a *universal* ground (or
more precisely, a universal *ungrounding*) for revolutionary praxis. This
negativism in Žižek's practice of critique, argues Motta, exhibits the
underside to his Prophetic knowing-subjectivity; if we noted above that
Žižek's arguments resisted the elements of prophecy insofar as the 'act
proper' constitutes the political event which reshuffles socio-political
co-ordinates necessarily unpredictably, prophecy still nonetheless subtly
re-enters as it is the figure of the revolutionary critic who 'knows' where
and how such an event may or may not happen, or, more specifically,
who 'knows' that it has yet-to-happen: Žižek's agent of revolutionary
critique becomes the denunciator of any (and seemingly all) *attempts* of
an 'act proper'. As Motta highlights, the agent of revolutionary critique
still nonetheless practices an ethics (which we connect with the inevitable *participation* in the territory that all revolutionary critique is), and
in Žižek's case, for Motta, this flows into an ethics of *non-listening* and
silencing of the other:

> [T]he tendency in Žižek's enactment of critique is to 'speak over'
> multiple perspectives in the name of achieving 'real' acts [. . .] This
> practice of critique fetishises the event as *the* political, reinforcing

the coloniality of Prophetic-knowing in which the 'knowing' subject has the right and duty to silence 'others' [. . .] Such a representational epistemological stance universalises a particular politics of knowledge and knowing-subjectivity constructed in and through onto–epistemological violence. (Motta, 2016: 37)

Such a practice, Motta notes, places the (Žižekian, or indeed more broadly the 'Prophetic knowing-subject of orthodox critique' (ibid.: 34)) revolutionary critic 'beyond critique and necessarily blind and deaf to receiving from the other' (ibid.: 39). This is a rendering of the subject of critique as transcendent, beyond the reach of critique; a non–immanent installation we seek to resist, as we noted earlier in this chapter, both through (1) the elements of our *mobile perspectivism* and *process epistemology*; and (2) to scaping's *participation* in the territory, rather than divorce from it ('*pure critique is a task for thought in the world rather than an interpretation by thought of the world*' (MacKenzie, 2004: xxiv)). For Motta, and indeed also for us, such negativism is a far cry from the sort of *affirmative work* of any revolutionary critique, which she articulates primarily through the figure the storyteller:

> Thus, for the storyteller to transform capitalism is a praxical task which implies a *stepping inwards to the contours of everyday life and inhabiting the fractured locus between processes of subjectification and active processes of decolonising subjectivity* [. . .] To step inwards involves committing to developing knowledge processes in which we collectively bring to awareness how systems of oppression wounds us and become embedded in our bodies, distort our emotions, separate us from our souls and limit our creative capacities [. . .] Critique for the storyteller, is not merely a process of contesting power relationships 'out there,' or decrying the ignorance of the other and building the conditions for a nihilistic authentic act of truth as in Žižek, but of unlearning social relationships, subjectivities and ways of life and learning new ones. (Motta, 2016: 40, our emphasis)

Frantz Fanon, too, highlighted the revolutionary (and rhythmic) role of the storyteller, which he discusses in the context of oral traditions:

> The contact of the people with the new movement gives rise to a new rhythm of life and to forgotten muscular tensions, and develops the imagination. Every time the storyteller relates a fresh episode to the public, he presides over a real invocation.

The existence of a new type of man is revealed to the public.
(Fanon, 2001: 194)

We will not discuss Motta's concept of the storyteller in any detail here:
her open pluralising gesture is taken by us as open to multiple such
figures. Nonetheless, Motta's arguments on the immanent *practice* of
decolonial-revolutionary critique (whether the storyteller, or other possible figures) is an explicit gesture of a revolutionary, and epistemological,
pluralism, which functions not only through *interventions* into dominant
colonial and capitalist ways of being and knowing, but also through
affirmative, open, reflexive, dialogical practices (centralising the importance of *listening*) in which the secure self is ever-and-always at risk (as
both *practitioner of* and *subject to* critique) (2016: 42–43). The sort of
affirmative, revolutionary, and decolonial work Motta conceptualises
operates on – here drawing on Gloria E. Anzaldúa (1987) – the border-
lands, taking us 'to our borders of self and certainty' (Motta, 2016: 43).
To use our similar terminology: for us, such work operates against what
we have called those rhythmic parameters of ontological security of the
milieu, namely, *on the border* of the milieu. On this question of listening,
and its force, Jean-Luc Nancy has situated the practice of listening as
a practice of *straining*, of going beyond the metastable confines of the
subject or self insofar as listening is always relational, involving a movement in which the self *opens* to the outside in such a manner that it is
constitutively put at risk. This involves a move away, for Nancy, from any
intentional-phenomenological subject (situated in space), towards what
he terms a *resonant* subject (moving through time), who thus has no ossified ocular 'point of view' but rather a *mobile* vibrationality (an 'intensive
spacing of a rebound' (Nancy, 2007: 21)). This resonant subject is one
that opens and returns to 'itself' through the vibrations and mobilities it
listens to and hears (including its own voice). This process of opening
and return is, for Nancy, rhythm:

> We should linger here for a long while on rhythm: it is nothing
> other than the time of time, the vibration of time itself in the
> stroke of a present that presents it by separating it from itself, free-
> ing it from simple *stanza* to make it into *scansion* (rise, raising of
> the foot that beats) and *cadence* (fall, passage into the pause). Thus,
> rhythm separates the succession of the linearity of the sequence or
> length of time: it bends time to give it to time itself, and it is in this
> way that it folds and unfolds a 'self.' If temporality is the dimen-
> sion of the subject (ever since Saint Augustine, Kant, Husserl, and
> Heidegger), this is because it defines the subject as what separates

itself, not only from the other or from the pure 'there,' but also from self: insofar as it waits for *itself* and retains *itself*, insofar as it desires (itself) and forgets (itself), insofar as it retains, by repeating it, its own empty unicity and its projected or . . . ejected [*projetée, ou . . . jetée*] unicity. (Ibid.: 17)

To listen is thus an opening to sense, towards the as-yet un-sensed and to affect, and thus to a subject 'broached by time' (ibid.: 39), metastable in its partial security and metastable through the partial sedimentations of its rhythms and desires. Listening is therefore to put oneself, one's habits of perception and thought, at risk, to open oneself to sense something different and to open oneself to the changes that might result. Scaping's attempted practice of revolutionary critique must also be a decolonial critique and practice of decolonisation, which, amongst other things, necessitates a critical openness and a practice of listening: scaping's revolutionary rhythmanalysis participates in the territory, and seeks to avoid precisely the sort of 'blindness and deafness' (Motta 2016: 38) that Motta charges the (non-immanent) Prophetic knowing-subject of orthodox critique with. As such, scaping's concern with its changeable and contingent positionality is only intensified; that is, scaping must fold into its own practice a critical openness, ethic of listening, and practices of decolonisation, aware that such a process is never finished 'once and for all'. The revolutionary process is also a decolonising process.

The notion of listening can hardly do justice to the breadth, scope, and depth of processes of *decolonisation*, and indeed we cannot do full justice to the growing range of work and practice conducted alongside this concept-in-formation. It will be useful, nonetheless, to situate *scaping* in conversation with the recent work of Ricardo Sanín-Restrepo, *Decolonizing Democracy*, in which he articulates a concept of (colonial) *power in a solid state*, which for him is crystallised in ossified institutional architectures and processes through which the ability to access and transform such institutions are, at least in part, blocked through what he calls an *encryption* process bound up in elitist language and *expert* knowledge (we partially gestured towards such a point, above, concerning the ability to *access* and *transform* technics), namely, through *research* (Smith, 2012). *Coloniality*, for Sanín-Restrepo, cannot be disassociated from encryption: 'in coloniality there is a primordial prohibition (political, juridical, racial) to the access and use of language' (2016: 9). *Solidity* is the *telos* and tendency of colonial power – by which Sanín-Restrepo is concerned with all aspects of Western sovereignty, nation-states, the notion of the *people*, capital, law, and the individual – and (what we would call) its arrhythmic ossification; and it is identified as being concerned with the 'utter destruction of difference' (ibid.: 13) or the 'nullification of singularity' (ibid.: 16) (*arrhythmia*: repetition with a minimum of difference).[21] Coloniality is the frame within which these other Western myths coalesce and contract. The production of a *people* being a production which is always the production of a norm of citizenship, a modelisation of the good, right, and proper subject (the subject who enjoys their subjection) which functions always – as we noted in the previous chapter on the notion of eurhythmia – as an exclusive disjunction and whose *telos* is that of the crushing of singularity. Any decolonising processes, in this schema, then, becomes concerned at least in part, with difference, which Sanín-Restrepo identifies with radical democracy ('in radical democracy everything that produces difference without eclipsing it counts as being' (ibid.: 45); 'Politics can only be considered when every being that makes a difference is considered as the condition of politics, *with no further qualification*' (ibid.: 105)); and with a political combat against those arrhythmic ossifications he identifies with coloniality and encryption, and which we have already identified with arrhythmic finalisms in the previous section concerned with social sculpture. Or, in other words, with a political environment of *inclusive disjunctions.* Sanín-Restrepo's radical democracy dovetails (and a dovetail is a not a subsumption) with our development of social sculpture above; namely, as concerned with *total access to the (r)evolutionary transformation of the social*, constituting a vast *opening* of the future to its participatory transformation:

> Democracy is thus the denial of the idea according to which every typology of distribution of power means a pre-existing model, an archetype; in other words, a refusal of any previous disposition or requirement to govern [. . .] Democracy is the annulment of any condition to govern and is the government of those that lack any quality or disposition to govern. (Ibid.: 167)

Revolutionary processes of decolonisation, the decolonisation of revolution. Neither are possible without open practices of listening or without the total access to the control and transformation of technics and the encryptive and elitist ossifications of power which extant colonial organological conditions arrange into a contemporary (seemingly) solid state (ibid.: 188).

It is fair to ask: Why 'revolution' at all? Latour's *We Have Never Been Modern* contains a succession of diatribes against the notion itself. We will not survey these here but will point to one of the most important criticisms he makes: 'Whether one wishes to conserve [the] past or abolish it, in either case the revolutionary idea *par excellence*, the idea that revolution is possible, is maintained' (1991: 47–48, our addition). Latour's claim is that the very notion of *revolution* – conceived as the possibility as the fundamental restructuring of social, political, economic (and so on) relations – remains trapped within a specifically *modernist* notion of temporality. This modernist notion of temporality is precisely what Bergson and Heidegger situated themselves against: a spatialised and divisible conception of time. For Latour, since we cannot *but* be caught in partial and local networks of human and non-human actors, the scope of our action 'permits scarcely anything more than small extensions of practices, slight accelerations in the circulation of knowledge, a tiny extension of societies, miniscule increases in the number of actors, small modifications of old beliefs' (ibid.: 48). Even if Latour is correct in his assessment of agential possibilities, however, this by no means commits us to a relinquishing of the very notion of revolution. The identification of the concept of revolution with a scientistic or modernist concept of time is by no means necessary. Treating the notion precisely as an Idea – recall that, for Deleuze, it is an 'excess in the Idea which explains the lack in the concept' (2014: 286) – we instead seek to reproblematise the notion of revolution through the practice of scaping, through rhythmanalysis. As MacKenzie notes on this, immanent critique 'constantly restages the relationship between problems and ideas without privileging any particular version of that relationship' (2004: 64). With Deleuze (here with Claire Parnet), perhaps we can consider that *another type of revolution can become possible*:

> Instead of betting on the eternal impossibility of the revolution and on the fascist return of the war machine in general, why not think that *a new type of revolution is becoming possible*, and that all kinds of mutating, living machines conduct wars, are combined and trace out a plane of consistence which undermines the plane of organization of the World and the States? (Deleuze and Parnet, in Deleuze and Guattari, 1983b: 113)

Indeed, did Deleuze not already in *The Logic of Sense* gesture towards such a reproblematisation of the concept of revolution, here entangling it with the notion of *rhythm* (to repeat the quote we deployed in a different sense in the previous chapter)?

> It is not at all the case that revolutions are determined by technical progress. Rather, they are made possible by this gap between two series, which solicits realignments of the economic and political totality in relation to the parts of the technical progress.

> There are therefore two errors which in truth are one and the same: the error of reformism or technocracy, which aspires to promote or impose partial arrangements of social relations *according to the rhythm of technical achievements*; and the error of totalitarianism, which aspires to constitute a totalization of the signifiable and the known, *according to the rhythm of the social totality existing at a given moment*. The technocrat is the natural friend of the dictator – computers and dictatorship; but the revolutionary lives in the gap which separates technical progress from social totality, and inscribes there his dream of *permanent revolution*. This dream, therefore, is itself action, reality, and an effective menace to all established order; it renders possible what it dreams about. (Deleuze, 2004a: 59, our emphases)

As did Guattari, here emphasising the relationship between revolution and futurity, as a continuous *cutting* into the future:

> The revolution to come will not be inscribed in the moulds of the past, it will not be synonymous with a 'step backwards' or with the freezing of the current situation, like that which is envisaged by the new technocratic mythology that is centered on the theme of a return to 'zero growth'! We think, on the contrary, that it will be entirely compatible with a tumultuous development in the sciences, of the forces of production, artistic creations, experiments of all kind, rupturing radically, it must be emphasised, with the forms that they had yesterday! (Guattari, 2016: 67)

The development of social relations, when subordinated to the rhythms of technical progress (reformism, technocracy), or frozen through a total subordination of the rhythms of the present (totalitarianism) are two modalities of *arrhythmia*: repetition with a minimum of difference or maximum rhythmic contraction, and a resistance to the multiplications of rhythm. The 'rhythms of technical achievement' and the 'rhythm of the social totality existing at a given moment' are *sedimented* through reformism and totalitarianism respectively. Revolutions – and the plural here is important – are not to-be-expected moments of the dialectical synthesisation of (teleological) historical movements. Revolutions, rather, are those ruptures or *becoming-otherwise* of the present. We can create and contribute to those *counter-actualisations* and *dramatisations* in order to effectuate such becomings, we can partake in the ridigification of the present 'according to the rhythms of technical achievement' (reformism), further still, we could contribute to the *intensification* and *totalisation* of the present 'according to the rhythm of the social totality' of today (totalitarianism).[22] Any of these movements are up for grabs, precisely because revolutions are not to-be-expected. The rhythms of totalitarianism are homogenising and totalising (hard authoritarianism): totalitarianism is a fast rhythmic colonialism. The rhythms of reformism are homogenising but not totalising (soft authoritarianism): reformism is a temperate rhythmic colonialism. Both are decidedly arrhythmic: resistant to polyrhythmia, resistant to new rhythms. Revolutionary rhythms are neither of these (heterogenising and singularising). Scaping's processual rhythmic-sculptural refrain proceeds from this conceptualisation.

We will close this section with a further explication of how the conceptualisation of 'revolutionary rhythms' will translate into this project. If reformism is a temperate rhythmic colonialism which tends towards the sedimentation of the rhythms of technical achievements, and if totalitarianism is a fast rhythmic colonialism which tends towards the homogenisation and totalisation of the rhythm of a given social totality, *revolutionary rhythms*, by contrast, will push against the moving targets which tend towards such varieties of colonialism through aesthetic interventionism. Revolutionary rhythms are heterogenising and singularising:

> [T]he idea of revolution is identified with the idea of process. Producing something that doesn't exist, a producing a singularity in the very existence of things, thoughts, and sensibilities. *It is a process that brings about mutations in the unconscious social field, at a level beyond discourse.* We could call it *a process of existential singularization.* The question is how to ensure that the singular processes – which almost swerve into the incommunicable – are maintained by articulating them in a work, a text, a way of living with oneself or with others, or the invention of areas of life and freedom to create. (Guattari, in Guattari and Rolnik, 2007: 259, second emphasis ours)

Further, this process of existential singularisation is not *totalising*. The commitment to what we have been calling a 'revolutionary pluralism' relates to a refusal to *unify* multiple revolutionary processes, insofar as one always responds, develops, launches, and creates *from* a milieu – which is to say revolutions are molecular – even if transversal and transductive relations can be established between milieus. As Gerald Raunig notes, making a similar point:

> The components of molecular revolution appear as actualizations of the components of the dividual: [. . .] dispersion, singularity,

similarity. Dispersion as an abstract line moving through single things instead of concentrating them as units. Singularity as singular subsistence instead of generalizing many single things in an original or universal substance. Similarity not as a step along the way to leveling, adapting, means to the end of sameness, but rather as a condition of the multi-formed, abstract line that permeates the co-forming. (Raunig, 2016: 183)

The co-ordinates we sculpt are, we hope, sites of revolutionary singularisation, but they are *not* static co-ordinates, nor are they by any means the only ones. Mobile co-ordinates translate, for scaping's purposes, into mobile counter-actualisation and dramatisation: more strategies, more pressure points, more opportunities for producing heterogenising and singularising rhythms (existential singularisation). This means that revolutionary rhythms will not simply counter, for example, capitalism's mode of acceleration with *deceleration*, but instead with local tactics comprising moments of acceleration and deceleration and the creation of new experiences of time. Revolutionary rhythms, to 'crack' hegemonic rhythms – to operate on their border – cannot themselves be static or unidirectional. Each co-ordinate is marked by differential rhythms, so, to 'crack' them, no one modality of resistance is enough. Since revolutionary rhythms are heterogenising and singularising, modes of resistance themselves are mobile, pragmatic, creative, and durative. If there is to be no revolutionary 'event' – in the sense of a 'moment' – scaping's *revolutionary pluralism* seeks to help create the ontological contours of *permanent revolution (permanent process)* though revolutionary rhythmanalysis; or, as we noted above, *revolutionary rhythms* will involve the creation of heterogenising and singularising vectors and temporalities which seek to proliferate the possibilities for new rhythms and new vectors. Is this not precisely a mode of pure critique, as MacKenzie terms it? ('Critique brings new modes of life into existence and it becomes pure when these new modes of life foster further creativity. The task of pure critique is not to judge but to create and create . . .' (2004: 88)). Once again: *scaping is not about developing a conceptually frozen ecology, but about the genesis of revolutionary vectors immanent in the possibilities of the present.*

There is no definite article prefixing revolutionary processes, nor a definite object of completion or arrival for such processes; *as* multiple, *as* heterogenising, *as* singularising, revolutionary processes are irreducible to either a definite subject or a definite object, or indeed to a theory of stages (Raunig, 2016: 183) with fixed co-ordinates enabling the epistemic judgement of 'progress'. Rather, revolutions are created, affirmed, and sustained through continual creation and affirmation; what Raunig calls the 'invention and multiplication of revolutionary practices and narratives' (ibid.: 184) through which, instead of any completion of *the revolution*, scaping instead, with Raunig, develops through an 'unending chain of instituent practices, the overtaking of the state apparatus [. . .] the institutionalization of the revolution becomes the invention of ever new monster institutions' (ibid.: 184–185). Where are molecular revolutions felt, desired, practiced, and affirmed? Raunig, here, is right to note that molecular revolutions are first of all connected to *everyday life*:

> The dividual lines of the molecular revolution transverse ways of living, modes of subjectivation, singular substances. *Molecularity means the pores of everyday life, transformation of the molecules of sociality, revolutionary transversing of things instead of universality.* (Ibid.: 187)

This, recall, is similar to Motta's point above: her figure of the storyteller is one who steps 'inwards to the contours of everyday life'. As a practice of *immanent critique*, scaping cannot assume any theory of *everyday life* as given. Indeed, this is the precise object of Chapter 3: a critique of the rhythms of everyday life.

e. Chapter 2 reprise

[26] To *scape* implies an inventive and constructive composition of the co-ordinates of the present in order to help generate potential holes, gaps, fissures, or cracks in extant dominating pulses, pushing them to their deterritorial border or region of ontological insecurity (*extemporaneous counter-actualisation*) in the pursuance of an emergent sculpting process of the new or of the creation of new worlds (*rhythmic dramatisation*).
[27] *Scaping is not about developing a conceptually frozen ecology, but rather, about the genesis of immanent revolutionary vectors along the contours of the present.* Scaping is an attempt to develop a *revolutionary rhythmanalysis.*
[28] Scaping will attempt an immanent critique of rhythms *through* a rhythmic method.
[29] Our *rhythmanalytic mobile perspectivism*, and notion of critique, emerges as a *process epistemology.* This has two senses:
(i) Insofar as it takes rhythms, tendencies, and processes as (mobile) 'objects' of analysis or selection.
(ii) Insofar as our rhythmanalytical approach is open to its own changeability, *open* to critique rather than beyond its reach, and as the task of critique is always one to be *repeated* (always differently), then the analyses, and practices of knowledge we embody, can never remain static.

[30] Mobile perspectivism is about the creation-ignition of new selections, their creative explication through *co-ordinate composition*, towards the creation of new milieus. The creation of new selections, new signs, new modes of understanding, all of these facets are geared in the practice of *scaping* towards the creative sculpting of *new milieus.*

[31] Scaping's triple response to the triple danger of non-immanence:

(i) Instead of rendering the *object of thought* as transcendent, scaping proceeds through the *composition* of co-ordinates. In so doing, it makes no claims to static representational mimesis: its mode of conceptual sculpting is *aesthetically interventionist*. In addition, by treating the map as an immanent participation 'in' and 'through' the territory, no ontological boundary is supernaturally (non-immanently) inserted between the subject and object of thought.

(ii) Instead of rendering the *activity of thought* as transcendent, scaping attempts to proceeds through immanent (or *pure*) critique which is creative or constructivist, constructing the idea of a rhythmic method in the critique itself and not placing this method 'outside' of the activity of thought as a given justificatory framework; in other words, scaping 'problematizes its own conditionality'.

(iii) Finally, instead of rendering the *subject of thought* as transcendent, scaping employs a *mobile perspectivism.*

[32] Scaping's naturalism is bound up with its situatedness 'within the territory'. Its compositional mapping is a practice which is 'in' the world, not 'of' (or 'outside') the world. Scaping's resistance to ontological and epistemological recourses to transcendence flows from its commitment to immanence.

[33] Scaping is not at all cybernetics, but seeks to confront the question of *cyberneticisation* through the question of technics in our digital epoch: digital technology having become, and continuously becoming, absolutely central to relations pertaining in our contemporary *mental ecology.* The mental milieu is the precise object of our practice of *mindscaping.*

[34] Scaping's three *ecological entry ways* (mental, social, environmental) are different *modes* of scaping insofar as scaping practices a *mobile perspectivism. The analytical delimitation of three distinct ecologies is not a firm ontological demarcation but a pragmatic application of scaping's mobile perspectivism.*

[35] The notion of *aesthetic interventionism* acquires momentum through the insight that particular *aesthetic regimes* are by no means beyond the capabilities of those subject to those regimes to transform it and sculpt it anew (the map participates in the territory).

[36] Aesthetic interventionism is a movement in line with the third synthesis of the future: it radically opens the past, present, and future. It seeks to *transform* and *sculpt* the territory along new vectors from the only

place it can: in the middle, through laying down new rhythms, attempting counter-actualisation and dramatisation. Such a transformation,
however, is ontologically risky. Opening the present is a precarious and
tenuous task which can generate new co-ordinates in the present. The
effects of counter-actualisation cannot be predetermined in advance,
and, hence, can generate dangers.

[37] *Counter-actualisation is an attempt to intervene into dominant aesthetic
conditions. Counter-actualisation is a virtualisation, not an actualisation.*

[38] *Extemporaneous counter-actualisation* is a situated mode of *aesthetic
intervention* which intervenes and interrupts extant dominating aesthetic
regimes and rhythms of life. *Aesthetic intervention temporally disrupts aesthetic conditions which pertain in a given context:* it is an aesthetico-temporal
interruption.

[39] Injecting new rhythms into the present – *rhythmic dramatisation* –
is a movement that partakes in the process of a new (differential)
actualisation.

[40] Rhythmic dramatisation is nothing other than a continuous (processual) affirmation of intensity and production of difference, a process
of individuation remaining constitutively open in its actualisation. The
notion of rhythm, here, allows for and envelops within its practice the
ever-present possibility of the effacement of difference and intensity,
but attempts to keep this spacetime for differentiation-intensification
open through the attached permanent possibility of *repeating anew* the
practice of rhythmic dramatisation made possible through new movements of counter-actualisation, that is, through the invention of new
problems.

[41] *The invention of new rhythms are sculptural processes; rhythmic dramatisation is the aesthetico-temporal sculpture of new habits, new processes, new
modes of perception, new thoughts, new ways of being*; all of which is to say
the milieu's participation in its *own* singularisation, intensification, or
differentiation.

[42] Rhythmic dramatisation – positioned as a type of social sculpture
through which *life rhythms* become indissociable from *sculpting the social* –
cuts into and sculpts the future *processually.*

[43] Rhythmic dramatisation may encompass 'limited finalities' – these
are those effects 'covering over' intensity which are to-be-expected – but
as a process it is invariably one of constant projection, attuned to the
future without subordinating its practice to some superior final cause. In
this specific sense, it is fair to label rhythmic dramatisation *objectless.* For
rhythmic dramatisation to be a process of *revolutionary investment*, it must
also constitute an affirmation of the immanent uses of the syntheses of
desire, affirming intensity and the production of difference, *against* the

overcoding of the pulsive flows of desire that pertain in the present, and works with the incalculable.

[44] *An 'act proper' – for us: extemporaneous counter-actualisation and rhythmic dramatisation – is revolutionary precisely insofar as it (a) reshuffles the co-ordinates of the possible through a redistribution of the sensible and (b) insofar as it does this, prevents the ontological movements of revolution from being rotational.* Such rotationality is prevented *precisely* insofar as the 'new' which emerges through rhythmic dramatisation is not reducible to those 'aesthetic regimes' from which it emerged.

[45] Scaping *immanently participates* in the territory, and to erect an onto-epistemological boundary between the agent of critique and the agent of praxis would be to *supernaturalise* the agent of critique as somehow 'beyond' or 'above' revolutionary praxis.

[46] Scaping's attempted practice of revolutionary critique must also be a decolonial critique and practice of decolonisation, which, amongst other things, necessitates a critical openness and a practice of listening.

[47] *Revolutionary rhythms are ontologically pluridirectional. Aesthetic interventionism attempts to effectuate revolutionary rhythms.*

[48] Revolutions – and the plural here is important – are not to-be-expected moments of the dialectical synthesisation of (teleological) historical movements. Revolutions, rather, are those ruptures and *becoming-otherwise* of the present. We can create and contribute to those *counter-actualisations* and *dramatisations* in order to effectuate such becomings, we can partake in the ridigification of the present 'according to the rhythms of technical achievement' (reformism), further still, we could contribute to the *intensification* and *totalisation* of the present 'according to the rhythm of the social totality' of today (totalitarianism). Any of these movements are up for grabs, precisely because the revolution is not to-be-expected.

[49] The commitment to what we have been calling a 'revolutionary pluralism' relates to a refusal to *unify* multiple revolutionary processes, insofar as each responds, develops, launches, and creates *from* a milieu – which is to say that revolutions are molecular – even if transversal and transductive relations can be established between milieus.

[50] If there is to be no revolutionary 'event', scaping's *revolutionary pluralism* seeks to help create the ontological contours of *permanent revolution*; *revolutionary rhythms* will involve the creation of heterogenising and singularising vectors and temporalities that seek to proliferate the possibilities for new rhythms and new vectors.

[51] There is no definite article prefixing revolutionary processes, nor a definite object of completion or arrival for such processes; *as* multiple, *as* heterogenising, *as* singularising, revolutionary processes are

irreducible to either a definite subject or a definite object, or indeed to a theory of stages.

Notes

1. For a further interesting discussion of *immanent critique*, as well as attempt to situate Jürgen Habermas in this tradition, see Stahl (2013). Further, this discussion of immanent critique could not proceed without acknowledging Foucault's brilliant lecture 'What is Critique?' (1997) as a silent partner.

2. To add a further explanatory disclaimer. We encounter here the distinction between *conceptualising* immanence and *opening* concepts *to* immanence; while the former encloses immanence within the concept, the latter is an infinite task. Indeed, this is one of the sources of Deleuze's differences with Hegel. For Deleuze, Hegel offers us a quasi-immanence of movement and becoming, fuelled by an illusory motor of negativity and oppositionalism and which, despite its movement, is too bound to identity and too quick to efface difference. One of the *precise* reasons why this might be called a quasi-immanence is insofar as it conceptually *encloses* immanence through the concept of the Absolute which thinks *through* our thought, which Jean Hyppolite terms 'complete immanence' (Hyppolite, 1997: 59). Complete immanence is that which, for Hyppolite, Spinoza could not achieve; but which, for Deleuze, is unachievable. As Beistegui notes, 'Rather than oppose Hegel (and we have learned from Derrida how ultimately self-defeating such an opposition must be), Deleuze chooses to carry out the genesis, or even the genealogy of the negative, to reveal its mechanism by returning to its unspoken origin [. . .] Chapter 5 of Difference and Repetition claims that the illusion of the negative lies in the fact that dialectics is able to recognise only the actual, or extended differences, in the real. In extensity, Deleuze claims, differences can indeed appear to be oppositions. But differences in extended time-space always presuppose their intensive depth, that is, differences that are inequalities, pure differentials without negation. Consequently, the illusion of the negative is not just transcendental: it is also physical. It is nature itself that produces these illusions, these effects of positivity' (2010: 26–27; see 24–27 for a broader discussion of these themes). It is also through this insight that we can speak of a Deleuzian naturalism.

3. We will not discuss this in any detail, but it is important to note that the slippery concept of immanence (and, indeed, purity) is not one we can claim to have 'achieved' through scaping. As Beistegui notes (2010: 13–17), critique's commitment to immanence *resists* re-installing transcendence partially through the acknowledgement that perhaps immanence cannot become an object of thought at all, functioning more as a *regulative ideal*, and is why we noted in the previous footnote that immanence 'as such' is unachievable.

4. The employment of the notion of perspectivism is an affirmative nod in the Nietzschean direction: 'From now on, my philosophical colleagues, let us

be more wary of the dangerous old conceptual fairy-tale which has set up a "pure, will-less, painless, timeless, subject of knowledge," let us be wary of the tentacles of such contradictory concepts as "pure reason," "absolute spirituality," "knowledge as such": hence we are asked to think of an eye which cannot be thought at all, an eye turned in no direction at all, an eye where the active and interpretive powers are to be suppressed, absent, but through which seeing still becomes a seeing-something, it is an absurdity and non-concept of eye that is demanded. There is *only* a perspectival seeing, *only* a perspectival "knowing"; the *more* affects we are able to put into words about a thing, the *more* eyes, various eyes we are able to use for the same thing, the more complete will be our "concept" of the thing, our "objectivity." But to eliminate the will completely and turn off all the emotions without exception, assuming we could: well? would that not mean to *castrate* the intellect? . . .' (Nietzsche, 2017: 88–89; also see Railton, 2012: 20–51).

5. See Heaney (2020) for an exploration of Whitehead's notion of rhythm alongside Stiegler's notion of the *noetic soul* deployed towards thinking about developing new institutional forms for the university.

6. In this sense, there are affinities between scaping and Karen Barad's quantum physics (specifically, Niels Bohr) informed materialist feminism. See Barad (2012: 52; 2007: 394).

7. We will not labour this much-discussed point any further any more than to perhaps loosen it. Did not Kant himself at least partially gesture to the centrality of *affect* to the cultivation of a certain type of sensibility which necessarily *precedes* the recognition of the 'moral law' when he noted, in *The Conflict of the Faculties* (1979: 75), that, 'It has to be made clear that we ourselves must work at developing that moral predisposition, although this predisposition does point to a divine source that reason can never reach (in its theoretical search for causes), so that our possession of it is not meritorious, but rather the work of grace?' This appears like a naturalist gesture (although it does not escape the supernaturalist impulse which animated so much of Kant's work), or more precisely a *libidinal* gesture: one must come to *desire* the moral law. As Deleuze notes: '*There is a single dangerous misunderstanding regarding the whole of practical Reason:* believing that Kantian morality remains indifferent to its own realization' (2008: 33).

8. In analytic philosophy, Bateson would be viewed as forwarding a type of *externalism*, and as in the growing traditions associated with *the extended mind* (Clark and Chalmers, 1998), the *embodied mind*, and the '4EA' tradition, which positions 'the mind' as embodied, embedded, enactive, extended, and affective (Varela, Thompson and Rosch, 2016). Though this is not to conflate the differences between these approaches. Whilst the classic extended mind hypothesis is largely functionalist in its view of the mind (the mind's potential 'enactive' importance is underplayed), 4EA's 'enactive' component highlights this potential. For more on this, see Gallagher (2013).

9. For a discussion of cybernetic aesthetics see Ikoniadou (2014b: 31–34), who similarly notes this primacy of informational ontology but ultimately seeks to go beyond it.

10. It is also of note that this mathematical theory of communication, which became fundamental to cybernetic theory, made (and continues to make in contemporary discussions) consistent use of the notion of entropy, which Shannon famously defined as a 'measure of uncertainty' (Shannon, 1998: 67) in a cybernetic system of communication, and through the proper measure of which it became possible to ensure, as close as possible, the mitigation against any loss of information that would occur in such a system in order to approximate the ideal of reproducing the information sent from one point and received at another as exactly as possible. We met this point in Chapter 1 when considering the potential inverse relation between noise and information. Information, for Shannon, is precisely this element of uncertainty or entropy; whereas for Wiener (1961) (the founder of cybernetics), information is a measure of organisation (as *opposed* to entropy, which relates to a level of disorganisation) (Hui, 2016a: 21). Simondon also, in engagement with the cybernetic tradition, utilises the notion of entropy, as well as that of *negative entropy* or *negentropy* (Iliadis, 2013; Heaney, 2019: 193–196), a term coined by Leon Brillouin (Malaspina, 2018: 4) ('The machine, as an element of the technical ensemble, becomes that which increases the quantity of information, increases negentropy, and opposes the degradation of energy' (Simondon, 2017: 21)), and extending from this, so Stiegler develops and utilises this terminology (Stiegler, 2018). Less discussed here, perhaps, is Guattari's use of the term negentropy to discuss the potential that, for example, art bore for what he termed existential resingularisation (Guattari, 2006: 131).

11. Interestingly, in a brief comment on cybernetic theory, Lefebvre too reproduces this analogy: 'Thus every organ has more or less complex self-regulations (such as feedbacks, scannings, and homeostases, to use the vocabulary of the cyberneticists who have helped to elaborate these concepts)' (2014b: 494).

12. Slavoj Žižek would call this question a question of *ideology*. His definition of ideology is not the traditional one, and is focused more on how subjects come to spontaneously relate to their social world (i.e., how subjects come to perceive certain things as 'given'): 'would it not be more appropriate to characterize as "ideological" any view that ignores not some "objective" reality undistorted by our subjective investment but *the very cause of this unavoidable distortion*, the real of that deadlock to which we react in our projects and engagements?' (2012: 3).

13. See Clisby (2015) for a thorough and clear depiction of the issues which surround the virtual-intensive-actual debate on Deleuze's ontology, of which there are a number of different accounts. Protevi (2013: 4–5), for example, reads it as a *tripartite* ontology with each of these respective terms operating as separate types of ontological 'registers'. How this depiction maps on to

a naturalist (and monist) ontology is not something we will discuss here, though there appears to be a problem with situating these three terms as 'ontological domains', as this appears to render each 'domain' independent and static. We might be better placed to speak in terms of *actualisation*, *intensification*, and *virtualisation* – terms that speak more clearly to the processual nature of Deleuze's ontology of becoming – rather than the rigid notion of static ontological domains. With this proviso (since we will often utilise the nouns) we can state the following. For Deleuze, the virtual is the realm of *pure difference*. This virtual field is a field of unactualised potentiality – a field of interacting forces, tendencies, and systems with metastability – potentiality which is partially and differentially actualised. The virtual, difference-in-itself, is Deleuze's ontological (non-transcendent) transcendental (2014: 189, 293). The intensive is the realm 'between' virtual and actual. It is *through* intensity that processes of differential actualisation occur, and it is *through* intensity that processes of differential virtualisation occur (Baugh, 1992: 139). The actual is the field of extensity, objects as the temporary suspension of intensity, forms, classification, and so forth. These three 'domains' are, at least on most readings, differentially related to each other: they are enmeshed in a process of continual co-constitution.

14. We must emphasise the *virtuality* of problems in Deleuze, the solution of which are processes of differential actualisation. We will explore this further in relation to the (virtual) Idea of the political and the (virtual) Idea of revolution. For more on this, see Deleuze (2014: 223, 235, 237–238) and Rölli (2016: 194).

15. Readers will note that, in the quote above discussing such a libidinal break, Deleuze and Guattari *do* use the term 'precise moment'. They do, however, directly follow this quote by acknowledging that 'Of course the schiz has been prepared by a subterranean labor of causes, aims, and interests working together' (1983a: 378). On this point, we must here emphasise more strongly than they do such laborious and rhythmic processes as a *condition* for such breaks in the case of extemporaneous counter-actualisation.

16. By the 'Idea' of the political, MacKenzie and Porter are here referring to the concept of the 'political' as a type of essentially contested concept: an endlessly provocative term which is never exhausted in attempts to represent it. The concept of the 'political' forces thought's movement and different approaches *dramatise* this concept in new ways, bringing it to life in new ways. This is the Idea's productive indeterminacy: its conceptual inexhaustibility is a functional part of the Idea as such. Deleuze states it with clarity in *Difference and Repetition*: 'It is excess in the Idea which explains the lack in the concept' (2014: 286); or further: 'We distinguish Ideas, concepts and dramas: the role of dramas is to specify concepts by incarnating the differential relations and singularities of an Idea' (ibid.: 283–284).

17. 'Partout une mise en scène à plusieurs niveaux' (Deleuze, 1968: 280).

18. This is conducted in a manner close to Guattari's own blurring of the distinctions between art and politics through the notion of the *readymade*.

For more on this, see Zepke's (2008) discussion of Marcel Duchamp, Guattari, and the notion of the readymade. Further, see Lünen (2016: 24) on how Beuys can be firmly differentiated from Duchamp. Stiegler, also, cites Beuys as both the 'echo and the antithesis' of both Warhol and Duchamp (2015: 69).

19. For more on the specific question of Beuys and the question of authority, see Verwoert (2008).

20. Towards, on orthodox Marxist theory, an eventual 'withering away' of the state.

21. To return to the question of *listening*: Sanín-Restrepo notes how *power in a solid state* not only distributes access to language, but by extension distributes access to a *voice*, that is, distributes access to *being heard*, or to being listened to (2016: 15).

22. A vital proviso must be added at this point. These three 'options' are not suggested to be mutually exclusive. Guattari, for example, took up this issue when discussing the distinction between campaigns which attempted to reform 'systematic injustices' and attempts at 'revolutionary struggle'. He noted the following: 'Let's take as an example the problem of shoring up a roof: the question that arises does not have to do with knowing whether shoring it up is revolutionary or not, but knowing whether we are running the risk that it will fall down on our heads. One can say the same about social relations. It's perfectly legitimate that the working classes and various interest groups use whatever means they can to resist oppressive systems. That's one thing; but articulating a politics of revolutions (in the plural), molecular revolutions, is quite a different thing. It's important to avoid the dualist, binary logic that sets Marxism/social struggle/union struggle against molecular revolutions, as exclusive alternatives' (Guattari, in Guattari and Rolnik, 2007: 261).

3

A Critique of the Rhythms
of Everyday Life

For Marx, to transform the world was also and above all to transform the human world: everyday life. When they interpreted the world, philosophies brought plans for transformation. Were we to fulfil philosophy, were we to change the process of philosophical becoming of the world into the process of the world-becoming of philosophy, would that not be to metamorphose everyday life? (Lefebvre, 2014b: 317)

[O]ne could go so far as to term this level of everyday life a colonized sector. (Debord, 2006: 193)

[E]veryday life has literally been 'colonized'. (Lefebvre, 2014b: 305)

The thesis of internal colonization states that the subsystems of the economy and state become more and more complex as a consequence of capitalist growth, and penetrate ever deeper into the symbolic reproduction of the lifeworld. (Habermas, 1987: 367)

An early 2014 edition of *Adbusters* – a culture jamming magazine, perhaps most famous for its call in early 2011 for the occupation of Wall Street (Harcourt, 2012; Mitchell, 2012)[1] – contains an image (or rather a *subvertisement:* Adbuster's term for their subversive practice of advertising: attempting to undermine rather than induce consumption) with a background of both colourful, cheerful, and variegated emoticons, alongside some black-and-white ones both less cheerful and less variegated. In thick black text written diagonally across the image is written *depression*, and a small text box below this word explains that 'Our apocalyptic future is not one devastated landscapes, but devastated mindscapes.'

Our rhythmanalysis of the mental environment – mindscaping – will now acquire movement through *slipping in* to our primary ecological entry way: the mental environment or mental ecology. (Though: it is important to note that we can only *partially* enter this milieu: we will not come to a totalising conception of it. We compose specific problems and we create specific solutions.) Mindscaping will be an inventive exploration of the mental ecology of the present. Recall: to *scape* implies an inventive and constructive composition of the co-ordinates of the present to help generate potential holes, gaps, fissures, or cracks in extant dominating pulses, pushing them to their deterritorial border or region of ontological insecurity (*extemporaneous counter-actualisation*) and in the pursuance of an emergent sculpting process of the new or of the creation of new worlds, new milieus (*rhythmic dramatisation*). It is in this sense that mindscaping will be an inventive exploration. To speak of a mental ecology will be to draw upon conversations about subjectivity (or *rhythmic processes of individuation*): consciousness, unconsciousness, memory, agency, affect (sensibility, perception, feeling, and emotion), and the co-emergence and co-constitution of the neurological, the cognitive, the psychological, the affective, and so forth.

Some guiding questions for this chapter will be as follows. What rhythms permeate our mental environment? What are the effects of these rhythms? How are rhythm and desire entangled in the mental environment today? What might it mean to speak about the *rhythmic production of subjectivity* or *rhythmic processes of individuation?*

In this chapter, we will explicate an operative concept of subjectivity, conceived as *rhythmic processes of individuation*, developed through the entangled processes of *rhythmic subjection* and *rhythmic containment*. This will involve a conceptualisation of *everyday life* (in a reading of Lefebvre) as the residue and product of various components of subjectification, and rhythmic processes of individuation as the production of meta-stability through the nexus of identity filtration, labour, and leisure, as well as pre- and supra-personal components (e.g., technics (memory) and imagination). The key conceptual task of this chapter is the development of a *rhythmanalytical critique of everyday life* through our conceptualisation of rhythmic processes of individuation, a task which was demanded in the conclusion of the previous chapter. Ultimately, this rhythmanalytical critique of everyday life will enable us – along with the conceptual developments of Chapters 1 and 2 – to explicitly *scape* the mental environment through the development and analysis of three ecologies of the mental environment: an attention-distraction ecology (Chapter 4), a happiness-depression ecology (Chapter 5), and a debt-credit ecology (Chapter 6). This is the task of Part II. By way of beginning this chapter, we will first develop some preliminary comments as to this notion of everyday life, primarily through an engagement with Lefebvre.

a. Everyday life

> As a body matures, it develops a repertory of stimulus-response circuits. The regularity of the normalized situations within which the body is placed is inscribed in it in the form of autonomic reactions. Same input, same output. Same stimulus, same response. On schedule. The circularity of the everyday. Training. 'Growing up.' Reactivity. (Massumi, 1992: 99)

We have on a few occasions already encountered the work of Lefebvre, whose importance for us stems primarily from his immense three-volume *Critique of Everyday Life* and his work on *Rhythmanalysis* (which itself can be positioned as a de facto fourth volume of the *Critique of Everyday Life* project). Throughout this book, the relationship between Lefebvre's work and our own will be subject to continuous modification and qualification, which all should be taken alongside the preliminary acknowledgement of the vast field of analysis and praxis he helped to produce by opening up the problems of everyday life and rhythm. How does Lefebvre produce the problem of the everyday? Or more precisely, what problems does the notion of the everyday help to generate? Designating the everyday as a *level* of reality – a mediating level between the economic *base* or forces of production and the *apex* or ideologico-political *superstructures* (2014b: 328, 339), superstructures which are themselves 'created at each instant of everyday life and social practice' (Lefebvre, 2014a: 79) – the everyday is, for Lefebvre, the vast *middle* which is marked by 'banality, triviality, *repetitiveness*', but it is also the source and site of profundity, creativity, change, and is that which must be transformed in any revolutionary process, it is 'what must be changed and what is the hardest of all to change' (Lefebvre, 2014b: 341); the everyday is 'the very soil on which the great architectures of politics and society rise up' (Lefebvre, 1976: 89). The everyday, for Lefebvre as for us, as both the ordinary, repetitive, and continuous, but also the extraordinary, spectacular, and discontinuous. The notion of rhythm allows Lefebvre to develop some claims on the specifically *modern* everyday. For example, he notes how pre-industrial or pre-capitalist everyday life was dominated and controlled by a planetary-cosmic polyrhythmia comprising cyclic time scales which, he claims, 'gave rhythm to an existence which was organically linked to nature' (Lefebvre, 2014b: 341). Industrialisation, on this account, introduces a historical break with this connection to cyclic time scales; the subject of modernity, *via* industrialisation, which is to say *via* industrial technics, becomes *detached* from the cyclic-rhythmic through the attempt to master and control *linear* time (ibid.: 342). Lefebvre claims that through industrial technics and partial, linear time scales (through which everyday life becomes *fragmented* and *broken* into, for example, the sequential completion of partial tasks), the rhythm of existence made possible by this connection to cyclic time scales is in a process of becoming lost (ibid.: 313). In short, the process through which industrial technics and linear time scales became embedded in the modern everyday constitutes, for Lefebvre, a *loss* of rhythm: 'Techniques which fragment time also produce repetitive gestures. *These do not and often cannot become part of a rhythm*: the gestures of fragmented labour, action which begin at any time and cease at any time' (ibid.: 342, our emphasis).[2]

There can never be a *total* loss of the cyclic in contemporary everyday life insofar as embrained bodies must pass through certain rhythms of subsistence in everyday life (Lefebvre's examples are hunger, sleep, and sexual reproduction); the example noted is that of the factory worker, whose experience of labour is fragmented, linear, and non-rhythmic, and who rediscovers the rhythmic through the family and its relationship to cyclic time scales, for example (ibid.: 344). The nightshift worker is a further case in point, whose working periods are nocturnal rather than diurnal. While Lefebvre does develop a distinction between the cyclic (rhythmic, natural) and the linear (non-rhythmic, non-natural, technical), it would be unfair to Lefebvre to claim that this flowed into a harsh dualism between nature and technics, although the tension is clear. Nonetheless, this division between the rhythmic and non-rhythmic *is* presented as oppositional.[3] With these points noted, Lefebvre's makes a key methodological claim on the critique of everyday life:

> Critique of everyday life studies the persistence of rhythmic time scales within the linear time of modern industrial society. It studies the interactions between cyclic time (natural, in a sense irrational, and still concrete) and linear time (acquired, rational, and in a sense abstract and antinatural). It examines the defects and disquiet this as yet unknown and poorly understood interaction produces. Finally, it considers what metamorphoses are possible in the everyday as a result of this interaction. (Ibid.: 343, 526)

So, we have a notion of everyday life with some key dimensions and relations: the relationship between the dimensions of the repetitive, continuous, and mundane, with those of the creative, discontinuous, and extraordinary; 'nature', or the non-technical (Lefebvre at times uses the term 'vital'); and the technical. The everyday, to repeat, is a 'level' for Lefebvre; but is *itself* constituted by levels, layers, degrees, or stages; for example, the biological-physiological everyday, the psychological every-day, the economic everyday; the 'everyday' as an object of analysis con-stituting a '*residual deposit*' and '*product*' of its various levels (ibid.: 351, 358). This double-determination of the everyday as a *product* (that is, as a qualitative *conjunction* of a multiplicity of distinct and fragmented activi-ties) and *residue* (which he also calls a common ground (Lefebvre, 2014c: 687)) is analysed by Lefebvre in relation to a specifically capitalist mode of production: 'Daily life is thus the product of the mode of production' (ibid.: 687). For us, extracting from this, our critique of the rhythms of everyday life is concerned with the everyday insofar as it constitutes, produces, and reproduces contemporary capitalist milieus through the relations between rhythm and desire; *the everyday as that which produces both capitalistic subjects and capitalistic milieus.*

In a more schematic form, Lefebvre designates three key layers of the everyday for his purposes, which will be useful for us to highlight, develop on, and differentiate from. The first is that which we have already mentioned: the relationship between the cyclic-rhythmic and the linear or non-rhythmic as it is confronted in contemporary capitalistic milieus. The second is one we will elaborate on further below: the relationship between *need* and *desire* in everyday life, and the (for Lefebvre, dialecti-cal) relationship between these; this level also pertains to the everyday relationship to commodities, consumption and other practices, pleasures, and so on. A basic example of this level in the everyday life of *modernity* is that of electrical lighting, and Lefebvre highlights mechanisms and tactics through which a global firm was able to generate the *need* for electric lighting in communities in China even in the absence of initial demand (Lefebvre, 2014a: 249–250; Elden, 2004: 116).[4] This dialectic between need and desire thus pertains to their mutual imbrication, and how certain processes can produce 'new needs'. The third layer Lefebvre describes as ideological – and is closer to what we will discuss in the next section when we turn to the question of the production of subjectivity or *rhythmic processes of individuation* – and is described as:

> [This level] is a set of practices, representations, norms and tech-niques, established by society to give itself to regulate conscious-ness, to give it some 'order,' to close the excessive gaps between the 'inside' and the 'outside,' to guarantee an approximate synchro-nization between the elements of subjective life, and to organize and maintain compromises. (Lefebvre, 2014b: 356, our alteration)

The *critique of everyday life* 'finds its points of impact' (loc. cit.), for Lefebvre, through directing itself towards these three levels (cyclic time/

linear time; desire/need; social/individual). This critique, as we have already noted, is above all a critique that seeks the revolutionary met-amorphoses of everyday life towards, for Lefebvre, (1) everyday life 'catching up' with what is possible (e.g., the technical); and (2) 'that the processes which have been distanced from' everyday life 'return and reinvest themselves within it' (ibid.: 357).

As *residue* and *product* of various interlocking and at times conflicting processes – its practices, relations, habits, repetitions, exchanges, cre-ations, and so on – *everyday life* is also indissociable from its rhythmic power. Everyday life itself is continually reproduced and transformed; it is processually composed of a metastable consistency of various rhyth-mic assemblages, 'cosmic rhythms, biological rhythms and rhythms of capital circulation' (Chen, 2018: 25) being only three key examples. To transform the rhythms of everyday life is to transform the milieu. There are some attenuations and deviations from Lefebvre's account of every-day life which will be important for us. For example, the (oppositional) distinction he offers between the rhythmic and the non-rhythmic is not one we can maintain, given our discussions in Chapter 1 on *arrhyth-mia* and *hyperrhythmia*. This distinction, and gap between the two, at times allows him to argue the revolutionary critique of everyday life as being concerned with reducing the 'disparities and time-lags' (Lefebvre, 2014b: 357) experienced in the everyday; or similarly that the everyday must 'catch up with what is possible' (loc. cit.). Lefebvre's reading of the lag between the rhythmic and the non-rhythmic (linear) and tech-nical is further buttressed by a criticism of the fragmentation of labour in which for him the 'traditional ethic' (ibid.: 363) of work is, or has been, weakened through the division of labour (increasing alienation), in a tendency towards techniques of automation in workplaces in which 'work' becomes ever more *passive* and produces ever more intense aliena-tion. Indeed, the question of *leisure* is not immune from this critique: the technical object fragments leisure as well as labour, and as such, *the con-temporary technical object functions as a quasi-agent of alienation in both labour and leisure, permeating everyday life.* Here, these questions of technology and of the technical object can be honed in on through the question of rhythm as, for Lefebvre, the technical object's imbrication within every-day life is nothing other than the injection of the *non-rhythmic* into the rhythms of everyday life:

> Only partially technicized, everyday life has not created its own
> specific style or rhythm. Unconnected objects (vacuum cleaners,
> washing machines, radio or television sets, refrigerators, cars, etc.)
> determine a series of disjointed actions. Small technical actions

intervene in the old rhythms rather like fragmented labour in productive activity in general. The equipment of everyday life finds
itself more or less in the same situation as industrial mechanization
in its early stages, in the period when specific tools had unique
and exclusive functions. If these gestures increase effectiveness –
productivity – they also split things up; they truncate, they make
mincemeat of everyday life; they leave margins and empty spaces.
(Ibid.: 369)

The stereotyped, mechanical repetition of gestures and signals differs from the rhythmed and periodic starting and restarting which
characterises vital activities. (Ibid.: 533)

Linear, non-rhythmic, technical time is *shallow*, lacks depth (ibid.: 372),
and is indissociable from what Lefebvre describes as the 'unreality of
alienation' (Lefebvre, 2014a: 189), an alien force controlling – or for
Lefebvre contributing to the destruction of – the rhythms of everyday
life. The relationship between the natural and the technical permeates
these aspects of Lefebvre's *Critique of Everyday Life*, but the identification of the *modern* technical with the non-rhythmic and linear effaces
the human imbrication with the technical, the technical which is itself
rhythmic (in the sense that Simondon had already developed in terms
of the evolution of technical objects through rhythms of technical
development of continuous and minor improvements and discontinuous and major improvements (Simondon, 2017: 40, 68)). The rhythms
of technics are not the rhythms of the human, but this difference does
not at all indicate a *non-rhythmicity* of the technical. In this sense, for
us, this 'first level' of the relationship between the cyclic and linear
is, rather, one of various interlocking and non-dialectical rhythmicities which we approach through tendential processes of *arrhythmia* and
hyperrhythmia in contemporary capitalistic milieus. We depart completely from Lefebvre when he claims that technicised everyday life
'has not created its own specific style or rhythm' (Lefebvre, 2014b:
369), and that technicised everyday life leaves 'margins and empty
spaces' (ibid.: 369), insofar as the *arrhythmic colonisation of everyday life* in
contemporary capitalistic milieus is bound up with the contemporary
technicised everyday (as we will develop in Part II). Furthermore, it
appears difficult to maintain that capitalistic milieus do not absorb and
reproduce these cyclic rhythms, nor produce new cyclic rhythms themselves. Consider, for example, rhythms of 'growth' (GDP), economic
cycles (e.g., bubbles), the crises produced – on Marx's analysis – by
the tendential falling rates of profit, rhythms of capital accumulation,

Schumpetarian bursts of creative destruction, and so on, all of which can generate fluctuations and developments in the rhythms of everyday life. A further point worth reiterating, too, insofar as Lefebvre employs a notion of time as an 'empty space' in everyday life, is an issue we already considered in relation to Bachelard's dialectic of Being and Non-Being – which is echoed by Lefebvre when he argues that, historically, time is the motor of negativity, that time is a 'profound act of negation' (ibid.: 470), that the process of historical transformations in, say, social structures, evidence the 'negativity of time [at] work' (ibid., our alteration) – which we approach instead in terms of multiplicity (see Chapter 1, section a).[5]

Turning to the 'second level' – that of the dialectic of desire and need – here we must also differentiate our approach from Lefebvre's, who places desire as a partial derivative of *need*, allowing for him the claim that, without need, desire remains *artificial*. For Lefebvre, desire *needs need* – that is, desire must develop a *transparent* relationship to need (ibid.: 330) – in order for desire to remain or become non-artificial. This dialectic of desire enables Lefebvre to claim the following:

> The consumer does not desire. He submits. He has 'strangely' motivated 'behaviour patterns.' He obeys the suggestions and the orders given to him by advertising, sales agencies or the demands of social prestige (not to mention worries about solvency, which are far from negligible). The circuit from need to desire and from desire to need is constantly being interrupted or distorted. These 'orders' from outside become subtly abstract fragments or absurdly concrete 'motivations.' Desires no longer correspond to genuine needs; they are artificial. (Ibid.: 304–305)

This is also echoed (but also in a slightly prophetic form concerning the question of cybernetics and control societies) by Vaneigem:

> [Consumer] society's need to market objects, ideas and model forms of behaviour calls for a decoding centre where an instinctual profile of the consumer can be developed to help in product design and improvement, and in the creation of new needs better suited to the consumer goods on offer. Market research, motivation techniques, opinion polls, sociological surveys and structuralism all contribute to this project, no matter how anarchic or feeble their efforts may as yet be. If we give them free rein, our cyberneticians can be counted on to remedy the lack of coordination and rationalization. (Vaneigem, 2012: 119)

These 'false' behaviour patterns – false insofar as they are the product of alien forces – display the very artificiality of the desire of the consumer; the consumer as both alienated and unaware (for 'Awareness of an alienation is already disalienation' (Lefebvre, 2014b: 502) in the dialectical logic of alienation-disalienation), due to the opaqueness of the relationship between desire and need, 'which conceals these relations from their consciousness and their actions' (ibid.: 330). That is, this artificiality is constituted, according to Lefebvre, insofar as the individual subject *does not* 'consciously' recognise and negotiate the contradictions pertaining to the milieu of consumable objects with which it is confronted and its relationship of need, enjoyment, and pleasure (and alienation-disalienation) relating to these objects. That is, a version of the *false consciousness* we already discussed (Chapter 2, section d). Desire, then, is 'activated' for Lefebvre only insofar as such *conscious work* is undertaken by the individual subject in the recognition and negotiation with such conflicts; this leads to a dialectical process between *desire* and *need*, where each co-transforms the other in a processual manner; an unfolding of new desires *consciously* confronted, some of which are then transformed into *new needs.* This unfolding of new needs was already present in the early work of Marx and Engels in *The German Ideology*, where they develop the question of need directly flowing from the problems generated by everyday life itself, situating the production of new needs as the production of history itself:

> But life involves before everything else eating and drinking, housing, clothing and various other things. The first historical act is thus the production of the means to satisfy these needs, the production of material life itself. And this indeed is an historical act, a fundamental condition of all history, which today, as thousands of years ago, must daily and hourly be fulfilled merely in order to sustain human life [. . .] [T]he satisfaction of the first need (the action of satisfying and the instrument of satisfaction which has been acquired) leads to new needs; and this production of new needs is the first historical act. (Marx and Engels, 2007: 48–49)

> The needs of work and of the worker, the need to work and work as a need – these modify sensory activities, and even the sensory organs themselves. The 'human world' which is created in this way is composed as much of human bodies and their physiological activities as it is of the range of works, products, objects and goods [. . .] It is a vast, uncertain and highly populated region, the region of everyday life. (Lefebvre, 2014b: 484)

This dialectical to-and-fro concerning need developed in an earlier form by Marx and Engels is taken on by Lefebvre as a creative process, a process through which life is 'metamorphosed into a creative consciousness, creating and created' (ibid.: 302) in a dialectic of desire and need. Desire, here, is the individualisation of need, with an inextricable intentional-teleological relationship to pleasure (ibid.: 484–485). Without this conscious and creative confrontation with desire, allowing its activation, consciousness's relationship to desire remains artificial and subject to the control of alien forces across the social fabric of capitalistic milieus through which desires are normalised, replacing, according to Lefebvre, 'previously diversified "lifestyles" by everyday ways of living which are analogous, if not identical' (ibid.: 305).[6] While there are, no doubt, strong affinities between our approach and Lefebvre's, there are still nonetheless clear cuts on this which are worth emphasising. For us, and as we emphasised in Chapter 2, our conceptualisation of desire is decidedly *not* reducible to a 'subject' of desire, nor necessarily to any process of 'conscious activation'. Indeed, desire is constitutive of the process through which the subject becomes constituted *as* a subject – and as subjected, as we will discuss in the next section – through a rhythmic process comprising a particular constellation of uses of the connective, disjunctive, and conjunctive syntheses of desire. Later, in *Rhythmanalysis*, Lefebvre conceptually reignites this relationship between desire and need, this time through rhythm, although desire still remains 'contained' in the subject-who-desires and as tied to particular teleologies (we partially quoted this at the top of Chapter 1):

> Desire, of which so much has been said (in psychic terms), is both work and the product of work. Yet it has its rhythm, it *is* a rhythm, whose goal (its end) is either placed outside, or remains internal to, its act (operation). Sensual desire enters into the first case, aesthetic desire into the second. Between need and desire there is a well-known difference, but there is no discontinuity [. . .] Need and desire, sleep and wake, work and repose are rhythms in interaction. (Lefebvre, 2015: 35–36)

Rather than coming 'after' the subject, in the domain of consciousness and subject to conscious activation, our plenitudinous and Spinozist conceptualisation of desire is rather about the *production* of the subject, the object, the social, and so forth, and is inseparable from an examination of the mechanisms by which desire's pulsive movements become subject to capture, contraction, and sedimentation by certain regimes; an analysis of the *production of milieus and the possibilities of orientation within and between milieus* (which Lefebvre does at least partially hint at when he notes the 'manufacture of consumers by those who hold the means of production and who produce for profit' (Lefebvre, 2014b: 321)). The 'artificial' relationship to desire harboured by Lefebvre's consumer is nonetheless a real relationship, producing new relations external to their terms; as Vaneigem notes: 'The world of falsehood is a real world; people kill and get killed there, and we had best not forget it' (2012: 78). Desire is *active* and *productive*; productive in the sense of *producing* the consumer-as-consumer in the process of rhythmic subjection, but also *reproductive* in the sense of *reproducing* tendencies of orientation within capitalistic milieus, thereby reproducing and securing the capitalistic milieus themselves.

At the risk of being unfair to Lefebvre, he was primarily interested in the question of how the capitalist mode of production becomes continually reproduced through everyday life. However, his deeming of desires as 'artificial' is as opaque (and vaguely moralist: what might a 'true' desire look like?) as it is non-immanent (insofar as the account of alienation developed by Lefebvre rests upon a species-being from which we are torn and distanced through the capitalist mode of production). Further, relegating practices to the domain of 'artificiality' belies and effaces the extent to which such practices are constitutive of the real production of subjectivity and reproduction of capitalistic milieus. Ascending desire to the realm of consciousness belies and effaces its productive character, its unconscious repetitions, its oozing flows and arrests, its rhythms which escape consciousness, the subtlety of its operations and effects, and, further, precludes the vital distinction between preconscious class interests and unconscious investments of desire we highlighted with Deleuze and Guattari in Chapter 2. Lefebvre's consumer does not lack desire, he is the product of desire and rhythm – the consumer's desires are not *alienated* or false, they are actual, and are produced through the interlocking capture of desire and rhythm – and, further, such desires are productive of not only the consumer *as* consumer, but reproductive of the capitalistic milieu which is reconstituted and resecured through each practice of consumption; consumption is an active practice of desire and securitisation, actively productive of capitalistic milieus, desire's pulsive flows having become captured within particular rhythmic parameters of ontological security within the capitalistic milieu. So much for the second 'level' of everyday life on Lefebvre's analysis.

The third 'layer' that Lefebvre describes is concerned with that constellation of practices, representations, norms, etc., concerned with the 'regulation' and 'ordering' of consciousness. Our independent development on this third layer, which we noted above as the question of the *production of subjectivity* or *rhythmic processes of individuation*, constitutes the object of the remainder of this chapter as we continue to define and problematise our approach to everyday life.

b. The rhythmic production of subjectivity or rhythmic processes of individuation

At the beginning of Chapter 1, when beginning to outline the *first synthesis of the living present*, we drew on Protevi's imbrication of life with rhythmic periodicities, negotiations, and transformations (2013: 161). We noted that the rhythmic-habitual practice of the first passive synthesis achieves 'connections between successive moments [and] produces a centre around which chaotic elements may become stabilised, the beginnings of order may crystallise, and from which the growing assemblage may be given a direction' (Turetsky, 2004: 144, our addition). We emphasised the interlocking of rhythm and desire within particular rhythmic parameters of ontological security. Such patterns, stabilisations, and productive processes provide us with conceptual instruments with which to express the rhythmic production of subjectivity; this discussion will function as our *slipping into* the questions of what rhythms permeate our mental environment, the effects of these rhythms, and the sort of symptoms and functions these rhythms produce in our rhythmic processes of individuation. Berardi and Stiegler will help us begin, who both immediately connect us to ongoing digitalisation of everyday life in our contemporary milieus:

> Let's call the *infosphere* the universe of transmitters, and the *social brain* the universe of receivers. The universe of receivers – human beings made of flesh, and frail and sensuous organs – is not formatted according to the standards of digital transmitters. Although the neural system is highly plastic, and can mutate according to the *rhythm of the infosphere*, the format of the transmitter does not correspond to the format of the receiver. So what happens? As the electronic universe of transmission interfaces with the organic world of reception, it is producing pathological effects: panic, over-excitement, hyperactivity, attention deficit disorders, dyslexia, information overload, and the saturation of neural circuitry. (Berardi, 2015: 41, third emphasis ours)

> [The process of *permanent innovation* as theorised by Bertrand Gille] results in a divorce, if not between culture and technics, at least between the *rhythms of cultural evolution* and the *rhythms of technical evolution*. Technics evolves *more quickly* than culture.

(Stiegler, 1998: 15, our addition, first two emphases ours; also see Gille, 1986: 34–66)

> In today's control societies (also modulation societies), aesthetic weapons play an essential role (this is what Jeremy Rifkin has referred to as 'cultural capitalism'): it has become a matter of controlling the technologies of *aisthēsis* (the audiovisual or the digital, for example), and, in this way, *controlling the conscious and unconscious rhythms of bodies and souls; modulating* through the control of flows these *rhythms of consciousness and life.* (Stiegler, 2014b: 2, third emphasis ours)

Berardi here identifies a 'gap' between the *rhythms of the infosphere* and the (seemingly, at present, limited) capacity of humans to internalise and obey such accelerated rhythms. This 'gap' argues Berardi, produces pathological effects in the mental environment through 'the saturation of neural circuitry'. Stiegler's language is less neuro-pathological and more combative. The rhythms of the infosphere comprise, for Stiegler, a vast aesthetic weaponry for social control, through which bodies and souls become controlled and disempowered through their relative incorporation and (conscious or unconscious) submission to and reproduction of these rhythms. Stiegler also emphasises how this 'divorce' in the rhythms of evolution of culture and technics respectively transforms retention, protention-anticipation, and decision-making as such (1998: 15). Indeed, this is also a point indebted to Simondon:

> Anxiety effectively arises from those transformations [technical transformations in the workplace] that provide a break within the rhythms of everyday life, making the old habitual gestures useless. (Simondon, 2017: 130, our addition)

In this sense, *affect* is crucial to rhythmanalysis ('Rhythms are composed out of an agglomeration of affects' (Chen, 2018: 47)). The relationship between distinct rhythmicities (organic rhythms, technical rhythms, rhythms of shock, adoption, and/or adaptation, and so forth) is not a problem distinct to our contemporary context, or to today's milieus. It constitutes a central problematic of *any* approach to everyday life, and to any critique of the rhythms of everyday life: everyday life constituted always by a vast polyrhythmia. As already highlighted above, Lefebvre cites the relationship between the 'rhythmic' and the 'linear' (non-rhythmic) as one of the key objects of analysis in his critique of everyday life. His claim here (from volume one of the *Critique of Everyday Life*, published in 1947) is strikingly similar to the Berardi and Stiegler quotes above, but from a milieu prior to cyberneticisation:

> The physiological functions of the 'modern' man's [sic] nervous and cerebral systems seem to have fallen victim to an excessively demanding regime, to a kind of hypertension and exhaustion. He has not yet 'adapted' to the conditions of his life, to the speed of its sequences and rhythms [. . .] His nerves and senses have not yet been adequately trained by the urban and technical life he leads. Modern concepts are like a kind of electrical supercharge to his brain [. . .] and, to pursue the metaphor, his nerves and senses are frequently short-circuited. (Lefebvre, 2014a: 139–140)

So, whereas Berardi's focus is on those pathological effects of the rhythms of social control today, Stiegler's focus is on how those rhythms of control are embedded in the functioning of our contemporary aesthetic regime, Lefebvre's focus is, rather – and distinct from our own – on the condition and experience of *alienation* which, on his immense analysis, constitutes everyday life.[7] Nonetheless, that all three highlight the centrality of rhythm is of clear pertinence for us. Each highlights one of the central problematics of our critique of the rhythms of everyday life; namely, the mechanisms and effects constitutive of the *mental ecology* of the present, and the ways in which perception, experience, rhythm, and desire are mobilised and disciplined, the effects of such rhythms (panic, anxiety, the modulation of the rhythms of everyday life), that is, the rhythmic processes of individuation constitutive of the epoch, the modalities and effects of the production of contemporary subjects. This is a decidedly *not* a psychologisation, however. Indeed, to speak of a *mental environment* is always already to situate the psychological in relation to the milieu. As Massumi notes:

> The subject is not psychological, it is not contained in any one mind. It is in the interactions *between* people. Which is not to say that it is simply interpersonal: it is also in the technology that defined the kinds of productive work our docility serves. Which is not to say that it is simply socioeconomic: it is also in the raw materials at the basis of that technology and in the genes that define the physical and intellectual potential of the human body. Which is not to say that it is material in any deterministic way: genes result from chance mutation. The subject is a transpersonal abstract machine, a set of strategies operating in nature and spread throughout the social field. It is a whole world composed of an

infinity of causal lines on countless levels, all fractured by chance. (Massumi, 1992: 26)

Guattari, in his *Three Ecologies*, also highlights this central problematic of what we are calling rhythmic processes of individuation in capitalistic milieus when he claims: '*Capitalistic subjectivity seeks to gain power by controlling and neutralizing the maximum number of existential refrains*' (2014: 34, our emphasis). *Existential refrains* are those sets of rhythmic practices through which connections are produced 'between successive moments [and a centre is produced] around which chaotic elements may become stabilised, the beginnings of order may crystallise, and from which the growing assemblage may be given a direction' (Turetsky, 2004: 144, our addition). In *A Thousand Plateaus*, Guattari and Deleuze conceptualise *the refrain* as a set of rhythmic and territorial practices through which what we have called *rhythmic parameters of ontological security* – constitutive of any rhythmic process of individuation – are produced, and by extension (and by *intension*) through which potential vectors of ontological transformation might be launched into: 'The polyphony of modes of subjectivation actually corresponds to a multiplicity of ways of "keeping time". Other rhythmics are thus led to crystallise existential assemblages which they embody and singularise' (Guattari, 2006: 15).[8] Existential refrains constitute the stylistics through which the rhythms of everyday day are lived, the modes of existence through which subjectivity comes to be produced (*polyphonic* subjectivity). The existential refrain, then, is about the *concretisation* and consolidation of a singularity, of a singular polyrhythmic nexus comprising the rhythms of everyday life *extracted* from the possibilities proffered by the milieu. The refrain is concerned with 'the detachment of an existential "motif" (or leitmotiv) which installs itself like an "attractor" within a sensible and significational chaos' (ibid.: 17). (Recall from Chapter 1: rhythm is an *answer* to chaos precisely in the sense that it generates *some* stable parameters of ontological security, some habits, some contractions, some relationship to the past, present, and future.) The subject is but a metastable rhythm (Nancy, 2007: 38–39).

So, when Guattari claims that capitalistic subjectivity seeks to gain power by 'controlling and neutralising the maximum number of existential refrains', his argument, in our terms, is that contemporary capitalistic milieus are decidedly *arrhythmic* – they function with narrow rhythmic parameters of ontological security – and as such operate through the production of *arrhythmic subjects* through the tight capture of rhythm and desire: a vast, systemic, and arrhythmic *closing of the future*. Capitalistic milieus, themselves arrhythmic, *orient the becomings of subjects' rhythmic processes of individuation to themselves become arrhythmic.* This involves a *gridding* of categorisations towards which bodies orient themselves in everyday life:

> A capitalistic subjectivity is engendered through operators of all types and sizes, and is manufactured to protect existence from any intrusion of events that might disturb or disrupt public opinion. It demands that all singularity must be either evaded or crushed in specialist apparatuses and frames of references. Therefore, it endeavours to manage the worlds of childhood, love, art, as well as everything associated with anxiety, madness, pain, death, or a feeling of being lost in the Cosmos. (Guattari, 2014: 33)

> A body only approaches its assigned category as a limit: it becomes more or less 'feminine' or more or less 'masculine' depending on the degree to which it conforms to the connections and trajectories laid out for it by society according to which coordinate in gender grid it is judged to coincide with. 'Man' and 'Woman' as such have only reality other than that of logical abstractions. What they are abstractions of are not the human bodies to which they are applied, but habit-forming whole attractors which society expects its bodies to become addicted. (Massumi, 1992: 87)

Let us be more specific on this. One of the central ways in which contemporary capitalistic milieus function, for Guattari, is through the production of various *vectors* or *components* of subjectification enveloped in a (relatively) standardised production of subjectivity and the attendant capture/delimitation of possible components of subjectification (or effects of these components) which deviate from the mass production of a delimited range of capitalist subjects. These 'vectors' or 'components' are 'mechanisms of identity filtration' available within rhythmic processes of individuation. By 'various types' we are gesturing towards the large *quantitative range* but narrow *qualitative scope* of existential refrains, or life rhythms, available in contemporary capitalistic milieus (and indeed, this is also why such standardisation is *relative*). On this point, for example, Lefebvre highlights that the 'private' life of the capitalist 'individual' is 'literally a life of "privation"' (2014a: 169) in the sense, on his account, of being *deprived* of meaningful connection or control over everyday life – deprived of control over his or her own self (ibid.: 268) – due to the individual's being directed by alien forces. *Private* consciousness, *privated* consciousness, constitutes for Lefebvre a *contractive* existence:

> Instead of expanding, of conquering the world, this consciousness shrinks in upon itself. And the more it shrinks, the more it seems to be 'its own'. Crass and complacent, the individual settles down amid his familiar surroundings. Consciousness, thought, ideas, feelings, all are seen as 'property' on a par with 'his' furniture, 'his' wife and 'his' children, 'his' assets and 'his' money. (Ibid.: 169)

Vaneigem, similarly, connects this image of private consciousness with the consciousness of isolation which, for him, is the experience of alienation: 'the consciousness of isolation is simply the private consciousness, the unforsakable shard of individualism that respectable people drag around like a piece of cumbersome but cherished property' (2012: 26). Such an existence – atomised-capitalistic-individualistic existence – is contractive, for Lefebvre, insofar as it is one reduced to relations of propriety between the subject and his/her property, and insofar as it splits the individual from the milieu through which they are constituted *as* individuals (Elden, 2004: 70); but also, we can add (and departing from the thematic of alienation) in the sense that the rhythms of everyday life become arrhythmic ('the individual settles down amid his familiar surroundings'), dictated by the 'asphyxiating straitjacket of fragmented activities' (labour/leisure; private life/public life; the marvelous/the everyday, etc.) (Lefebvre, 2014a: 170). This 'asphyxiating straitjacket' Lefebvre describes dovetails with Guattari's account of the 'control and neutralisation' of existential refrains, constituted by the delimited qualitative scope of existential refrains possible in capitalistic milieus and *covered over* or *effaced* by a seemingly large quantitative range. Putting this another way, Berardi likewise argues that 'individualism' in capitalistic milieus is nonetheless a process of standardisation (control and neutralisation): the 'competitive consumerist individual is extremely standardized in his or her goals, tastes, and desires' (2015: 312), which Lefebvre humorously describes, drawing on Nietzsche's analogy in *Thus Spoke Zarathustra* (Nietzsche, 2003: 189–190), as individuals as grains of sand:

> Typically the middle classes are individualistic social groups made up of 'human sand'. Each grain is quite distinct and separable. And taken together they form a mass – indeed the heaviest and most impenetrable of masses. A sandbag can stop bullets! What is comical about this is that each grain of human sand thinks itself to be not only distinct, but infinitely original. But nothing is more like a grain of sand than another grain of sand. Bourgeois individualism implies the dreary, ludicrous repetition of individuals who are curiously similar in their way of being themselves and of keeping

themselves to themselves, in their speech, their gestures, their
everyday habits (meal times, rest times, entertainments, fashions,
ideas, expressions). (Lefebvre, 2014a: 172)

If Lefebvre, here, is perhaps too reductionist in terms of the actual broad
quantitative range of existential refrains possible in contemporary capitalistic milieus, we can attenuate this with the claim that this *relatively
standardised* process is one through which the maximum number of existential refrains in capitalistic milieus are nonetheless subordinated to a
logic through which these existential refrains themselves become processes of the continuous *securitisation* of these milieus. In this sense, we
do not claim that the subject occurs as simply as an *imprint*, or passive
effect, of the milieu, insofar as the subject immanently participates in
the milieu. The subject, developing and becoming in her rhythmic processes of individuation and rhythms of everyday life, is no sheep, and is
not (as Michel de Certeau puts in his *The Practice of Everyday Life*) 'graz-
ing on the ration of simulacra the system distributes to each individual'
(Certeau, 1988: 166). The subject's actualisation of singular rhythms of
everyday life in her existential refrain is a process of differential actualisation. As active, productive, and creative activity, experimental existential
refrains are a permanent threat to the capitalist milieu; they are 'actively
machinic, opening onto the most heterogeneous Universes of references'
(Guattari, 2006: 66). The point, therefore, is that capitalistic milieus do
not simply delimit ways of life, in other words, but rather they capture
their heterogenisation *into* a logic of securitisation, or what Guattari calls
the 'capitalistic homogenesis of generalised equivalence, which leads to all
values being valued by the same thing, all appropriative territories being
related to the same economic instrument of power, and all existential
riches succumbing to clutches of exchange value' (ibid.: 55).

Capitalistic homogenesis, for us, then, is a term we can use to denote this
process of control and neutralisation of existential refrains and its logic
of securitisation, by which we mean a logic through which *everyday life
continuously reproduces and securitises the capitalistic milieu*. The qualitative
scope of existential refrains, the possibilities of rhythms of everyday life,
constitutes the key problematic as we attempt to *mindscape* the rhythms
of everyday life. Each of the chapters in Part II will be devoted, in distinct ways, to the ways in which we might break through the *arrhythmic*
squeezing of such possibilities in contemporary capitalistic milieus, to
create new rhythms of everyday life, new habits, new ways of being,
new milieus, and thereby to create new worlds. This problematic will be
explored through our reading of rhythmic processes of individuation –
itself grounded and explored through our reading of rhythm and desire

(Chapter 1) and methodological *fiat* of scaping (Chapter 2) – we will develop in this chapter.

Subjectivity is conceptualised here as that which becomes established 'at the crossroads of multiple components, each relatively autonomous in relation to the other, and, if need be, in open conflict' (Guattari, 2014: 23).[9] That is, as *rhythmic processes of individuation* ('Sensation, affectivity, and rhythmicity should be considered as accompanying, enveloping, and generating subjectivity, perhaps revealing all of perception as intensely affective' (Ikoniadou, 2014b: 58)). Everyday life is the ever-moving spacetime through which rhythmic processes of individuation, always embodied, move. Traversed by movement, affect, sensation, and cognition, and comprised infra- or pre-personally of opticality, proprioception (the 'muscular memory of relationality' which is the 'cumulative memory of skill, habit, posture' (Massumi, 2002: 59)), tactile sensibility, and visceral sensibility, embodied everyday life moves through variable states of passional intensity, at times cognised through emotions. Massumi terms the combination of proprioception and viscerality *mesoperception*, or simply *sensation:*

> Mesoperception is the synesthetic sensibility: it is the medium where inputs from all five senses meet, across subsensate excitation, and become flesh together, tense and quivering. Mesoperceptive flesh functions as a corporeal transformer where one sense shades into another over the failure of each, their input translated into movement and affect. Mesopercetion can be called *sensation* for short. (Ibid.: 62)

Affect being that virtual and transpersonal modality of synesthetic perspective, of which emotion is but an intense embodied contraction (ibid.: 35). *Affective ecologies* (we engage with three in Part II) are thus those ecologies of the mental environment traversed by transpersonal affective components which we *sense* in our rhythms of everyday life. In *Francis Bacon: The Logic of Sensation*, Deleuze engages with this same question of the body registering intensity and affect in movement through sensation. Or more precisely, the question of what, across these differential levels of sensation, enables their (ever temporary) metastable unicity. We take such a metastable unicity as being the precise crossroads where subjectivity becomes constituted, or, more precisely, where rhythmic processes of individuation become partially stabilised. Massumi underlines sensation as the becoming-flesh of the body's affective engagement with the world, and to this we can add how Deleuze situates *rhythm* as the component which traverses and provides contact between sensations. Discussing the role of the painter as being able to *render visible* this rhythmic unity of the senses, Deleuze notes:

> But this operation is possible only if the sensation of a particular domain (here, the visual sensation) is in direct contact with a vital power that exceeds every domain and traverses them all. This power is rhythm, which is more profound than vision, hearing, etc. Rhythm appears as music when it invests the auditory level, and as painting when it invests the visual level [. . .] What is ultimate is thus the relation between sensation and rhythm, which places in each sensation the levels and domains through which it passes. This rhythm runs through a painting just as it runs through a piece of music. It is a diastole-systole: the world that seizes me by closing in around me, the self that opens to the world and opens the world itself. (Deleuze, 2016: 30–31)

The intersection of sensation, affect, and rhythm is that crossroads through which our rhythms of everyday life acquire metastability and vibrational consistency ('Sensation is vibration' (ibid.: 32)), pointing towards what Deleuze calls that 'rhythmic unity of the senses' (ibid.) or what Massumi discusses in terms of how proprioceptive elements 'fuse into a rhythm' and 'unity of movement' (ibid.: 183) producing a *vector:* existential refrains.

Indeed, like Lefebvre's definition of the everyday as 'residue' and 'product' of its distinct activities, the subject (or more precisely the account of the process through which subjectivity is continually produced, reproduced, and transformed) is developed here as *residue and product of the rhythms of everyday life*, rhythms with affective cadences and colours. Writing here in the context of a rhythmic and phenomenological analysis of poetic expression, but usefully for our purposes, Abraham notes that the '*meaning [sens]* or *value* of a rhythm is the affective tonality it calls forth, allowing us to describe it as graceful, solemn, pounding, ethereal, or others' (1995: 25). What these vectors or components might be are multiple, relatively autonomous (though often connected), and impersonal – and we do not here submit these processes to any determinism or rigid structuralisation – but will include: language, social, political, juridical, economic, educational, technological, cultural, medical, therapeutic, and religious institutions in historical contexts (comprising the rhythmic contraction and normalisation of patterns of practice around certain stable points; certain interlockings of rhythm and desire); the embrained body/embodied brain of the subject and its historical context (here we can point both to genetic and epigenetic factors, as well as to the social positionality of the subject along intersectional (Crenshaw, 1989, 1995) lines of class, embodiment, race, sex, gender, age, and family history); the rhythms pertaining to everyday 'labour' and 'leisure' (including the navigation of different types of transport (technologies of mobility), different patterns of light exposure, and different types of architecture through which these labour-leisure rhythms are rendered possible); as well as technology and differential distribution of technological (or *technic*-ological) access (what Stiegler terms, drawing on Husserl, *tertiary retentions*, and into which we can include, as an example, *digital-communicative technologies*).[10] Nor, indeed, can we *totalise* our conception as we will be developing it (recall from Chapter 2, section a: *if the scope of critique is to be total, critique must be non-totalising in its creations, always opening up the possibility for future movements of critique (composition, sculpture)*). Our analysis of rhythmic processes of individuation – here in the case of the 'production of subjectivity' – therefore is concerned with what is produced through the connections, disjunctions, and conjunctions of these relatively autonomous components, a production which occurs through the interlocking (and potential capture) of rhythm and desire.

These components are never determinants: they are *transducers* or *inducers*. As *inductors*, these components solicit actualisation through the coding and capturing of time and desire ('Call the rigging of becoming *induction*' (Massumi, 2002: 63)). Induction pertains to the proffered field of potentiality in which the body finds itself in the milieu; this field of potentiality induces a field of possible rhythmics, the *telos* of which is that of the targeted unity of being, what we will discuss at various points in Part II as the securitised, capitalist, egoic *I* engaged in the pursuit of happiness. *Induction*, in the sense we are using it, pertains to the solicited filtration of affective, semiotic, etc., components in our rhythms of everyday life precisely towards the *telos* that integrates these components into a 'stable ground' of individuality.

Transduction here pertains to the body's function to convert actualised sensation transversally across domains (ibid.: 42); the body acts within an induced field of possibility and itself acts to transduce and transmit through sensation, affect, and actuality. Massumi even speaks of the body as contributing to processes of 'rhythmic transduction' (ibid.: 118) between and across electromagnetic, organic, and technical domains. For Simondon, the living being is essentially a transducer, storing chemical energies and actualising them 'during the course of different vital operations' (2017: 155). Transduction is a *modulation*, involving elements of structural change and amplification processes (Hui, 2016a: 191). To give an initial example, the whole field of cyberspace can be positioned, in part, as a '*dynamic field of transduction*' (Simondon, 2017: 124) inso-far as its interconnectivity enables sensation and affect to be triggered, induced, and amplified, en masse, through the event of relation between bodies and the continuous stream of information.[11] Simondon describes networks – networks of technical objects – as producing an 'extremely concrete and actual solidarity, existing instant by instant through the interplay of multiple conditions; through the technical networks, the human world acquires a high degree of internal resonance' through which the technical milieu is not just an ensemble of means, but also 'an ensemble of conditionings of actions and incitements to act' (2017: 229). Transduction operates across domains or zones of intensity.

This initial and non-exhaustive listing highlights the intense com-plexity of conceptualising subjectivity in this multiplicitous manner. Our rhythmic conceptual apparatus provides us with an *assemblage of enunciation* through which to scape this complex terrain and compose it anew. We will conceptualise two distinct but interlocking processes of individuation in contemporary capitalistic milieus through the notion of everyday life: rhythmic subjection and rhythmic containment.

c. Rhythmic subjection

That social authority (whether religious, economic, political, technolog-ical, institutional, cultural, aesthetic, or scientific) mobilises our bodies, souls, minds, dreams, imaginations, and so on; that they nudge, direct, or command us in certain directions and towards our internalisation and reproduction of the norms and injuncts of these authorities, is by no means a new idea or novel analytical focus point. Nonetheless, this ana-lytical dramatisation must always be redone *anew*, insofar as the condi-tions of the present are never static. This is an admission, in other words, that the task of this chapter is historically and politically situated, but it is also a claim for its permanent and always heightened relevance.

Rhythmic subjection is the term we will use to conceptualise some of the meeting points at the crossroad of those 'multiple components' through which embrained bodies become partially and temporarily mobilised *as subjects*, which is to say *as subjected* to elements of social authority today through:

1. Affective, emotional, and cognitive identification *with* or *in relation to* (including *against*) social authority and the grids of intelligibility (including collective grids of intelligibility, such as race, gender, eth-nicity, as well as codes of meaning and value-systems) they supply. These constitute particular deployments and sedimentations of the

conjunctive synthesis of desire as lived in the rhythms of everyday life. (Recall: the conjunctive synthesis is concerned with the emergence of the subject, who identifies herself with the impersonal flows of desire and the particular relations that pertain between connective and disjunctive syntheses in that case; or, more precisely, with what has been *recorded* or *inscribed* on the body without organs.) We will term this *identity filtration*, insofar as these processes of affective, emotional, and cognitive identification display mechanisms of subjective filtration of what the subject *is* and *is not* in a spacetime and in a milieu.

2. The spatio-temporal-material rhythms that bodies must negotiate and pass through to subsist. For now we will call this *labour* (of course, including reproductive and domestic labour).

3. Those activities that fall outside of the realm of labour, variously including that which is biologically necessary (rest, sleep), as well as various forms of consumption. Speaking broadly, this includes the spectrum of available *coping mechanisms* – which are rhythmic mechanisms insofar as they are time-limited and habitual – and how these mechanisms are governed, as well as those activities outside of the sphere of necessary labour. For the purposes of brevity we will refer to these elements at different points as simply 'rest' and 'leisure'.

Although these three components do not *exhaust* the rhythms of everyday life – indeed, recall Lefebvre's claims on everyday life constituting both a *residue* and *product* – we situate these as being nonetheless crucial components of the rhythms of everyday life in contemporary capitalistic milieus. Filtration, subsistence, coping/existence/leisure. The immediate connection between *subjectivity*, rhythms, and *subjection* is to gesture towards our multiplicitous conception of subjectivity *as a rhythmic process of subjection*.

Rhythmic subjection is our development of Maurizio Lazzarato's work on *social subjection* as a mode of subjectivity production under capitalism today. Drawing primarily on Guattari, Lazzarato's conception of social subjection is of the manifold apparatuses through which we *become* subjects, or through which we *become* subject-ed; the notion of *subjection* is vital here insofar as constitutes the establishment of hierarchies. He claims the following:

> Subjection plays an essential role, because it allows capitalism to establish different molar hierarchies: a first hierarchy between man (as a species) and nature and a second hierarchy within culture between man (gender, white, adult, etc.) and woman, child, and

so on. These two hierarchies are the antecedents fundamental to the more specifically economic hierarchies. (Lazzarato, 2014: 35)

So, subjection is about the establishment and rigidification of molar hierarchies (such as certain molar identities).[12] However, we should not take this to mean that these hierarchies are stable or fixed, insofar as they are continuously generated, reproduced, and transforming. These hierarchies are generated, reproduced, and transformed, we argue, at the intersection between *identity filtration, labour, and leisure* (we do not presume a hierarchy or priority to these three components); which is also to say *through the rhythms everyday life.*

Recall our quote from Guattari above: capitalistic milieus demand 'that all singularity must be either evaded or crushed in specialist apparatuses and frames of references' (2014: 33). These 'specialist apparatuses' and 'frames of reference' are precisely what we mean by mechanisms of *identity filtration*: the general form or spectrum of possible *existential refrains* (ways of life, life rhythms) and the stylistics through which this spectrum is negotiated (labour and leisure). Such a spectrum of existential refrains is also indissociably implicated with the technical environment through which the embrained bodies in particular milieus must orient their becomings. Lefebvre highlighted a dimension of this point, in the specific case of milieus *post*-Industrial Revolution, when he noted that: 'Technological or industrial civilization tends to narrow the gap between lifestyles (we are not talking about living standards) in the world as a whole' (Lefebvre, 2014b: 313). Lazzarato notes how social subjection involves the production of the *entrepreneurial-agential individual* who exercises *choice* and *risk* in socio-economic interaction and assumes *responsibility* for these choices and risks in their biological lifetime. This subject is mobilised, constituted, and produced through conscious signifying semiotics, the egoic 'I', relative levels of 'human capital' and 'entrepreneurship', and pre-constituted 'preferences' which are expressed through its consumption (demand) of goods and services and through voting and migration patterns (Tiebout, 1956). Social subjection produces a normative (normalising) grid of social interaction: intersubjectivity in a realm of communicative representation (language), economic representation (economic data and political economy), and political representation (for example, though not necessarily, democratic institutions).

In other words, social subjection is a process of production, a process of producing individuated subjects befitting capitalistic milieus, with certain rhythms and desires, subjects with properties, characteristics, and attendant positions in historically constituted social hierarchies (male/female, white/non-white, skilled/non-skilled, able-bodied/non-able-bodied, capitalist/worker, debtor/creditor, etc.), and who are *responsible* for *their capitalisation* on *their lifetime* (labour and leisure). Labour being the site through which *supply* is governed (where the subject(ed) must produce goods and services), and leisure being the site through which *demand* is governed (where the subject(ed) must desire and consume goods and services). Such abstract 'specialist apparatuses' or 'frames of references' are noticeably devoid of content: any and all modes of existence might be abstractly captured within this schema.[13] Nonetheless, these abstract apparatuses grid and *orient* the becomings, i.e., the rhythms of everyday life, of those subject to processes of rhythmic subjection in contemporary capitalistic milieus.

As Lazzarato also notes: 'To be employable means to match one's behavior and lifestyle to the demands of the market' (2017: 35). A grid functions as a *tuner* of rhythm. What we can further subtract from such an abstract and political schema is that it is a *generalising* and *neutralising* mode of (subjectivity) production; *everyday life* becomes the differential actualisation of, and rhythmic negotiation with, these general models. As general models, they may provide a large quantitative range of existential refrains, but their qualitative scope is nonetheless narrow and delimited. This is our reading of Guattari's claim: 'Capitalistic subjectivity seeks to gain power by controlling and neutralizing the maximum number of existential refrains' (2014: 34). *Orienting the rhythms and desires of everyday life* is constitutive of this process of control and neutralisation.

Let us return to the process of rhythmic subjection more closely through an example of how such generalised models of identity fil- tration can function. Entrepreneurial subjection, as Lazzarato will at times refer to it (2014: 9), is *responsibilising* of the self: the subjected is incentivised to take responsibility for the acquisition of one's own human capital (employability, skills, physical health, psychical health).[14] (Responsibilisation functions as a part of the processes of identity filtra- tion and as a libidinal investment thereon.) This is evidenced, though in different forms, through both the functioning of welfare states and contemporary austerity states. Under the increasingly defunct capitalist-welfare state (which Guattari terms *assistentialist*) the relations of dependence between the state and the welfare recipient involved 'pro- duce[s] an infantilized subjectivity' (Guattari and Rolnik, 2007: 208) in which the state is the *mediator* through which *all becomings must pass.* In other words, a subject's rhythms of everyday life *pass through* the state in order to achieve subsistence and existence. In the capitalist welfare state, the state acts as a normative guide, advising us on eating habits, sexual preferences, child raising, educational choices, and so on. The assisten- tialist or welfare state, according to Guattari, 'begins by organizing a segregation that drives a considerable part of the population out of the economic circuits. In a second stage the state comes to the rescue, giving assistance to those people, but on condition that they go through the system of control' (ibid.: 209–210).

The point to be taken here is that welfare state mechanisms are structured in such a manner so as to incentivise, for example, the unemployed subject to identify himself as a subject who needs to be rescued or as a beneficiary of unemployment insurance. In either sense, it is the unemployed subject who is *responsibilised* for their plight of unemployment, responsibilised in the sense that the embrained body in question is incentivised to *libidinally invest in their responsibilisation*: it is in this sense that responsibilisation (differentially) functions as a mechanism for identity filtration. Guattari would have placed the mechanism of responsibilisation as ones of the many 'machines of culpabilisation' which have become 'necessary to stabilise the social field of capitalism' (Guattari, 2016: 8). Today, the assistentialist state is not what it once was. Especially in the post-2008 context of austerity and precarity,[15] the state is no longer willing to 'come to the rescue' quite so often, and so the mechanisms of control have altered and intensified. As we noted above, the hierarchies Lazzarato gestured towards are, for us, *continuously generated, reproduced, and transformed* in the ever-moving present. As Lazzarato puts it, speaking of this post-2008 context:

> In the current crisis, for the majority of the population, 'work on the self' means no more than 'entrepreneurial' management of unemployment, debt, wage and revenue cuts, reductions in social services, and rising taxes [. . .] Capitalism obliges individuals to assume the 'superegos' necessary for filling hierarchical roles and functions, whether those of the unemployed, factory workers, retirees, consumers, or cognitive workers. (Lazzarato, 2014: 53–54)

Under conditions of austerity-precarity, the libidinal mechanism of responsibilisation still functions in relation to how embrained bodies ought to relate to 'their failures' in relation to labour and leisure (unemployment, high debt levels, poor credit ratings, depression, anxiety, ill-health, smoking, and so on). One example of this that is central to Lazzarato's analysis is that of *debt*. He argues that the creditor/debtor relation is the core of capitalistic social subjection insofar as the promise the debtor makes to the creditor to reimburse his debt *produces* memory and affects such as guilt, responsibility, loyalty, and trust: the *filtration* of these affective and semiotic components in the debtor's rhythmic subjection are crucial to the fulfilment of the promise (ibid.: 48). For us, these affective components are inseparable from particular modalities and territorialisations of the pulsive flows of desire. Whenever we utilise the terminology of 'identity filtration' or 'concretisation' of certain mechanisms of identity filtration, we are here explicitly connecting this movement with those moments of identification and libidinal investment (with or against grids of intelligibility proffered by the milieu) that applications of the conjunctive synthesis of desire are.

We can call debt, to return to the example, a mechanism of *rhythmic subjection* precisely insofar as debt governs the subject(ed)'s rhythms of everyday life towards the concretisation of particular mechanisms of identity filtration: (1) debt governs and squeezes the present through continuous repayment mechanisms and deadlines, and, so, the possibilities of *everyday life* that the subject can negotiate; (2) debt governs, contracts, and selects a portion of the past through crystallising a subject's 'worthiness' of credit and liquidity through its *informational memory* of previous borrowing and consumption patterns; (3) debt governs the future through channelling this informational memory (which is a type of tertiary retention) into 'credit ratings', and, so, into the subject's ability to develop and act on a plan of life (or a subject's ability to cultivate a singularising existential refrain).

In short: *debt functions as a mechanism of rhythmic subjection through rhythmic contraction.* Recall our definition of *arrhythmia* from Chapter 1: we termed *arrhythmic* those pulsive flows of desire that are *captured*, exhibiting the *minimum of rhythm* or the *maximum of rhythmic contraction* in its functioning (repetition with a *minimum* of difference). Arrhythmia freezes the virtual structure of the past, delimits patterns of practice in the present, and so *forecloses* the future. *Is such freezing and foreclosure not precisely what the contemporary indebted subject experiences?* Such an arrhythmic *contraction* of possibilities that the indebted subject experiences *towards* the *securitisation* of the capitalist milieu in which it is experienced. *Debt provokes the indebted subject to orient its becoming towards the continual securitisation of the capitalistic milieu.* Debt, in this sense, functions as a mechanism that seeks to generate and continuously reproduce capitalism's ontological security (both materially, through material impoverishment and precarity, and subjectively, through the crushing and distressing psychic impacts of continuous indebtedness). We do not need to agree with Lazzarato's identification of debt as *the* central mechanism of subjection, but its importance is clearly crucial.

This example of debt will be revisited in more detail in Chapter 6 but functions here to introduce how our practice of mindscaping, as a *rhythmic ecology*, will slip into the milieu of the mental environment through an analytical focus on the rhythms and processes of everyday life, and to substantiate more clearly how capitalism controls and neutralises existential refrains: through the capture of rhythm and desire, through actual processes of rhythmic subjection. Moving on, we will now develop a second vector pertaining to the production of subjectivity and the mental environment today: *rhythmic containment.*

d. Rhythmic containment

Rhythmic containment operates on different registers to *rhythmic subjection.* The latter's focus is on identity filtration on a personal level through which the subject(ed) negotiates everyday life (labour and leisure): the government of individuals. The former is focused on processes of governance on pre- and supra-personal levels (particularly, though not exclusively, through *technics* or *tertiary retentions*): the government of *dividuals* (Deleuze, 1992). Lazzarato's term for this, which we are again modifying, is *machinic enslavement*:

> [E]nslavement employs modeling and modulating techniques that bear on the 'very spirit of life and human activity.' It takes over human beings 'from the inside,' on the *pre-personal* (pre-cognitive and preverbal) level, as well as 'from the outside,' on the *supra-personal* level, by assigning them certain modes of perception and sensibility and manufacturing an unconscious. Machinic enslavement formats the basic functioning of perceptive, sensory, affective, cognitive, and linguistic behaviour. (Lazzarato, 2014: 38)

The Guattarian emphasis on the *machinic* is indicative of a refusal to reduce the machinic to the technical, insofar as this runs the risk of reinstating a human/machine binary (for Lazzarato, 'the machine is a prerequisite to technique' (ibid.: 81)). We have already encountered elements of this machinic analysis on pre- and supra-personal levels in Chapter 1, through our discussion of Deleuze and Guattari's notion of *desiring-machines.* Guattari's machinism goes beyond desiring-machines, encompassing technical machines, biological machines, linguistic machines, musical machines (to name just some examples), machinic conjunctions productive of new machines – *abstract machines* or *machinic assemblages* – which function through relating these heterogeneous machines and giving the machinic ensemble a direction (Guattari, 2006: 34–35). The technical milieu (in the Simondonian sense) would constitute a machinic assemblage, as would, indeed, and in a more heterogenous and complex fashion, contemporary capitalistic milieus. So, *desiring-machines* function only as a component part of the machinic assemblages that contemporary capitalistic milieus are.

Connecting this machinic notion explicitly to the production of subjectivity in his *Chaosmosis*, Guattari highlights the machinic dimensions entering into the production of subjectivity, encompassing, as we have highlighted numerous times, libidinal investments (there are 'investments of desiring machines producing a subjectivity adjacent to these components' (ibid.: 34)), as well as mechanisms of *semiotic production* (which we discussed above in terms of the relationship between signifying semiotics and social subjection), cultural production (media), and, most important for this section and for this notion of rhythmic containment, *asignifying semiological dimensions* 'that trigger informational sign machines' which function independently of denotation and signification, and thus 'escape from strictly linguistic axiomatics' (ibid.: 4). Asignifying semiotics are not to be confused with or reduced to *signals*, which in Lefebvre's theory of the semantic field of everyday life are those *command-functions* which function as closed systems within milieus (Lefebvre's prototypical example is that of traffic lights; signals obey a rule of *exclusive disjunction*, yes/no, either/or, permission granted/permission denied; they produce reflex actions and their central effect is one of conditioning (Lefebvre, 2014b: 572)). Lefebvre did, however, point in the direction of asignifying semiotics: he explicitly argues that *signs* (constitutive of signifying semiotics) and signals – which were born with, in, and through industrialisation (ibid.: 594) – are irreducible to each other; that signals are meaningless (in the sense of having nothing to do with conveying meaning), and are concerned rather with an unambiguous order-transmission, that the signal '*itself has no signification*' (ibid.: 573). This connection between signals and industrialisation is, for Lefebvre, an indication that signals function as one of those aspects of the *linear* or *non-rhythmic* everyday life we met above. Indeed, Lefebvre points further in the direction of asignifying semiotics when he imagines that, one day, signals may perhaps coalesce into a 'gigantic machine' of control, in which 'cyberneticists will simply formulate and put into action' (ibid.: 594). Guattari's *asignifying semiotics*, similarly, operate machinically, through triggering operations through what he describes as a *diagrammatic function* of part-signs. There is neither the need, time, nor possibility of *interpretation* (nor negotiation) in the case of asignifying semiotics: they *machinically function*, they produce effects:

The indicative matter of a-signifying semiotic machines is constituted by 'point-signs'; these on the one hand belong to a semiotic order and on the other intervene directly in a series of material

machinic processes. Example: a credit card number which trig-
gers the operations of a bank auto-teller. The a-signifying semiotics figures don't simply secrete significations. They give out stop
and start orders but above all activate the 'bringing into being' of
ontological Universes. (Guattari, 2006: 49)

An instance of a non-signifying semiotic would be a mathematical
sign machine not intended to produce significations; others would
be a technico-semiotic complexus, which could be scientific,
economic, musical or artistic, or perhaps an analytic revolutionary
machine. (Guattari, 1984: 75)

It is here therefore that, despite their similarities, Guattari's asignifying semiotics distinguishes itself from Lefebvre's signals, revolving crucially around the former's *machinic* (and therefore non-anthropocentric
approach) and the latter's anthropocentrism. Lefebvre's signal 'can only
be directed at a single sense organ' (Lefebvre, 2014b: 572); that is, it is
the human, and the human's relative levels of conditioning expressed
in their response to the signal, which is key for Lefebvre. There is no
focus or sustained attention given to the technical milieu in the case of
signals (indeed, Lefebvre emphasises that his example of the traffic lights
is totally arbitrary; this signal could as effectively be given by a spray of
perfume); nor is there attention paid to interactions *between non-human
machinic or technical components.*[16] As such, Lefebvre's account of the signal
fails to take into account the complexity of technics and the role technics
can play in the production of subjectivity: subsumed within Lefebvre's
general categorisation of the technical as the non-rhythmic, his account
is reductionist. Further, the interactions between non-human machinic
components, which Lefebvre excludes from his analytics through reducing signals to necessarily being directed at a human sense organ, will
become crucial to our own account of the 'surrounding components' of
identity filtration-labour-leisure in helping to determine a field of action
and to orient the becomings of refrains within the milieu. For Guattari,
these non-human machinic components are also crucial to the analysis
of asignifying semiotics as such.

So, to return more closely to the notion of rhythmic containment:
rather than focusing on rhythmic processes of individuation through the
nexus of identity filtration, labour, and leisure, in which conscious and
affective components are at work (which encompasses signifying semiotics, described by Guattari as a '"dictatorship" of dominant significations'
which enter into those machines of culpabilisation (2016: 8)), the angle
here is rather of those pre- and supra-personal components surrounding

this identity filtration-labour-leisure nexus. Some examples of asigni-fying semiotics here will help to clarify this: stock market levels and fluctuations, GDP and inflation figures, public and private debt levels, binary code, algorithmic data processing and data banks generally, and so on. Discussing asignifying semiotics, Genosko discusses in particular Guattari's example of the magnetic strips on credit/debit cards:

> There isn't any room for interpretation in the strings of num-bers and characters on a typical magstripe: framed by start and stop sentinels, field separators between system/bank/account/ and redundancy check, all of which are recognized automat-ically, and have limited numbers of characters. In themselves a-signifying signs have no meaning but they operationalize local powers. (Genosko, 2008: 14)

This operationalisation occurs without the mediation of subjectivity, and is a process triggered by a-signifying semiotics enabling (or not) an 'authorization process at a distance' (Genosko, 2016: 23). Indeed, the following famous quote from Deleuze's *Postscript on the Societies of Control* is one that imagines a cybernetic Guattarian city, where mobility is con-trolled (local powers are operationalised) through asignifying semiotics and their diagrammatic functioning, and which *automatically* authorise (or do not) one's possibilities of orientation within the milieu:

> Félix Guattari has imagined a city where one would be able to leave one's apartment, one's street, one's neighbourhood, thanks to one's (dividual) electronic card that raises a given barrier; but the card could just as easily be rejected on a given day or between certain hours; what counts is not the barrier but the computer that tracks each person's position – licit or illicit – and effects a universal modulation. (Deleuze, 1992: 7)

One's dividual electronic card enables the networked algorithmic inter-action between non-human technical components that diagrammatically activate permissions and proscriptions in Guattari's imagined cyber-netic city of control. These permissions and proscriptions – unlike in Lefebvre's signals – which could, at least in principle, be disobeyed or questioned, even if the commands are 'understood' (Lefebvre, 2014b: 573) – are produced independent of the embrained body (if one's bank card is swallowed, one cannot negotiate with, disobey, or question the ATM). In contemporary capitalistic milieus, and amidst growing levels of the cyberneticisation of everyday life, our critique of the rhythms of everyday life cannot but pass through an account of the mechanisms of *automatic* control/modulation, of which asignifying semiotics are an important component.

So, *rhythmic containment* focuses on those processes of control on pre- and supra-personal levels *not* through mechanisms of identity filtration, labour, and leisure, but rather through the surrounding conditions of these mechanisms on pre- and supra-personal levels. These surrounding conditions form a crucial part of the 'inputs' through which identity filtration (and thus *rhythmic subjection*) itself operates. Rhythmic containment, in other words, will focus on the 'surrounding components' of identity filtration, labour, and leisure which form crucial co-ordinates in the rhythms of individuation. On this, Berardi notes how subjection as a process emerges somewhere 'in-between' the pre- and supra-personal; that is, subjection emerges processually and cannot be totally divorced from pre-personal elements (such as the neurological limits of the brain or the field of possible action within the *milieu* in question) or supra-personal ones (his example is that of cultural imagination and thought) (Berardi, 2015: 249).[17] Though, to emphasise, this is not to position one mechanism as somehow prior or more 'fundamental' than the other, insofar as these levels are co-constituted, co-emergent, and co-implicated in the rhythms of individuation. Our approach bears strong similarities to Protevi's in *Political Affect* (2009); his oft-repeated refrain for his triple analysis is that of 'above, below, and alongside' the subject. If capitalism 'seeks to gain power by controlling and neutralizing the maximum number of existential refrains' (Guattari, 2014: 34) in a tendential process of *capitalist homogenesis* then the registers of the pre-personal ('below') and supra-personal ('above') discussed in this section allow for a potentially tighter grip on such control and neutralisation.

In Guattari's (and Deleuze's) terms, machinic containment works on the *deterritorialised* components of subjectivity; machinic containment's role in the subjective ecology of capitalism is the constitution of an embrained body that works 'for the machines' (understood as the machines which regulate capital flows and for continuous capital valorisation): an *automatisation* of practices which tend to *securitise* capitalistic milieus. How so? Stiegler will help us draw this out, as well as highlighting the importance of *rhythm* in such a conception. What Stiegler calls sensibility's 'machinic turn' speaks precisely to this point, and he connects sensibility's 'machinic turn' both with the industrialisation of culture and the connected proliferation of technic-ological devices and tools bound up with the 'production' and 'consumption' of culture on pre- and supra-personal levels (in particular, today, digital devices and tools). He claims the following:

> This machinic development of the senses represents a great rup-
> ture as, from now on, not everything has to pass by way of the
> hand or the voice: it is possible to *listen to music without knowing
> how to make it*, and it is now almost always listened to in this
> way [. . .] [This] allows for the separation of producers and con-
> sumers, the machinic systemization of all forms of symbolic and
> sensible expression is able to put all kinds of aesthetic spheres
> into the services not only of social control, but also of control
> societies – where it is a matter of capturing the attention of souls
> so as to control the behaviour of bodies, with the intention of
> getting them to consume goods and services. (Stiegler, 2015: 12,
> our addition)

By this, he is gesturing towards the increasing *machinic control of expression*
which subordinates or *reduces* expression (whether intra- or interper-
sonal) to consumption or production, and thus as oil to the machines of
capital valorisation. How is such a process of subordination (of expression to consumption) effectuated on pre- and supa-personal levels?
For Stiegler, this is effectuated through the *exteriorisation* of *the nervous
system*, *memory*, and *imagination* (the pre-personal as 'below' the subject;
the supra-personal as 'above the subject', which are entangled insofar as
the psychic, social, and technical interact to 'retain' memory and produce psycho-social imaginaries).[18] By *exteriorisation* Stiegler is referring
to both the *condition* and *effect* of expression:

1. Exteriorisation of the nervous system (pre-personal): Exteriorised
   technologies are themselves *conditions* for linguistic-communicative
   expression; *learning* to utilise and transform such technologies *affects*
   and transforms the nervous system as well as the technologies utilised (as do all material learning processes) ('The temporality of the
   human [. . .] presupposes exteriorization and prostheticity' (Stiegler,
   1998: 172)). Such technologies, the differential *access* to these technologies, as well as the related *transmission* of access to these technologies, form crucial components in the *possible field of action* bodies can
   enter into in the milieu in question, and indeed how the milieu *orients the becomings* of those within it ('this transmission [of knowledge]
   is determined by the explicitly technological forms recording forms
   of knowledge, by the conditions of *access* they provide' (ibid.: 210,
   our alteration)). So exteriorisation here functions as a condition for
   expression; learning to utilise such technologies transforms the nervous system (here we are also entering a conversation with the literature on *neuroplasticity*, which we will return to later in this chapter),

and expressive utilisation of such technologies has the potential to *affect* and *transform* such exteriorised technologies themselves.

2. Exteriorisation of memory and the imagination (supra-personal): Exteriorised technologies, further, are *effects* of imagination and themselves are the material traces of expression (i.e., *memory*); by extension, *learning* to utilise and transform such technologies *affects* and transforms (and sometimes *delimits*) imagination and memory. Taking again the example of linguistic-communicative technologies, the early Ludwig Wittgenstein aptly expressed the co-constitution of such technologies with imagination and memory in his famous aphorism: '*The limits of my language* mean the limits of my world' (2001: 68).

In a context of the increased prevalence of digital tertiary retentions, the concern here is how the accelerated temporalities such technologies obey affects nervous systems, the brain, imagination, and memory, tightening the 'control' and 'neutralisation' of existential refrains (Berardi, 2015: 243).[19] On this, Berardi cites *time* as the primary 'battlefield' between the organic time of the human and inorganic – and much faster – 'cybertime', the misalignment between which exacerbates, amongst other effects, 'stress, aggressiveness, anxiety, and fear' (ibid.: 187). Berardi goes as far as to claim that the digital revolution constitutes a *trauma* in the mental environment (ibid.: 238), limiting memory through the decreased time of elaboration (and therefore limiting possibilities of criticism), and by extension, limiting the imaginative possibilities in the mental environment. We will address these points in more detail later in this chapter. For now, let us return more closely to draw some threads together in our development of *rhythmic containment*. Our argument thus far has been the following. We have identified two levels. First, the pre-personal ('below' the subject), as an assemblage of components of subjectification that are crucial in the rhythms of individuation. We have focused on the example of the nervous system (and the possible field of action bodies can enter into in their *milieus*) as a set of such components that are affected and transformed by contemporary technological conditions (such as the explosion of digital tertiary retentions): the imbrication of tertiary retentions with the nervous system and with neurology. Second, the supra-personal ('above' the subject), as an assemblage of components of subjectification that are, too, crucial in the rhythms of individuation. We have focused on the examples of *memory* and *imagination* as pre- and supra-personal components that are, too, conditioned (though we do not say *determined*) by the technological environment of the *milieu*.[20] Indeed, as we will often discuss in Chapters 4, 5, and 6, the construction of new imaginaries is a crucial component in the creation of new rhythms of everyday life. As Massumi notes, 'thought-as-imagination departs from the actual, dips into the fractal abyss, then actualizes something new' (1992: 101). Or, at least, it *can* do so. The accelerated temporalities of digital tertiary retentions not only alter social memory and the imaginative possibilities of the mental environment, but also the social relations and the possibilities for developing and acting on a plan of life as such. In other words, the control and neutralisation of the maximum number of existential refrains.

These have only been introductory gestures as to the processes and functioning of *rhythmic containment*. We will finish this introductory example revisiting the example of *debt*, which we will return to in greater detail in Chapter 6. Debt also functions in relation to rhythmic containment, that is, to the pre- and supra-personal levels of the rhythms of individuation. Recall how we positioned debt as a mechanism of rhythmic subjection, in particular through its triple relationship to the three syntheses of time; debt functions in this way to freeze the past and foreclose (or, more specifically, delimit) the future. When we introduce the notion of *rhythmic containment* we can more specifically focus on how debt socially functions on pre- and supra-personal levels. Before doing this, however, it is important to highlight how debt operates as a (now *digital*) tertiary retention: as informational and digitalised memory of the past which has material effects on the present and future. The very notion of debt is indissociable from memory, and, by extension, possible imagined futures.

On the pre-personal level, for the subject caught within the *rhythms of repayment* (repayment schemes which are pre-decided by impersonal and authoritative financial machines), debt functions as an apparatus of temporal capture that affects what mechanisms of identity filtration become available to her. Such *rhythms of repayment* are that which the indebted subject must constantly answer to and be accountable for function in a manner not unlike the *rhythms of confession* (which are, apparently, pre-decided by impersonal and authoritative theological machines) through which the Christian subject repays his sins against God and becomes a Christian subject (or a subjected Christian). In other words, when the rhythms of debt repayment come to dominate the rhythms of individuation, anxiety, stress, desperation, guilt, fear, and permanent insecurity (in short: psychic and material disempowerment) are the predictable effects which manifest in the mental environment. These effects, however, are themselves *crucial* in the production of responsibilised indebted subjects; governing the pre-personal is in part the governing of 'modalities of perception, ways of feeling, seeing and thinking' (Lazzarato, 2015: 179).

This is the intense intertwinement of rhythmic subjection and rhythmic containment. What is 'governed' – or *rhythmically contained* – in the case of debt is not the 'subject' as such, but rather dividual or modular components of the subject (quantitatively synthesised into datasets detailing credit history and repayment reliability, earning history, projected earning potential, and so on). This is effectuated through the arrangement of the *possible field of action* – a field of action partially constituted by the differential access (along lines of privilege, usually) to technics, and which constitute the everyday rhythms of identity filtration, labour, and leisure – so as to both *induce* or *solicit* our interiorisation of our guilt-for-debt (rhythmic subjection) but also further arrange our field of action for the continuous reinforcement of this interiorisation in the service of capital valorisation:

> On the one hand, we are constructed as 'subjects,' assigned to our 'nature' as responsible and guilty individuals (guilty for indebtedness). We must interiorize this responsibility and guilt and assume the consequences by atoning for our faults, paying and reimbursing our creditors. On the other hand, we are instituted as 'dividuals' into elements, parts, cogs, of the 'debtmachine.' 'Dividuals' do no more than 'respond' to the signals emitted by the spread, adapt in real time to the variations of the new circumstances of austerity and recession. (Ibid.: 209–210)

Moving on: on the supra-personal level we can gesture towards the social memory and social imaginary of debt. Take, for example, the post-2008 European context of sovereign debt crises (Baker and Underhill, 2015; Schmidt, 2014) channelled into rationales of national and continental austerity programmes, as well as technocratic governance, a channelling which functioned as the creation of collective culpability, guilt, and insecurity for crises generated by the systematic and institutional functioning of debt in the financial system as such. In the post-2008 context of financial 'crisis' – i.e., when the rhythms of the financial system were pushed to their region of ontological insecurity – the 'meaning' of that debt was *reterritorialised* onto guilty and culpable citizens who 'acted inappropriately' within the confines of an appropriate financial system. Such an artificial reterritorialisation fails to account for – or rather *covers over* in the social memory and imaginary (the supra-personal) – the manner in which debt is a *central* and *crucial* mechanism of contemporary capital valorisation (and thus the empowerment of some) and continuous deterritorialisation. Through securitisation, trading, and commodification, debt provides temporary liquidity and purchasing power to the *debtor* (at the cost of the foreclosure of the future and psychic disempowerment) and enhances the wealth and privilege of the *creditor* (and thus the opening of the future and psychic empowerment). Debt is what Guattari termed one of the 'non-signifying cogs of the system' (1984: 171): a mobile tertiary retention that functions like oil to financial, consumption, and production machines. This creditor/debtor distinction is not totalising, but the key point to be taken from it is that *creditors are those who have access to and have learned how to utilise and transform financial technologies, and, by extension, transform extant conditions of memory and imagination; creditors have privileged access to the pre- and supra-personal.* Debtors do not have such access. Creditors have privileged technological access to the financial machine, through which they partially arrange the field of action available to debtors *in the service of* rhythmic containment: 'Debt is guilt, and as guilt, it is entering the domain of the unconscious, shaping language according to structures of power and submission' (Berardi, 2015: 165).

e. Conclusion

> no ecology of late capitalism, given the variety of forces to which it is connected by a thousand pulleys, vibrations, impingements, dependencies, shocks, and threads, can specify with supreme confidence the solidity or potential flexibility of the structures it seeks to change. (Connolly, 2013: 36–37)

We concluded Chapter 2 with the immanent demand not to treat everyday life as *given*, to explicate and problematise it with our rhythmanalytical assemblage of enunciation. The task of this chapter, therefore, was to bring us closer to a position where we could begin to *scape* various ecologies of the mental environment today with conceptual instruments befitting a revolutionary rhythmanalytical critique of everyday life. With these conceptual instruments developed, and our task defined, we will now move on to Part II.

f. Chapter 3 reprise

[52] Our critique of the rhythms of everyday life is concerned with the everyday insofar as it constitutes, produces, and reproduces contemporary capitalist milieus through the relations between rhythm and desire; *the everyday as that which produces both capitalistic subjects and milieus.*
[53] As *residue* and *product* of various interlocking and at times conflicting processes – its practices, relations, habits, repetitions, exchanges,

creations, and so on – *everyday life* is indissociable from its rhythmic power. To transform the rhythms of everyday life is to transform the milieu.

[54] Desire is *active* and *productive*; productive in the sense of *producing* the consumer-as-consumer in the process of rhythmic subjection, but also *reproductive* in the sense of *reproducing* tendencies of orientation within capitalistic milieus, thereby reproducing and securing the capitalistic milieus themselves.

[55] Consumption is an active practice of desire and securitisation, actively productive of capitalistic milieus, desire's pulsive flows having become captured within particular rhythmic parameters of ontological security within the capitalistic milieu.

[56] The relationship between distinct rhythmicities (organic rhythms, technical rhythms, rhythms of shock, adoption, and/or adaptation, and so forth) is not a problem distinct to our contemporary context. It constitutes a central problematic of *any* approach to everyday life, and to any critique of the rhythms of everyday life: everyday life constituted always by a vast polyrhythmia.

[57] '*Capitalistic subjectivity seeks to gain power by controlling and neutralizing the maximum number of existential refrains.*'

[58] Existential refrains constitute the stylistics through which the rhythms of everyday day are lived, the modes of existence through which subjectivity comes to be produced. The existential refrain, then, is about the *concretisation* and consolidation of a singularity, of a singular polyrhythmic nexus comprising the rhythms of everyday life *extracted* from the possibilities proffered by the milieu.

[59] Capitalistic milieus, themselves arrhythmic, *orient the becomings of subjects' rhythmic processes of individuation to themselves become arrhythmic.*

[60] This *relatively standardised* process of subjectivity production process is one through which the maximum number of existential refrains in capitalistic milieus are subordinated to a logic through which these existential refrains themselves *securitise* the capitalist milieu. Simultaneously, the subject's actualisation of singular rhythms of everyday life in her existential refrain is a process of differential actualisation. As active, productive, and creative activity, experimental existential refrains are a permanent threat to the capitalist milieu.

[61] Capitalistic milieus do not simply delimit ways of life, in other words, but rather they capture their heterogenisation *into* a logic of securitisation: *capitalist homogenesis.*

[62] Like Lefebvre's definition of the everyday as 'residue' and 'product' of its distinct activities, the subject (or more precisely the account of the process through which subjectivity is continually produced, reproduced,

and transformed) is developed here as *residue and product of the rhythms of everyday life*.

[63] Subjection is about the establishment and rigidification of molar hierarchies. These hierarchies are generated, reproduced, and transformed at the intersection and nexus between *identity filtration, labour, and leisure*, which is also to say *through the rhythms of everyday life*.

[64] The affective components constitutive of identity filtration are inseparable from particular modalities and territorialisations of the pulsive flows of desire.

[65] Rhythmic containment is concerned with those pre- and suprapersonal components surrounding this identity filtration-labour-leisure nexus; this works on the *deterritorialised* components of subjectivity; containment works towards *the automatisation of practices which tend to securitise capitalistic milieus*.

Notes

1. More specifically, the image is from Issue #112 (vol. 22, no. 2), March/April 2014.
2. This line of thought is reflected, too, in Raoul Vaneigem's *The Revolution of Everyday Life:* 'The life we have now is broken up – a broken line [. . .] No moment radiates now as moments did in the cyclical time of earlier societies. Time for us is a thread: from cradle to grave, from memories of the past to anticipations of the future, an endless survival strings out its succession of instants and hybrid presents, all gnawed at by the time that slips away and the time yet to come. The feeling of living in symbiosis with cosmic forces – a sense of simultaneity – vouchsafed joys to our forebears that our way of passing through the world can scarcely provide. What remains of such a joy? All we have is the headiness of our transit, of our efforts to keep in step with the times. You must move with the times – or so we are told by those who profit if we do' (Vaneigem, 2012: 75). It is important to note that Vaneigem quickly follows this claim with 'Not that we should lament the cyclical time of old' (ibid.). Published in 1967 while a member of the Situationist International, Vaneigem's *Revolution of Everyday Life*, a key text of May 1968 alongside Debord's *Society of the Spectacle*, does not contain this notion of the *everyday*, or *la quotidienne*, in its title, although the notion is important in the text. Its original title is *Traité de savoir-vivre à l'usage des jeunes générations*, or *Treatise on Knowing How to Live for the Younger Generations*. Indeed, the relationship between the Situationists and Lefebvre is complex (Lefebvre's theory of 'moments' formed a critical impetus for the Situationist method of 'constructing situations') and is not one we will be discussing. For more on this, see Trebitsch (2014: 287–298).
3. A further distinction Lefebvre makes pertinent to this issue, but which we will not discuss in detail, is that between what he calls the *controlled* and

uncontrolled sectors. These are vast terms. The latter pertains to 'everything which human activity has so far been unable to orientate and consolidate, everything not yet "produced" through man and for man' (Lefebvre, 2009: 125), and which he explains in relation to facets of nature, spontaneity, and the unconscious, for example. The former is that which humans *do* control, and which Lefebvre describes in relation to the activity of production and to mechanistic approaches (such as, and this is our example, linear time) which seek to 'establish relations subject to human control' aimed at 'establishing a determinism' (ibid.: 123).

4. Artificial lighting is (and continues to be) a technical shock which confronts human-organic diurnality and challenges the Sun as a circadian zeitgeber (Heaney, 2023: 14–17; also see Otter, 2008).

5. It is of note, here, that Lefebvre defines his *theory of moments* as 'the product of a violent protest against Bergsonism and the formless psychological continuum advocated by Bergsonian philosophy' (Lefebvre, 2014b: 636).

6. Lefebvre calls this spectrum of available existential refrains 'diverse' yet 'identical'. We will instead, in the following section, emphasise a large *quantitative range* (which does not reduce to 'identity') but narrow *qualitative scope* of existential refrains. We would dispute that any large quantitative range could be reduced to identity, especially, as we will highlight in Chapter 4, insofar as solicited ontological heterogenisation functions within contemporary capitalistic milieus.

7. It is of note, here, that for Lefebvre the alienation connected to technology is of a *new* form; he describes *technological alienation* as both new and unforeseeable (Lefebvre, 2014b: 508). This, therefore, sharply distinguishes his approaches from Stiegler's, for whom alienation – his preferred term being proletarianisation – is constitutive of the human relation with the technical object as such; a position, of course, hugely indebted to Simondon (Stiegler, 2017: 129–135; also see Turner, 2023: 116–123).

8. The original French retains this sense: 'La polyphonie des modes de subjectivation correspond, en effet, à une multiplicité de façons de "battre le temps". D'autres rythmiques sont ainsi amenées à faire cristalliser des agencements existentiels, qu'elles incarnent et singularisent' (Guattari, 1992: 30).

9. Guattari's usage of the term 'relative autonomy' has hints of both Karl Marx and Louis Althusser, although this will not be explored this here. See Althusser (1976: 138, 169, 170, 177).

10. Here, Stiegler underlines the following: 'Just as the living being has a collective history in the sense of a genetic history informed and inscribed in a *phylum* – a phylogenesis – and an individual history – an epigenesis – regulated by its indetermination in confrontation with a singular milieu and regulating in turn its morphogenesis, the technical object calls into play laws of evolution that are immanent to it, even if, as in the case of the living being, they are effected only under the conditions of an environment, to wit, here, that of the human and the other technical objects' (1998: 71).

11. Although we will not discuss it here, Massumi develops both transduction and induction (in a rereading of Simondon) together with a notion of *cataly-sis.* Catalysis pertains to the modes through which these processes of induction/transduction are actualised or triggered in processes that have passed certain threshold points. Speaking of systems where chemical reactions are occurring, Prigogine and Stengers explain that catalysts function to 'modify the reaction rate' (1984: 133) in a given system, enabling new paths of development and new speeds of reaction to emerge. Often with a small dose of a particular catalyst, reactions can grow into a loop in a non-linear fashion. The catalyst functions to destabilise a given equilibrium state and the catalytic loops which emerge (in which 'the product of a chemical reaction is involved in its own synthesis' (ibid.: 145)) are reactions indicative of process of self-organisation, and which are crucial in, for example, metabolic processes and in molecular biology generally. In Massumi's more expanded schema, catalysis is the event of synthesis, or relation, of disparate elements, a 'fusional production of a primacy of relation' (Massumi, 2002: 165), without general model: 'There is no general model for the catalysis of an event. Every time an event migrates, it is re-conditioned. In the home space, the television and the images it transmits are inductive signs. The images are also transducers. And they contribute to the catalysis of the domestic event' (ibid.: 81).

12. The distinction between the *molecular* and the *molar* is not at all, or is not simply, a question of *scale.* Rather it pertains to organisation, perceptibility, and boundedness. *Molarity,* as such, relates modes of organisation which are the *effect* of molecularity. One example here would be that of the *subject,* whose (quasi-)molarity is produced as an effect of those syntheses of desire and time we discussed in Chapter 1; the pre-constituted subject endowed with certain properties (sex, race, gender, class) is the molar quasi-subject. For more on this, see Merriman (2018).

13. For a discussion of how such abstract grids feed not just into policy documents and decision-making, but into the processes of everyday life in the specific example of contemporary neoliberal university in the UK, see Heaney (2015, 2016).

14. Professions, as Guattari notes, are 'totally gridded and modelized into hierarchies of systems of exams, CVs, and so on' (Guattari and Rolnik, 2007: 215).

15. This is not to situate the 2008 financial crisis as a hugely pivotal transformation, but rather to situate it as an important part of a tendential trend away from Keynesian welfare capitalism. This tendential trend is evidenced through sequential historical events: Richard Nixon's removal of the gold standard (and subsequent liquidification of debt), the elections and reigns of Margaret Thatcher and Ronald Reagan respectively, General Pinochet's neoliberal regime, the popularity of Ayn Rand's *Atlas Shrugged* (especially in Silicon Valley), Tony Blair's neoliberalisation of the Labour Party in the United Kingdom (particularly through the removal of 'Clause 4' from the Labour Party's constitution), to name only a few examples. Indeed, as

Thomas Piketty notes, the redistributive tendencies of many states in the twentieth century was, historically, a blip which made little difference in the distribution of wealth and power (2014: 21–22).

16. A related term in the literature here worth exploring further, but which we do not devote any space to here, is *interobjectivity*. See Latour (1996) and Hui (2016a: 160–167).

17. This is also to gesture in agreement with Guattari's argument (1984: 111–119), *pace* Jacques Lacan, against the structuralisation and ridigification of the unconscious; rather, the unconscious is positioned here as part of historical, political, economic, social (and so on) processes; pre- and supra-personal elements through which the 'subject' historically emerges (or does not, as the case may be).

18. Interestingly, in *Chaosmosis*, Guattari draws affirmatively on Leroi-Gourhan, who we met earlier (Chapter 2, section b), and who is (perhaps alongside Derrida and Simondon) one of Stiegler's key reference points, emphasising the importance of the technical ensemble (involving the human-technical object relation) to the activation and rhythmic evolution of technical objects (Guattari, 2006: 36). The human interaction with the technical object in the technical ensemble, importantly for Guattari, occurs through a-signifying semiotics, through 'equations and plans which enunciate the machine and make it act in a diagrammatic capacity on technical and experimental apparatus' (ibid.); the conjunctive operation through which the technical ensemble is activated constituting, then, a new machine comprised of human and non-human components.

19. For more on this, see Kalle Lasn's *Meme Wars* (2012), a book published by *Adbusters*, which focuses on this precise question of how contemporary mechanisms of 'control' of the nervous system, memory, and imagination interact in a manner that 'neutralises' existential refrains (to use our language).

20. Indeed, in the quote at the opening of this section, Lazzarato's claim that machinic enslavement 'formats' behaviour is, we think, overly deterministic. We resisted this already through our deployment, with Massumi, of the terms *transduction* and *induction*, as well as our developing of his ideas on this through our notion of rhythmic containment. It is also through Bergson, the question of neuroplasticity, and the notion of *aesthetic interventionism* that we will resist such determinations.

Part II

Mindscaping the Rhythms of Everyday Life

4

Distraction-Attention Ecology

So an ATTENTION ARMS RACE is set up: the more a market society becomes mediatized, the more it must dedicate a significant proportion of its activity to the production of demand, investing ever greater resources into the machinery of attention attraction. (Citton, 2017: 55)

Recall that we conceptualised *rhythmic subjection* through the interlocking of identity filtration, labour, and leisure, an interlocking of temporal and libidinal investment: the subject produced as a residue and product of her rhythms of everyday life. As we have already mentioned, the explosion (in scale, scope, and speed) of digital tertiary retentions has altered, and continues to alter exponentially, the mental environment that we co-occupy in everyday life. Digital tertiary retentions are becoming the increasingly hegemonic focal point through which *labour* (the sites of supply or production) and *leisure* (the sites of demand or consumption) are funnelled; that is, digital tertiary retentions are increasingly surrounding everyday life, the mechanisms of identity filtration, and, so, rhythmic processes of individuation as such. Broadly speaking, for initial purposes, this indicates an interlocking of the tendencies of contemporary capitalist homogenesis (the delimitation of existential refrains and securitisation of the capitalistic milieu) and what we called in Chapter 2 (with Hörl) the digital cyberneticisation of everyday life. This interlocking is what Hörl gestures towards when he notes that 'the all-encompassing cyberneticization and computerization of our form of life has brought with it a new form of closure, a new dogmatism, and a new form of bondage through mediation and processuality' (Hörl, 2013: 123).

The tautological term 'social media' (as if any media, that is, any mode of communication, could be *a*social), is helpfully defined by Dominic Pettman as the 'simultaneously limitless and circumscribed ways we interact via newly enmeshed communications and entertainment technologies' (2016: xi). What does he mean by this? For Pettman, social media is *limitless* insofar as social media is differentially navigated by every individual, and insofar as it *tends* towards the limitless temporal colonisation of everyday life (where both labour and leisure increasingly *necessitate* the interaction with digital tertiary retentions). It is *circumscribed* insofar as this differential navigation is narrowed both (1) in terms of who has access to the control of these technics (only a material digital elite has access to the means and capabilities to *transform* such technologies) and (2) phenomenologically (the 'digital divide' evidences the relative circumscription of who can even *access* and *experience* (let alone transform) such technologies (Norris, 2001)).[1] This circumscription is gestured towards by Sanín-Restrepo as an encryptive process that blocks access to the sort of communicative organological conditions and processes that are crucial for his decolonising radical democracy:

> Even though we are connected irremediably in a network of ever-extending information, as a *General Intellect*, the cultural language of the machine remains encrypted: its flows and commands are still dependent on the hunger of the market, and its core intellect remains a highly scarce material. Hence, information can only become democratic when the machine – as a point of absorption of power-knowledge – is itself decrypted and politically liberated. (Sanín-Restrepo, 2016: 116–117)

What is the spectrum of available existential refrains, or rhythms of individuation, available to those who find themselves in a milieu increasingly dominated by digital tertiary retentions? Before developing on this, let us first delineate how we will be approaching the notions of attention and distraction. We are here treating distraction not in opposition to attention, but rather treating distraction-attention as entangled. That is, as ecologically enmeshed. *Attention*, derived from the Latin *attend-ere*, pertains to a sustained temporality, or *duration*, of care (Stiegler, 2012: 1): attending to something is a modality of caring for something with its own temporality and its own stylistics and rhythm. As a caring for *something* (one cares for others, one cares for oneself, one cares for the milieu), attention is an exercise of force and desire – Yves Citton, with Paul Valéry, insists that attention is 'by nature pressure, prolongation, effort, *conatus*' (Citton, 2017: 77, our emphasis; Valéry, 1974) – that is, it (at)*tends* in particular directions, and 'calls for an exit from oneself' (Citton, 2017: 78). This is the case even when one attends to oneself, insofar as paying attention to oneself involves a split in the attentive subject. For example, when one pays attention to one's habits, potentially with a view to altering them, this necessitates an 'exit' from oneself in the sense that it involves thematising one's habits and making a distinction

between these habits (what one habitually does) and one's future, transformed habits (what one aims to habitually do). Attention can sometimes be demanded *of* us, whether through the interruptive shock of a
sudden noise, a personal health scare that demands that we *pay attention*
to what we ingest and how often (and how) we move our bodies, an
upcoming and potentially important election cycle, the notification of
a new email from our phone vibrating in our pocket, the red icon containing a number in the top right-hand corner of your social media
feed, and so forth. We also know that attention is paid *to* us: CCTV
cameras (whose feeds may then be processed by increasing experiments
with facial recognition technology); public and private monitoring and
surveillance; YouTube, Netflix, Amazon et al.'s continuous algorithmic
machines of observation and recommendation, and so on. One is always
already the subject *and* object of attention. Attention, and here we agree
with Citton, 'can only be understood and explained within a certain
field of forces in which it reacts to exterior constraints' (ibid.: 78).

Attention pertains to a duration of care with its own particular rhythmics, to the exercise of force and desire which *tends* in particular directions (attention always implicating *duration* and *direction*, that is, force,
time, and desire), and such an exercise is indissociable from the milieu,
insofar as *the milieu orients becomings in part through the orientation of attentional energy.* Attention participates in its felt environment, indissociable from its affectivity, and embodied through muscularity, tactility, and
viscerality: 'In the experience of reading, conscious thought, sensation,
and all the modalities of perception fold into and out of each other.
Attention most twisted' (Massumi, 2002: 139).

As attention implicates specific durations and directions (attention is
finite), it is disrupted or threatened whenever, for example, attention is
demanded at all times and from all directions. This brings us to *distraction*.
Derived from the Latin *distractionem*, distraction pertains to being pulled
in distinct directions, of indecision, or being 'dragged apart', or 'separated'. Distraction has its own affective modalities through which the
body engages with itself: 'scratching, fidgeting, eyes rolling up or around
in their sockets as if they were endeavoring to look back in at the brain'
(ibid.). If attention is demanded at all times from all directions, the potential for attentional durations of care is threatened. Distraction is *in no sense*
in opposition to attention, entangled as they are in an attention–distraction
ecology. Being attentive to an object of concern or a demand necessitates a level of distraction from *other* objects or demands; and, conversely,
'being distracted *by an object*' pertains to that object *receiving a temporal level
and certain intensity of attention. Being attentive to x necessitates that one is being
distracted by x.* We *pay attention* to the oncoming ambulance by being (at

least initially) *distracted* by its sirens. Likewise, we may *not* be distracted by the oncoming ambulance if we are *too attentive* to (or too distracted by), for example, the smartphone in our hands. There is only ever a continuous alteration between attention and distraction in variable tendencies and towards differential results, not least through our digital environment ('Surfing sets up a rhythm of attention and distraction' (ibid.)). The milieu proffers a multiplicity of signals which seek to *distract* and *demand attention*, and our orientation in these milieus relates to our *filtration* of which signals are worthy of such attention.

The question of filtration pertains to what we already discussed in Chapter 1, namely, the mobilisation of libidinal energies, and how desiring-machines connect and combine its flows with other desiring-machines, contracting and sedimenting certain *pulsive patterns* (induction and transduction). Furthermore, the governance of *repetition* in the milieu, exhibiting such pulsive patterns, is the process through which the milieu becomes securitised, inscribed in memory, and directed towards futural reproduction. In terms of our rhythmic ecology, attention emerges as a vital libidinal force through which attentional patterns are governed within the milieu. *How* attention is paid and *what* it is paid to are therefore ecological concerns, arising in milieus orienting becomings and attentional energy. What we pay attention to, or do not pay attention to – our 'attentional habits' (Citton, 2017: 174) – forms a key component in our rhythmic processes of individuation.

We will conceptualise the attention-distraction ecology through their tendencies and how these tendencies are manifested in contemporary capitalistic milieus. The extreme tendency of distraction is a case of being distracted by a multiplicity of objects and demands to the extent that the subject's attention becomes distributed and temporally minute in relation to each object: indecision and anxiety. The extreme tendency of attention is a case of taking so much care of particular objects of concern or demands to the extent that the subject's attention becomes extensive and fixated in relation to particular objects or demands: obsession, addiction, paranoia, and neurosis. These different tendencies relate to different mechanisms of attentional filtration. When developing this account of our contemporary *distraction-attention ecology* we are already in the realm of *affect* (of anxiety, care, obsession, and so on). Developing these initial comments on the attention-distraction ecology, in our first co-ordinate, distraction-subjection-containment, we will explore what effects this contemporary distraction-attention ecology has in the mental environment. Or more precisely: how do rhythmic subjection and containment function in relation to this attention-distraction ecology? What roles do our attentional energies have in contemporary capitalism?

a. [CC1]: distraction-subjection-containment

> The entire West has lost those instincts out of which institutions grow, out of which the future grows; perhaps nothing goes so much against the grains of its 'modern spirit.' One lives for today, one lives very fast – one lives irresponsibly: it is precisely this which one calls 'freedom.' (Nietzsche, 1968: 94)

Friedrich Nietzsche's *The Twilight of the Idols*, from which the above quote was taken, was first published in 1889. This prophetic statement speaks to the entanglement between the *accelerated experience of the present* ('one lives very fast'), the erasure of *memory* ('The entire West has lost those instincts out of which institutions grow . . .'), and the connected *closure* of the future ('. . . out of which the future grows'). Nietzsche's claim here feeds directly to the composition of our first co-ordinate, which will be effectuated through a rhythmanalysis of the intersection or crossroads between *distraction*, *rhythmic subjection*, and *rhythmic containment*, a crossroads we term the attention-distraction ecology: distraction-subjection-containment.

We will make three claims here. Each of these claims bears a direct relation to Nietzsche's. First, that the contemporary distraction-attention ecology tends towards a continuous *capitalist-technological interruption of the first passive synthesis*, an interruption which captures time and desire (in this context: our libidinal energies and attentional habits) in the service of capitalist homogenesis, insofar as distraction and attention are *continuously technologically insinuated* and insinuated at an accelerated rate for the purposes of capital accumulation. Second, that this distraction–attention ecology bears an important relationship to the constitution of *memory* insofar as memory is becoming increasingly *exteriorised in digital tertiary retentions* (wherein digital technological apparatuses are only within the capabilities of an elite to transform and control). Third, that this distraction-attention ecology is placing increasing demands on the embrained bodies of contemporary subjects to an extent which it runs the risk of *erasing the future*; that is, the *rhythmic contraction of our contemporary distraction-attention ecology has the potential to erase collective possibilities for the collective imagination and sculpting of alternative futures*. This neutralisation of attentional, affective, subjective, and social possibilities highlights the *arrhythmic* tendencies of contemporary capitalistic milieus. Each of these points will be elaborated in conversation with our notions of rhythmic subjection and rhythmic containment.

Claim One: the contemporary distraction-attention ecology tends towards a continuous capitalist-technological interruption of the first passive synthesis of the present, capturing time and desire.

The first passive synthesis of the living present, which we met in Chapter 1, constitutes the set of rhythmic periodicities, negotiations, and transformations, achieving 'connections between successive moments [and producing] a centre around which chaotic elements may become stabilised, the beginnings of order may crystallise, and from which the growing assemblage may be given a direction' (Turetsky, 2004: 144, our alteration). The first passive synthesis of time, as well as the operations of particularly the first (connective) and second (disjunctive) syntheses of desire, produce a level of *rhythmic contraction*, or stability, in which the capture and delimitation of pulsive flows serve to code rhythmic parameters of ontological security. The coding of desire's pulsive moments is also to code what patterns of practice are launched into, repeated, or avoided. The habits of everyday life which we negotiate serve such a purpose: mechanisms of identity filtration spread between patterns of labour and leisure can generate stability, closure, and predictability, helping to enable the pursuance of a *singular existential refrain* or self-styled aesthetics of existence. The habits of everyday life, for many increasingly, do not allow for such closure and stability. Further, in the advent of the explosion of digital tertiary retentions and devices, such closure and stability are being consistently and permanently interrupted, disrupting the secure consolidation of rhythmic parameters of ontological security, insofar as our libidinal energies and attentional habits are increasingly at the service of capitalist homogenesis and capital accumulation. This, on our reading and which we argue, is due to the *temporal colonisation* of mechanisms of identity filtration and through its contribution to an arrhythmic erosion of the labour/leisure distinction.[2] This mutation in the distraction-attention ecology renders closure and stability increasingly difficult to attain.

There are plentiful examples that we could point to on this. We noted how *rhythmic subjection* functions through providing grids of self-intelligibility ('frames of reference') for subjects to negotiate in relation to in everyday life. Entrepreneurial self-production is, today, and increasingly, not possible without the simultaneous production of a 'virtual' or 'online' self. Social media platforms – such as TikTok, Facebook, YouTube, Twitter/X, Instagram, LinkedIn, Snapchat, Tinder, various blogging platforms, and so on – comprise a sprawling digital semiotic environment for the constitution of one's individuality (that is, a sprawling digital semiotic environment of rhythmic subjection). These platforms provide the 'frames of reference' through which one's subjection is continuously solicited, whether through online avenues of self-entrepreneurialism (where one can 'sell oneself' as a worthy labourer) and/or through self-objectification (where one can 'sell oneself' as an informed and engaged citizen, a desirable sexual partner, or whatever the platform in question demands). Insofar as contemporary rhythmic subjection is not possible without the continuous negotiation and involvement with digital tertiary retentions and digital devices, we can say that the phenomenological experience of digitised social relations tends towards the *erosion* of the online/offline distinction.[3] Citton terms this attentional capitalism's 'ontology of visibility', which '*measures a being's level of existence by the quantity and quality of its perception by others*' (Citton, 2017: 45–46). As such, one can *always* be producing goods and services (consider the literature on the *cognitariat* (Berardi, 2005) or *immaterial labour* (Lazzarato, 1996), for example), one can *always* be selling oneself as a worthy labourer, one can *always* be 'catching up' with social commitments, one can *always* be selling oneself as a desirable sexual partner, one can *always* be consuming. Indeed, in contemporary capitalistic milieus, one *ought* to be doing precisely all these things at all times, insofar as one's digital visibility and prominence is a measure of one's worth (Citton, 2017: 46). All of these activities constitute continuous investments in one's 'human capital', that is, they constitute one's investment in future monetary, social, sexual (etc.) returns. In short: one can *always* be engaged in both 'labour' and 'leisure' through digital mechanisms of identity filtration and the frames of reference they provide. This is also to claim that the erosion of the online/offline distinction tends towards the erosion of the labour/leisure distinction (though we by no means reduce the erosion of the former to the erosion of the latter).

We noted above that the extreme tendency of distraction is a case of being distracted by a multiplicity of objects and demands to the extent that the subject's attention becomes distributed and temporally minute in relation to each object: indecision and anxiety. We also noted that the extreme tendency of attention is a case of taking so much care of particular objects of concern or demands to the extent that the subject's attention becomes extensive and fixated in relation to particular objects or demands: obsession, addiction, paranoia, and neurosis. Both of these extreme tendencies are manifest in the contemporary mental environment and can be read as *effects* of the capitalist-technological interruption of the first passive synthesis rendered possible through the proliferation of digital tertiary retentions and digital devices.[4]

On the extreme tendency of distraction. Through digital tertiary retentions and digital devices, and their insisting permanence, the *felt* interaction with these devices and retentions is, for many, that of a hyper-urgency of 'the now', or, in other words, a permanent struggle in 'the now' to be 'up to date'. This accelerated hyper-urgency of the now – and the attached phenomenological injunction to 'keep up' – onto-temporally functions so as to *resist* or *interrupt* the passive and contractive synthesis of the present, and, by extension, to disturb the mechanisms of expectation and securitisation as such. Libidinal-attentional energy, thus, has become increasingly caught within a perpetual feedback loop of *excitation*. Mark Fisher refers to this hyper-urgency of the now as one of 'digital micro-slices' (2009: 25) which Pettman echoes through terming it a phenomenology of 'staggered or delayed micro-experiences' (2016: 19).[5] Hui, in this vein, describes it as a 'hyper-ecstasy that celebrates speed while simultaneously being haunted by the anxiety of not being there' (2016a: 47). We term it the *capitalist-technological interruption of the first passive synthesis*. Without contraction and expectation – that is, without the first passive synthesis of the living present – rhythmic parameters of ontological security are not reproduced with stability or predictability, or are squeezed into smaller and smaller microtemporalities, and can thus be pushed to their deterritorial border. Whether doomscrolling or navigating a more 'curated' feed of content for positive affect, the experience of scrolling down or consistently refreshing the 'newsfeed' (of Facebook, Twitter, Instagram, etc.) is indicative of such a permanent libidinal-attentional thrust of excitation. As Marcus Gilroy-Ware (2017: 35) notes: 'You don't know exactly what your scrolling or clicking will reveal, but you know there will always be *something else*, and this provides you with an incentive not only to keep scrolling, but to keep coming back.' Through such generalised permanent excitation, *insecurity* becomes the norm, producing *indecision* and *anxiety*. Consider the anxiety coupled with the horror of being 'offline' for any prolonged period for many, or the extreme anxiety and panic that would ensue were the internet to be taken permanently offline. Connolly notes that attention to the presence of the *rift* or *gap* between the experienced present and the (lack of) secure future expectations, "*does sow anxiety in those who seek closure* [. . .] Anxiety, indeed, can be read as a sign or symptom of the rift, during a time when many are not prepared to come to terms affirmatively with it" (Connolly, 2002: 146, our emphasis). Alvin Toffler, too, highlights how accelerated experiences of change disrupt expectations, and therefore the available patterns of life as such. While identifying the human's bio-physical 'internal rhythms' (1970: 47) as being crucial, he additionally isolates rates of cultural change, and the mechanisms of expectation generation made possible by the rhythms of everyday life. These build within us a 'series of expectations about the duration of events, processes of relationships' (ibid.). Confronted with and contributing to acceleration, the embrained body confronts this deterritorial border in undetermined and differential ways, although certain trends are apparent. We will come back to this later in this section, but, in short: the insisting permanence of digitised social relations and their colonisation of everyday rhythms of identity filtration, labour, and leisure tends towards the extreme case of distraction: the conjunction of permanent distraction and permanent subjection. This conjunction constitutes a *capitalist-techno-logical interruption of the first passive synthesis*, disrupting secure passive con-tractions and expectations, producing permanent excitation, indecision, and anxiety in the mental environment.

On the extreme tendency of attention. We can read this in relation to the indecision and anxiety produced in the mental environment through the extreme tendency of distraction. The 'horror' which we noted would follow were a condition of compulsory 'offlineness' to emerge is a strong sign of a collective *addiction*, *obsession*, or *neurotic attachment* to the internet, despite the effects of anxiety, insecurity, and indecision that 'permanent onlineness' produces through the interruption of the first passive synthe-sis. The addictions, obsessions, or neurotic attachments that emerge are patterns of practice regarding attempts to 'keep up' with the accelerated pace of digital tertiary retentions and their continuous innovative turn-over and transformation. Toffler highlights this type of response as one whereby a subject has 'internalized the principle of acceleration', who thereby anticipates that 'situations will endure less long', and as such, 'is less frequently caught off guard and jolted than the person whose dura-tional expectancies are frozen, the person who does not routinely antic-ipate a frequent shortening in the duration of situations' (ibid.: 48–49). However, such *increased shortening* of the duration of situations, we argue, tends to disrupt the contraction of expectations as such.

In other words, the processes tracked here indicate that the 'hyper-urgency of the now' disrupts the mechanism of expectation as such (producing indecision and anxiety in many), but in the attempt to *recon-stitute* expectation, addiction, obsession, and neurotic attachment to the 'hyper-urgency of the now' emerge as simultaneous effects. Just as passive contractions and expectations are continuously disrupted, so attempts to 'chase' secure expectations are continuously disrupted (as soon as one closes one's laptop after having 'caught up', one is already behind). A vicious feedback loop of libidinal excitation, as we already mentioned, of anxiety, indecision, addiction, obsession, and neurotic attachment, produced by mechanisms of permanent distraction, subjection, and attention, are continuous effects of a mental environment increasingly dominated by digital tertiary retentions, their continuous innovative turnover, and deployment in a milieu that extracts surplus value from attentional energies.

These trends manifest differentially, and we do not submit this to any sort of determinism, nor to any necessary logical order. For example, for generations who experienced the explosion in digital tertiary retentions after having already constituted certain rhythmic parameters of ontological security, the effort to 'keep up' may take much more *conscious* 'work on the self' (an *attentive* process requiring a further split in the attentive subject, which we mentioned above) and a felt lag between the pace of change and the ability to internalise such change. For generations whose initial processes of acculturation as such took place in this environment of the explosion of digital tertiary retentions, their rhythmic parameters of ontological security might already be attuned to a different rhythmics, i.e., a different combination of time and desire, and, so, the pace of change is experienced differently. In addition: addictive, obsessive, or neurotic attachment to digital tertiary retentions and their speed become more difficult to identify when these symptoms become *normalised* in the mental environment (an important point to which we will return). In short, the insisting permanence of digital tertiary retentions and their colonisation of everyday rhythms of identity filtration, labour, and leisure also tends towards the extreme case of attention: the connection of permanent attention and permanent subjection. This conjunction also constitutes another element of the *capitalist-technological interruption of the first passive synthesis*, disrupting secure passive contractions and expectations insofar as the continuous turnover of digital tertiary retentions themselves resists the secure constitution of rhythmic parameters of ontological security, producing addiction, obsession, and neurotic attachment in the mental environment.

In other words, we occupy a mental environment that displays symptoms of extreme distraction (anxiety, insecurity, indecision) and extreme attention (obsession, addiction, neurosis). The content of reactions to such extreme addiction and/or distraction is differential: from addictive work patterns (and drugs to enhance such work patterns, such as cocaine and 'study drugs'), obsessive and potentially neurotic Tweeting, Facebooking, or Tindering (to name three prominent examples), all of which display an attempt to 'keep up' with the accelerated temporalities of the digital and 'chase' the digital interruption of the first passive synthesis; to reactive *flights* from these temporalities displayed in those who practise social media abstinence or 'dopamine fasts', who go 'off the grid' or champion 'slowness', 'tradition', or 'stability' (including drugs which can 'slow' the experience of time) in the face of the uncertainty the digital interruption of the first passive synthesis generates.[6] Given this, it is no wonder Lazzarato argues that 'drugs and addiction count among the ontological conditions of capitalism' (2015: 144). Furthermore, Laurent de Sutter situates these toxic feedback loops of addiction as emerging from a capitalism devoted to the permanent stimulation of subjects, which the internet constitutes our key contemporary example of:

> Every capitalism is, necessarily, a narcocapitalism – a capitalism that is narcotic through and through, whose excitability is only the manic reverse of the depression it never stops producing, even as it presents itself as remedy. (Sutter, 2018: 43)

Claim Two: the capitalist-technological interruption of the first synthesis further constitutes the rhythmic containment of memory.
The second passive synthesis of memory, which we met in Chapter 1, enables the present to 'pass'. Memory occurs in the present, and differentially actualises the past in the present, altering the virtual structure of the past as such. The past becomes an active element in the present ('continuously becoming') under the second passive synthesis, not a static or fixed past which 'is'. When explicating this, we did so alongside the *disjunctive synthesis of recording*, Deleuze and Guattari's second synthesis of desire, and buttressed this with a discussion of *technics*, broadening our discussion of memory beyond the human's organic and retentional finitude. Recording constitutes the inscription, or production, of memory. In what Holland describes as the 'alternating rhythms of attraction and repulsion between the organ–machines and the body-without-organs' (1999: 31), recording functions as an arrest and release of the libidinal energies of the connective synthesis. Recall, further, that a milieu of ontological security is one which attempts to *freeze* or *control* memory, delimiting patterns of practice in the present so as to ensure ontological security as the milieu moves through spacetime. Such a freezing, in other words, is a process through which a double effect is generated: (a) establishing ontological security in the present; and (b) attempting to control practices so as to continuously generate such security in the future; that is, a *control and neutralisation* of the future. We intersected this conceptual development in Chapter 1 with the examples of gender performativity, ethno-national practices of community and memorialisation, and biological-organic rhythms. Our second claim in this section, on the accelerating alteration of the function of the second synthesis of memory and the libidinal mechanisms of this process, pertains to (a). Our next (third) claim in this section will pertain to (b). Let us focus on (a) for now.

The exteriorisation of memory into tertiary retentions is not a novel development. Indeed, Stiegler's organological methodology seeks to examine the interactions and transformations between humans and tertiary retentions as another vector in the process of (non-individualist) evolution as such, or more specifically between psychic individuation, collective individuation, and technical individuation. The advent of *digital* tertiary retentions is but a recent part of this process, but it is an advent through which the speed of innovation and turnover of tertiary retentions is accelerating, producing an alteration in the function of memory. How so, and in what sense? Stiegler's answer to this is a complex one, but it will be useful to enter this question through his approach. The process of *exteriorisation* is the process through which ideas, imaginations, dreams, etc., can become discretised and concretised into the rhythms of the everyday (such concretisations are, in our terms, *aesthetic interventions*). The most oft-repeated example of this is *writing*. The *library* functions as a store of memory in exteriorised tertiary retentions (books, journals, etc.), but also the exteriorisation of the nervous system (the pre-personal), and by extension, the imagination (the supra-personal) (Stiegler, 2014b: 70–71). The imagination, here, is exteriorised (and, by extension, partially neutralised and controlled) by filing processes, indexes, the linguistic-communicative technologies available to the library, and so on. The disjunctive synthesis of recording, on our reading, in part functions through the production of technics. We met this already above, with our development of exteriorisation as a *condition* and *effect* of imagination which takes place in a context of surrounding tertiary retentions.

Today, imagination is increasingly exteriorised through digital tertiary retentions. Insofar as digital tertiary retentions are retentions that only an elite can control and transform, we argue that digital exteriorisation *today* constitutes a process of the *rhythmic containment of memory*. (Recall: rhythmic containment focuses on the 'surrounding components' of identity filtration, labour, and leisure which form crucial co-ordinates in the rhythms of individuation.) This tendency towards *rhythmic containment* is 'embodied by search engines which' rhythmically contain by 'accentuating mimetic behaviour and generalizing a ratings logic in what claim to be personalized access procedures – as with Google' (ibid.: 72). This is effectuated through pre- and supra-personal control of digital tertiary retentions. We noted at the top of this section how digital communications technologies were socially, materially, and phenomenologically circumscribed insofar as only the owners of the means of communication have access to the means and capabilities to *transform* digital tertiary retentions and direct their function, and insofar as there is a divide (the 'digital divide') amongst those who can even *interact* with and experience, let alone *transform*, digital tertiary retentions.

What does it mean for us to claim that such a circumscription of the access to transform such technologies constitutes memory's rhythmic containment, especially insofar as digital tertiary retentions have been positioned, by many, as the harbinger of a potentially new democratic (e-)culture? It constitutes memory's rhythmic containment insofar as *expression is subordinated to containment*, or, in other words, *containment is becoming the condition of expression in the realm of digital tertiary retentions*. Rather than the signalling the advent of a new participatory e-community, digital tertiary retentions today offer only a simulation of this, simulated e-communities in which the function is to extract surplus value from attentional energies. As Citton notes: '*if a product is free, then the real product is you!* More precisely: your attention' (2017: 9).

Recall what we noted above in Chapter 3: exteriorisation is both the condition and effect of expression. Exteriorised technologies, as a residue or trace of technical memory, are those that embrained bodies *learn* to utilise in order to express themselves in the milieu in question (such a *learning* process is a transformational one for the embrained body on the pre-personal level). Indeed, it is this imbrication of technics and psychic interiority that renders possible the coding of desire's pulsive moments in terms of permanent attentional excitation. Further, exteriorised technologies are themselves *effects* of expression and creation (this is their memorial trace) that can both create imaginative conditions, but also curtail them (supra-personal). But we can be much more specific than this. Our very navigation of the digital communicative environment is a source of monetisation, it is a form of immaterial labour for which the majority of participants receive no remuneration (for participants who can *utilise* but not *transform* or *control* such technologies). The most useful examples of this are Facebook, TikTok, Instagram, YouTube, Twitter/X (etc.), platforms which singularly tailors each user's experience (that is, what appears on their 'Newsfeed', what advertisements they receive, and so on) according to algorithmic calculations based on *previous* consumption, clicking, listening, and *looking* patterns (as well as patterns others have displayed) and on the future corporate *solicitation* of continuing or increasing such patterns.[7] Jonathan Crary captures some of these elements:

> The most advanced forms of surveillance and data analysis used by intelligence agencies are now equally indispensable to the marketing strategies of large businesses. Widely employed are screens or other forms of display that track eye movements, as well as durations and fixations of visual interest in sequences or streams of graphic information. One's casual perusal of a single web page can be minutely analyzed and quantified in terms of how the eye scans, pauses, moves, and gives attentive priority to some areas

over others [. . .] Incalculable streams of images are omnipresent 24/7, but what finally occupies individual attention is the *management of the technical conditions that surround them:* all the expanding and determinations of delivery, display, format, storage, upgrades, and accessories. (Crary, 2014: 48–49, our emphasis)

The sprawling semiotic environment of digital tertiary retentions is *phenomenologically filtered through algorithms that monitor, pre-empt, and seek to capture and control our habits of interaction with these technologies*, and, as such, the judgements (conscious or not) we make while traversing digital space (e.g., the judgement to purchase this or that product, or to look at a particular advertisement, or to post on social media). To express oneself (and, indeed, *paying attention* to something is a mode of expression) through the utilisation of digital tertiary retentions – and, as we already noted, it is becoming increasingly socially compulsory to do so – one must *pass through the rhythmic containment of memory.* That is, through mechanisms of algorithmic control and neutralisation that solicit consumption of goods and services and the production of information which can be utilised in personalised marketing schemes, and, by extension, the *continuous insinuation* of attention, expression, consumption, and production. Or to put this differently: in a state of permanent libidinal excitation through the capitalist-technological interruption of the first passive synthesis, our rhythms of attention towards the digital environment constitute a disjunctive practice of recording, releasing libidinal energy through the production of retentions (commodifiable information), which are themselves used to circumscribe and further tailor our newsfeeds so as to solicit further attentional energy in the future. Facebook itself famously and dubiously conducted experiments examining the impact of the algorithmic personalisation and manipulation of the newsfeeds of users and whether such manipulation could spread affective contagions (Kramer et al.: 2014).[8] Such algorithmic experimentation has also been conducted by Facebook in relation to voting, and by dating app OkCupid in relation to purposefully setting up predicted 'bad dates' (Pettman, 2016: 84). Continuous interaction and injunctions to 'express oneself' in and pay attention to the sprawling semiotic environment of social media are only possible today through processes of rhythmic containment. Our utilisation of digital tertiary retentions is the *continuous* production of monetisable information – which is then stored as *memory* in digital tertiary retentions – to solicit further consumption and the production of further information for *future* (increasingly self-tailored) consumption. Pettman notes this with clarity:

Thus the traditional dystopian scenario of the nineteenth and twentieth centuries changes in the age of social media, no longer a bleak, black-and-white world of uniform movement and homogenous expression, but a colourful, 'fun,' personalized experience, in which we all dance to our own drum [. . .] We are invited to blaze our own pathway through the world, so long as we leave our legible (and leverageable) data shadow in our wake. Social media allows, even encourages, self-tailored lines of flight; all the better to *re*territorialize these into a continuous coding operation that can then anticipate, and incorporate, such options into the database. (Ibid.: 87–88)

Aldous Huxley's *Brave New World* and George Orwell's *1984* are (disciplinary) dystopias of compulsory visibility (Foucault, 1991), of ontological homogenisation and the delimitation of self-expression. They lacked the imagination of a dystopia of compulsory visibility *with the addition of* compulsory self-expression (and solicited ontological heterogenisation) which could then incorporate those mechanisms (through the digital storage and memory of attentional habits) of self-expression into its very functioning and perpetuation. Digital tertiary retentions, controlled by the owners of the means of communication, here both solicit and capture compulsory ontological heterogenisation into their mechanisms and functions with continuous insinuations to express through (unpaid) production (such as a user's navigation of a social media feed) and consumption, and, thus, contribute to capital accumulation.[9] We met this point in Chapter 3, where we noted the large *quantitative range* but narrow *qualitative scope* of existential refrains available in contemporary capitalistic milieus: capitalist homogenesis.[10] Ontological heterogenisation, expression, is *subordinated* to rhythmic containment, for the purposes of its capture into the field of economic exchange, digital memory or digital tertiary retentions, and capital accumulation.

Through this, *lifestyles* and their constitutive rhythms are continuously insinuated and captured by digital tertiary retentions for the purposes of capital accumulation. Not only is the pre-personal (such as the nervous system) captured by the compulsory injunction to learn to utilise technologies that one cannot transform or control, but so too is the supra-personal (such as the imagination). The imagination is captured through digital tertiary retentions becoming the increasingly hegemonic focal point *through which* imagination is concretised, and, relatedly, through which imagination is captured, neutralised, and subordinated to capital accumulation. The rhythmic containment of memory is a process through which the existential refrains are *controlled and neutralised* through their quick *capture* and, sometimes, pre-emptive solicitation made possible by algorithms and digital tertiary retentions.

Digital tertiary retentions function as a vast active database which not only 'stores', or exteriorises, memory, but which has an active ethico-political-economic function insofar as such retentional apparatuses are controlled by the owners of the means of communication or a material-digital elite. The insisting permanence of digital tertiary retentions in the contemporary mental environment has the effect of constituting or contributing to the ontological security of capitalism's rhythmic processes of subjective neutralisation and control, as well as material capital accumulation. The plastic and dynamic nature of what can be 'captured' into processes of capital accumulation have, as we noted, a broad *quantitative range* but narrow *qualitative scope* insofar as existential refrains which *do not* seek to contribute to capital accumulation are increasingly subjected to capture, control, and neutralisation through, amongst other things, the rhythmic containment of memory (which, to say the same thing in a different way, is the attempted capture of the pre- and supra-personal through digital tertiary retentions). Such modes of governance *delimit* patterns of practice for those in capitalistic milieus, ensuring (or attempting to ensure with a vast digital weaponry) the disempowerment of those who might wish to transform such milieus; the control of digital tertiary retentions constitutes the control of one of the most crucial retentional apparatuses in the mental environment. The control of memory, and the extended attempt to control, neutralise, and capture existential refrains into ones which contribute to capital accumulation constitutes the continuous solicitation to *contribute to the ontological security of the capitalistic milieu*, and is expressive of the *arrhythmia* of contemporary capitalist milieus. This was the central point to be made in relation to the rhythmic containment of memory. We will now turn to our third claim of this section, which pertains to the future.

Claim Three: the combination of the capital-technological interruption of the first synthesis and the accelerating digital exteriorisation of memory is a process which tends to foreclose the future.
An accelerating present, the erasure of memory, and the closure of the future. This is what we have extracted from Nietzsche's claims on speed and time above, and such is our argument in this section. Our third claim in this section will develop from the previous two and consider what effect the capitalist-technological interruption of the first synthesis and the accelerating digital exteriorisation of memory have in relation to the future.

We noted in Chapter 2 that arrhythmia exhibits the minimum of rhythm or maximum rhythmic contraction, functioning in order to freeze the virtual structure of the past and delimit patterns of practice, and as such, *foreclosing the future*. What we call arrhythmia is that tendency for milieus, organisations, patterns of practice, relational systems (and so on) to *delimit* the practice, *freeze* the past, and, so, *foreclose* the future, insofar as pulse functions to code rhythmic parameters of ontological security. The ontological security of a milieu pertains to this triple temporal relationship, and the constant processual work required to constantly *re-secure* ontological security. Through the notion of pulse, we also discussed the rhythmic flows and arrests of desire around these coded parameters, noting the constitution of a milieu as being bound up with the governance of libidinal flows through which the milieu is rhythmically secured over time: through repeated patterns of practice mechanised through desire. Such a delimitation, freezing, and foreclosure is precisely what Guattari is gesturing towards when he underlines the production of subjectivity in capitalism as one that 'controls and neutralises' the maximum number of existential refrains (homogenesis). Our analysis of the distraction-attention ecology, with specific emphasis on the effect of digital tertiary retentions (retentions which are controlled and profited on by a digital elite), underlines specific ways in which these processes of delimitation (of the present), freezing (of the past), and foreclosure (of the future) function in this specific ecology; taken together, we describe this as the arrhythmic nature of contemporary capitalistic milieus. Recall: *arrhythmic* tendencies pertain to the neutralisation of attentional, affective, subjective, and social potentialities.

We will develop here what we mean when we announce this tendency towards the foreclosure of the future under the contemporary distraction-attention ecology. We have already highlighted numerous effects of this ecology, effects which are psychically, politically, socially, and economically disempowering: indecision, anxiety, insecurity, obsession, addiction, paranoia, and neurosis. Berardi (2015: 207) postulates that the extremity of these effects signals a *mutation* or even a *trauma* (ibid.: 238) in the mental environment. We have also highlighted how the accelerated tendency of the exteriorisation of memory in digital tertiary retentions has effects on both the pre- and supra-personal levels, effects which solicit and induce those who find themselves in capitalistic milieus to contribute consistently to enhancing the milieu's ontological security.

These effects are ones which consistently feed off the permanent insecurity the capitalist-technological interruption of the first passive synthesis generates, a permanent insecurity which *forecloses* the possibilities of *imagining* alternative futures, insofar as such imaginative processes minimally require security (contraction and expectation), memory, access to the technologies of memory, and an openness to experimentation and surprise through a level of *sustained care or attention to* the future. That is, *imagining* the future seems to require that we can *pay attention to, or be distracted by, dream, or imagine a desired future*. To open the imaginative plane of a new world requires attentional energies. Such attentional processes are consistently blocked and prevented through the capitalist-technological interruption of the first synthesis and the *capture* of attention-distraction for the purposes of capital accumulation. Crary notes an element of this well in connection with reverie:

> One of the forms of disempowerment within 24/7 environments is the incapacitation of daydream or of any mode of absent-minded introspection that would otherwise occur in intervals of slow or vacant time. Now one of the attractions of current systems and products is their operating speed: it has become intolerable for there to be waiting time while something loads or connects. When there are delays or breaks of empty time, they are rarely openings for the drift of consciousness in which one becomes unmoored from the constraints and demands of the immediate present. There is a profound incompatibility of anything resembling reverie with the priorities of efficiency, functionality, and speed. (Crary, 2014: 88)

Toffler, similarly, argued that the accelerative thrust of technological 'progress' results in less and less time for 'extended, peaceful attention to one problem or situation at a time' (1970: 40). Guattari (2014: 25) likewise, and finally, notes how such an accelerative thrust might work against any *investment* in a common future when the unconscious is captured by mechanisms of pre- and supra-personal control.

The central point to be taken here is that the 'control and neutralisation' of the maximum number of existential refrains is the process through which the present is delimited, the past is frozen and/or captured, and, so, the future is foreclosed in part through the *blockage* or *interruption* of imaginative processes. In the case of the distraction-attention ecology, these processes are explicitly manifest in the capitalist-technological interruption of the first passive synthesis, and the affectively disempowering effects these help to produce, as well as the control of the digital retentional apparatuses which surround mechanisms of identity filtration, labour, and leisure on pre- and supra-personal levels by a digital and material elite.

To conclude this section, we will isolate an additional rhythmic–affective tendency, a limit-case, being insinuated through the mechanisms and tendencies we have been developing: that of *sleeplessness* and/or *insomnia*. Sleep constitutes a vital component in the organic navigation of the rhythms of everyday life. It does not constitute a vital component, it seems, in the insinuations to consume and produce in the surrounding environment of digital tertiary retentions. Crary notes that the proliferation and continuous function of 24/7 markets – *economic exchange and capital accumulation as social processes which never stop* – functions as a war on the rhythmic–organic (biorhythmic) necessity of sleep itself: it is an ongoing technosocial experiment in the mass rejection of diurnality. Contemporary capitalistic milieus *resist* diurnality. Crary terms the 24/7 marketplace (made possible and ever faster, we should note, though the *contraction* of spacetime, and therefore communication across spacetime, made possible by digital technologies) a 'static redundancy that disavows its relation to the rhythmic and periodic textures of human life' (2014: 9). Further still, he identifies the tendency of the 24/7 marketplace as one which *forecloses* the future and imaginative processes beyond those that can contribute to the ontological security of capitalist milieus:

> What is new is the sweeping abandonment of the pretense that time is coupled to any long-term undertakings, even to fantasies of 'progress' or development. An illuminated 24/7 world without shadows is the final capitalist mirage of post-history [. . .] *24/7 is a time of indifference*, against which the fragility of human life is increasingly inadequate and within which sleep has no necessity or inevitability. (Ibid.)

Indeed, a 2016 marketing campaign by McDonald's highlights the insomniac tendencies of capitalistic milieus, and their injunctions to consume and produce 24/7. The campaign's tagline: 'We Are Awake'; its theme tune: 'The Rhythm of the Night.'[11]

This war on the organic necessity of sleep itself, capitalism's insomniac tendencies, is part a broader process through which the possibilities of sculpting alternative futures is being confronted and eroded in milieus dominated by digital tertiary retentions. They are being confronted by a combination of retentional apparatuses (which are being innovated at an accelerating rate and are controlled by a material–digital elite) and by the continuous disruption of contraction and expectation, and, therefore, mechanisms of identity filtration as such. Such processes, at present, *tend* to produce permanent insecurity, felt anxiety, and indecision, as well as obsession, addiction, paranoia, and neurosis.

Distraction-subjection-containment is a complex and multi-faceted co-ordinate which will demand complex and multi-faceted interventions. We will now turn, therefore, to some processes of *extemporaneous counter-actualisation* and *rhythmic dramatisation* that are being, and can be further, enacted in order to re-sculpt the distraction–attention ecology and compose new futures in the mental environment.

b. Minority experiment one: copyfarleft co-operatives/ collectives

> The real task is to find the institutional and technological means of self-control and autoproduction while simultaneously avoiding a slide into bureaucratic sclerosis or romantic cyberbabble. (Genosko, 2003: 21)

Our first two claims in relation to the distraction–attention ecology were the following:

Claim One: the contemporary distraction-attention ecology tends towards a continuous capitalist-technological interruption of the first passive synthesis of the present, capturing time and desire.

Claim Two: the capitalist-technological interruption of the first synthesis further constitutes the rhythmic containment of memory.

The insisting permanence and increasingly compulsory interaction with and utilisation of digital tertiary retentions help produce a mental environment wherein both the extreme tendencies of distraction (indecision, anxiety) and attention (obsession, addiction, paranoia, neurosis) manifest. Distraction and attention are continuously and simultaneously insinuated at an accelerating rate, and this insinuation is in part conducted through processes of rhythmic containment, through which *containment is becoming the condition of expression in the realm of digital tertiary retentions.* Also recall that an *extemporaneous counter-actualisation* of the co-ordinate distraction–subjection–containment would constitute a *virtualisation*, not an actualisation. Counter-actualisation constitutes an *affirmation*, an affirmation which affirms its *disjunction* with extant rhythms, paving the way for the rhythmic-sculptural creation of the new (Deleuze, 2004a: 204, 243). In other words, counter–actualisation constitutes *affirmative work*, but so as to affirm its *disjunction* with the present, opening spacetime for dramatisation. An extemporaneous counter-actualisation at the intersection of distraction, subjection, and containment would, minimally, constitute a *disentangling of the subordination of expression to containment*. Such a disentangling could be pursued in a number of ways, but it would preliminarily involve strategic and tactical manoeuvres in relation to digital tertiary retentions so as to redistribute the sensible (Rancière, 1989: 22) and sculpt the attention–distraction ecology anew.

What possibilities for such affirmative work present themselves in the distraction-attention ecology in contemporary capitalistic milieus? Or what affirmative work might already be being conducted in this ecology? There will be and are multiple strategies and vectors that might be pursued; and, indeed, as we will consistently emphasise, none of the strategies we *pay attention* to here can be considered as universally generalisable, precisely because of the extent to which expression is, today, subordinated to containment. In this sense, we cannot commit *dogmatically* or *principally* to any of the specific strategies of affirmative work we pursue, insofar as the conditions of the present are never static, and insofar as such strategies could be pursued in heterogeneous ways. The hope is, simply, that multiple tactics and pressure points can be pursued to generate a cumulative *effect* that we might be able to call an *extemporaneous counter-actualisation*, rupturing the experience of the present, disentangling the subordination of expression to containment, helping to open a spacetime for rhythmic dramatisation. With this noted, we will explore one potential vector of such affirmative work; *minority experiment one: copyfarleft co-operatives/collectives*.

The question of copyfarleft is a confrontation with the question of intellectual property and copyright. Indeed, the question of intellectual property is a particularly apt one to discuss, given the context in which academic labour such as this project is produced (in the realm of the contemporary neoliberal university and its continuous practice of monitoring and appraising the production of this particular object of intellectual property (largely through digital tertiary retentions)), and given the potential this particular tertiary retention might bear for commodifiability (however slim). In this sense, this project itself, of course, is caught within the processes through which expression is subordinated to containment.[12] The *disentangling* of this subordination has a potential vector of effectuation through *copyfarleft* production, based, amongst other works, on Dmytri Kleiner's *The Telekommunist Manifesto*. The subordination of expression to containment, as we have already noted, is a subordination through which (increasingly compulsory) online activity – whether this is conducted as 'leisure' (such as in social media) or 'labour' (such as in cognitive labour) – is monetised and utilised for purposes of capital accumulation, and it is a process through which our expression *supports the ontological security of capitalism*. To begin this process of *disentangling*, Kleiner notes the following:

> New ways of producing and sharing, then, are a precondition of any change in the social order. These new methods of production and sharing require the creation of new kinds of relationships, new productive relations, to constitute a new economic structure that is able to give rise to a new kind of society. No social order, no matter how entrenched and ruthlessly imposed, can resist transformation when new ways of producing and sharing emerge. (Kleiner, 2010: 9)

In other words, this process of *disentangling* is a creative and temporal process through which we create new modes of production and new modes of exchange in a realm increasingly dominated by digital tertiary retentions, and through which we seek to *decouple* the subordination of expression to containment, which is no small task. Recall that the tendency towards rhythmic containment is partially 'embodied by search engines which' rhythmically contain by 'accentuating mimetic behaviour and generalizing a ratings logic in what claim to be personalized access procedures – as with Google' (Stiegler, 2014b: 72). Such control is effectuated by a material and digital elite who has privileged access to digital tertiary retentions, the ability to control, transform, and profit from their utilisation through the extraction of surplus value from attentional energies; such political and organological conditions constrain communicative processes and possibilities (Sanín-Restrepo, 2016: 187). On the pre-personal level, disentangling the subordination of expression to containment might be pursued through the creation of modes of exchange which *evade* algorithmic capture for the purposes of capital accumulation. On the supra-personal level, we already noted that imagination is, today, increasingly *captured* by digital tertiary retentions and folded into processes of capital accumulation, and, so, a *disentanglement* of the subordination of expression to containment on the supra-personal level could be effectuated through *co-operative ownership* and *participation* in the supra-personal; common access to the ability to utilise, control, and transform digital tertiary retentions.

Our practices of *extemporaneous counter-actualisation* will confront the conditions of the present, helping to *break* the circuits that our expression is caught in today, and can only do so through an awareness of their situatedness, that is, through an immanent practice. Gary Hall, in his *Pirate Philosophy: For a Digital Posthumanities*, highlights the key problem in relation to *complete* (that is, dogmatic) anti-intellectual property stances today, effectively charging them with non-immanence:

The difficulty with the anticopyright stance is that it may be effective only from a position either outside the capitalist legal system or after its demise. Certainly when it comes to academic publishing, gestures of this kind risk playing into the hands of the neoliberal philosophy that states universities should carry out the basic research the private sector does not have the time, money, or inclination to conduct for itself, while nevertheless granting businesses easy access to that research and the associated data for commercial application and exploitation. (Hall, 2016: 8)

Responding to this concern, what might a *copyfarleft* approach look like? How might it help disentangle the subordination of expression to containment? Let us quote Kleiner's detailed response to the first question, and then we will conclude with a response to the second:

In order for copyleft to mutate into a revolutionary instrument in the domain of cultural production, it must become 'copy-far-left'. It must insist on workers' ownership of the means of production. The works themselves must be a part of the common stock, and available for productive use by other commons-based producers. So long as authors reserve the right to make money with their work, and prevent other commons-based producers from doing so, their work cannot be considered to be in the commons at all and remains a private work. A copyfarleft license must not restrict commercial usage, but rather usage that is *not* based in the commons. Specifically, copyfarleft must have one set of rules for those who are working within the context of workers' communal ownership, and another for those who employ private property and wage labor in production. A copyfarleft license should make it possible for producers to share freely and to also retain the value of their labor product. In other words, it must be possible for workers to earn remuneration by applying their own labor to mutual property, but impossible for owners of private property to make profit using wage labor. Thus, under a copyfarleft license, a worker-owned printing co-operative could be free to reproduce, distribute, and modify the common stock as they like, but a privately owned publishing company would be prevented from having free access [. . .] Copyfarleft only prohibits subtraction from the commons, not contributions to it. (Kleiner, 2010: 42)

Copyfarleft suggests an alternative remunerative approach for organisations or institutions to adopt, as well as a revision of standards of intellectual property (the production of knowledge and culture) that might be able to be effectuated within contemporary capitalistic milieus. The process of *disentangling* the subordination of expression to containment here would be effectuated in, we suggest, two ways. First, through *disentangling* pre-personal intervention for the purposes of *accessing* digital tertiary retentions (pre-personal intervention which is then utilised to algorithmically generate monetisable information and advertising patterns, continuously inducing consumption and production). A copyfarleft co-operative would *block* such informational abstraction for the purposes of capital accumulation, in effect through applying different 'rules' to those who 'opt in' to the copyfarleft co-operative, and another set of 'rules' to capitalist enterprises that still employ wage labour and seek capital accumulation. Those who 'opt in' to a copyfarleft co-operative could share freely among other co-operative members their and each other's work, receiving remuneration for contributions they make to the co-operative. Those who do not 'opt in' (such as private enterprises in capitalistic milieus operating through wage labour, profit maximisation, and capital accumulation) would be blocked from having free access. Second, through common ownership and remuneration, there would be *common participation in the supra-personal* in and through copyfarleft collectives. That is, the processes of production and consumption would not be driven by a digital-material elite for the purposes of capital accumulation, quite simply because all those who 'opt in' to the copyfarleft collective would have access to, and the ability to transform, the digital tertiary retentions through which the copyfarleft would operate.[13] It is through this mechanism that the *subordination of expression to containment* is disentangled: total retentional access.

As such, and further: proliferated, variegated, and differential actualisations of copyfarleft collectives bear the potential for pushing distraction-attention ecologies in contemporary capitalistic milieus to their deterritorial border, or region of *ontological insecurity*, through processes which contribute to the material security of participants in such a collective, and which exclude capital accumulation. In other words, such practices could form local networks that not only produce new rhythms of everyday life (an *aesthetic intervention*), but can *contribute to the ontological insecurity of capitalism* through contributing to the disentangling of expression and containment. *Entrance into* and *participation in* a copyfarleft co-operative could constitute an 'opening of technicity' (Stiegler, 2015: 120); that is, an *extemporaneous counter-actualisation* of *distraction-subjection-containment*. Such affirmative work is, no doubt, not short-termist; *sustained* care and *attention* to such projects would be necessary to operate on their border, to ignite and proliferate inclusive revolutionary processes, and to work on sculptural processes in order to sculpt the attention-distraction ecology anew. We will now pay a little more attention to this sculptural dimension.

c. Sculptural process one: the sculpting of co-operative networks

> A change in technics entails a modification of what one could call the political constellation of the universe. (Simondon, 2017: 231)

Our third claim in relation to the distraction-attention ecology was the following:

Claim Three: the combination of the capital-technological interruption of the first synthesis and the accelerating digital exteriorisation of memory is a process which tends to foreclose the future.

Our first *sculptural process* is related to the creation of *copyfarleft co-operatives/collectives* we developed in section 4b. Indeed, for such a creation to help open the spacetime for *rhythmic dramatisation*, our suggestion here is that they be coupled with *the sculpting of co-operative networks.* Let us revisit Kleiner, who we introduced in our first *minority experiment*, who captures some of the motivating ideas here:

> Capitalism depends on the state to impose control within the network economy, particularly to control relations through authorized channels, and thereby capture value that would otherwise be retained by its producers. In order to change society we must actively expand the scope of our commons, so that our independent communities of peers can be materially sustained and can resist the encroachments of capitalism. (Kleiner, 2010: 12)

Let us be more precise. What might it mean to participate in the *collective sculpting of co-operative networks?* As with all of our gestures here, we do not seek to *totalise* or necessarily prioritise the experiments we suggest; rather, as we noted in Chapter 2, *scaping is not about developing a conceptually frozen ecology, but, rather, about the genesis of revolutionary vectors immanent in the (virtual) possibilities of the present.*[14] One of the vectors of such a process would nonetheless involve the creation of networks through which all have the ability and means to partake in the technical milieu. The collective sculpting of co-operative networks could, we suggest, mobilise around three temporally oriented, yet nonetheless entangled, tactical points. First, through confronting the conditions of the present in the attention–distraction ecology we scaped in section 4a (the *erasure* of attentional time generated through the capitalist-technological interruption of the first passive synthesis, and expression increasingly becoming conditional upon rhythmic containment). Second, through the co-creation of new co-operative *retentional apparatuses* and *long-term circuits.* Third, through a collective sculpting of a *common investment* towards the future. Due to their entanglement, we will discuss these together.

There are already a number of examples that we can highlight for introductory purposes, specifically, confronting the conditions of the present we scaped. Take, for example, the anonymous-software and encryption practices that are being created in order to *circumvent* the surveillance (which is a mechanism of containment) present in largely corporate and state-owned networks today, such as the web browser Tor. Or the growing popularity of so-called 'mesh networks', which will be our main example here. Mesh networks are decentralised networks that enable digital connectivity between all participants in the network, and that do not require connection to the corporate- and state-owned 'grid' in order to enable such connectivity. (In such cases, we might even speak of a *complete disentanglement of the subordination of expression to containment.*) Mesh networks are *co-operative* in the sense that *each network participant* strengthens the network through their participation. In mesh networks, it is possible for independent 'nodes' in the network to be connected to every other router (which is also to say that the network can operate *without a centre*). This strengthens the networks insofar as such multi-connectionality can create what is termed 'full redundancy'; that is, an enhanced reliability of the network. At Occupy Wall Street, for example, a mesh network was established in Zuccotti Park by Isaac Wilder and Charles Wyble named 'The Free Network Foundation'.[15] The Free Network Foundation continued its operations, creating co-operative networks where each member pays only the costs for the maintenance of the network (for example, server maintenance) (see Akmut, 2019). It is possible that in operational mesh networks, no internet service provider (ISP) is required; the network *is* the ISP. In effect, what this generates is the possibility of digital connectivity outside of the corporate- and state-owned 'grid'. This would be no small feat, insofar as for many in capitalistic milieus today, such connectivity and expression must *pass through rhythmic containment*, as Astra Taylor reminds us in *The People's Platform*:

There is philosophical, political, and schizoanalytical project
flows through private pipes. However, using the Internet for the
consumption of culture or to search for information is nearly as
essential to participating in modern life as having electricity or
plumbing in your home (try going to school or applying for a job
without it). (Taylor, 2014: 254, our addition)

Such a sculptural process would, no doubt, would take on the order
of decades. There are a few key points we wish to underline here.
Mesh networks are only one potential example, and there are numerous experiments exploring solutions to such problems of connectivity:
community networks remain an open field of experimentation (see
Barcelo et al., 2012; Belli, 2018). The aim to offer frameworks and
how-to guides, common in such experiments, is an important element
through which milieus can navigate the process of planning, developing, and running similar projects themselves; i.e., such guides can
function as an epistemological-technical proliferation of not just how
network architecture currently functions, but also how it may function differently. That is, they can function as an 'opening of technicity'
(Stiegler, 2015: 120). Further, such projects, to the extent that they are
focused on the creation of sustainable and *long-term circuits*, invite us to
invest in a *common future*. The co-creation of such an *investment* bears
the potential of enabling *rhythms* to emerge from our contemporary
pulsed arrhythmia: engendering such an investment would constitute
the formation of *attentional time* (which is being saturated by digital
tertiary retentions controlled by a digital and material elite, saturating
attentional time (Stiegler, 2010b: 6–8)), produce solidarity – though
not sameness – across present lines of social disjunction which co-
operatively run the network, and the shared pursuance of shared, but
differential, singularising existential refrains; that is, *a collaborative sculpting of the mental environment.* Insofar as such sculptural processes would
be pursued through an *investment in a common future*, we can also say
that such processes would thereby focus on the question of *long-term
circuits* or *sustainability.* We say this insofar as, say, milieus in which the
mental environment *forecloses* or *blocks* any investment in a common
future – such as contemporary capitalistic milieus – *efface* the question
of long-term circuits and of sustainability. In contemporary capitalistic milieus, the capitalist-technological interruption of the first passive
synthesis constitutes such a *blockage* to long-term circuits. This claim
bears strong affinities to Stiegler's one of the *systemic stupidity* of capitalistic milieus: 'The consumerist model has reached its limits because
it has become systemically short-termist, because it has given rise to

a *systemic stupidity* that *structurally prevents the reconstitution of a long-term horizon*' (2010a: 5).[16] Taylor highlights some specific digital, cultural, and material blockages to long-term circuits:

> Too often people assume that digital content will last forever, immateriality and reproducibility encouraging the false impression that anything uploaded to the cloud is safely stored for posterity. In reality, we lose an estimated quarter of all working links every seven years and digital files can quickly become incomprehensible due to the swift churn of technological obsolescence. Sustainable culture includes building archives that will allow people to explore cultural heritage for years to come. (Taylor, 2014: 216–217)

Importantly, such a focus on sustainability, as Taylor highlights, would 'concern itself with every layer of our communications infrastructure, from the creative works distributed online to the Web sites we visit to the mud and wires that make our connections possible' (ibid.: 225). To reiterate: such a project can only be pursued collaboratively, processually, and in the long term. The co-operative forming of mesh and other decentralised networks, locality-based network typologies, that is, the collective sculpting of co-operative networks, has the potential to produce a *libidinal investment in a common future*, the *creation of long-term circuits* – requiring the creation of new rhythms – *and the expansion of access to digital tertiary retentions*, as well as the expanded access to engagement with and transformation of such technologies. While mesh networks, and The Free Network Foundation in particular, have been our central focus here, there are further distinct examples we could mention. Taylor also mentions co-operatively owned music streaming websites, documentary distributing websites, community agricultural associations, and community broadband initiatives (ibid.: 222, 226). An important point worth adding to this, before concluding this section, is related to how such processes can reach across lines of social disjunction. A key issue we mentioned above in relation to the distraction-attention ecology was the digital divide (the differential distribution of who can even *access*, let alone *transform*, such digital technologies). The digital divide is in effect generated by this systemic stupidity we referred to above, as Taylor notes, insofar as 'private investment markets would rather cherry-pick districts packed with well-to-do customers than invest in broadband infrastructure to serve poor and sparsely populated regions' (ibid.: 226). The short-termism through which capitalistic milieus function *block* the collective sculpting of sustainable, long-term, and inclusive circuits.

Here, rhythmic dramatisation through the sculpting of co-operative net-works, if pursued, would be locally determined, organised, and run; that is, an *adoption* (and therefore *transformation*) of the conditions of the present. In this sense, such sculptural processes are slow and piecemeal, but as Guattari reminds us: '*revolution is either processual or it isn't revolution*' (Guattari, in Guattari and Rolnik, 2007: 260).

d. Conclusion

The broad creation of *copyfarleft co-operatives* and the *sculpting of co-operative networks* would, at least initially, constitute micropolitical work. As objects of collaborative attention, they bear the potential of the genera-tion of new solidarities and the formation of new attentional networks in the rhythms of everyday life in their very process of creation and institution. Insofar as contemporary capitalistic milieus weaponise and commodify our attentional energies in the service of a vast arrhythmia to which we all contribute, our attentional energies themselves must become an object of revolutionary struggle in the mental environment. As such, these tactics can be positioned as contributing to the generation of new sites where our attentional energies can be directed outside of their arrhythmic weaponisation, and to the foundation of the sorts of new technical sites of collaboration (new transindividual collectives) and exchange that we will need to create an inclusive revolutionary future, and through which we can *sediment* the memory of such processes in a constitutively open and long-term manner. This would be to create new relatively stable matrices of emergence (Massumi, 2017a: 11) in the functioning of our milieus-to-come; that is, movements that were held together rhythmically. The creation of new rhythmic parameters of ontological security would be to relatively securitise these new atten-tional milieus, new attentional relations, without which these projects will likely collapse through the *reintegration* of libidinous and attentional energies in the service of the capitalistic milieu. In order to sustain these new milieus and matrices of emergence, in other words, the point is to generate relations that are held together with relative stability, to create variations *irreducible* to the capitalistic milieu, and new attention ecologies in the mental environment.

e. Chapter 4 reprise

[66] Attention pertains to a duration of care, to the exercise of force and desire which *tends* in particular directions (attention always implicating *duration* and *direction*, that is, force, time, and desire), and such an exercise

is indissociable from the milieu, insofar as *the milieu orients becomings in part through the orientation of attentional energy.*

[67] *The contemporary distraction-attention ecology tends towards a continuous capitalist-technological interruption of the first passive synthesis of the present, capturing time and desire.*

[68] The extreme tendency of distraction is a case of being distracted by a multiplicity of objects and demands to the extent that the subject's attention becomes distributed and temporally minute in relation to each object: indecision and anxiety. We also noted that the extreme tendency of attention is a case of taking so much care of particular objects of concern or demands to the extent that the subject's attention becomes extensive and fixated in relation to particular objects or demands: obsession, addiction, paranoia, and neurosis. Both of these extreme tendencies are manifest in the contemporary mental environment, and they can be read as *effects* of the capitalist-technological interruption of the first passive synthesis rendered possible through the proliferation of digital tertiary retentions and digital devices.

[69] The insisting permanence of digitised social relations and their colonisation of everyday rhythms of identity filtration, labour, and leisure tends towards the extreme case of distraction: the conjunction of permanent distraction and permanent subjection. This conjunction constitutes a *capitalist-technological interruption of the first passive synthesis*, disrupting secure passive contractions and expectations, producing permanent excitation, indecision, and anxiety in the mental environment.

[70] The insisting permanence of digital tertiary retentions and their colonisation of everyday rhythms of identity filtration, labour, and leisure also tends towards the extreme case of attention: the connection of permanent attention and permanent subjection. This conjunction also constitutes another element of the *capitalist-technological interruption of the first passive synthesis*, disrupting secure passive contractions and expectations insofar as the continuous turnover of digital tertiary retentions themselves resist the secure constitution of rhythmic parameters of ontological security, producing addiction, obsession, and neurotic attachment in the mental environment.

[71] *The capitalist-technological interruption of the first synthesis further constitutes the rhythmic containment of memory.*

[72] The sprawling semiotic environment of digital tertiary retentions is *phenomenologically filtered through algorithms that monitor, pre-empt, and seek to capture and control our habits of interaction with these technologies,* and, as such, the judgements (conscious or not) we make while traversing digital space.

[73] In a state of permanent libidinal excitation through the capitalist-technological interruption of the first passive synthesis, our rhythms of attention towards the digital environment constitute a disjunctive practice of recording, releasing libidinal energy through the production of retentions (commodifiable datasets), which are themselves used to circumscribe and further tailor our newsfeeds so as to solicit further attentional energy in the future.

[74] Aldous Huxley's *Brave New World* and George Orwell's *1984* are (disciplinary) dystopias of compulsory visibility, of ontological homogenisation and the delimitation of self-expression. They lacked the imagination of a dystopia of compulsory visibility *with the addition of* compulsory self-expression (and solicited ontological heterogenisation) which could then incorporate those mechanisms (through the digital storage and memory of attentional habits) of self-expression into their very functioning and perpetuation. Digital tertiary retentions, controlled by the owners of the means of communication, here both solicit and capture compulsory ontological heterogenisation into their mechanisms and functions with continuous insinuations to express through (unpaid) production and consumption, and, thus, contribute to capital accumulation. Ontological heterogenisation, expression, is *subordinated* to rhythmic containment, for the purposes of its capture into the field of economic exchange, digital memory or digital tertiary retentions, and capital accumulation.

[75] *The combination of the capital-technological interruption of the first synthesis and the accelerating digital exteriorisation of memory is a process which tends to foreclose the future.*

[76] To open the imaginative plane of a new world requires attentional energies. Such attentional processes are consistently blocked and prevented through the capitalist-technological interruption of the first synthesis, the *capture* of attention-distraction for the purposes of capital accumulation.

[77] Minority experiment one: copyfarleft co-operatives collectives. *Affirmative work towards the disentangling of the subordination of expression to containment.*

[78] Sculptural process one: the sculpting of co-operative networks. Collaborative processes building long-term, sustainable circuits and the potential *complete disentanglement* of the subordination of expression to containment.

Notes

1. However, we must tread carefully on this point, at the risk of rendering digital social media a phenomenon isolated on one side of an 'in-or-out'

digital divide. Marcus Gilroy-Ware highlights research that indicates that the countries with the highest levels of Facebook 'penetration' in 2015 were the Philippines, followed by Mexico and Turkey (Gilroy-Ware, 2017: 74). So, our point here is not to reduce the notion of the 'digital divide' to an exclusive disjunction, insofar as such a reduction would be untenable.

2. We by no means romanticise nor reify the labour/leisure distinction here, indeed, quite the contrary. We use the distinction here for pragmatic reasons (mainly that of historical situatedness and clarity).

3. As early as 1996, Slavoj Žižek discussed the possibilities that cyberspace offered for ontologically problematising the distinction between a 'real' and 'virtual' self. Does the 'online self' constitute an ontological 'diversion' from one's 'authentic self', or does virtuality provide an opportunity to allow one's 'authentic self' to emerge? Through Lacan, Žižek offers a response that centres on the *essential* 'splitedness' of the subject, explained through the Lacanian void or Real, which we will not be discussing here.

4. Further, we do not intend to *reduce* these effects of extreme distraction and extreme attention to digital tertiary retentions and devices, but their role is crucial.

5. The cultural phenomenon of 'Fear of Missing Out' (FOMO) is a manifestation of this trend. Toffler, already in 1970, gestured towards the growth in such a trend: 'Some people are deeply attracted to this highly accelerated pace of life – going far out of their way to bring it about and feeling anxious, tense or uncomfortable when the pace slows. They want desperately to be "where the action is". (Indeed, some hardly care what the action is, so long as it occurs at a suitably rapid clip.)' (1970: 44).

6. Again, these are *not* totalising explanatory gestures: they are partial and situated.

7. Although we will not explicitly discuss this here, we could easily bring into this discussion the post-Foucauldian literature on *algorithmic governmentality*; indeed, *rhythmic containment* and *algorithmic governmentality* are approaches to the same social processes. Whereas the latter's focus is primarily on knowledge/power relations broadly speaking, the former pivots closer focus to how such processes of governmentalisation feed into the *rhythms of individuations* and the production (and delimitation) of supra-personal imaginaries. For more on this, see Reigeluth (2014), Rouvroy (2013), Bueno (2016), and Vignola (2016).

8. The abstract's first sentence states: 'We show, via a massive ($N = 689,003$) experiment on Facebook, that emotional states can be transferred to others via emotional contagion, leading people to experience the same emotions without their awareness.'

9. See Shannon Winnubst's (2012) interesting discussion on how the capture of ontological heterogenisation potentially poses a problem for elements of queer theory that might praise resistance to normalisation; the capture

of ontological heterogeneity (i.e., resistance to normalisation) here is the precise *incentivisation* and *capture* of such resistance.

10. Here we must note that the apparent heterogenesis incentivised through expressive attentional platforms such as Instagram is an operation of capitalist *homogenesis* precisely insofar as we defined the latter as pertaining the large *quantitative range* but narrow *qualitative scope* of existential refrains possible within contemporary capitalist milieus.

11. See Ben Fordesman's 'McDonald's "We Are Awake'": http://benfordes man.com/portfolio/mcdonalds-we-are-awake (accessed 17 April 2019).

12. See Heaney (2015, 2016, 2017) and Heaney and Mackenzie (2017) for further explorations of the context of the contemporary university.

13. We do not here indicate that digital tertiary retentions would be the only commonly owned technology, but we are focusing on such tertiary retentions for our present purposes.

14. For a related Simondon-focused discussion of makerspaces, see Mazzilli-Daechsel (2019).

15. For more on this group, see the Motherboard film *Free the Network: Hackers Take Back the Web* (2012).

16. For an exploration of the conceptual relationships between Deleuze's and Stiegler's conceptions of stupidity, and their relation to the contemporary university, see Heaney (2017).

5

Happiness-Depression Ecology

As we developed in Part I, our rhythmanalytical scaping of ecologies of the mental environment pays particular attention to the *affective economy* which differentially functions in empowering or disempowering ways depending on one's material, social, phenomenological (and so on) situatedness. Our focus here will be on the *happiness-depression ecology* particular to contemporary capitalistic milieus. Treating these terms ecologically, that is as *entangled*, and as situated within the milieu is to foreground social situatedness in relation to the affective quality of everyday life:[1] the entanglement of the affective quality of everyday life, psychic pain, and social situatedness within the milieu.

We will first draw some definitional brushstrokes to initiate our scaping of this ecology. The psychic ecology of depression is constituted in part through certain rhythmics of thinking and feeling. Imprisoning cyclic loops of permanent negative (largely self-critical) self-talk and self-thought – coupled with an affective quality and tempo of either numbness or anxiety (as a certain objectless fear, potentially attaching itself to any object of thought, in which the fear of anxiety can itself produce anxiety) – come to dominate the psychic struggle that becomes the very rhythms of everyday life of the depressed subject. The sense of self, or the sense of being an *I*, becomes the seemingly inescapable site of psychic suffering. The cycles of numbness become associated with aspects of social withdrawal, self-silencing (produced in part through hardened rhythms of thought which associate the depressive experience as indicative of a personal failing or weakness, and therefore a source of shame),[2] a sense of meaninglessness and relative levels of catatonia, to name some examples. The cycles of anxiety often contract into a processual and objectless fear of the present, where the passage of time itself becomes feared. These mutually reinforcing aspects of numbness and anxiety constitute a contractive rhythmics for the depressed subject, which often opens onto obsessive, or even addictive, reterritorialisations in order to break through the psychosomatic binds of numbness and anxiety (for example, cycles of obsessive work patterns, excessive drug use, etc.).

The felt possibility of what kind of existential refrains are possible within the milieu are highly contracted for the depressed subject, whose libidinal flows are arrhythmically bound by tight codes in feedback loops. In contemporary capitalistic milieus, which seek to code these flows in particular ways, depression becomes both an effect of the manner in which these milieus orient becomings, an object of commodification and accumulation (and therefore supportive of the reproduction of the capitalistic and depressogenic milieu), as well as a process of disempowerment. Consider what *existential refrains* are possible, imagined, and have become desirable in our contemporary milieus. Rhythmic processes of individuation, at the crossroads of multiple components of identity filtration, labour, and leisure (the rhythms of everyday life), take place in mental environments traversed by possible *existential refrains* that are differential actualisations from the contemporary (supra-personal) imaginary. We have already noted on several occasions the large *quantitative range* but narrow *qualitative scope* of existential refrains available in capitalistic milieus, that is, the manner in which contemporary capitalistic milieus orient becomings and seek to code the flows of desire through time. This is another way of saying that whilst there is a relatively open space of 'content' through which we can 'fill' these processes of individuation (different products to consume, different careers to pursue, different leisure habits), they are nonetheless filtered through dominant mechanisms of individual and entrepreneurial self-actualisation (in both production and consumption), self-optimisation, effective investment in one's human capital, the fulfilment of one's hedonic desires, and contributions to capital accumulation and gross domestic product (GDP) growth; all of which, in a phrase, is the *pursuit of happiness.*

In this sense, the *happiness-depression* ecology is an ecology of the mental environment produced in capitalistic milieus: (the) *happiness* (of the *I*) is (re)produced as the specifically capitalist object and measure of life. In this sense, it is perhaps serendipitous, though nonetheless interesting, that periods of prolonged contraction in GDP are termed periods of *depression*; these are economic periods in which the rhythms of production and consumption are seriously disturbed and are pushed to their region of ontological insecurity, periods of *economic unhappiness* or periods in which the (capitalistic) *pursuit of happiness is blocked*, shocks usually absorbed through the acceleration of capital accumulation: capitalistic milieus produce and rely upon crises and depressions in the socio-economic environment precisely to the same extent that they do so in the mental environment, in the psychic ecology of everyday life. Not only does such economic rhetoric make a clear connection between growth (material accumulation, increased consumption, increased production) and happiness, it by extension depicts the *remedy* for a lack of growth (whether in a recession or a depression) as simply being more material accumulation, more consumption, and more production (rather than, say, a creative confrontation with such a notion of economic growth and its implicit or explicit connection to this notion of happiness as such). Economic depression is, to put it simply, a period in which the narrow qualitative scope of existential refrains under contemporary capitalism is starkly evidenced through the lack of existential stylistics available once the mechanisms of capitalistic production and consumption are threatened or no longer operate effectively.

That the *remedy* for depression is material 'growth', and that such processes of material growth constitute our contemporary *pursuit of happiness* – in the socio-economic environment and mental environment – is by no means a novel point to make. Nonetheless, it does have some novel manifestations in the present, particularly in relationship to the explosion of reports on mental illness, records on rising levels of anti-depressant and anti-anxiety medication usage, rates of suicide, as well as when these are contextualised within our current technical epoch and the development of psychotherapeutic and psychopharmaco-logical techniques. To take just one of these examples, Berardi high-lights that, according 'to the *World Health Organization*, in the last 45 years suicide rates have increased by 60% worldwide [. . .] [the years of] the thorough submission of attention time to the rhythm of the economic machine' (Berardi, 2015: 304, our alteration). Developing on these contemporary manifestations, our rhythmanalysis of the happiness-depression ecology will focus on the rhythms and processes through which depression in the mental environment is bound up with and governed through mechanisms of rhythmic subjection and rhyth-mic containment. Let us now turn to our co-ordinate for this chapter: happiness-subjection-containment.

a. [CC2]: happiness-subjection-containment

> If a certain physical context (such as work or poverty) is causing pain, one progressive route would involve changing that context. But another equivalent would be to focus on changing the way in which it is experienced. (Davies, 2015: 35)

> Depression is a 'brain-based' disorder and is the principal source of workplace disability, attacking the individual's ability to concentrate and work productively. Today's brain-based economy puts a premium on cerebral skills, in which cognition is the ignition of productivity

and innovation. Depression attacks that vital asset. (Wilkerson, in
HR Leadership Forum, 2014: 3)

We will make three claims in this section. First, that the contemporary happiness-depression ecology tends towards the rhythmic subjection of depression, that is, the production process of the depressed
subject. Second, that this happiness-depression ecology is becoming
increasingly imbricated with the rhythmic containment of memory,
and the government of and intervention in psychic ecologies on pre-
and supra-personal registers, further enhancing the rhythmic subjection of depression. Third, that the tendential effect of these productive
processes is a mental environment of *adaption*, rather than *adoption*.
Contemporary capitalistic milieus, this is to say, are machines for the
continuous and permanent production of depression and disempowerment, producing depression and seeking to govern its reintegration into the functioning of that milieu in a toxic and arrhythmic
feedback loop.

Claim One: the contemporary happiness-depression ecology tends towards the
rhythmic subjection of depression.
Sigmund Freud's *Mourning and Melancholia* (1957) classically distinguishes
these two concepts in terms of the directions and uses of psychic and
libidinal energies following the experience of a 'loss'. For Freud, mourning, initiated by grief, is ignited through a conscious loss of some object
of libidinal attachment, and the work of mourning involves devoting
attention to re-scaffolding the *I* after the trauma of this loss. Melancholia,
or depression, for Freud, relates however to an 'object-loss which is with-
drawn from consciousness' (1957: 245). Freud normalises the former
while pathologising the latter. Alongside this pathologising distinction,
Freud adds some further distinctions indicative of melancholia rather
than mourning: excessive negative self-regard and internalisation of psychic pain, self-hate, feelings of inferiority, and so on, in which the *I* itself
becomes the site of psychic struggle: 'In mourning it is the world that has
become poor and empty; in melancholia it is the ego itself' (1957: 246).
As Elizabeth A. Wilson notes, however, Freud does not claim that the
inward turn constitutive of melancholia makes melancholia a completely
'closed system', and that types of 'aggression turned outward is a crucial
part of the traffic between ego and world, and that we need to keep this
mode of relationality alive in theories of depression' (Wilson, 2015: 74).
Additionally, it should be highlighted that the depressed subject often
experiences a myriad of psychosomatic alterations: the numbness and
anxiety which we mentioned above, but also other rhythmic disturbances

such as that of changing appetites, altered sleeping habits, sexual desire, and even cardiac arrhythmia (Volkan, 2009: 95).

Freud's individualisation and pathologisation of depression, diagnostically and therapeutically (where the object-goal of which is to construct secure affective scaffolding and ontological security for the *I*), forms a useful starting point for our scaping of the happiness-depression ecology in relation to rhythmic subjection today. Indeed, the conceptual and therapeutic individualisation conducted by Freud in this text bears strong similarities to contemporary psychotherapeutic trends of individual responsibilisation in relation to depression. (Recall, further, how *responsibilisation* can function as part of the process of identity filtration, which we noted with Lazzarato in Chapter 3.) But what precisely is it that individuals are responsible *for* in the contemporary context? Our response to this has already been gestured towards: today, individuals are responsible for making *profitable investments on their human capital*, in which to invest in one's human capital is to pursue happiness: the capitalist promise of the alignment or synchronisation of affective and material prosperity. Such investments are by no means limited to one's labour, but extends to one's leisure, one's personal relationships, one's consumption habits, one's education, one's practice of child-rearing, and so forth (Becker, 1990, 1993a, 1993b; Schultz, 1960, 1971).

Sites of human capital are responsible *for their personal* (psychosomatic and material) *resilience and growth*. A firm whose entrepreneurial owner has made profitable investments on that firm's capital is a firm that has *resilience* (to recessionary or depressive shocks in the economic environment) and a firm that *continually* (or *perpetually*) *grows* (also see Han, 2015: 42). Such, likewise, is the site of human capital: the affective quality of happiness possessed by the secure capitalist *I* becomes a measure of one's self-investment. The *responsible* and *entrepreneurial* individual is he who makes profitable investments on his human capital, cultivates resilience against external shocks, and through this resilience and profitability, continually 'grows' (accumulates economic, human, and social capital (to name only three examples)). There is a model and *telos* in the mental environment of the capitalist milieu: the secure *I* engaged in the pursuit of happiness, the hero of our myth.[3] If an individual has not made such profitable self-investments, then *of course* that individual is responsible for his lack of resilience against external shocks, *of course* that individual is responsible for his lack of growth (or psychic vulnerability). The coded libidinal flows of the entrepreneurial individual engaged in permanent self-investment constitute a foundational *pulse* of contemporary capitalistic milieus, consistently re-securitising them: capitalist oxygenation through the rhythms of everyday life. The depressed subject is thereby enframed to be a result of poor individual investment decisions.

The analogy being drawn here between the firm and the individual is not one that our rhythmic ecology can adopt. Nonetheless, to say that such an analogy *functions* as a mechanism of rhythmic subjection in the contemporary mental environment is to make a different point. Barbara Ehrenreich, in her famous *Smile or Die*, highlights how this analogy tends to function:

> But if early capitalism was inhospitable to positive thinking, 'late' capitalism, or consumer capitalism, is far more congenial, depending as it does on the individual's hunger for *more* and the firm's imperative of *growth*. The consumer culture encourages individuals to want more – cars, larger homes, television sets, cell phones, gadgets of all kinds – and positive thinking is ready at hand to tell them they deserve more and can have it if they really want it and are willing to make the effort to get it [. . .] If optimism is key to material success, and if you can achieve an optimistic outlook through the discipline of positive thinking, then there is no excuse for failure. The flip side of positivity is thus a harsh insistence on personal responsibility [. . .] the promoters of positive thinking have increasingly emphasized this negative judgment: to be disappointed, resentful, or downcast is to be a 'victim' and a 'whiner.'[4] (Ehrenreich, 2010: 8–9)

William Davies wonderfully terms this as the 'entanglement of psychic maximization and profit maximization' (2015: 177). Today's pursuit of happiness – and we are taking here the limit-case of happiness in our happiness-depression ecology functioning through mechanisms of responsibilisation – is the effective and efficient management of one's human capital involving competitive and individualist self-actualisation, the material satisfaction of one's material desires, and profitable investments that enhance one's resilience and ensure growth towards the attainment of the affective quality of happiness produced in the supra-personal imaginary. The self-entrepreneur, 'who accepts the rule of the competitive game' (Lazzarato, 2017: 20), thrives off his personal responsibility for his resilience and growth, including his psychic or conscious well-being: *libidinal flows coded in such a manner as to make the support of the ontological security of the capitalist milieu coincide with the pursuit of happiness in the rhythms of everyday life.* It is important to note, here, that it is not necessarily entrepreneurial to be engaged in labour at all times: to acquire social and cultural capital, for example, one must be 'well rounded' or

have a 'work-life balance'. The self-entrepreneur maximises his mar-
ginal rate of productivity and efficiency in part through strong social
and communication skills (Lazzarato, 1996: 137), and by taking enough
'time off' (time filled with patterns of consumption and the acquisition
of various forms of cultural capital (such as the acquisition of John Stuart
Mill's famous *higher pleasures* (Mill, 1906: 12–14)) so that he can remain
affectively invested in the cultivation of his human capital, all in order
to ensure his perpetual growth: obeying the injunction to 'be yourself'.

Depression functions as a flip side of this, as the other limit-case in a
happiness-depression ecology which functions through personal responsibilisation. Depression constitutes the *failure* of the individual to manage
his human capital, his *failure* to be adequately ruthless and competitive,
such a subject is *soft* or *fragile*, not resilient, and, further, such a subject *contracts* rather than *grows*. Such is the ruthlessness of the happiness-
depression ecology in many contemporary capitalistic milieus. What
existential refrains are available to the *depressed*, or *contractive*, subject in
these capitalistic milieus? This can be answered with a clarification on the
use of the term *contraction* in this case. In previous sections and chapters,
we have repeatedly noted how the first synthesis of the living present
requires the mechanism of *contraction* for the generation of repetition and
expectation, and, so, for the production of rhythmic parameters of ontological security. Contraction in this sense helps generate security. Recall,
further, how we noted that pulsive flows establish ontological security
through connections as well as the contraction and delimitation of iterative or periodic repetition: secure rhythms of everyday life. Libidinal and
temporal contraction being vital for the constitution of ontological security. However, the contemporary depressed subject today faces a rhythmic assault on this mechanism of contraction, and, so, faces a context
of *felt* permanent insecurity, materially, socially, physically, psychically,
and at times all of these. This applies, although differentially, to the contemporary *precarious* subject who has *no* guarantee that their economic
and social security is forthcoming, and to many in the *cognitariat* who
work in relatively well-paid jobs with relatively higher levels economic
and social security (this is not to ignore the fact that many are *simultaneously* precarious workers and cognitive workers).[5] Consider, further,
the corporate worker whose rhythms of everyday life are traversed by a
pressure-cooker working environment which quickly sweeps away anything like the possibility of a distinction between labour time and leisure
time, and who, further, while receiving higher levels of economic and
social security than the precarious worker, is nonetheless in a milieu of
fear, competitiveness, and insecurity insofar as those are the atmospheres
generated in the hierarchical strata of corporate environments. Or, and

importantly, the felt permanent insecurity of those who are the objects of systemic paranoiac violence, discrimination, and exploitation (racially, materially, sexually, culturally, and so forth). The experiences of racism become embedded in the rhythms of everyday life of those subject to it, constituting a process of material, social, and psychic disempowerment within the milieu (Brown et al., 2000; Williams and Williams-Morris, 2000; Reid-Musson, 2018); individual pathologisation of the depression that emerges from these particular rhythms of everyday life serves only to efface the conditions of this emergence and potentially reinforce aspects of it in the context of institutionalised racism and inequalities in therapeutic distribution (Monk, 2015).

Depression is not entirely reducible to these suggested surrounding contexts, and as such, the experience of depression resists theoretical homogenisation – relative as it is to the manner in which the milieu orients becomings – but it is certainly not an implausible or unpredictable response to these contexts, especially with the insisting rhetoric of personal responsibilisation soliciting filtration. In addition, work at the intersection of clinical psychiatry, molecular psychiatry, and neuropsychiatry continues to search for, and represent, neural correlates of depression – for example: changing brain structures and function during depression (Leuchter et al., 1997), the involvement of different regions of the brain (Nestler et al., 2002; Fitzgerald et al., 2008), the potential suppression of neurogenesis due to stress as precipitative of depression (Jacobs et al., 2000), and the neurobiology of depression more generally (Laasonen-Balk et al., 2004; Saarinen et al., 2005, cited in Volkan, 2009: 97) – but here our focus is concerned more with the conditions through which contemporary capitalistic milieus continuously produce depression in the mental environment, which, while always neurologically actualised, is not auto-produced by the brain.

The sense in which the *depressed subject* is *contractive* is not in the sense of having stable rhythmic parameters of ontological security. Rather, the depressed subject is contractive precisely in the sense that the depressed subject is *rhythmically subjected as responsible for her depression*, as *responsible for her lack of resilience and growth*, and as responsible for the narrowing (contracting) range of existential refrains available the milieu she navigates, and often therapeutically attended to through individualising work which seeks to secure re-scaffold the secure *I* engaged in the pursuit of happiness. (Recall the quote we used at the top of this section, which identified depression as a 'disorder' which harms 'productivity', constitutes an attack on the vital profitable 'asset' that is the brain of the embodied worker.) As responsible for her lack of resilience and growth, the depressed subject *experiences* a *contracting* range of existential refrains, a felt powerlessness or frozenness, indecision, sometimes unworthiness, a lack of desire or directedness towards the future, and, by extension, experiences the *rhythms of everyday life* as demands which she is unsure she will be able to navigate without breakdown; as such, the *rhythms of everyday life* often become a milieu for *the continuous production of anxiety*. Through responsibilising mechanisms of identity filtration, the depressed subject often practices what Byung-Chul Han calls an 'auto-aggressivity' (Han, 2017: 7) through which perceived psychosomatic and/or economic 'failure' is taken as indicative of a personal abnormality or failure to play the entrepreneurial game well, a game which encompasses life and the pursuit of happiness as such in contemporary capitalistic milieus. What is contracted, through responsibilisation, is the quantitative range of existential refrains (already qualitatively narrow) that can be rhythmically negotiated in a given capitalistic milieu with security. Let's lean again on Berardi:

> Depression thus presents itself as a sickness of responsibility in which the feeling of insufficiency dominates [. . .] Depression is intimately linked to the ideology of self-fulfilment and the happiness imperative. And depression is also a way of identifying, in the language of psychopathology, a kind of behaviour that wasn't clearly identifiable as pathological outside of the competitive, productivist and individualistic context. There is no competition without defeat, without failure, but the social norm cannot recognise the normality of failure without putting into doubt its ideological foundations, without putting into doubt its economic efficiency. (Berardi, 2005: 61–62)

When the *rhythms of everyday life* become a process for the *continuous production of anxiety*, the depressed subject finds it increasingly difficult to *direct* itself towards the future insofar as the present is experienced as one of depression and as anxiety-provoking. The rhythmic subjection of depression is the production of the depressed and anxious subject who is responsibilised for her 'failure' to fulfil the 'happiness imperative' of today (that is, enhanced resilience and perpetual growth). For Lazzarato, *depression* constitutes our contemporary malady:

> Neurosis is the pathology of a bygone capitalism: the 'malady' of the twenty-first century manifests itself in 'depression': the powerlessness to act, to decide, to undertake projects; passive individual resistance to generalized mobilization, to the injunction to be active, to have plans, to get involved. (Lazzarato, 2015: 186–187)

The rhythmic subjection of depression here functions as an *effacement* of the mechanisms which render *necessary* (as the Berardi quote noted) that 'failure' (and intense economic punishment for this failure) and disempowerment are a crucial part of the functioning of capitalistic milieus as such. That is, it effaces how (1) economic failure is a necessary component of the capitalistic game; and (2) how processes of responsibilisation and individualisation of depression function importantly to maintain the continuous reproduction of capitalistic milieus. The function of rhythmic subjection in a *disempowering* sense tends towards a trend of *adaptation* rather than *adoption* (which we will come back to later in this section), regardless of the location one finds oneself in the happiness-depression ecology. This is also to say, as with the distraction-attention ecology, that the tendency is one through which it is becoming increasingly difficult to sculpt alternative futures and alternative mental environments.

Claim Two: this happiness-depression ecology is becoming increasingly imbricated with rhythmic containment, that is: (1) the depressed subject's necessary submission to pre- and supra-personal intervention for the purposes of therapeutics; and (2) the capture and commodification of depression as well as its subordination to capital accumulation. Not only does this double process leave the capitalistic milieu untransformed, it also enhances its very ontological security.

In order to develop this second claim, on the relationship between the happiness-depression ecology and rhythmic containment, we will shift our focus to the pre- and supra-personal elements, those 'surrounding mechanisms' of the rhythms of everyday life. A key focus of this section is the examination of the processes through which the extreme tendency of depression is *insinuated* and *captured* into mechanisms of rhythmic containment. In other words, those processes through which *containment becomes a condition for depression- and anxiety-focused therapeutics.*

We treat therapeutic technologies here in a broad sense, but we will be taking a few key examples. These will include psychopharmacological therapeutics, therapeutics based on research in neuroplasticity, and brain imaging technologies, all of which are developments in contemporary neuroscience which have filtered out not just to mental health therapeutics, but also in marketing strategies.

The pre- and supra-personal levels are extensively engaged with by psychopharmacological therapeutic technologies. Increasingly, and this is our claim here, *the depressed subject is solicited to submit themselves to rhythmic containment as a condition for therapeutic practices.* Such a solicitation is indissociable from a mental environment coloured by the insistence of personal responsibilisation for experienced depression, from a felt failure in relation to one's level of self-investment in attaining the affective quality of happiness in everyday life, and by extension, for the felt necessity of *personal* transformation required to 'overcome' depression. The *telos* of capitalist therapeutics builds from the ground of personal responsibilisation and is libidinally charged through coded desires that submit to this ground, towards a state in which the secure capitalist *I* is re-scaffolded so as to resume its pursuit of happiness (earning money, spending money). To 'submit' oneself to containment as a condition for therapeutics is to submit oneself to intervention on the pre- and supra-personal levels to assist in the 'overcoming' of depression or the cultivation of 'resilience'. We will take three examples to discuss such pre-personal interventions: therapeutic technologies which lean on research from neuroplasticity (specifically, we will focus on certain types of '*mindfulness*'), psychopharmacology, and brain imaging more generally; the supra-personal element pertains to the contextualisation and socio-diagnostic norms of how 'depression' and other mental health issues are treated (individual pathologisation), as well as their *telos* of normalisation (therapeutic recovery, affective re-scaffolding of the *I*, and the continued pursuit of happiness). All of this is to say that this ensemble of pre-personal interventive strategies and supra-personal imaginaries which condense in the treatment of the depressed subject are, like any process of recording, aimed towards the *inscription* and *sedimentation* of particular habits, desires, practices, and memories in the depressed subject. The *contracting* possibilities of existential refrains for the depressed subject constitute a limit-case of the *arrhythmic tendencies* of capitalist milieus. Recall: we called *arrhythmic* those pulsive flows of desire which are *captured*, exhibiting the *minimum of rhythm* or the *maximum of rhythmic contraction* in its functioning (repetition with a *minimum* of difference, or *metre*). Arrhythmia freezes the virtual structure of the past, delimits patterns of practice in the present, and, so, *forecloses* the future. *Arrhythmic*, in the terms we developed in Part I, therefore, is not to be conflated with the *absence* of rhythm, but rather its metric minimum, its freezing, its resistance to multiplications of rhythm (eurhythmia, polyrhythmia). The depressed subject, in this sense, is produced *precisely* in line with the arrhythmic manner in which capitalistic milieus govern time and desire. The capitalist pursuit of happiness is a machine of sadness and disempowerment in the mental environment, and while the range of existential refrains may nonetheless expand through capitalist therapeutics, they are in the service of reintegrating the depressed subject into a milieu of a generalised *arrhythmia*.[6]

Moving on to our examples. The advent of neuroplasticity in neuroscience treats the brain, as the term suggests, as relatively *plastic*, which is to say as relatively *open to intervention and transformation*: when it comes to the brain, neuroplasticity forwards evidence that 'neither structure nor function were inscribed in the genes or fixed at birth' (Rose and Abi-Rached, 2014: 11). The acquisition and development of (organic) memory in the human, including learning processes, necessitates neuroplasticity (Kandel, 2009; Lewis, 2016: 194–198), especially so prior to around twenty-five years of age. The brain, subject to periodic (rhythmic) injections of new patterns of thought, can transform its habitual functions. New contractions, retentions, expectations, and, potentially, projections. Cognitive Behaviour Therapy (CBT), as the name suggests, is behaviour-focused therapy that, unlike many 'talking therapies' which operate through a level of subjective archaeology, is focused primarily on identifying potentially harmful thought patterns, and seeks to re-channel the libidinal flows and rhythms of thoughts and feelings in such a way as to reduce harmful patterns and magnify useful ones. Rather than a protracted qualitative 'depth' process of self-archaeology as in psychoanalytic methods, CBT often involves continuous practices of quantifiable 'surface' self-reporting (where patients are asked to accord numerical values expressive of the intensity of various thoughts and feelings) and the assignment of practices to be engaged in by the patient outside the therapeutic context (emerging both from a rejection of the Freudian unconscious and a growth in more quantitative-empirical methods in psychology). There are a wide variety of CBT variants, ranging from directed CBT which focuses on addictions, anxiety, depression, and so forth, to particular styles of CBT practices which practise slightly different methods, focusing on 'Acceptance and Commitment' (used sometimes, for example, as a therapeutic intervention into how individuals might cope with chronic pain (McCracken and Vowles, 2014)), 'Dialectical Behaviour Therapy', 'Mindfulness' based CBT, and 'Mindfulness Based Stress Reduction', to name just some examples. While Stoicism has undoubtedly been a key influence on the development of CBT, we will focus on the influence of certain elements of Buddhist meditation practices in contemporary variants of CBT ('mindfulness' or 'clear awareness' is translated from the Pali word *sati*, a central aspect of, for example, discourses and methods in the Theravāda tradition in Buddhism, and techniques of *vipasanā* (the Pali term usually translated as 'insight') in which *sati* is cultivated). Neuroscientific research has investigated the correlation between meditative practices and changing states of the brain (Lutz et al., 2004; Brefczynski-Lewis et al., 2007; Lutz et al., 2008a; Lutz et al., 2008b, cited in Harris et al., 2009) and continues to investigate these links (see, for example, Daniel Goleman and Richard J. Davidson's work *Altered Traits: Science Reveals How Meditation Changes Your Mind, Brain, and Body* (2017)). Further, research into clinical applications continues to investigate the applications of techniques of mindfulness, or the CBT umbrella generally, into mental health treatment (often alongside medication) (Shapiro et al., 2008; Wiles et al., 2012; Nakagawa et al., 2014; Pickert, 2014; Wiles et al., 2014; Nakagawa et al., 2017).

In the process of exportation from ancient Buddhist traditions to Western and secularised therapeutic techniques, some of which we will now explore, there is, no doubt, a diminution in the depth and scope of practices deployed: i.e., they become integrated into the capitalistic milieu. Goleman and Davidson highlight this by suggesting a distinction between 'deep paths' of meditation – in the aforementioned Theravāda Buddhism and Tibetan yogis (Level 1) and more secularised versions which retain many of the more intensive elements of the practice (Level 2) (see, for example, Harris (2015)) – and the 'wide paths' – under Level 3 they suggest those therapeutic techniques we already mentioned; under a further watered down Level 4 they put the current trends in mindfulness integrated with digital technology; and Level 5 contains their own project called 'Healthy Minds', which seeks to offer meditative practice to as many people as possible, but which is also integrated into ongoing scientific research (Goleman and Davidson, 2017: 3–4). For the purposes of this section, our focus in particular will be on Levels 3 and 4, which, we argue, have become increasingly integrated in the reproductive functioning of contemporary capitalistic milieus.

That is, the sense in which we are approaching mindfulness in this section will pertain in particular to its mechanisms of capture – the ways and manners in which the promotion and deployment of mindfulness techniques function to *support the ontological security of capitalistic milieus* – rather than engaging or igniting processes of revolutionary transformation.[7] CBT is a set of therapeutic techniques which functions in a space *between* both contemporary developments in the research on neuroplasticity and as a practice that actively promotes many of the methods of mindfulness. Mindfulness, and indeed much of the positive psychology literature (although these are by no means synonymous), in a great many cases functions to promote 'new thought patterns' through which the subject engaged in these therapeutic tactics is encouraged and solicited to cultivate a *distance* from one's feelings of depression and/or anxiety, a *distance* from one's rhythms of everyday life which are often so destabilising for the depressed subject, and, by extension, a *distance* from or *indifference* with respect to the very milieu or context which formed a crucial part in the production of the depressed subject, which remains strictly within the context of individualising psychiatric mechanisms in contemporary capitalistic milieus. The distance that is cultivated is a distance *from* the milieu, and, so, the process is one that can be fairly described as a process of *self-criticism* and *self-transformation*, while maintaining (or seeking to re-establish) a secure *I* which functions as the affective basis upon which future happiness will be pursued.[8] The individualising capitalist therapeutic intervention is dominantly framed in the supra-personal imaginary as a process of *correcting*, but maintaining, the capitalist *I*, the affective foundation for the pursuit of happiness: investing in one's mental health functions as an investment in one's human capital.

This retreat to the secure *I*, nonetheless, demarcates a non-immanent ontological independence of the subject(ed) from the milieu; the problem for the depressed subject, according to the practice of such strategies, is not the milieu, but it can be reduced to the way in which the depressed subject *relates* to its milieu. It is therefore the depressed subject's *responsibility* to cultivate an *alternative mode of relation* to its milieu through injections of 'new thought patterns' which her plastic brain will, in time, hopefully, habituate to. In other words, if we can say that the depressed subject's experiences a libidinous and rhythmic crisis in her rhythms of everyday life through the crushing psychic pain of depression, in which there is a lack of *synchronisation* or *misalignment* of her desires and rhythms with respect to how the milieu seeks to orient her becomings, then the individualised therapeutic process can be positioned as a process of *realignment* or *synchronisation* with respect to the proper desires and rhythms befitting the demands of the milieu. This is a profoundly arrhythmic synchronisation, however. Such techniques are ones of pre-personal intervention on the plastic elements of the brain. The depressed subject who practises mindfulness is solicited to submit her brain to pre-personal therapeutic intervention and transformation. Such responsibilisation pervades the 'self-help' and positive psychology literature, some of which identifies 'positive outlooks', the cultivation of optimism, and self-belief with material reward (Konings, 2014: 46) and increased efficiency and focus.

The submission to such pre-personal intervention through the practice of such therapeutic technologies is usually a submission practised out of a felt necessity for the depressed subject's need for therapy due to distressing psychic disempowerment, and, indeed, the point here is *not* that therapeutic interventions cannot reduce the intensity of the psychic struggle in the depressed subject's rhythms of everyday life, nor indeed do we reject the claim that transforming one's psychosomatic habits can result in the transformation of one's experience. Nonetheless, a key *function* of this solicited submission is a continuous process of the depressed subject's self-criticism and self-transformation so that she may 'better function' in the depressogenic milieu. Or, put tersely, a process through which the subject is solicited to cultivate *indifference* with respect to the milieu she occupies. As such, this solicited submission is a process through which the conduct of the depressed subject is conducted: 'developments in neuroscience have become entwined with what one might term "human technologies" – strategies for the government of conduct drawing upon empirical knowledge of the brain and beliefs about its relation to conduct' (Rose and Abi-Rached, 2014: 7). Capitalistic milieus, through this, remain unchallenged, while the depressed subject's therapeutic process – which requires submission to pre-personal intervention as a condition – is one of *adapting* to a depressive milieu. Davies captures this decontextualised therapeutic practice well:

> Treating the mind (or brain) as some form of decontextualized, independent entity that breaks down of its own accord, requiring monitoring and fixing by experts, is a symptom of the very culture that produces a great deal of unhappiness today. Disempowerment is an integral part of how depression, stress and anxiety rise. And despite the best efforts of positive psychologists, disempowerment occurs as an effect of social, political and economic institutions and strategies, not of neural or behaviour errors. To deny this is to exacerbate the problem for which happiness science claims to be the solution. (Davies, 2015: 250)

Psychopharmacology is similar, in this sense, to mindfulness and CBT, though its techniques of intervention are not consciously practised 'new thought patterns' but pharmaceutical products or technologies, potentially constituting a more 'direct' set of neurochemical interventions. Indeed, as already mentioned, it is often the case that psychopharmacological interventions are conducted alongside practices such as CBT so as to enhance the effectiveness of such pre-personal interventions, a process through which the depressed subject must continuously submit to pre-personal intervention on the behavioural and neurochemical levels in her rhythms of everyday life so that she may 'recover', and so that she may fully pursue happiness once more. Fluoxetine (Prozac) is perhaps the most widely known antidepressant and example of such a pharmaceutical technology. It is a selective serotonin reuptake inhibitor (SSRI) which functions, as the name suggests, through preventing serotonin – a neurotransmitter which helps in the regulation of, amongst other things, mood – from being reabsorbed, causing an increase in serotonin levels in the brain over time. The precise functioning of SSRIs is still not clear, and their effects often vary from one user to the next between a number of tendencies (ibid.: 166).

Antidepressants, and other similar medications (such as anti-anxiety medications) constitute a *molecular and neurochemical intervention* at the pre-personal level. Rose and Abi-Rached forebodingly call psychopharmacology the development of a 'new relation [. . .] between governing the brain and governing the soul [. . .] [The] mind could be modulated by molecular interventions' (2014: 8). Some of the early claims on the usefulness of Fluoxetine were around its apparent ability to help inject *psychic energy* into the rhythms of everyday life, to alter our neurochemistry to the extent that we could feel less *contractive*, less inadequate, less anxious, over time producing an energetic numbness, rather than the catatonic numbness which so often characterises depression: so that we may support the capitalistic milieu in a state of numbness. Nonetheless, the medicalisation and personalisation of depression as an illness potentially resolvable through psychopharmacological intervention is, once again, part of the process of responsibilisation we have been discussing: a pre-personal intervention which tightens the grip of rhythmic subjection, which restores rather than banishes the capitalist *I*, which seeks to reintegrate the libidinal flows and rhythms of everyday life of the depressed subject into ones which befit the milieu, all of which constitutes a psychopharmacological machine that dulls potential revolutionary flows through individualising responsibilisation. The depressed subject who has had her brain transformed by, say, a combination of CBT and psychopharmacological interventions is a subject who has been incentivised to *adapt* to the depressogenic capitalistic milieu; she will have become a better worker, a more content worker, more able to pursue the cultivation of resilience and personal growth (psychic and profit maximisation); that is, the image of happiness proffered in the supra-personal imaginary. Not only does the capitalistic milieu remain relatively unchallenged, but its security is enhanced by this transference.

To develop this further, and also to demonstrate how these interventions consistently reach beyond medical interventions, we will now turn to our third example: brain imaging techniques, made possible by new digital tertiary retentions, specifically Position Emission Topography (PET) scans and functional Magnetic Resonance Imaging (fMRI). Those who have access to these technologies are enabled to observe the brain 'as it processes experiences' to develop a *memory* of patterns of response, stimulation, and so on, and to subsequently develop mechanisms of intervention based on this *memory* of response patterns (the function of *recording* on tertiary retentions, therefore, emerges again as a crucial element). It is important to note that the *access* to these technologies is prominent among mental health screening research and practice, but also by advertising firms and researchers. Those who can access such technologies of observation thus have a privileged access to constructing possibilities of intervention on the pre-personal level. (The combination of brain imaging technologies with advertising firms constitutes the field of *neuromarketing* (*The Lancet*, 2004; Renvoisé and Morin, 2007), practitioners of which seek to intervene on the brain's pre-personal decision-making instincts for the purposes of soliciting consumption.) We will not focus on this example any longer than this quick gesture towards it, mainly to highlight the intense entanglement between strategies of knowledge production (research) on mental health and the brain, and how these research practices are situated in capitalistic milieus in which the combination of psychic and profit maximisation (our pursuit of happiness) is the imperative for ensuring the continual ontological security of capitalistic milieus.

In Tony D. Sampson's *The Assemblage Brain* he develops a discussion of the 'rhythmic brain', which will help us further contextualise contemporary techniques of neurogovernance within contemporary capitalistic milieus. In this account, he develops an account of the close relationship between the idea of *care* (whether taken in terms of industries tasked with care – health and social care, mental health care, education, etc.) as performing a rhythmic–attentional function. All therapeutics are particular mechanisms of care. Caregivers 'direct the rhythm of imitation' (2017: 175), helping to provide effective rhythmic parameters of ontological security (he uses the term 'affective scaffolding', which we have deployed throughout this chapter) to subjects. The caregiver is not always or necessarily one individual, which is why he expands this to develop the notion of '*systems of care*, namely, systems that intervene in the rhythmic flows between brains and sensory environments, providing alternative scaffolds' (ibid.). Given that any milieu is precisely that which provokes the organism to orient its becoming, any milieu functions as a *system of (rhythmic) care* or carelessness, providing (or failing to provide) affective scaffolding for the rhythms of everyday life. The capitalist *I* engaged in the pursuit of happiness through continuous investment in their human capital constitutes our contemporary *arrhythmic* scaffolding. Relating this more closely to contemporary capitalistic milieus, Sampson notes:

[C]ontemporary post-industrial sensory environments [. . .] play a significant role in once again rupturing harmony and repositioning subjects in the rhythmic flows of digital culture – although seemingly deterritorializing the copresence of the crowd brain, the quickening rhythm of digital culture brings together (or reterritorializes) cells, brains, people, crowds, publics, masses, and ubiquitous technologies into nascent sensory terrains. (Ibid.: 174)

What Sampson calls contemporary capitalist *neuropower* is a system of carelessness in which systems of care are increasingly subordinated to supporting the ontological security of the capitalistic milieus themselves, and in which we find further examples through elements of psychiatric and psychopharmacological interventions in mental health discussed. Consider the following quote from Nikolas Rose and Joelle Abi-Rached, which succinctly surveys the contemporary supra-personal imaginary pertaining to the contemporary research on the brain:

> A range of new practices is emerging around the governing of human 'embrained' existence – new experts advising us how to live with, manage and improve our brains; biopolitical activism and identity formation around capacities or disorders located in the brain; new modes of responsibilization urging individuals to care for their brain; and a new consumerization of the brain, offering us all manner of products, devices, exercises and the like to keep our brains healthy and maximize our brain power. In what some have termed 'the age of neurological reflexivity', we are urged to recognize not only that our brains shape us, but also that we can and should act on our brains through our conscious decisions: reshaping our brains to reshape ourselves. (Rose and Abi-Rached, 2014: 16; see also Rose and Abi-Rached, 2013)

The developments in neuroscience that we have been discussing have altered the contemporary imaginary on what the brain might be capable of. Take, for example, the literature on *neuroenhancement* and *transhumanism* (Kurzweil, 2005), both of which, in distinct ways, attempt to imagine, and argue for, how we might be able to create and control future evolutionary developmental vectors and hugely enhance our human (all too human) capabilities through further entangling our species with digital tertiary retentions and prosthetics. This normative push for neuro-enhancement is perhaps most forcefully argued by Julian Savulescu and Ingmar Persson, who claim that (moral) neuro-enhancement is not only desirable but also *urgently necessary* (2008, 2012, 2013). This imaginary of neuro-enhancement is not simply one of 'improving' our neurological capabilities, but also one of 'normalising' our brains when they show 'decreased' neurological capabilities. Insofar as it is a project for the professed 'improvement' of the evolutionarily and biologically limited, and finite human, genetic, and neural interventions which seek to rewrite the brain's pleasure centre are decidedly not off the table for transhumanists (Bergsma, 2000: 406–409), especially given the human's proneness to psychic suffering.

A consequent component of individual responsibilisation and neuro-reductionism of depression (in which we are responsible for our brains) in the contemporary supra-personal imaginary is the treatment of mental ill-health as presenting an *economic* problem, or more specifically, as something which is harmful to the proper functioning of capitalistic milieus: mental ill-health as a risk to economic health. Poor mental health is increasingly seen as a key reason for 'lost' productivity – as an indicator of 'decreased' neurological performance in many cases – as the quote at the top of this section indicates. Around 20 per cent of employees in North America and Europe consider themselves 'mentally disengaged' from their labour (such disengagement costs an estimated US$550 billion a year). In the UK, the 'cost' of mental health issues to the economy sits at around £117.9 billion per year (related to absence, disengagement, reduced productivity, medical costs, etc.) (McDaid and Park et al., 2022); the period from 1993–2014 saw a 35 per cent rise in adult reporting of severe mental health issues in the UK, with a concentration in younger people and women (Gilroy-Ware, 2017: 103). Further, the World Health Organization, in 2001, predicted that mental health disorders 'would have become the world's largest cause of disability and death by 2020' (Davies, 2015: 107). Employment emerges as one of the specifically capitalist therapeutic responses, with happiness as its proper *telos*, or what Sara Ahmed calls the *promise* of happiness, producing a certain attachment to the future, which can create 'a political and personal horizon that gives us an image of the good life' (Ahmed, 2008: 12) ('The desire for happiness sends happy objects forth, creating lines and pathways in their trail, as if we might find happiness by following these paths' (Ahmed, 2010: 161)). In the throes of COVID-19, this narrative was complicated, insofar as happiness lay beyond the horizon of crisis management. Fear, bereavement, and isolation were, for many, amplified in their affective intensity, atop our already-disrupted quotidian rhythms. Whatever relationship we had to our linear and cyclical rhythms prior to lockdowns, they were for many disrupted, transformed, blurred. For those able to work at home, or who in any case remained domesticated, new behaviour protocols were recommended for our self-optimisation: the daily walk, stretching, managing your dopaminergic rhythms. The capitalist subject invests in Stoic techniques during times of crises.

As Dawn Lyon and Rebecca Coleman (2023: 34; also see Nash and Lyon, 2023) chart in their rhythmanalysis of everyday life during periods of lockdown, spatial confinement literally *shrunk* the quotidian.

The capitalist milieu's large quantitative range of existential refrains was *contracted* further through this spatial delimitation: movement and mobility, as a vector through which the capitalist milieu promises a smooth space for happiness pursual, was in this sense disrupted. Nonetheless, this recent narrative complication of the pursuit of happiness presented by this period of crisis is nothing new: capitalism's promise is in this sense *permanently deferred* in that it is permeated, consistently, by crises. How, then, should the capitalist subject pursue their well-being and happiness?

In an independent review commissioned by the UK Government's Department for Work and Pensions entitled *Is Work Good for Your Health and Well-Being?*, Gordon Waddell and A. Kim Burton argue that no direct evidence can be used to argue that work is either beneficial or harmful to well-being, and indirect evidence suggests it is beneficial (Waddell and Burton, 2006: 21), and express scepticism that mental ill-health has any direct correlation with work volume (in terms of hours worked) (ibid.: 23). Noting, further, that stress (a partial measure of psychological well-being) produced through work is similar to stress produced through job insecurity, but at lower levels compared to, for example, unemployment or regional deprivation (ibid.: 24), they argue that the benefits of work can be said to outweigh the risks in terms of psychological well-being, and work even has therapeutic benefits and helps in the process of individuals achieving secure individual identities linked to their social roles and status (i.e., the securitisation of the egoic *I* in pursuit of happiness through stable employment rhythms). *Happier* workers are *more productive* workers, and productive workers are happier workers (Davies, 2015: 106–107). In line with those interventions conducted at the pre-personal level on the depressed subject, we see in such research (which is a part of the supra-personal imaginary) a localisation and responsibilisation of depression in the embrained body of the subject, whose 'happiness' is (quantitatively) measured by the level of *affective investment* he or she has in her rhythms of everyday life. Measuring depression by lost productivity and affective investment effaces any potential that continuous injunctions towards continuous productivity and perpetual growth might help in the production of the depressed subject who fails to live up to such insisting and constant demands. Indeed, to reiterate the point, insofar as the contemporary supra-personal imaginary pertaining to mental ill-health commonly treats it as largely *ontologically independent* from the capitalistic milieu in which such processes are generated, it is decidedly non-immanent, a blockage which maintains the arrhythmia of contemporary capitalism and its capture of the future.

Mechanisms of supra-personal intervention, however, go further than this non-immanent epistemological practice. There are further mechanisms, bound up with digital tertiary retentions, which capture and commodify depression- and anxiety-centred therapeutics to further insinuate consumption, production, capital accumulation, and, so, for the *continuous* or *perpetual* reproduction of the ontological security of capitalism. The specific example we will focus on here is that of interconnected digital tertiary retentions such as smartphones, laptops, tablets, etc., and their *gamified* 'lifestyle' applications. *Gamification* here refers to online applications or devices which allow a person to compete with others, or with yourself, and achieve digital rewards or increased 'rank' ('medals', 'achievements', 'levels', etc.). It is important to note that many of these applications can themselves be considered as *digital therapeutic technologies*, through which the system of care proffered by the milieu is one outsourced to technics or is exteriorised. What is gamified here are the *rhythms of everyday life* themselves, which are increasingly subject to data collection, quantification, and, so, rhythmic containment; the digital awards received are the constant *simulation* of the cultivation of resilience and perpetual growth, that is, a simulation and solicitation towards the rhythms of everyday life being dominated by the *constant investment in one's human capital*, reward systems which interlink with the dopamine rush and which thus can tie us into new feedback loops. Gamification also constitutes an affective *stimulation* on the pre-personal level, producing the sense of micro-accomplishments (run streaks and badges), exhibiting a 'specific temporality marked by immediate experiences of success and reward' (Han, 2017: 49).

Through the utilisation of gamified applications, individuals conduct, amongst other things, personalised mood tracking, exercise tracking (Fitbit, WHOOP), meditative practices (Headspace, Calm, Ten Percent Happier), sleeping and eating habits (Sleep Cycle, MyFitnessPal), alcohol consumption (Untappd), personalised GPS tracking, all of which is used by providers to build up 'a careful picture of which regions, lifestyles, forms of employment or types of consumption generate the greatest mental well-being' (Davies, 2015: 5). Such applications, as with the strategies of brain imaging used in neuromarketing, are utilised so as to solicit, in the future, *future* lifestyle choices, *future* potential employment ventures, *future* types of consumption, and so forth (the control and neutralisation of the maximum number of existential refrains). That is, these digital therapeutic technologies solicit pre- and supra-personal intervention for the purposes of access to those therapeutics, and seek to capture and commodify such therapeutics for capital accumulation through gamifying the rhythms of everyday life as ones constantly soliciting perpetual 'personal growth'. Recall Pettman's point that we highlighted in Chapter 3: we are encouraged to practise 'self-tailored lines of flight; all the better to *re*territorialize these into a continuous coding operation that can then anticipate, and incorporate, such options into the database' (2016: 87–88). The injunctions to self-experiment and self-record – fuelled and supported in part by neuroscientific research into psychopharmacology, brain imaging, neuroplasticity, and by gamified applications – are increasingly important tools for governments, intelligence agencies, and corporations to manage potential security threats (detecting abnormal behaviour), to incite productivity and dull psychic pain (happier, more productive, affectively engaged, and self-managing self-entrepreneurs), and for consumption (self-tailored advertisements and 'one-click' consumption), and, therefore, perpetual growth and capital accumulation: the pursuit of happiness. Or: the perpetual reproduction of capitalism's ontological security, and decidedly not as a system of care. The happiness-depression ecology is one in which depression is not only continuously produced by capitalistic milieus, and effaced through individualisation, but through which *responses* to this depression are captured for the purposes of *supporting the security of these capitalistic milieus themselves.*

Claim Three: these processes of rhythmic subjection and rhythmic containment, in relation to the happiness-depression ecology, tend towards the production of a milieu in which existential refrains are ones of adaption rather than adoption.
We have made a few gestures towards the distinction between *adaption* and *adoption* evidenced in some of the tendencies we have been discussing in our contemporary happiness-depression ecology. This is a distinction important to Stiegler, which he again develops from Leroi-Gourhan (1993: 245–251), and is a distinction related to Stiegler's organological methodology which examines the interactions and transformations between humans and tertiary retentions (or technical objects) as another vector in the evolutionary process. What Stiegler calls *adoption* involves the ability – to develop it in our terminology – to *produce, access, control, and transform* tertiary retentions (i.e., participate in or contribute to culture); an 'adoption' of a milieu involves an *engagement with* and *transformation of* the milieu in question. For Stiegler, our ability to produce, access, control, and transform tertiary retentions is intimately connected to our ability to invest in and sculpt alternative futures, as Gerald Moore highlights with clarity here:

> The extent of our adoption of technics, namely our access to the technologies through which society operates, is what determines our ability to participate in the construction of the institutions

and values in which our artificial environment consists. Given the overwhelming inertness of our genetic inheritance, it is also through the adoption of different technics (clothes, books, and so on) that we differentiate (or 'transindividuate') ourselves within a group. By enabling the active construction of a future, an 'à-venir' that is not simply that passive acceptance of what one 'becomes' ('deviant'), adoption is what makes technical evolution irreducible to Darwinian adaptation. (Moore, 2013: 25)

In Chapter 1 we mentioned the habitual and non-reflective manner in which our relationship to technical objects can become inscribed in the flows of desire, what Simondon called a 'minority' status of technics. Drawing on Simondon, we can say that 'adoptive' processes in relation to our relationship with technics must overcome this minority status. He notes:

The prime condition for the incorporation of technical objects into culture would thus be for man to be neither inferior nor superior to technical objects, but rather that he would be capable of approaching and getting to know them through entertaining a relation of equality with them, that is, a reciprocity of exchanges; a social relation of sorts. (Simondon, 2017: 105)

If *adoption* is an engagement with and transformation of the milieu, a transformation itself incorporating a transformed relationship to technics, *adaption* or *adaptation* is a *response* to the milieu through which *we* change according to the standards of the milieu (technics remaining in a 'minority' status). Adaption is the process whereby it is the *self* who transforms so that he or she may 'fit' in the milieu: treating the milieu as transcendent or unchangeable. Adaption as (ontological) indifference with respect to the milieu, and as arrhythmic integration. The happiness-depression ecology we have scaped in this section is traversed by vast and extensive mechanisms of governance through which we are solicited to pass through a process of responsibilisation for depression, through processes of self-criticism and self-transformation, and through processes of rhythmic containment (where submission to containment is becoming a condition for therapeutics, and then utilised to solicit further consumption, production, and capital accumulation), thereby maintaining and reproducing the ontological security of depressogenic capitalistic milieus. These are our *adaptive* responses to capitalistic milieus and, in the specific case of the happiness-depression ecology, our adaptation to these milieus involves not only that we transform ourselves according to the standards of the milieu (the cultivation of resilience, perpetual growth, psychic and profit maximisation), but that we *affectively invest* in the milieu as it is or however it becomes: this is what, above, we called the process through which the depressed subject's desires and rhythms are *realigned* or *synchronised* in a manner befitting the demands of the milieu. This capture of desire solicits, this is to say, not only that we *submit* to our exploitation but that we become libidinally integrated within its functioning: the 'ideological imperative to enjoy one's adaptation conveniently fits consumer capitalism's channeling of redemption into the purchase and consumption of short-term pleasure' (Moore, 2013: 31). Such are the processes through which the maximum number of existential refrains are 'controlled and neutralised' in our happiness-depression ecology (also see Berardi, 2015: 253).

It will be useful to end this section on a terminological note, or potential terminological tension, that may have been raised here. We have claimed that *adaption* involves a level of *affective investment*, or capturing of desire. We have also claimed, however, that adaption constitutes *indifference* with respect to the milieu. While this may appear initially unclear, these two claims are reconcilable insofar as they operate in two distinct senses and insofar as they pertain to the levels of practice and temporality. In order to be clearer about this, it is important to note that practices of *adoption* – which we will revisit a number of times – will preliminarily involve elements of an *investment* in the future, of the *transformation* of the milieu, the production of new supra-personal imaginaries, and the collaborative sculpting of new mental environments. The capture of desire in capitalistic milieus, however, has nothing at all to do with such long-term projects. Indeed, as we noted in the previous chapter, the obverse is the case. Insofar as desire is captured in contemporary capitalism and its milieus, its flows are *blocked* from igniting *differential transformations* of these very milieus. Or, put differently, *desire, in such cases, invests in its own (ontological) indifference and individuality with respect to the milieu, supporting and enhancing the ontological security of capitalism.*

b. Minority experiment two: milieu therapeutics/ institutional schizoanalytics

The revolutionary pole of group fantasy becomes visible [. . .] in the power to experience institutions themselves as mortal, to destroy them or change them according to the articulations of desire and the social field, by making the death instinct into a veritable institutional creativity. For that is precisely the criterion – at least the formal criterion – that distinguishes the revolutionary institution from the enormous inertia which the law communicates to institutions in an established order. As Nietzsche says; churches, armies, States – which of all these dogs wants to die? (Deleuze and Guattari, 1983a: 63)

Our first two claims in relation to the happiness–depression ecology were the following:

Claim One: the contemporary happiness-depression ecology tends towards the rhythmic subjection of depression.

Claim Two: this happiness-depression ecology is becoming increasingly imbricated with rhythmic containment, that is: (1) the depressed subject's submission to pre- and supra-personal intervention for the purposes of therapeutics; and (2) the capture and commodification of depression as well as its subordination to capital accumulation. Not only does this double process leave the capitalistic milieu untransformed, it also enhances its very ontological security.

How might we conduct an extemporaneous counter-actualisation in relation to happiness–subjection–containment? How might we redistribute the sensible in relation to this ecology from its current insisting rhetoric of personal responsibilisation, and the compulsory submission to containment for therapeutics?

For Berardi, a key source of the generation of depression in contemporary capitalistic milieus is the rhetoric of personal responsibilisation, felt economic insecurity, and injunctions towards permanent competition (2015: 46). However, as the research on *neuroplasticity* seems to indicate, our embrained bodies have a level of openness to transformation, which, as we argued above, is today tending towards *adaptive transformations* of accelerated, distracting, competitive, and depressive capitalistic milieus rather than an *adoptive transformation* of these milieus themselves. An extemporaneous counter-actualisation in relation to happiness-subjection-containment, building on this, would involve affirmative work that sought to collectively elaborate the intense entanglement and increasing ubiquity of depression in contemporary capitalistic milieus; such affirmative work could have the effect of *transferring* the object of therapeutics away from *just* the depressed subject, but a conduct of *common therapeutics* or *milieu therapeutics*: such would constitute the practice of co-creating a *caring milieu*. Insofar as such methods must be *immanently effectuated*, it is not the case that the transformation of the milieu would *ipso facto* dissolve the experience of depression, nor would it preclude individual therapeutics as such, nor practices such as mindfulness. A revolutionary strategy in the mental environment, here, must involve the creation of therapeutics that operate transversally between the subject and the milieu. Such milieu therapeutics would nonetheless, we could minimally predict, *transform* the aesthetic experience of the milieu (i.e., would constitute an *aesthetic intervention*), transforming the responsibilising *rhythmic subjection* of the depressed subject. Such *common therapeutics* bears the potential for the co-production of connections in the mental environment that we can call *solidaristic*. Such is one of the key motivations for our second potential vector of affirmative work; *minority experiment two: milieu therapeutics/institutional schizoanalytics*.

In a mental environment saturated by the insisting permanence of digital tertiary retentions, anxiety, depression, and increased social disjunction, and hyper-individualised modes of therapeutics, the collective production of such milieu therapeutics seems extremely difficult to ignite. However, we do find examples of such milieu therapeutics being conducted as minority experiments in Northern Ireland, Israel-Palestine, and the western Balkans; three sites of intense conflict and social disjunctivisation in the twentieth and twenty-first centuries, where, admittedly, the focus of such common therapeutics is more focused on healing intense divisions between groups.[9] Such examples of *milieu therapeutics*, however, in our elaboration of our second minority experiment, we will explicitly connect more broadly to practices of *schizoanalysis*. Consider the following quote, where Berardi is discussing Guattari:

> Guattari's philosophical, political, and schizoanalytical project aimed at re-focalization and singularization, *not adaptation*. Indeed, the goal of prevailing psychotherapeutic techniques was to enable the suffering organism to *adapt* to its social and technical environment [. . .] Guattari's schizoanalysis is based on the idea that healing is a process of singularization, not one of conformity. But this process of singularization implies a complex dynamics of the mutual transformation of the social environment and of individual minds. (Berardi, 2015: 253, our emphasis)

What might it mean to fold together these two notions of *milieu therapeutics* and *institutional schizoanalytics*, as we are doing now? Ian Buchanan will help us respond to this question. As he notes, schizoanalysis can 'usefully be considered an "incomplete project" because it exists in a state of "permanent revolution"' (2013: 163–164). Experimenting with the institution, or with institutional creation and processual transformation, as an *in principle incomplete process* functioning in part through *common therapeutics*, would constitute an experiment in *institutional schizoanalytics*. Such experimental institutional practices could, for example, be experimented with in the university, community education centres (and the formation of community education co-operatives), community psychotherapeutic initiatives, and other sites of knowledge and culture production (including but not limited to: publications, media production generally, and so forth), as well as through therapeutic and care-based initiatives.

The creation of new supra-personal imaginaries on what future 'well-being' might look like, how mental health care is situated and treated within the milieu, as well as the creation of new therapeutics in the service of existential singularisation, rather than normalisation, would in this sense become the objects of a common project of transformation in the mental environment; in short, that the psychic ecology of everyday life becomes an object of political struggle towards new, sustainable, and participatory mental environments. *Schizoanalytic institutions* might, to suggest some initial examples, function as experimental institutions that subjected their own functioning to *common therapeutics*. One example of such a common therapeutic might be what Connolly suggests as *role experimentation*. Role experimentation is the subjection of one's *rhythms of everyday life* within and between institutions to collective experimentation; role experimentation shuffles the common *disjunctivisation of rhythms of everyday life* enforced through hierarchical, materially, and psychically disempowering class, gendered, racialised (and so forth) divisions, producing new associations, new connections; that is, the co-production of solidarity, a pre-personal mode of therapeutics:

> [A]n institution is an organized hierarchy of roles in relation to energies and activities that overflow them, such as gossip, back-door deals, confusion, whistle-blowing, care, revenge, and secrecy; roles mediate between identities and institutions [. . .] such experiments can filter into the sensibilities, beliefs, identities, and larger political activities of those who initiate and respond to them [. . .] Indeed as such oscillations proceed, moments of stuttering, unfocused shame, laughter, and hesitation periodically arise, drawn from the element of noise that inhabits the spaces between roles and role bearers. There is no zone of complete neutrality in a world of role performances. Obedient performances in cumulative effect tend to support the existing regime as they insinuate its dictates into collective habits of perception, judgment, and action [. . .] *Our lives are messages. Role experimentation can disrupt and redirect the flow of authority, habit, institutional regularity, and future projection. It can also encourage others to look more closely at their own performances in this or that domain.* (Connolly, 2013: 184–185, our emphasis)

Such role experimentation could be effectuated through rotational roles in co-operatively run institutions (consider, for example, a co-operatively run university, or the famous La Borde clinic, in which Guattari prac-tised, and in which the 'patients' actively participated in the running of), through which the operative hierarchies – and the mental envi-ronments such hierarchies contribute to as well as other elements of the milieu – are continuously subject to confrontation and transforma-tion; the institution in a state of 'permanent revolution'. This resonates with the work of the SenseLab Project, which in its very institutional functioning seeks to:

> avoid reproducing not only hierarchy, but any self-perpetuating governing structure [. . .] The idea is to activate tendencies agitat-ing at the infra-individual level, in order to bring them to expres-sion in such a way that they play out transindividually, in collective experimentations whose improvisational character prevents what takes place from being attributable to individuals. (Massumi, 2017a: 38)

Importantly, as Massumi and Erin Manning also note, the question of 'failure' would in turn become the object of experimentation and negoti-ation. Rather than 'failure' becoming categorised as abnormalisation, we can think instead of incorporating our collaborative failed experiments as indicating the beginning of *new* rhythms of thought and practice; failure, that is, as incorporated into a rhythmic process and as *part* of that process, rather than as an harbinger of individualised reterritorialisation ('I am a failure') and pathologisation:

> Failures, for the SenseLab, have come to be thought of as oppor-tunities for the emergence of new techniques of experimentation: they push the collective toward an engagement with the limit of what can be thought/created in a particular context. Techniques of relation access their creative potential most when they oper-ate at the edge of what they are preconceived to do. For this to happen, they must embrace the eventuality of their own fail-ure as a creative factor in their process. (Manning and Massumi, 2014: 103)

To give another example: we noted in Chapter 2 how scaping's folds into its practice a critical openness, ethic of listening, and practices of decolo-nisation, aware that such a process is never finished 'once and for all', and that the revolutionary process is also a decolonising process. Earlier in this chapter, evidence was cited pertaining to the different mental health experiences of different subjects across lines of race and gender. To this we can add Brittney Cooper's (2016) reflections on the racialised politics of time, where she articulates what we could call a rhythmic reading in which racialised hierarchies dictate: the relative speed and slowness of reparative work; social inclusion; lifespans; and geographic displacement through processes of gentrification (to name some examples). The point we wish to emphasise here, and building on this, is that any attempt at institutional schizoanalytics/milieu therapeutics would necessitate the development of such an ethic of listening within the functioning of institutions and within new therapeutic practices as such. This listening could not simply be that of the practitioner-patient model: as we noted in Chapter 2, through *listening*, the secure self and meaning as such is ever-and-always at risk, and subject to attack through the production of a *new* sense (of self, of meaning). The ever-present possibility of such transformations produced by an ethic of open listening interlocks with the open nature of revolutionary processes: the revolutionary potential of listening. For us, in this sense, any putative revolutionary processes that did not centralise practices and processes of listening would lock themselves into arrhythmia. Jean-Luc Nancy highlights this point on listening incisively:

> To be listening is to be inclined toward the opening of meaning, hence to a slash, a cut in un-sense [*in-sensée*] indifference at the same time as toward a reserve that is anterior and posterior to any signifying punctuation. In the spacing out of the opening [*entame*], the *attack* of sense resonates, and this expression is not a metaphor: the beginning of sense, its possibility and its send-off [*coup d'envoi*], its address, perhaps takes place nowhere but in a sonorous attack: a friction, the pinch or grate of something produced in the throat, a borborygmus, a crackle, a stridency where a weighty, murmuring matter breathes, opened into the division of its resonance. (Nancy, 2007: 27)

Listening, in Nancy's sense here, pertains to a practice of *opening* oneself ('to be inclined towards the opening . . .') to that which is not known or has not been felt, an opening that leaves one vulnerable to sensing that which has not been sensed before. In other words, an opening to *learning*. Our point in drawing on this is to underline that the sort of transformative and collaborative practices we are discussing minimally require such practices of listening, opening to learning from others, through which none emerges untransformed.

Moving on. If role experimentation can be said to function 'within' and 'between' institutions as embrained bodies pass through and between them in their *rhythms of everyday life* (which is, in part, a mode of pre-personal therapeutics), our second example of institutional experimentation considers how *institutional schizoanalytics* produces a relationship between the institution and the milieu, which is decidedly *not* a relationship of indifference. We can call this example the *collective schizoanalytic singularisation of the institution*; the participation of the institution in the supra-personal imaginary (which is *cartographic* precisely in the sense that the *map participates in the territory*) (see Guattari, 2014: 26).

Such a process of schizoanalytic singularisation would constitute an institution engaged in *process of heterogenesis.* In other words, *actively engaged in the transformation of its milieu; creative adoption* rather than *evolutive adaption.* To return to the example of the SenseLab, Massumi notes that the hope of such a project involves an institutional expansion into forms of mutual aid (2017a: 39) through which institutions 'can contrive an effective freeing' (loc. cit.) from arrhythmic processes continually resecuritising capitalistic milieus. Institutions, with their at best seemingly *viscous* habits and structures, and as sites which function through the coding of desire and time, can become sites of veritable revolutionary transformation: the gathering of bodies and rhythms that institutions are, as such, indicates this (permanent) virtual potentiality, harbouring the potential for what Raunig calls 'an unending chain of instituent practices', and through which 'the overtaking of the state apparatus becomes a consolidation of constituent power, the institutionalization of the revolution becomes the invention of ever new monster institutions' (Raunig, 2016: 184–185).

But what do these two examples, and our folded practice of *milieu therapeutics* and *institutional schizoanalytics*, have to do with counteractualising the processes of rhythmic subjection and rhythmic containment in the happiness-depression ecology? Recall that rhythmic subjection, today, functions to *efface* the 'failures' that are central to the functioning of capitalistic milieus (in the pursuit of happiness, psychic and profit maximisation, and self-investment) – what Alliez calls the 'infinite becoming-unequal proper to the capitalistic universe (of subjectivity)' (1996: 154), or what Lazzarato calls the '"formal game" between inequalities – a game that must be instituted, and continually maintained and sustained' (2017: 7), which are the milieu's very conditions for 'competition' to be incited and for any 'successes' to emerge – and as a tendential trend towards adaption rather than adoption. That rhythmic containment, today, functions through the continuous insinuation of depression and its capture by digital and psychopharmacological, as well as non-immanent and individualising, therapeutic technologies, tending towards the enhancement of the capitalistic milieu's ontological security. Role experimentation, as just one mode of pre-personal therapeutics, seeks to shuffle institutional roles, and, as such, towards one in which the 'success/failure' binaries upon which competitive capitalistic milieus are organised dissolve into *adoptive* processes of collaborative and continual institutional transformation.

The social necessity of psychic and material 'failure' must become an object of revolutionary attack in our *counter-actualisation* of the happiness-depression ecology; in so doing creating a movement in line with the third synthesis of the future: radically opening the past, present, and future, shuffling the initial co-ordinates for decision-making, shuffling the micropolitical coding of rhythms and desire. Moreover, processes of schizoanalytic singularisation, as practices through which the institution is engaged in the participation in the supra-personal imaginary and transformation of the milieu, would be heterogenetic processes that push capitalistic milieus to their deterritorial border, disrupting their ontological security; such institutions would not cultivate 'resilience' and 'adapt' to capitalistic milieus, but engage in their transformation through processes that dissolved the rigidly hierarchical distribution of economic, political, socio-institutional, and psychic privilege upon which capitalistic milieus are presently enhanced through: capital instituting, as it does, a war of each individual against each other, and of each individual within himself. Once again, our claim here is that *participation in or creation of milieu therapeutics/institutional schizoanalytics* could constitute an 'opening of technicity' (Stiegler, 2015: 120) – institutions as arrangers and arrangements of organological conditions – transforming the mental environment and experience of the institution; that is, an *extemporaneous counter-actualisation* of *happiness-subjection-containment*.

c. Sculptural process two: sculpting caring milieus

> Schizoanalysis, rather than moving in the direction of reductionist modelisations which simplify the complex, will work towards its complexification, its processual enrichment, towards the consistency of its virtual lines of bifurcation and differentiation, in short towards its ontological heterogeneity. (Guattari, 2006: 61)

Our third claim in relation to the happiness-depression ecology was the following:

*Claim Three: these processes of rhythmic subjection and rhythmic contain-
ment, in relation to the happiness-depression ecology, tends towards the production of a milieu in which existential refrains are ones of adaption rather
than adoption.*

In section 5b, we offered the example of *milieu therapeutics/institutional
schizoanalytics* as an example of what an *extemporaneous counter-actualisation*
might be in the contemporary happiness-depression ecology. In this
example, we turned our attention to potential experiments that might
be conducted in universities, educational, and other institutions. We will
follow this example again, but will consider more precisely what it might
mean to participate in the *collaborative sculpting of milieus of care.* To begin
this consideration, we can first reiterate the point we made in the previous section, connecting the *short-termism* of capitalistic milieus with *systemic stupidity*, systems of carelessness in which therapeutic technologies
consistently reek to (re-)establish the affective scaffolding of the capitalist
I so that she may pursue happiness once more. Stiegler explicitly makes
this connection in *Taking Care of Youth and the Generations*:

> To take care means caring for an equilibrium always at the limit of
> disequilibrium, even 'far from equilibrium,' and it is also caring for
> a disequilibrium: it is taking care of *movement* [. . .] [Today] calls
> for a sociotherapy that is nothing less than the conceiving of a new
> age of the formation of care and attention for facing the care-less-
> ness of a global consumer society that we know is condemned to
> vanish. (Stiegler, 2010b: 180)

As with section c in Chapter 4, our suggestion here is that such a sculptural process could mobilise around three temporally orientated and
entangled strategic points. First, through confronting the conditions of
the present in the happiness-depression ecology we scaped in section 5a;
second, through the co-creation of new co-operative *therapeutic technologies*; third, through a collective sculpting of a constitutively open and
adoptive milieu which can *commonly* pursue heterogeneous futures and
thereby 'ward off', in Guattari's words, 'the entropic rise of a dominant
subjectivity' (2014: 46).

That our sculpting of milieus of care confronts the conditions of the
present is connected to our much earlier point, namely that the *rhythms of
everyday life* are in no sense *ontologically independent* from the milieus that we
navigate. Recall that insofar as the contemporary supra-personal imaginary pertaining to depression deterritorialises depression (and thereby,
therapeutics) as the *fault* of the depressed subject (who is responsibilised,

individualised, experiences a contracting range of existential refrains, and so forth) and as to some extent neurologically 'resolvable'. In this sense, the therapeutics that tendentially dominate the mental environment are also functionally *careless*, insofar as these therapeutics tend towards the continuous production of the adaptive and resilient subject and towards the increased ontological security of depressive capitalist milieus. This is functionally so when, for example, mindfulness techniques are deployed individualistically and narrowly instrumentally, towards making us less stressed, more efficient, more productive, more focused, and more able to pursue happiness. As we noted, mindfulness strategies and techniques are by no means reducible to such individualisation (and in terms of its place in Buddhism, broadly speaking, the obverse can be said to be the case); and, indeed, there is literature exploring 'shared mindfulness' (Krieger, 2005). Admittedly, the context of this research is more special-ised (it examines the communication tactics of aviation pilots in 'cockpit crisis' situations), but gestures towards, and helps us begin to elaborate, the co-creation of co-operative *therapeutic technologies*.

To repeat a clarificatory point we made earlier: this is not at all to *exclude* the potential necessity of therapeutic technologies which particu-lar embrained bodies could deploy within their particular psychosomatic positionality. The evolved milieu of the human body and the human brain is thrown − today into the context of a post-industrial milieu − into an array of challenges, affordances, incentives, and disincentives which the rhythms of everyday life constitute an attempted response to. As such, and given that experienced rhythms of thoughts and feelings are at least a cen-tral component of psychic suffering and the affective quality of everyday life − see, for example, Killingsworth and Gilbert's work, which concludes with the claim that 'a human mind is a wandering mind, and a wandering mind is an unhappy mind. The ability to think about what is not hap-pening is a cognitive achievement that comes at an emotional cost' (2010: 932) − then new therapeutic technologies must concern themselves with tactics at the level of the body-brain nexus as well as at the level of the milieu. Recall what we mentioned earlier with Goleman and Davidson's distinction between the 'deep' and 'wide' paths through which meditative practices can be pursued. Guattari was prescient on and prefigured such a distinction whenever a similar meditative 'vogue' was prominent:

> Consider the practice of transcendental meditation now so fashion-able in the United States: we may find it developing into an organ-less body opening desire out onto an a-signifying outside world, or, equally, closing in upon a signifying activity that alienates indi-viduals in line with the values of authority. (Guattari, 1984: 151)

Overwhelmingly, contemporary capitalist milieus are functioning increasingly to incorporate such practices in line with the latter option. This is, however, by no means determined. For our purposes, the point is to move towards the transformation of the 'object of care' from the subject *to* the subject *and* the milieu transversally. What becomes the object of care, or object of collaborative attention, is not the subject and the subject's relation to the milieu – or, rather, not just this – but the mental environment, the local milieu as such, and how it might be transformed. The object being, in this case, the creation of a new shared mental environment and new modes of relation; a *new milieu*. The co-creation of co-operative therapeutic technologies could, in this sense, incorporate a collective schizoanalytics of – or a co-operative therapeutic technological focus on – the mental environment that those in the milieu in question co-occupy, co-creating a collective object of attention or care which could then be subjected to experimental action and social sculpture in each case.

In contemporary capitalistic milieus, confronting the conditions we scaped in section 5a, and to continue the work of our second minority experiment, such co-operative therapeutic technologies could pass through a schizoanalytics of continuous injunctions towards continuous productivity, perpetual growth, and the abnormalisation of 'failure' (despite its structural necessity in capitalistic milieus) so as to co-create 'new micropolitical and microsocial practices, new solidarities, a new gentleness' (Guattari, 2014: 34) through which 'new existential configurations' (Guattari, 2014: 30) – new ways of being – could be created. This, it seems minimally, requires *long-term attention* and *patience*, which is also to say again, *care*. For such existential configurations (singularising existential refrains) to emerge – that is, for adoptive milieus to emerge – the collective sculpting of milieus of care cannot proceed either through eschatological (finalist, non-immanent, transcendent) 'general models' nor, relatedly, though the exclusion of 'abnormal particulars' from the process of social sculpture. Such general models and exclusionary practices, operative in (though not only in) contemporary capitalistic milieus, constitute a *blockage* to singularising existential refrains, that is, it is partially through these components that existential refrains are 'controlled and neutralised'. Further, any such model or any such practice runs the permanent risk of lapsing into *carelessness*. In effect, such 'models' and practices which 'abnormalise particulars' are in part an effect of *impatience* and/or *systemic carelessness*. This *impatience* and *carelessness* of capitalistic milieus is manifested through its demand 'that all singularity must be either evaded or crushed in specialist apparatuses and frames of reference' (Guattari, 2014: 33), which we articulated previously as the large *quantitative range* but narrow *qualitative scope* of sustainable existential refrains available in contemporary capitalistic milieus. As urgent as such practices may be, the revolutionary sculptural transformation of our capitalistic milieus is a cross-generational and long-term task. The space-time for rhythmic dramatisation here is produced through the collective sculpting of milieus of care, patient milieus, milieus which are *shared* and *solidaristic*, but are nonetheless – or better yet, are *thereby* – *heterogenetic*. Guattari again pre-figured us on this:

> Given a gridding of equipment, what politics of a collective assemblage is it possible to envisage? Where to begin? *Obviously only the preparation of collectively elaborated monographs could allow such questions to be suitably tackled!* [. . .] [Our analytic] task would not be limited in this domain to an external examination, to 'expert' interventions, but which would have to facilitate the collective taking in charge in determinate micropolitical domains. (Guattari, 2016: 36, our emphasis)

Returning to the exclusionary 'frame of reference' pertinent to us: the competition-success-failure nexus which we have met a few times, or quite simply the *pursuit of happiness*, a crucial assemblage of components in the contemporary supra-personal imaginary. This nexus constitutes a generalising frame encompassing the central importance of material reward, personal responsibility for success and failure, as well as the imperative to compete, consume, produce, and through this self-actualise and self-optimise; the depressed subject's *rhythms of everyday life* in capitalistic milieus involve continuous daily negotiation with these pervading mechanisms of identity filtration, negotiated, crucially, from a particular positionality that tendentially affects these rhythms in different ways. The impatience and carelessness of this dominant frame of reference or 'dominant subjectivity' is evidenced in the tendential, and often ruthless, *blockage* effectuated on those who do not 'fit' such models quickly and successfully; contemporary capitalistic milieus, in this specific sense, *do not care*. This is evidenced in the insinuation as well as the commodified *capture* of depression we scaped in section 5a, but of which there are plenty more examples. Indeed, our *sculpting of caring milieus*, creatively confronting this blockage, would seek to *engender singularising participation in the supra-personal imaginary*, such an engendering functioning through *care*, *patience*, as well as the collective sculpture of '*dissensus* and the singular production of existence' (Guattari, 2014: 33). Capitalistic milieus, today, in part through *systemic careless* and *impatience*, block the collective sculpting of sustainable, long-term, inclusive, and participatory circuits. Here, we pursue a process of rhythmic dramatisation through *collectively elaborated and co-operative therapeutics*, functioning as a caring, open, and patient process through which we can collectively sculpt the milieu anew. In this sense, such sculptural processes are slow and piecemeal, but as Guattari reminds us: '*revolution is either processual or it isn't revolution*' (Guattari, in Guattari and Rolnik, 2007: 260); and Beuys underlines:

> [T]he formula 'every man [sic] is an artist' [. . .] refers to the transformation of the social body. Every man [sic] can, indeed must, take part in this transformation if we are to succeed in this great task. Because if one voice is missing in the work on this social plastic which first must be expressed, I say if one voice is missing, if it does not participate, we will have to wait a long time for the transformation, for the new societal construction. (Beuys, 1994: 24, quoted in Stiegler, 2015, 72, our additions)

d. Conclusion

The explosion in depression, anxiety, suicide, and so forth, constitutes one of the most serious and difficult issues with which we are currently confronted in contemporary capitalistic milieus – both in terms of the tendential effect these trends have in the sense of psychological well-being and in terms of the ways in which libidinal energies are rhythmically reintegrated into further perpetuations of milieus that do not care – our response to which will play a key role in shaping the milieus-to-come. The distressing and disempowering impacts of the experience of depression, anxiety, and other forms of mental distress, as well as the hardened psychic ecology through which it is actualised, is a differential but nonetheless *shared* experience in the mental environment. We can affirm these differences while retaining aspects of this shared experience in a process of creating new solidarities and creating new *caring* milieus that situate our psychic ecologies within these shared mental environments and towards new futures that centre participation, collaboration, listening, and sensitivity to singular experiences. Our depression, happiness, and psychic ecologies can become, this is to say, the object of a new political struggle.

e. Chapter 5 reprise

[79] The *happiness-depression* ecology is an ecology of the mental environment produced in capitalistic milieus: (the) *happiness* (of the *I*) is (re) produced as the specifically capitalist object and measure of life.

[80] Capitalistic milieus produce and rely upon crises and depressions in the socio-economic environment precisely to the same extent that they do so in the mental environment and psychic ecology of everyday life.

[81] Contemporary capitalistic milieus are machines for the continuous and permanent production of depression and disempowerment, producing depression and seeking to govern its reintegration into the functioning of the milieu in a toxic and arrhythmic feedback loop.

[82] The contemporary happiness-depression ecology tends towards the rhythmic subjection of depression.

[83] The *responsible* and *entrepreneurial* individual is he who makes profitable investments in his human capital, cultivates resilience against external shocks, and, through this resilience and profitability, continually 'grows' (accumulates economic, human, and social capital); the model and *telos* in the mental environment of the capitalist milieu: the secure *I* engaged in the pursuit of happiness, the hero of our myth.

[84] As responsible for her lack of resilience and growth, the depressed subject *experiences* a *contracting* range of existential refrains, a felt powerlessness or frozenness, indecision, sometimes unworthiness, a lack of desire or directedness towards the future, and, by extension, experiences the *rhythms of everyday life* as demands which she is unsure she will be able to navigate without breakdown; as such, the *rhythms of everyday life* often become a milieu for *the continuous production of anxiety*, often therapeutically attended to through individualising work which seeks merely to securely re-scaffold the *I* engaged in the pursuit of happiness.

[85] The rhythmic subjection of depression functions as an *effacement* of the structural economic mechanisms which render necessary that 'failure' (and punishment for this failure) and disempowerment is a crucial part of the functioning of capitalistic milieus as such. That is, it effaces how (1) economic failure is a necessary component of the capitalistic game; and (2) how processes of responsibilisation and individualisation of depression function importantly to maintain the continuous reproduction of capitalistic milieus.

[86] The happiness-depression ecology is becoming increasingly imbricated with rhythmic containment, that is (1) the depressed subject's necessary submission to pre- and supra-personal intervention for the purposes of therapeutics; and (2) the capture and commodification of depression as well as its subordination to capital accumulation. Not only does this double process leave the capitalistic milieu untransformed, it also enhances its very ontological security.

[87] To 'submit' oneself to containment as a condition for therapeutics is to submit oneself to intervention on the pre- and supra-personal levels to assist in the 'overcoming' of depression or the cultivation of 'resilience'.

This ensemble of pre-personal interventive strategies and supra-personal imaginaries that condense in the treatment of the depressed subject are, like any process of recording, aimed towards the *inscription* and *sedimentation* of particular habits, desires, practices, and memories in the depressed subject. The capitalist pursuit of happiness is a machine of sadness and disempowerment in the mental environment, and while the range of existential refrains may nonetheless expand through capitalist therapeutics, they are nonetheless in the service of reintegrating the depressed subject into a milieu of a generalised *arrhythmia*.

[88] These processes of rhythmic subjection and rhythmic containment, in relation to the happiness-depression ecology, tends towards the production of a milieu in which existential refrains are ones of *adaption* rather than *adoption*.

[89] An extemporaneous counter-actualisation in relation to happiness-subjection-containment, building on this, would involve affirmative work that sought to collectively elaborate the intense entanglement and increasing ubiquity of depression in contemporary capitalistic milieus; such affirmative work could have the effect of *transferring* the object of therapeutics away from *just* the depressed subject, but a conduct of *common therapeutics* or *milieu therapeutics*: such would constitute the practice of co-creating a *caring milieu. Such common therapeutics bears the potential for the co-production of connections in the mental environment that we can call solidaristic. Such is one of the key motivations for our second potential vector of affirmative work; minority experiment two: milieu therapeutics/ institutional schizoanalytics.*

[90] The social necessity of psychic and material failure must become an object of revolutionary attack in our *counter-actualisation* of the happiness-depression ecology; in so doing creating a movement in line with the third synthesis of the future: radically opening the past, present, and future, shuffling the initial co-ordinates for decision-making, shuffling the micropolitical coding of rhythms and desire. Moreover, processes of schizoanalytic singularisation, as practices through which the institution is engaged in the participation in the supra-personal imaginary and transformation of the milieu, would be heterogenetic processes that push capitalistic milieus to their deterritorial border, disrupting their ontological security; such institutions would not cultivate 'resilience' and 'adapt' to capitalistic milieus, but engage in their transformation through processes that dissolved the rigidly hierarchical distribution of economic, political, socio-institutional, and psychic privilege upon which capitalistic milieus are presently enhanced through: capital instituting, as it does, a war of each individual against each other, and of each individual within himself.

[91] As urgent as such practices may be, the revolutionary sculptural transformation of our capitalistic milieus is a cross-generational and long-term task. The spacetime for rhythmic dramatisation here is produced through the collective sculpting of milieus of care, patient milieus, milieus which are *shared* and *solidaristic*, but are nonetheless – or better yet, are *thereby* – *heterogenetic*. Our *sculpting of caring milieus*, creatively confronting this blockage, would seek to *engender singularising participation in the supra-personal imaginary*, such an engendering functioning through *care*, *patience*, as well as the collective sculpture of '*dissensus* and the singular production of existence', a process of rhythmic dramatisation through *collectively elaborated and co-operative therapeutics*, functioning as a caring, open, and patient process through which we can collective sculpt the milieu anew.

Notes

1. It is also to gesture in agreement, broadly speaking, with elements of Kate Pickett and Richard Wilkinson in *The Spirit Level* (2009) as to the relationship between *relative*, *felt*, and *known* levels of material inequality and felt unhappiness and depression in contemporary capitalistic milieus (or which they explore further in their more recent *The Inner Level* (2018)).

2. It is of note that Freud claims the precise opposite in the case of depression. He argues that the melancholic is defined in part by a lack of shame in most cases, and more so by self-exposure rather than self-silencing (Freud, 1957: 247). Psychological research, however, continues to associate self-silencing, and experiences of being silenced, with depression. Such research regularly frames the question of self-silencing and depression in gendered terms (Jack, 1993; Witte and Sherman, 2002; Tan and Brooke, 2008; Romero-Canyas et al., 2013; Swim et al., 2010), although evidence has shown correlation between the two across genders and cultures (Gratch, Bassett, and Atra, 1995; Cramer, Gallant, and Langlois, 2005; Flett et al., 2007). Interestingly, some of this research links tendencies of self-silencing directly to the milieu (rather than individual pathologisation) (Jack and Ali, 2010; also see Alleyne, 2004), and to traumatic experiences (such as pervasive systemic racial discrimination or experiences of war (Ritter, 2014)), supporting micropolitical work in order to combat it.

3. The reference to social capital is a nod to Pierre Bourdieu. For Bourdieu, 'Social capital is the sum of the resources, actual or virtual, that accrue to an individual or a group by virtue of possessing a durable network of more or less institutionalized relationships of mutual acquaintance and recognition' (Bourdieu, in Bourdieu and Wacquant, 1992: 119).

4. The point made here on 'early' (or 'industrial') capitalism is a claim Ehrenreich makes in agreement with Max Weber (2001) who, in his *Protestant Ethic and*

the Spirit of Capitalism, identified this stage of capitalism as bound up with more punitive structures and delayed gratification, and not on continual consumption and entrepreneurial optimism.

5. This equation of precarity and non-guarantism is made by Guattari and Antonio Negri in *Communists Like Us*: 'The non-guaranteed [i.e., precarious] constitute a fundamental point of support for the constitution of capitalist power: it is in terms of them that the institutions of repression and marginalization find their consistency' (Guattari and Negri, 1990: 76, our addition).

6. For a discussion, with Deleuze, of a notion of joy irreducible to pleasure, including some comments on the specifically *sad* dynamics that capitalistic milieus produce and are oiled by, see Heaney (2018).

7. For an extremely useful survey of some of these different approaches to the term 'mindfulness', see Helen Spencer-Oatey (2013).

8. It is on this point that the distinction between the 'deep' and 'wide' paths can be sharpened. Broadly speaking (we cannot do justice to the different schools and traditions here), Buddhism tends to emphasise the non-dual nature of experience, that is, the lack of a sharp distinction between subject and object, and thereby, egolessness (the Pali term is *anattā*, often translated as 'non-self'; the term *atta* is usually translated as 'self'). Consciousness experiences the *thought* of an *I* repetitively, and comes to grasp and identify with it, (mistakenly) grasping the *I* as if it were a permanent point of egoic-securitisation. Buddhism, in turn, emphasises *impermanence* foundationally (the Pali term being *anicca*): meditative practices can often involve engaging in a search for the secure *I*, which by definition fails, rhythmically flowing as it does in and out of consciousness. The *I*, and the grasping to an impermanent anchor of egoic-securitisation, constitutes in Buddhism the foundation of psychic suffering or unsatisfactoriness (here, the Pali term is *dukkha*), not the necessary foundation for the pursuit of happiness, as in contemporary capitalistic milieus. Buddhism, further, tends to recognise and centralise this reality of human suffering or unsatisfactoriness, especially psychic suffering, rather than efface it. Indeed, the dissolution of the subject/object distinction and experience of egolessness can combine into a worldly pursuit where the diminishment of worldly suffering emerges as a spiritual practice (for example, in Shāntideva's *Bodhicharyāvatāra* (*The Way of the Boddhisattva* (2006)). *Anattā, anicca*, and *dukkha* constituting, in the Theravāda Buddhism school for example, the three 'universal charateristics' (*ti-lakkhana*), of existence, derived from various statements in the teachings of the Buddha in *The Dhammapada* (Easwaran (trans.), 2007).

9. On this, see Dudouet, Fischer, and Schmelzle (2008) in relation to the western Balkans and Israel-Palestine, and Kelly (2005) in relation to Northern Ireland.

6

Debt-Credit Ecology

The infinite creditor and infinite credit have replaced the blocks of mobile and finite debts. There is always a monotheism on the horizon of despotism: the debt becomes a *debt of existence*, a debt of the existence of the subjects themselves. A time will come when the creditor has not yet lent while the debtor never quits repaying, for repaying is a duty but lending is an option. (Deleuze and Guattari, 1983a: 197–198)

The king's treasures: today we would say the nation's accounts, the gross national product, or the budget [. . .] Money is bereft of meaning, it has all the meanings. It is blank and polysemous. Money is pure number and naked calculation. They are faculties. Abstraction. (Serres, 1995: 38–39)

A rhythmanalysis of the debt–credit ecology in the mental environment may appear as an unclear object of analysis insofar as it invokes economic relations and processes at the level of the social environment and does not initially seem to map onto the sorts of libidinal and affective ecologies that concern Chapters 4 (attention-distraction) and 5 (happiness-depression). However, as we have known since, at least, Nietzsche, economies of indebtedness are as much moral, legal, and libidinal economies as material ones:

Have these genealogists of morality up to now ever remotely dreamt that, for example, the main moral concept '*Schuld*' ('guilt') descends from the very material concept '*Schulden*' ('debts')? [. . .] Throughout most of human history, punishment has *not* been meted out *because* the miscreant was held responsible for his act [. . .] but rather [. . .] it was out of anger over some wrong that had been suffered, directed at the perpetrator [. . .] held in check and modified by the idea that every injury has its *equivalent* and can be paid in compensation, if only through the *pain* of the person who injures. And where did this primeval, deeply-rooted and perhaps now ineradicable idea gain its power, this idea of an equivalence between injury and pain? I have already let it out: in the contractual relationship between *creditor* and *debtor*, which is as old as the very conception of a 'legal subject' and refers itself back to the basic forms of buying, selling, bartering, trade and traffic. (Nietzsche, 2017: 40–41)

The creditor-debtor relation, for Nietzsche, marks a perverse libidinal economy in which creditors institute hierarchies inasmuch as they extract pleasure from this very hierarchy and from the psychic, socio-legal, and economic punishments that are meted out to the debtor: 'Through punishment of the debtor, the creditor takes part in the *rights of the masters*: at last he, too, shares the elevated feeling of being in a position to despise and maltreat someone as "inferior"' (Nietzsche, 2017: 42). Pleasure extracted: recorded in the flows of desire, producing new feedback loops, the pleasure of hierarchy as the *telos* of our pursuit of happiness. Debt is indissociable from this history of the 'cruelest mnemotechnics' (Deleuze and Guattari, 1983a: 185). And who, precisely, is the creditor, who partakes in this cruelty? The creditor is the one who can be trusted, who can be believed, who has *credence* in the milieu, derived from the *credential* of being a *creditor*: such is the *creed* of the capitalistic milieu:

> [M]erchants, bankers and money changers [. . .] speculate on the future as much as they quantify time by assigning every object and every duration with a value, a price; with the generalized use of that extraordinary multiplier that was the bill of exchange. This was nothing more than a title, a draft drawn on time (and not a mere instrument of payment linked to a commercial operation requiring a different currency: the operation of exchange), associating *credit* with *credence* – confidence [*confiance*] with belief [*croyance*], the *fiduciary* with *fideism* [. . .] Such is the general economy of representation in its earliest emergence. (Alliez, 1996: 218)

Credit, credence, trust, confidence, and faith: the creditor is the one who pulls the milieu into the future, and who can judge the debtors in the milieu. The sphere of indebtedness, and of the creditor-debtor relation, does not limit itself to particular contracts, and comes to permeate the processes constitutive of the milieu. One becomes indebted to Christ, the community, society, leader, capital, etc., and it is to this or that object that one must sacrifice oneself for, pay compensation to, or redeem oneself in the eyes of for existing. 'Punishment' as such is produced differentially depending on the creditor whom one has offended: prison, hellfire, or permanent indebtedness and material impoverishment. Capitalistic milieus naturalise the Christian infinity of supernatural punishment in hellfire with an infinity of indebtedness in the rhythms of everyday life; it is our permanent and necessary indebtedness which constitutes our *fallenness* and *sinfulness* under the surveilling gaze of banks, financial institutions, and our own practices of economic and moral accounting made necessary by, at minimum, the bank account:

> The capitalist axiomatic ensures that no virtual-actual circuit other than its own will reach full amplitude, simply by requiring that every body considered to be of any worth, regardless of who or what it desires, have its own bank account. (Massumi, 1992: 139)

Systems of indebtification are libidinally pulsed with machines of guiltification and responsibilisation, rhythmically operating, inducing and transducing the interiorisation of these affective dynamics: the creditor-debtor distinction being produced through the social function of the *promise*, a promise inscribed in *memory*, and which must be fulfilled through new habits in everyday life (rhythms of (re)payment: the monthly credit card bill, the weekly confession) (Deleuze and Guattari, 1983a: 185). Blocks of debt in contemporary capitalistic milieus – as inscripted memories of alliances sealed and punishments-to-come, and which enable retentions, selections, and the coding of desire ('a memory straining towards the future' (ibid.: 190)) – are '"parcels of destiny" [. . .] [which render] *debt infinite*' (ibid.: 192, our addition) and permeate the rhythms of everyday life of the indebted subject. Indeed, low credit-worthiness and high levels of 'delinquent' debt (when debts remain unpaid, when rhythms of repayment have not been satisfied, when one's indebtedness intersects with one's life) have been linked to increases in the risk of death (Argys, Friedson, and Pitts, 2016): indebtedness becoming the necessary, yet fatal, debt of existence as such. So, debt is immediately *retentional* and *protentional* – both a tertiary retention and a tertiary protention – as Hui notes: 'debt [is] at the same time a retention and a protention; debt is not purely retentional since it also anticipates and *commands* a return – should this be out of moral or legal obligation' (2018: 146, our addition). Across the creditor-debtor ecology in contemporary capitalistic milieus, credit (creditors, accreditation) functions as machine of hierarchy, through processes of rhythmic subjection and containment towards individualisation and the privatisation of indebtedness (Harney and Moten, 2013: 61), and as one of those 'machines of culpabilisation' which have become 'necessary to stabilise the social field of capitalism' (Guattari, 2016: 8), which we will explore further below. Developing on these definitional brushstrokes, our rhythmanalysis of the debt-credit ecology will focus on the rhythms and processes through which indebtedness in the mental environment is bound up with and governed through mechanisms of rhythmic subjection and rhythmic containment. Let us now turn to our co-ordinate for this chapter: debt-subjection-containment.

a. [CC3]: debt-subjection-containment

> Man is no longer a man confined but a man in debt. (Deleuze, 1995: 181)

In Chapter 3, we made some comments as to what a rhythmanalysis in relation to debt might look like, paying specific attention to the relationship between debt and time. The creditor-debtor ecology, today, is an ecology bound up with differential (hierarchical) *access* to financial technologies. For Lazzarato (2015: 84), the creditor-debtor distinction in contemporary capitalistic milieus is a hierarchical and asymmetric distinction through which debt becomes an inexpiable, unpayable, and fundamental component to contemporary capitalism, a distinction which pedals continuous indebtedness, and, as such, functions as oil to processes of capital accumulation. In other words, debt in contemporary capitalistic milieus *cannot* be explained within an exchangist conception, insofar as exchangist conceptions of debt require that debts can *in principle* be paid (principle of equality) and that such exchange operates in a 'closed system' (Deleuze and Guattari, 1983a: 187) (principle of closure), neither of which pertain to the creditor-debtor relation today. While debt, when individualised and territorialised through regimes of credit, appears as payable, indebtedness within the contemporary regime of credit *as such* (and therefore the creditor-debtor hierarchy) is inexpiable insofar as it is foundational to contemporary capitalistic milieus: the creditor/debtor distinction functioning as foundational (and therefore in principle unpayable within the rhythmic parameters of ontological security of the capitalistic milieu) and within a continuously expanding (rather than closed) system of indebtedness tending towards the infinite (what Massumi terms the 'expanded field' (continuously expanding) of capital in which debt is a crucial apparatus of capture (2017a: 22–23)). Debt functions through a principle of inequality and a principle of openness, which is to say through continuous processual expansion.

Capitalistic milieus produce debt as their life blood, expanding the fields and intensities of indebtedness as a principle of expansion, capture, and accumulation. To be a creditor is to have access to 'credit money' (a stock), that is, access to certain privileges in relation to financial technologies: the ability to make decisions on the flows and conditions of production, the distribution of spoils, tax levies, and so forth (Lazzarato, 2015: 126). The creditor is in a position of having the ability to *access and transform* financial technologies: the ability to anticipate and shape the future. This is effectuated through, for example, the creditor's *granting access to credit* (i.e., the creation of a new block of indebtedness and flow of temporary purchasing power with interest) to the debtor. The granting of access to credit is immediately a process through which debt is privatised, isolated, and reduced to the *I*, where the *I* becomes rhythmically subjected, induced, and transduced through a process of subjection (and mechanisms of surveillance) towards machines of libidinal and material culpabilisation: 'the renewed reign of credit, a reign of terror, a hail of obligations to be met, measured, meted, endured' (Harney and Moten, 2013: 63). This process of *granting access to credit* is what Stefano Harney and Fred Moten call *governance*, involving the capture into regimes of accounting, accreditation, and calculability; where the existential balance sheet of the debtor's rhythms of everyday life can be produced, stored (inscribed), and deployed in such a manner as to (relatively) enhance or contract the debtor's range of possible existential refrains. Credit money 'rhythmises economic and social life' (Chen, 2018: 122) through this function of temporal colonisation.

To be a debtor is to only have access to 'commodity money' (a flow), that is, money which participates in the conditions set by credit money. Commodity money enables *access* to financial technologies (and their exchange), but the debtor cannot transform or control such technologies. Debtors can only access 'impotent monetary signs of the general equivalent, of money as means of payment' (Lazzarato, 2015: 125). Frédéric Lordon captures this distinction with clarity:

> The fundamental difference is that money as wages is accessed in the form of *flow*, namely, in quantities that allow for the short-term reproduction of labour power but do not allow a glimpse beyond this limited horizon, whereas money as financing is accessed in the form of a *stock*, namely, with the hope of crossing the critical threshold of the process of accumulation by self-sustaining valorisation (in which capital grows by itself, thanks to its capacity to extract surplus-value). Thus, the capitalist has privileged access to *money-capital*, rather than simply to money. (Lordon, 2014: 19)

Those who only have access to money in the sense of a *flow* are those whose exchange partakes only in the *actual*: commodity-money is actual money, exchange within pre-defined zones, within the closed elements of an open financial system. Money as financing, credit money, or simply *Capital*, 'with a capital C: money begetting more money, accumulating interest, building factories' (Massumi, 1992: 130), is money operating between the virtual and the actual, inscribing particular memories and deploying it to control the field of possible futures; that is, money operating at the borders of the system of indebtedness as such, seeking to direct the expansive process: finance and the arrhythmic colonisation of the future. The infinite speed of financial trading, too, poses a challenge to the polyrhythmic nexus of the body. For example, Borch, Hansen, and Lange note how the 'roundtrip' time for data transmission in a financial market between Chicago and New York is 8.1 milliseconds, compared to the 300–400 milliseconds that the blink of a human eye takes (2015: 1092; also see Heaney, 2023: 24–28). High frequency trading is but a game of rhythm and chance, in which chance is combated through 'being algorithmically present in markets in order to be able to sense their rhythms and proactively adjust the strategies on this basis' (Borch, Hansen, and Lange, 2015: 1093). Their game is finance, credit. Credit money 'locks up possibilities within an accepted framework while at the same time projecting them into the future. For finance, the future is a mere forecast of current domination and exploitation' (Lazzarato, 2012: 71).

Tòkos, or interest, that process through which money begets money and founds intensive indebtedness, arrhythmically captures the processes of exchange and desire insofar as they become subordinated to the continuous instantiation of the creditor-debtor hierarchy; that is, financial and libidinal flows are relatively directed along the expansive path of indebtedness set by finance:[1]

> Interest is no more than the number of a movement of (monetary) growth following the desire for money that binds individuals to each other in the radical injustice of a debt that nothing can acquit [. . .] Interest is the effect of a disproportion establishing inequality in terms of a caesura by which the permanence of money no longer coincides with the social *presence* of need, or with the immanence of an end with each act of exchange, but with the *différance* of a power. (Alliez, 1996: 10)

Our creditor-debtor ecology is *not* totalising. As with the digital divide we mentioned in Chapter 4, there are milieus in which *access* to financial technologies in the first place (i.e., the ability to even *acquire* debt, the ability to be *granted* credit) is a privilege, and, indeed, one of the perks of being a 'creditor' is the ability to acquire vast amounts of debt for the purposes of capital accumulation. Our rhythmanalysis of the creditor-debtor ecology recognises the situatedness of this very ecology.[2]

We will make, once again, three claims in this section. First, that debt functions as a mechanism of rhythmic subjection through the temporal squeezing it effectuates on the *rhythms of everyday life*, responsibilising debtors and rendering them 'guilty' for their debts. Second, that debt functions as a movement of rhythmic containment through the increasing *subordination of the pursuit of existential refrains to compulsory indebtedness*, and through systems of pre-personal and supra-personal control. Third, that debt *forecloses* the future for debtors, and *opens* the future for creditors, and, so, for the *continuous transference of privileged access to the means to control and transform financial technologies, supporting the ontological security of the capitalist milieu*.

Claim One: debt functions as a mechanism of rhythmic subjection through (1) continually reproducing the creditor-debtor hierarchy; and (2) the temporal squeezing it effectuates on debtors' rhythms of everyday life, having a contractive effect on possible existential refrains.
The very notion of debt is bound up with future-oriented commitments (promises) and the possibility of redemption (the fulfilment of promises). Debt, that is, functioning as a promise of repaying (with interest) the credit one has been granted, as a promise that *in the future*, the debtor will be redeemed for having to accrue debt in the first place (with interest). The strong distinction between the debtor and creditor in capitalistic milieus, which we highlighted above, however, problematises the possibility of such redemption at all. As Lazzarato notes, in these milieus, the creditor-debtor distinction is one based on a fundamental *subjection* of debtors to creditors, whereas the very possibility of *redemption* necessitates that it is at least in principle possible for *all* debt to be paid (and therefore the annulment of the debtor's general subjection to the creditor), if even only temporarily. Such 'total' redemption is not possible when the creditor-debtor hierarchy is essential to the functioning of capitalistic milieus *as such*; debt functions within vertically constituted regimes of credit in capitalistic milieus and the differential access to actual money and virtual money. This *blocks access* to the virtual.

This hierarchical and asymmetric social positionality functions as a starting point through which debtors enter this relationship of subjection, and which cannot in principle be resolved under contemporary capitalist financial technologies insofar as these technologies are premised upon the constant liquidity that new debt provides, fuelling the expansive openness we mentioned above. Through every credit card transaction, for example, the creditor-debtor distinction is further instantiated and reproduced. Each transaction provides *more* credit money for creditors (for example, through providing opportunities for securitisation), and the accumulation of debt (and interest) for debtors: debt is a principle of financial expansion. Whether the debtor is utilising her transactions for purposes of production or consumption is beside the point, insofar as *subjection* to the creditor-debtor hierarchy is the *condition* of engaging in such economic activity in the first place, and a state of personal or individualised indebtedness the *consequence*: indebtedness becoming the rule of the game. For Lazzarato, this creditor-debtor relationship of subjection is so fundamental to the reproduction of contemporary capitalistic milieus – a relation of subjection 'between owners (of capital) and non-owners (of capital)' (Lazzarato, 2012: 8) – that to obliterate the distinction would involve 'exiting capitalism altogether' (Lazzarato, 2015: 88). This is our first point in relationship to our first claim in this section; namely, that *since* the creditor-debtor distinction is indissociable from the perpetuation of contemporary capitalistic milieus, that *in principle*, credit-based-debt functions as a process of *perpetual rhythmic subjection of debtors to creditors*, and as a continuous reproduction of the creditor-debtor hierarchy.

As *perpetually rhythmically subjected to creditors*, debtors, in today's capitalistic milieus, are continuously solicited to *accrue* debt in order to make investments on their human capital, resilience, and perpetual growth; and are also continuously solicited to *repay* their debts and 'take responsibility' for their risks. As David Graeber notes, such a responsibilising injunction is applied differentially depending on social positionality. Corporations or financial institutions, for example, often evade such responsibility:

> In this world, 'paying one's debts' can well come to seem the very definition of morality, if only because so many people fail to do it. For instance, it has become a regular feature of many sorts of businesses in America that large corporations or even some small businesses, faced with a debt, will almost automatically simply see what happens if they do not pay – complying only if reminding, goaded, or presented with some sort of legal writ. (Graeber, 2012: 377)

The process of responsibilisation, or 'guiltification', is a process that is applied largely depending on one's position in relation to the debt-credit ecology. We met this point earlier in relation to the post-2008 European context of sovereign debt crises, where culpabilisation and guiltification was reterritorialised largely onto states, or, more precisely, on to the non-credit-owning populations in those states through austerity regimes, austerity regimes necessary for redemption for collective indebtedness. As continuously solicited to *accrue* and *repay*, the *rhythms of everyday life* for the contemporary indebted subject are ones surrounded by debt-based injunctions. The indebted subject's rhythms of everyday life are ones through which mechanisms of responsibilisation and guiltification – which themselves are mechanisms of identity filtration in processes of rhythmic subjection – are continuously solicited and demanded. Under such a continuous process, the indebted subject is induced towards such responsibility and such guilt, that is, transduced towards the internalisation and reproduction of the creditor-debtor hierarchy through the filtering of the affective and semiotic components of responsibility and guilt into his rhythms of everyday life; a libidinal and rhythmic contraction. One *feels* one's indebtedness in the mental environment: psychic pain, anxiety, guilt, resentment. The creditor, too, *feels* that he is owed his just repayment, with interest. The debtor's responsibility is to *fulfil* the promise he made to the creditor, and the affective component of guilt enters primarily as a *libidinal* and *motivational* mechanism to spur repayment-activity and psychic disempowerment, and also when such a fulfilment appears unlikely or difficult. This is a continuous process of rhythmic subjection, which not only transforms the indebted subject as one who identifies with 'his' responsibility and 'his' guilt, but which effectuates a temporal and ontological squeezing or *contraction* on what possible existential refrains he may enter into. If one fails on one's debt payments, one can often begin a feedback process of worsening credit ratings, financial disempowerment, and further contraction. The indebted subject moves through an increasingly *squeezed* present insofar as he is continuously responsible for repayments, deadlines, financial checks, and so on; all the while, the indebted subject is a potential target for *further* debt accrual through, say, acquiring further debt in order to fulfil previous debts (as with the potential vortex of indebtedness entered into through balance transfer credit cards, payday loans, and other forms of predatory financial mechanisms), for further consumption, or for potential avenues of production. In other words, the indebted subject is required to transform himself to fit the standards of the milieu, and simultaneously support the ontological security of the milieu that generated his precarious and insecure position of indebtification.

The possibilities of everyday life become increasingly *contracted* in a milieu dominated by indebtedness, insofar as they become increasingly controlled by the debtor's ability (or lack thereof) to fulfil his promises to his creditors. All of this is to say that when the *rhythms of debt repayment and debt accrual* come to dominate the rhythms of everyday life, anxiety, stress, desperation, responsibility, guilt, fear, and permanent insecurity are the predictable effects that manifest in the mental environment. Recall that the *pulse* of the milieu *codes the flows of desire*, and that the coding of desire's pulsive moments is also to code what patterns of practice are launched into, repeated, or avoided. Given the necessity of operating within the realm of actual money, and increasingly needing to access indebtedness to *invest in one's human capital*, the indebted subject's self-investment – his pursuit of happiness – becomes bound within a tight grid of moral and economic accountability. Credit-based-debt promises only the freedom of the capitalist *I*. The indebted subject's conduct is conducted through these financial technologies, demanding that everyday life, and the project of life itself, become filtered through these systems of accountability and their psychic internalisation. These have increasingly come to permeate multiple sectors: privatised social insurance, privatised (and stock market dependent) pension schemes, university tuition fees, real estate loans, and so forth, in tandem with increasing levels of economic precarity and insecurity. Investing in one's human capital and pursuing a liveable life increasingly necessitates that one becomes rhythmically subjected and constituted as the indebted subject; that is, that one's desires and rhythms become *integrated* into the continual reproduction of the capitalistic milieu, extensively subjected to the realm of actual money and intensively subjected to rhythms of becoming-capitalist:

> In the debt economy, to become human capital or an entrepreneur of the self means assuming the costs as well as the risks of a flexible and financialized economy, costs and risks which are not only – far from it – those of innovation, but also and especially those of precariousness, poverty, unemployment, a failing health system, housing shortages, etc. [. . .] The debt economy, then, is characterized by a twofold expansion of the exploitation of subjectivity: extensive (since not only are industrial work and tertiary sector concerned but every activity and condition) and intensive (since it encompasses the relationship to the self, in the guise of the entrepreneur of the self – who is at once responsible for 'his' capital and guilty of poor management – whose paradigm is the 'unemployed'). (Lazzarato, 2012: 51–52; also see Massumi, 1992: 132)

Bound within the reproduction of only its own flows and the attempt to capture any that might escape, the creditor-debtor ecology arrhythmically colonises everyday life. Such affective mechanisms libidinally energise the creditor-debtor ecology and are crucial components through which indebtification is a process of *perpetual rhythmic subjection*. This *perpetuality* of contemporary indebtedness, combined with the necessity of seeking and/or achieving *redemption*, and the processes of internalisation which are solicited as necessary affective components in order to direct the subject's practice towards redemption as a *felt* responsibility, is not unlike, as we have already mentioned, infinite Christian indebtedness (and Christian processes of guilt-internalisation), as Lazzarato notes (and which we hinted at with the quote from Deleuze and Guattari at the top of the chapter):

> Christianity 'struck us with the infinite,' which comes down to saying that we are in a social system in which there is no end to anything, in which indebtedness is for life [. . .] Christianity, by introducing the infinite, completely reinvented the system of debt which capitalism would inherit [. . .] The particularity of Christianity lies in the fact that it places us not only within a system of debt, but also within a system of 'interiorized debt.' (Lazzarato, 2012: 77–78)

Perpetual rhythmic subjection functions here, again, as an *effacement* of the structural economic mechanisms which render the ability to *escape* the creditor-debtor hierarchy itself an impossibility within contemporary capitalistic milieus. Debt is both *essential* oil to the cogs of capitalistic production and consumption machines, and therefore essential for the perpetuation of the ontological security of capitalistic milieus themselves, though nonetheless indebtedness is positioned as that which the indebted subject must *feel guilty for*, or nonetheless, in the final analysis, *is* guilty for: the creditor's judgement. The indebted subject must repay, and when his *rhythms of everyday life* become saturated by perpetual rhythmic subjection to debt, repayments, and further solicitations for increasingly toxic forms of debt accrual, he experiences a temporal squeezing that has a contractive effect on what possible existential refrains he may launch into. Blocked from accessing virtual money, and therefore blocked from controlling his future, the indebted subject in contemporary capitalistic milieus remains caught within the delimited zone of actual money. That is, debt, considered in this way, is a mechanism for the 'control and neutralisation' of the maximum number of existential refrains. We will now move onto our second claim.

Claim Two: debt functions as a mechanism of rhythmic containment: the subject in contemporary capitalistic milieus is increasingly required to submit to pre- and supra-personal intervention, and compulsory indebtedness, in order to pursue their own existential refrain.

Some economic data on contemporary debt levels is a useful entry way into this second claim, underlining as it does the extent, depth, and breadth of indebtedness across a multiplicity of connected capitalistic milieus. American federal student loan debt is currently just over US$1.6 trillion, and since 2010 has surpassed American credit card debt as one of the primary sources of American indebtedness (as of Q1 2023, American credit card debt was around US$986 billion) (Federal Reserve Bank of New York, 2023). To put this in some context, Greece's public debt during the European sovereign debt crises was approximately €323 billion, a debt for which the EU and the IMF imposed, and continue to effectively impose, strict sanctions and austerity packages for years to come, involving continuous financial reviews of their public accounts, the selling of public assets, and tightening budget constraints, to name some examples. Greece serves as a partial but important example for the shifting architecture of European financial macro-governance.[3] In France, *interest* payment on 'national debt' is one of the highest items of the French national budget, taking in almost all income tax revenue (Lazzarato, 2012: 18). In the UK, household debt (private debt, consumption debt) is consistently higher than disposable income (ibid.: 19).

Debt, and its vast financial technologies, are increasingly difficult to avoid in the pursuance of an existential refrain. Further, debt is inseparable from tertiary retentions (increasingly digital), which store the *memory* of debt. Indebtedness is a system of (selected) memory. Such memory is utilised to submit debtors to particular rhythms of repayment and in the calculation of the debtor's 'worth' in relation to previous financial records ('credit ratings') to decide what type of debt the debtor is 'worthy' of, in a dividualised and machinic process of rhythmic containment. Marx was extremely prescient on this:

> *Credit* is the *economic* judgment on the *morality* of a man. In credit, the *man* himself, instead of metal or paper, has become the *mediator* of exchange, not however as a man, but as the *mode of existence of capital* and interest [. . .] Within the credit relationship, it is not the case that money is transcended in man, but that man himself is turned into *money*, or money is *incorporated* in him [. . .] Instead of money, or paper, it is my own personal existence, my flesh and blood, my social virtue and importance, which constitutes the material, corporeal form of the *spirit of money.* (Marx, 1975: 215)

This (necessary) *submission* to one's financial data being stored and deployed in and through tertiary retentions is a submission process of pre-personal intervention in the material-economic sense of an intervention which enables the contraction or enhancement of possible existential refrains. Further, in the sense in which systems of moral-economic accounting come to play a role in the subject's rhythmic processes of individuation towards their individual interiorisation of responsibility for this moral-economic balance sheet and a felt guilt in the face of the continuous surveillance of capital (towards which they do not even have to confess their sins, insofar as creditors have privileged access to the technologies with produce these balance sheets). These processes of inscription, in other words, function as an *automatic confessional process.*

Recall that recording is the process through which particular practices, habits, desires, become *inscribed* in the functioning of, say, a subject within a milieu. Coding is therefore a practice of inscription or recording, enabling the repetition of that which has been recorded and the contraction of time and desire in the secure reproduction of the milieu straining towards the future. The necessity of bank accounts and the increasing necessity of permanent indebtedness in the pursuance of existential refrains in contemporary capitalistic milieus as such can be positioned within a political economy of memory and a political economy of the future through which automatic confessional processes render their financial flows and 'interests' permanently *sensed* by capital (Harney and Moten, 2013: 66) and, as such, permanently open to continuous intervention towards the futural alignment of their rhythms and desires (a new credit card, an extension of credit limit, an overdraft charge, a notice of non-payment, debt collection, payday loans and other predatory lending practices) in the expanding field of indebtedness (finance). That is, such data is centrally also utilised by creditors, through financial technologies, as a process of supra-personal intervention insofar as access to these tertiary retentions enables creditors to *control the future* through financial, legal, and economic mechanisms: 'debt appropriates not only the present labor time of wage-earners and of the population in general, it also preempts non-chronological time, each person's future as well as the future of society as a whole' (Lazzarato, 2012: 46–47).

Debt covers the 'surrounding components' of the *rhythms of everyday life*, as a memory 'bank' of one's previous conduct and as that which delimits or opens what future is possible, and indeed imaginable, for the indebted subject. This memory is also used by creditors in tactics of securitisation (that is, the process through which debts are packaged and sold and used in the pursuance of further capital accumulation). *Securitisation as rhythmic containment: foreclosing the future of the debtor and enhancing the future of the creditor.* Indeed, we see in practices of lending (the creditor's granting access to credit to the debtor) the skewed and asymmetric nature through which people even *access* credit (along lines of race, class, gender, and so forth), and the 'debt trap' that often follows such easy access to credit. Further, these debts themselves allow creditors to enhance their financial portfolios and further reproduce and intensify the creditor–debtor hierarchy. As Raunig notes, speaking specifically on the subprime mortgage crisis: 'The better asset values of the wealthy were supported by the growing debts of the impoverished, so that mathematical risk models ultimately determined who had a roof over their head' (2016: 148; also see Appadurai, 2016).

For the debtor, these tertiary retentions (the records of debt promises they have made and how they fulfilled/did not fulfil these debt promises) function (increasingly algorithmically) so as to, in many cases, contract and select narrow elements of the debtor's past so as to control and neutralise what existential refrains he might be able to pursue (subordinating him to certain rhythms of repayment); for the debtor, these tertiary retentions function in an *ontologically contractive* sense. For the creditor, these tertiary retentions function so as to, often, *enhance* what existential refrains the creditor might be able to pursue; when one is a creditor, debt is an asset that can be packaged, commodified, transformed, sold, and used for purposes of further capital accumulation (for the creditor, the debtor's debt enables the creditor to create new rhythms of accumulation). For the creditor, these tertiary retentions function in an *ontologically expansive* sense. The creditor, in this sense, *relies* upon the debtor to expand the field of capital. To quote Marx again:

> [T]he life of the poor man and his talents and activity serve the rich man as a *guarantee* of the repayment of the money lent. That means, therefore, that all the social virtues of the poor man, the content of his vital activity, his existence itself, represent for the rich man the reimbursement of his capital with the customary interest. Hence the death of the poor man is the worst eventuality for the creditor. It is the death of his capital together with the interest. One ought to consider how vile it is to *estimate* the value of a man in *money*, as happens in the credit relationship. As a matter of course, the creditor possesses, besides *moral* guarantees, also the guarantee of *legal* compulsion and still other more or less *real* guarantees for his man. (Marx, 1975: 215)

Tapping into streams of existing indebtedness and creating new possibilities for indebtedness for the purposes of profit and accumulation constitutes a veritable *innovative opportunity* for creditors. Consider, for example, *FinTech*, a growing area of 'innovation' in contemporary capitalistic milieus which seeks to increasingly integrate banking and financial services with digital tertiary retentions (particularly through smartphone applications). Services can range from orthodox banking services, services which enable smooth international transfers, applications for financial trading and investment, and schemes of 'peer-to-peer lending and human capital financing', taking 'aspects of the so-called "sharing economy" and [applying] them to the realms of debt and credit' (Thornton and Haiven, 2016: 70, our addition). The *telos* of such machinic assemblages when pertaining to the debt-credit ecology is to mobilise debtors to launch into further vectors of indebtedness through modes of pre- and supra-personal intervention towards the securitisation of the capitalistic milieu (see Lazzarato, 2014: 96–97).

When it comes to the debtor, access to the liquidity that debt provides is an increasingly important form of access that enables her to develop and act on a plan of life as such in many capitalistic milieus. This is due to the processes of gradual substitution of the 'social rights' offered by the welfare state (which are not immune from criticism, as we already noted) being replaced by the 'right of indebtedness'. The trend is one that moves away from a 'right to education' to a 'right to education, on the condition of indebtedness', from a 'right to healthcare' to a 'right to healthcare, on the condition of indebtedness', from a 'right to a liveable life' to a 'right to a liveable life, on the condition of indebtedness', from a 'right to a liveable wage' to a 'right to credit-based consumption', from a 'right to a home' to a 'right to a mortgage' (indeed, the right to home-ownership forms an important part of the *pursuit of happiness* of the capitalist *I*, the American dream (Malinen, 2016: 75; Donovan, 2013)). The financialisation of everyday life is inseparable from the indebtification of everyday life.

Insofar as indebtedness is increasingly a compulsory process through which one must pass in order to cultivate an existential refrain, and insofar as debt is bound up with imbricating our personal financial records – records which function as automatic confessions of our economic sins – onto tertiary retentions which decide our 'worthiness' for debt, the contemporary indebted subject is increasingly required to submit to pre- and supra-personal intervention *for* the acquisition of indebtedness *for* the pursuance of an existential refrain. Rhythmic containment to debt is becoming the condition for pursuing an existential refrain as such. As such, the pursuance of existential refrain involves, for debtors, that they *contribute to the ontological security of capitalism* through their participation in, and reproduction of, the creditor-debtor hierarchy. Debt works on the *deterritorialised* components of subjectivity through these processes of automatic confession (moral-economic accounting) and continual incentive-structure rebalancing, towards the production of an embrained body that works 'for the machines' in a general tendency we have been noting towards the *automatisation of practices which tend to securitise capitalistic milieus.*

Claim Three: debt forecloses the future for debtors, and opens the future for creditors, and, so, for the continuous transference of privileged access to the means to control and transform financial technologies.
The imbrication of debt with time makes it difficult to discuss how debt functions in contemporary capitalistic milieus without reference to how it curtails the possibilities of sculpting alternative futures for debtors and enhances such possibilities for creditors. Indeed, whether debt is submitted to or confronted through revolutionary attack, it will by necessity occupy our future. As such, we have already in this section strongly signalled this third claim, though we can focus on it in a little more detail. Creditors, as we noted, are those who have privileged access to credit money, the control and transformation of financial technologies, and to the pre- and supra-personal mechanisms of rhythmic containment in the creditor-debtor ecology. Recall that the process of *recording* is a process through which memory can become *inscribed* into technics and into the flows of desire, enabling repetition and the contraction of habit. *Recording, therefore* – to reiterate – *emerges as a condition for retention and transmission.* The inscription and recording of creditor-debtor hierarchies function in contemporary capitalistic milieus to, precisely, *retain* and *transmit* these asymmetries into a perpetual future. Stiegler makes a similar point discussing tertiary retentions generally in his *For a New Critique of Political Economy*:

> When technologically exteriorized, memory [such as debt] can become the object of sociopolitical and biopolitical controls through the economic investments of social organisations, which thereby *rearrange psychic organizations* through the intermediary of mnemotechnical organs, among which must be counted machine-tools [. . .] and all automata – including household appliances, as well as the 'internet of things' and the communicating devices that would soon invade the hyperindustrial market. (Stiegler, 2010a: 33–34, our addition)

Creditors are those with access to such technologically exteriorised memory, and, as such, to mechanisms of socio-political and biopolitical control through which existential refrains are controlled and neutralised. The creditor's hierarchical position in the creditor–debtor ecology itself, however, can be situated in a future-oriented analysis. What futures are possible whenever only a privileged few have the ability to access, control, and transform such a vital technology in the functioning of contemporary capitalistic milieus? We can begin to respond to this question by positioning our current context in relation to an example from the seventeenth century, to the foundation of the UK's central bank, the Bank of England. It is worth quoting Graeber at length here in order to flesh out this important example:

> In 1694, a consortium of English bankers made a loan of £1,200,000 to the king. In return they received a royal monopoly on the issuance of banknotes. What this meant in practice was they had the right to advance IOUs for a portion of the money the king now owed them to any inhabitant of the kingdom willing to borrow from them, or willing to deposit their own money in the bank – in effect, to circulate or 'monetize' the newly created royal debt. This was a great deal for the bankers (they got to charge the king 8 per cent annual interest for the original loan and simultaneously charge interest on the same money to the clients who borrowed it), but it only worked as long as the original loan remained outstanding. To this day, this loan has never been paid back. It cannot be. If it ever were, the entire monetary system of Great Britain would cease to exist. (Graeber, 2012: 49)

It is of note that this arrangement was of crucial importance in providing liquidity for the fortification of the English state's military apparatus (the navy in particular). No doubt, we are in a very different milieu today, not least due to the fact that the Bank of England, as is the norm with contemporary central banks, is no longer formally a private corporation and is instead an 'independent' public organisation controlling monetary policy (monitoring inflation, adjusting interest rates, conducting quantitative easing, attempting to ensure 'economic strength and stability' and 'growth'). Nonetheless, this unpaid loan remains the (necessary) condition upon which economic exchange in GBP depends. Further, our contemporary context is host to a different milieu of tertiary retentions that surround the mechanisms of identity filtration, labour, and leisure. A third key difference is in relation to the fact that we now occupy a post-Nixonian context of *fiat money*. Nonetheless, the UK, as Graeber notes, still bears the material and memorial trace of this arrangement in the foundation and continuing vital importance of the Bank of England itself, which bears a monopoly on the issuance of banknotes. In this arrangement the creditor-debtor hierarchy was instantiated and crystallised into the functioning of the British state in such a manner that (and we do not here underestimate the importance of private financial institutions in any regard) the Bank of England *itself* constitutes a retentional apparatus that only an elite can access and transform. Further, it is a retentional apparatus – or perhaps more clearly: an ensemble of tertiary retentions and financial technologies – through which this historical privilege is *transferred* or *conferred* to future creditors. We do not say 'maintained' precisely because these technologies are constantly undergoing mutations and transformations depending on social, historical, political, and economic contexts. What *is* maintained is that *the privileged access the control and transformation* of these financial technologies *in the future*.

What is *also* maintained is the debtor's position of *perpetual subjection* to creditors. Today, as we have already argued, debtors have access only to actual-commodity money, not virtual-credit money, and insofar as this subjection continues to operate, we can identify this as a *tendency of perpetual subjection of debtors to creditors* and as the *perpetual transference of a class privilege*. In other words, an *arrhythmic closing of the future*.

The crucial point we are developing here is that not only does the position of 'debtor' perpetually and rhythmically subject and enslave specific subjects, contracting their futures, holding them accountable for their financial 'sins', and closing their future (control and neutralising possible existential refrains); but insofar as the creditor-debtor ecology is based upon hugely inaccessible financial technologies that debtors have no access to control or transform, this status as a 'debtor' is *perpetually transferred onto future generations*. Conversely, the position of 'creditor', as a privileged position through which the scale and scope of one's existential refrains are enhanced, is a position through which creditors *perpetually hold debtors to account* and, further, through their privileged access to financial technologies, creditors *perpetually transfer this privilege to future generations*. Given this analysis, the continuing ontological security of capitalistic milieus is perpetually enhanced and expanded through all transactions between creditors and debtors in everyday life. As we already noted, this political economy of memory is therefore immediately a political economy of the future: the debt-credit ecology is one consisting of processes with revolutionary potential.

b. Minority experiment three: strike debt

Our first two claims in relation to the debtor-creditor ecology were the following:

Claim One: debt functions as a mechanism of rhythmic subjection through (1) continually reproducing the creditor-debtor hierarchy and (2) the temporal squeezing it effectuates on debtors' rhythms of everyday life, and, as well as through processes of individualisation and culpabilisation, having a contractive effect on possible existential refrains.

Claim Two: debt functions as a mechanism of rhythmic containment: the subject in contemporary capitalistic milieus is increasingly required to submit to pre- and supra-personal intervention, and compulsory indebtedness, in order to pursue their own existential refrain.

In 2015, the television series *Mr. Robot* (2015), created by Sam Esmail, began broadcasting. In it, the protagonist – Elliot Alderson (Rami Malek) – works for a cybersecurity firm 'by day' but is engaged in ad hoc vigilante-style hacking 'by night'. Elliot is a proficient and obsessive hacker, who also experiences, amongst other things, depression, substance addiction, and intense social anxiety. One of the key plots of the first season is Elliot's involvement in a hacking group called 'f_society' (which appears to be broadly modelled on *Anonymous*) engaged in a project trying to create the 'biggest wealth redistribution in history' through *striking, cancelling, or forgiving debts.* Their ability to plan such a project is made possible by f_society's hacking abilities; that is, their ability to *break* the circuits through which debt functions today (predominantly through 'memory' stored as digital tertiary retentions, which their hacking abilities enable them to access). Through hacking processes, f_society's project is, to put it simply, to *delete the informational memory of debt stored on digital tertiary retentions*; which, today, would constitute a deletion or *striking* of the debts themselves. The premise of this television series provides a smooth segue into our next proposal for affirmative work; *minority experiment three: strike debt.*

Mr. Robot participates in the contemporary supra-personal imaginary on debt, or, more specifically, on what might be technically possible in terms of *striking debt.* However, there are others more engaged in direct action: take the example of Strike Debt, a decentralised network which emerged from Occupy focused on participating in processes that cancel or forgive debts, and which released a how-to guide entitled *The Debt Resisters' Operation Manual* (Strike Debt, 2014a) and which formed the basis of the 'Rolling Jubilee' project that has abolished nearly US$32 million in debt; or The Debt Collective, which also emerged from Strike Debt, and which is attempting to develop collective projects focusing on politicising finance/debt, exploring the possibility of constructing debtors' unions (The Debt Collective, 2016: 84). Strike Debt has connections – though is not reducible to – the work and participation of

Andrew Ross, author of *Creditocracy: And the Case for Debt Refusal*. In this book, Ross forcefully argues the following:

> Making loans that clearly can never be repaid in full is a more delinquent act than being unable to pay. Making a killing off vital common goods like education and healthcare and public infrastructure is venal, anti-social conduct, to be condemned and not indemnified. The money we borrowed from banks was not theirs to begin with – it was created as interest-bearing debt, only when we signed the loan agreement. The long record of fraud and deceit on the part of bankers disqualifies their right to be made whole – it is more moral to deny them than to pay them back. The banks, and their beneficiaries, awash in bonuses, profits, and dividends, have already been paid enough. Since the creditor class produces phony wealth, fake growth, and thus no lasting prosperity to society as a whole, it deserves nothing from us in return. Loading debt onto the citizenry inflicts grievous damage on any democracy, no matter how durable it appears to be. When a government cannot – or will not – respond, then taking debt relief for ourselves, by any means necessary, may be the most indispensable act of civil disobedience. (Ross, 2013: 128–129)

For our purposes, the minority experiment of *striking debt* would function as an *extemporaneous counter-actualisation* in the creditor-debtor ecology in at least two senses: (1) through the collective participation and creation of *new* supra-personal imaginaries on debt, and, through this, the transformation of the rhythmically subjected and contained indebted subject (once again, such collective participation has the potential for the co-production of *solidarity*); (2) through the epistemological-technical proliferation on how debt functions (as a predominantly digital tertiary retention) in contemporary capitalistic milieus, striking debt could function, once again, as an 'opening of technicity' (Stiegler, 2015: 120). Although we are using the singular term of 'strike debt' here, by this we are gesturing not solely towards the particular activity we mentioned above with *Mr. Robot* or varieties of it (namely, the gaining of access to and deletion of informational memory), but rather a more generalised politics of debt that opens itself up to variegated strategies and tactics: striking debt as already described constitutes one set of tactics, as are *debt strikes* (collective action of targeted non-payments which *The Debt Collective* promotes), and other forms of debt-centred political action. The counter-actualisation of the creditor-debtor ecology would constitute the *breaking* of the automatic circuits through which debt functions to economically (the automatic confessional function made possible thorough rhythmic containment) and morally (through processes of rhythmic subjection) orient the becomings of bodies in contemporary capitalistic milieus and through which we have acquired arrhythmic habits of thought and practice *as if* such indebtedness were necessary. Such automaticity or necessity is only *relative* automaticity, insofar as it is *rendered* such only through how the milieu orients becomings; counter-actualisation functioning as *de-automatisation*. Such automaticity in our libidinal and material circuits can become the object of a revolutionary attack:

> We must recapture this second innocence [through freeing ourselves from an *a priori* and quasi-theological debt of existence], rid ourselves of guilt, of everything owed, of all bad conscience, and not repay a cent. We must fight for the cancellation of debt, for debt, one will recall, is not an economic problem but an apparatus of power designed not only to impoverish us, but to bring about catastrophe. (Lazzarato, 2012: 164, our addition)

Let us take (1) and (2) from above in turn.

On the first claim. Consider the following, an introductory statement by Strike Debt titled 'Principles of Solidarity' which, they claim, was adopted by consensus at a general meeting in New York:

> Strike Debt is building a debt resistance movement. We believe that most individual debt is illegitimate and unjust. Most of us fall into debt because we are increasingly deprived of the means to acquire the basic necessities of life: education, health care, and housing. Because we are forced to go into debt simply in order to live, we think it is right and moral to resist it. We also oppose debt because it is an instrument of exploitation and political domination. Debt is used to discipline us, deepen existing inequalities, and reinforce gendered, racial, and other social hierarchies. Every Strike Debt action is designed to weaken the institutions that seek to divide us and benefit from our division. (Strike Debt, 2014b)

Importantly, striking debt, or any minority experiment which focused on the politicisation of indebtedness, would not be simply reducible to the technical operations or know-how required in order to strike, cancel, or forgive debt. If it were, such a process would leave the mental environment surrounding debt (including insisting mechanisms of individualisation, responsibilisation, and the production of guilt) relatively untransformed, which may leave the creditor–debtor hierarchy *as such* in place. Our minority experiment of *striking debt*, this is to say, involves processes through which indebted subjects *singularise alternative supra-personal imaginaries* on the experience of indebtedness. Through such processes of singularisation made possible by movements organised around the experience of indebtedness, alternative mechanisms of identity filtration might be collaboratively produced; more specifically, we might imagine the production of *solidarity* around the experience of indebtedness, and the *transference* of responsibility onto the diffuse financial mechanisms through which contemporary capitalistic milieus operate (mechanisms which *necessitate* debt, and continuously reproduce the creditor-debtor hierarchy) rather than the individualising and responsibilising mechanisms that dominate the supra-personal imaginary in contemporary capitalistic milieus. The production of new supra-personal imaginaries and transindividual connections is also a process of producing new pre- or infra-individual connections around memories of indebtedness. Such practices would encounter the *differential* experience of indebtedness. The American indebted subject's experience of indebtedness would not be reducible to the Greek indebted subject's experience of indebtedness. Nor would an American indebted subject who has been racialised as white's experience of indebtedness be reducible to an American indebted subject who has been racialised as black's experience of indebtedness.

The statement quoted from Strike Debt above pays witness to how processes of social disjunction function to *block* the co-production of solidarity (through the operation of exclusive disjunctions). Nonetheless, that indebted subjects are (albeit differentially) rhythmically subjected and rhythmically contained in the creditor-debtor ecology could serve as a basis for the co-production of solidarity around inclusive disjunctions; the production of associations in the mental environment through partially shared experiences of the *contraction of existential refrains*, which is an *effect* of the creditor-debtor ecology. Insofar as such collective production (singularisation of alternative supra-personal imaginaries and the co-production of solidarity) participates in the creation of new supra-personal imaginaries – and the transformation of the mechanisms of identity filtration as such – this collective production functions as a type of *milieu therapeutics*, transforming the aesthetic experience of the milieu, and (heterogeneously) transforming the responsibilising rhythmic subjection of debt. The work of Harney and Moten, who we met earlier in this chapter, has forcefully gone in this direction in a radical rethinking of the notion of debt beyond our own credit-based indebtedness. They develop an affirmative, productive, and affective reading of our *indebtedness* to each other, a qualitative (and non-quantifiable) *transindividual* and

deterritorialising indebtedness produced in and through our intersec-
tions and interactions with each other in the rhythms of everyday life:

> It is not credit we seek nor even debt but bad debt which is to
> say real debt, the debt cannot be repaid, the debt at a distance, the
> debt without creditor, the black debt, the queer debt, the criminal
> debt. Excessive debt, incalculable debt, debt for no reason, debt
> broken from credit, debt as its own principle [. . .] [D]ebt is social
> and credit is asocial. Debt is mutual. Credit runs only one way.
> But debt runs in every direction, scatters, escapes, seeks refuge.
> (Harney and Moten, 2013: 61)

All that we discussed in section a of this chapter pertains precisely to
what Harney and Moten call 'credit', which is why we have focused
on a few occasions on the fact that our contemporary indebtedness is
credit-based debt, and on the fundamental creditor/debtor hierarchy
constitutive of contemporary capitalistic milieus. Their notion of debt
exceeds the techniques through which we are bureaucratically, libidinally,
temporally, and materially integrated within machines of credit-based
indebtedness, creating a new concept of debt through which it functions
as its own affective and productive principle, unlocked from the automaticity of individualisation, guiltification, culpabilisation, confession,
and disempowerment through which our credit-based indebtedness is
filtered today. Raunig calls debt a 'terrain of molecular revolution' (2016:
151) in conversation with Harney and Moten, highlighting how this
ceaseless rhythmic flow of mutual indebtedness is cut off from (falsely
restorative) regimes of credit and guilt. This productivity combined with
its unaccountability pushes us towards an 'offensive practice of making
debts' (ibid.: 152), rather than simply a defensive manoeuvre in the face
of credit. Indeed, this is one of the reasons why such *minority experiments*
concerned with the politicisation of debt and making debt into an object
of revolutionary attack cannot remain at the level of debt forgiveness or
cancellation, as they run the risk of *remaining* within the credit-based
regime of *restoration*, which we highlighted, with Nietzsche, as the foundation to the forms of credit-based indebtedness we have been discussing
throughout this chapter: 'Restored credit is restored justice and restorative justice is always the renewed reign of credit [. . .] To seek justice
through restoration is to return debt to the balance sheet and the balance sheet never balances' (Harney and Moten, 2013: 63). Even a radical
process of total debt cancellation, in other words, would remain *adaptive*
rather than *adoptive* without dissolving the debtor-creditor distinction
and composing the mental environment anew.

We mentioned above how political experiments in the debt-credit ecology could help function towards the co-production of solidarity in the mental environment, and the de-automatisation of the circuit of individualisation of indebtedness. It is worth quoting Harney and Moten at length on this point:

> Debt at a distance is forgotten, and remembered again. Thinking of autonomism, its debt at a distance to the black radical tradition. In autonomia, in the militancy of post-workerism, there is no outside, refusal takes place inside and makes its break, its flight, its exodus from the inside. There is biopolitical production and there is empire. There is even what Franco 'Bifo' Berardi calls soul trouble. In other words there is this debt at a distance to a global politics of blackness emerging out of slavery and colonialism, a black radical politics, a politics of debt without payment, without credit, without limit. This debt was built in a struggle with empire before empire, where power was not with institutions or govern-ments alone, where any owner or colonizer had the violent power of a ubiquitous state. This debt attached to those who through dumb insolence or nocturnal plans ran away without leaving, left without getting out. This debt got shared with anyone whose soul was sought for labor power, whose spirit was borne with a price marking it. And it is still shared, never credited and never abiding credit, a debt you play, a debt you walk, and debt you love. (Ibid., 2013: 64)

These productive and complex flows of mutual indebtedness, paid attention to, can pierce into the mental environment through the supra-personal imaginary, solidarity produced through shared expe-riences and the inclusive disjunction of the difference of these expe-riences: a caring and listening milieu. (It is of note here that the *Debt Resisters' Operation Manual* includes suggestions on assemblies focused on sharing experiences of indebtedness through stories as testimonies, which in addition to providing a space for the dein-dividualisation of our indebtedness, also opened up a shared space for the production of new, non-credit-based debts through mutual forms of support, sociality, or care (The Debt Collective, 2016: 92).) Our transindividual indebtedness in our rhythms of everyday life can be refigured as a productive principle and solidaristic flow of our milieus-to-come, and thereby a principle which is itself con-stitutively open and processual, open always to further elaboration through everyday life as such:

Psychic and collective retentions, however, can produce meaning and sense (that is, desire and hope) only as long as they are *individuated by all and hence shared by all* on the basis of processes of psychic individuation that form, from out of relations of co-individuation, social processes of transindividuation, creating relationships of solidarity that are the basis of sustainable (and intergenerational) *social systems.* (Stiegler, 2016a: 33)

On the second claim. The technical operation of striking debt is one that could be pursued in a number of ways. One such example was explored by John Oliver – a comedian and television host engaged in political analysis and satire – in his HBO series *Last Week Tonight with John Oliver* (2016). In June 2016, Oliver devoted a section of his show to exploring the connection between indebtedness and healthcare in the US; the former being, for many, the *condition of access* for the latter. Using tactics and strategies that have been popularised largely by Strike Debt (though Oliver made no explicit reference to them in his piece), Oliver and his colleagues created a debt acquisition company and purchased just under US$15 million worth of medical debt. This debt was being securitised, commodified, and traded for purposes of capital accumulation; Oliver and his colleagues were able, therefore, to purchase the debt for a 'cutprice' of less than US$60,000. At the end of the segment, Oliver *forgave* the debts, cancelling those particular medical debts of around 9,000 Americans. Although this piece focused narrowly on the inequities of the debt- and insurance-based healthcare funding system in the US – and remained firmly within the restorative remits of our credit-based indebtedness (i.e., capitalism with a human face) – it could nonetheless be expanded and function as an important *pedagogical* toolkit of precisely how debt functions and operates (and can be functioned and operated with) in contemporary capitalistic milieus. Such strategies constitute an 'opening of technicity' (Stiegler, 2015: 120) insofar as they utilise the tactics deployed in practices of debt securitisation and capital accumulation *in order to contribute to the ontological insecurity of capitalism.*

Strike Debt's *Debt Resisters' Operation Manual*, another example of a pedagogical toolkit constituting an opening of technicity, highlights this element of what they call 'public education' both through communications but also through action, mainly in the form of rolling debt jubilees. Technical and political experiments that hack into and break our indebtedness are, as Raunig noted, a terrain of molecular revolution: the seeming inexpiability of the debtor-creditor hierarchy, if radically counter-actualised, could help create the spacetime for the elaboration of new revolutionary processes that went beyond them. As we emphasised at the end of the previous section, the debt-credit ecology forms part of a political economy of memory that is also a political economy of the future that is operated, in part, through the ensemble of technics constituting financial technologies ('Memory is always the object of a politics, of a criteriology by which it selects the events to be retained' (Stiegler, 2009: 9)). Our debt-credit ecology, today, consists in a political war on memory and the future leveraged through privileged abilities to access, control, and transform the technical milieu, but which is always already a war on the present insofar as it actualised through the indebted subject's contracted rhythms of everyday life. A revolutionary politics of the debt-credit ecology must, in this sense, concern itself crucially with the technics through which our becomings our oriented.

Such practices of striking debt *opens* the future for indebted subjects, insofar as their range of existential refrains is *enhanced* through debt forgiveness, and, indeed, problematising the debtor-creditor hierarchy as such. Our claim here is that the minority experiment of *striking debt* – involving the singularisation of alternative supra-personal imaginaries on debt, the transformation of the rhythmically subjected indebted subject, and the *breaking* of the circuits debt is in in contemporary capitalistic milieus – would constitute an *extemporaneous counter-actualisation* of *debt-subjection-containment*.

c. Sculptural process three: the sculpting of new modes of exchange

Recall our third claim from section 6a:

Claim Three: debt forecloses the future for debtors, and opens the future for creditors, and, so, for the continuous transference of privileged access to the means to control and transform financial technologies.

In section 6b, we developed the example of *striking debt* as a venture into what an *extemporaneous counter-actualisation* might look like in the debtor-creditor ecology. This example focused on collaborative *affirmative work* in the creation of new supra-personal imaginaries on debt, the co-production of solidarity, and the 'opening of technicity' (Stiegler, 2015: 120). Here, we will try to sketch out how the *sculpting of new modes of exchange*, as our third sculptural process, might take shape. Such a collaborative sculpting process could be conducted alongside the affirmative work on *striking debt*. Collaborative sculpting processes of alternative modes of exchange (involving the *investment* of participants, but also, insofar as these strategies confront contemporary capitalistic milieus, may indeed require *capital* investment) with various forms of experimental tactics we discussed above in terms of *debt strikes* conducted periodically. So, (1) continuous *debt strikes*, coupled with collaborative sculpting processes which simultaneously (2) created and experimented with new modes of exchange; and (3) gradually 'sucked' capital investment into these collaborative processes, constituting a triple strategy for pushing capitalistic milieus to their region of ontological security as it pertains to the creditor-debtor ecology, towards the fundamental dissolution of the creditor-debtor hierarchy in our milieus-to-come, developing new rhythmic parameters of ontological security for our milieus-to-come.

The creditor-debtor hierarchy pertains, in large part, to the skewed distribution of access to financial technologies (virtual money and actual money), and to the dominance of the abstract mode of exchange constitutive of capitalistic milieus, reducible to the general equivalent. Minority experiments such as those of *striking debt* constitute partial contributions to the alleviation of this skewed distribution. The *collaborative sculpting of alternative modes of exchange* would centralise the creation and operation of modes of exchange collaboratively and deliberatively decided within and across milieus. What we suggest here is that the process of co-operatively inventing and practising new modes of exchange could mobilise around the three temporally oriented strategic points we have been focusing on. In this specific ecology, this could take practical shape through: first, confronting the conditions of the present in the debtor-creditor ecology we scaped in section 6a (requiring, at least initially, operating at the edge of the parameters of contemporary capitalistic milieus); second, through the co-creation of *sustainable*, long-term circuits of exchange *irreducible to any putative general equivalent*; third, through a collaborative and solidaristic *investment* in creating the conditions for singularising existential refrains. These would constitute a new political economy of memory and protentionality; new forms of exchange that centred the politics of the archive and invested in the milieu's collaborative orientation of itself into the future; that is, the collaborative formation of new strategies of investment and the creation of new expectations (Stiegler, 2016b: 483).

The continuous transference of privileged access to the means to control and transform financial technologies forms part of the mechanisms of rhythmic subjection and rhythmic containment through which existential refrains are continuously and perpetually controlled and neutralised. Any process that sought to collaboratively sculpt new modes of exchange would encompass co-operative reflexive production as to how these modes of exchange *affect* the mental environment: our future modes of exchange would *pay attention* to (care for) the ways in which modes of exchange always run of the risk of generating new hierarchies, new exclusions, and new arrhythmias, and make such blockages an object of revolutionary attack. Today, the indebted subject faces a *contracting range of existential refrains* but does not participate in the hierarchies that differentially distribute privilege and punishment through financial technologies. The collaborative sculpting of new modes of exchange creatively confronts these technological conditions through the *co-operative control* and *participatory management* of newly created financial technologies; as well as a constant *reflexive rebound* between the use of such technologies and the effects they might have in the mental environment. This is also to call the *elaboration* of these technologies a *schizoanalytic* process; Guattari highlights, speaking in the context of linking schizoanalytics to institutions more generally, that this *reflexive rebound* process is one of his primary concerns, that is, 'the continuous development of [an institution's] practices as much as its theoretical scaffolding' (2014: 27, our addition). Through this *patient* process, modes of exchange would always be up for revision, transformation, or indeed *erasure* if a new mode of exchange were to emerge that began to produce, say, toxic effects in the mental environment. Such modes of exchange would, in this sense, be *fluid*, but a fluidity which flowed from the process of social sculpture as such; that is, flowing from the *participative, deliberative, and processual* elements of the process.

We cannot be exhaustive or indeed overly predictive about how this might be practised in advance, but two points are worth mentioning. First, as a process of social sculpture, the collaborative invention of new modes of exchange would operate through an *extension* of access to technologies of exchange, and could only be transformed collaboratively in the milieu in question, or across milieus collaboratively. In other words, the fluidity or processual sculpture of new modes of exchange flows from the slow, piecemeal, and patient process of their elaboration and practice, with an attentive focus on creating the conditions for singularising existential refrains; a collaborative *enhancement* of futures linked to a *common investment* in the future ('What is important is the process: desire for the future' (Massumi, 1992: 106)). Second, for such modes of exchange to be sustainable, deliberative, and conducive to the creation of long-term circuits of exchange, they would not, in this sense, be reducible to any general equivalent. This is due to these modes of exchange being determined by their participants within and across milieus, which blocks any abstract 'general equivalent' colonising the rhythms of exchange (as with contemporary financial technologies). The *reduction* of 'objects' (commodities) and 'time' (of production) to a general equivalent is, indeed, one of the key practices of *enframing* through which capitalistic milieus colonise the globe (see Heaney, forthcoming). Such a *totalising enframing,* in our terms, manifests *paranoiac control* in the mental environment, rendering all possible objects and all possible time 'exchangeable' through the general equivalent. In contemporary capitalistic milieus permeated by the informationalisation or cyberneticisation of everyday life, there is a total quantitative reductivity of value to exchange value, in which 'anything can be reduced and dissolved, thereby becoming "virtual" in the contemporary (and hollow) sense of the term' (Stiegler, 2017b: 85): a fluidisation of value is what follows from general equivalency, whereby value is *measured* through the ever-moving boundaries of capital accumulation and expansion. Jean Baudrillard, in *The Impossible Exchange*, seeks to make a version of such fluidity the principle of exchange as such:

> All current strategies boil down to this: passing around the debt, the credit, the unreal, unnameable thing you cannot get rid of. Nietzsche analysed the stratagem of God in these terms: redeeming man's debt by the sacrifice of His son, God, the great Creditor, created a situation where the debt could never be redeemed by the debtor, since it has already been redeemed by the creditor. In this way, He created the possibility of an endless circulation of that debt, which man will bear as his perpetual sin. This is the ruse of God. But it is also the ruse of capital, which, at the same time as it plunges the world into ever greater debt, works simultaneously to redeem that debt, thus creating a situation in which it will never be able to be cancelled or exchanged for anything [. . .] This irruption of radical uncertainty into all fields [here, the economic field] [. . .] is not at all a negative fate, so long as uncertainty itself becomes the new rule of the game. So long as we do not seek to correct that uncertainty by injecting new values, new certainties, but have it circulate as the basic rule. (Baudrillard, 2001: 8–9, our addition)

By enfolding 'uncertainty' as the 'rule of the game', one could be forgiven for seeing such uncertainty as *precisely* what unfolds – through financial speculation, debt securitisation, capital accumulation, and so on – in contemporary capitalistic milieus: up to a point, the values of capital appear forever moving and expanding. Indeed, we noted this above with Massumi, drawing on his claims about the 'expanded field' (2017a: 22) of capital in which debt functions as a mechanism of capture. This capture is the continuous *attempt* to *control* uncertainty. In other words, in contemporary capitalistic milieus, uncertainty is *permanently subjected* to a totalising quantitative enframing, which is to say, subjected to a general equivalent of numerical calculability; the attempt to confront uncertainty through controlling risk:

> [The neoliberal economy rides] waves of *meta*stability through
> the turbulence of a permanently uncertain environment. A
> metastability is not so much a provisional stability as a wave
> patterning [. . .] It does not try systematically to shelter itself from
> the storm [. . .] Faced with the spectre of catastrophe, it does
> not turn self-protectively inward. It fully assumes the risks of its
> ontogenetic outside. (Massumi, 2015a: 53, our addition)

In this sense, uncertainty circulates, no doubt, but this uncertainty is
subjected to *paranoiac control* and reductionism; uncertainty is that which
must be 'controlled' or 'known'. Stiegler highlights this as a question
of *trust*:

> [T]he *reduction* of trust (and of time, that is, of belief in a future) to
> pure calculation, which would be capable therefore of eliminating
> everything incalculable, is what *radically destroys all trust*, because it
> destroys all *possibility of believing*: all possibility of believing in the
> indetermination of the future, in the future as indeterminate and
> in this indetermination as a *chance*, an *opening* to the future as to its
> improbability, that is, to the future as *irreducibly singular*. (Stiegler,
> 2011a: 45)

So, in this sense, the reduction of exchange to calculability is a manifestation of the attempted *paranoiac control* of uncertainty in and between
contemporary capitalistic milieus: capital accumulation is indissociable,
in other words, from *reactive fear* which seeks to keep insecurity at bay,
assuming the risk of the ontogenetic outside in order to control it. We
do not here 'prescribe' Baudrillardian uncertainty as the general rule of
the game through which collectively sculpted modes of exchange must
operate, nor do we seek to *exclude* calculability from any future mode of
exchange; rather, the point worth underlining here is that the *reduction
of modes of exchange to any calculable general equivalent* is a reduction which
excludes the emergence of singularising existential refrains and which
erodes or *blocks* solidaristic associations in the mental environment insofar as it *erodes trust* and manifests paranoiac control. Milieus consist of
matrices of emergence through which they rhythmically move through
spacetimes, and the centrality of modes of exchange within and between
milieus are crucial in the sense that it is largely through such modes
that milieus acquire directionality and orientation: different modes of
exchange would produce different milieus. As such, for our collective
sculpting of new modes of exchange to be *sustainable*, to create *long-term
circuits of exchange*, and to create a *solidaristic investment in a common future*,

it will nonetheless co-operatively and deliberately *confront* this question of uncertainty, and, indeed, a *common investment in the modes of exchange operative in the milieu as such*. Exchange, investment, sustainability: these processes of social sculpture would as such, as already indicated, pass through the question of *value*: what is of value to the milieu? How are these values themselves to be valued? We mentioned this in Chapter 2 when we noted that scaping, as a rhythmic ecology open to the virtual, seeks to constitute an opening to the creation of new ecologies of value and new modes of libidinal investment; and that opening onto the question of value would not be to non-immanently instate a 'set' of values prior to ecological production, but rather, as Massumi notes, to open onto value insofar as values themselves reach no 'final resting point' (2017b: 356). This lack of a resting point, the sense in which (qualitative) value always exceeds and escapes any attempt at (paranoiac) quantitative reduction, points towards a notion of *qualitative surplus value* (ibid.: 360). Indeed, this incalculable qualitative surplus value dovetails with our incalculable mutual indebtedness, to use Harney and Moten's terms.

The hope is that such a process of social sculpture could help in the long-term formation of the conditions of singularising existential refrains. To give some examples. Massumi has highlighted the potential of blockchain technology in the development of decentralised modes of exchange that do not require mediation through banks and other financial institutions, and the possibility of exploring ways in which these technologies could be harnessed and developed in order to expand onto modes of exchange that do not reduce to quantitative equivalence (2017a: 35–36). The ecological credentials of cryptocurrencies in this domain, however, remains contested. In this direction, there is also the increasing development of community currencies (which are not necessarily territorialised, though as yet have often been) that centralise democratic participation, a confrontation with social exclusion, as well as taking account of other negative externalities (such as environmental impact) (Bindewald and Steed, 2015). Massumi points towards the potential of hacking the *derivative*, which in contemporary capitalism arrhythmically captures the future, as a potential mode of futural investment (protention) through which our common investment in a sustainable future could be filtered without reduction to a general equivalent; he considers whether the derivative could be reimagined through qualitative derivatives involving 'non-ownership-based, self-motoring speculative processes "backed" by collectively produced, creatively induced affective intensity: a creative process engine run on the collective generation of surplus-value of life' (2017b: 37). (It is of note that these experiments are being developed in a project entitled the *Three*

Ecologies Seed Bank, which would be combined with the activities of an alter-university called the *Three Ecologies Institute*, developing out of the SenseLab.) Raunig, similarly, considers whether the logic of the dividend could be hacked beyond metrics and beyond property and dispossession, through which distribution takes on an 'ever broader and wilder' (2016: 149) form. Stiegler seeks to respond to the questions of value and new modes of exchange through the development of what he calls *contributory* economies or economies of contribution, drawn and developed from the group he co-founded in 2005 called *Ars Industrialis* (Stiegler, 2014a: 11–15). To develop contributory economies requires, for Stiegler, a new political economy of adoption through which we create new criteria for valorisation (an opening, in other words, to a virtual ecology of value):

> [A]doption is not a simple *adaptation* to becoming, but its projec-
> tive transformation into a possible future as the implementation of
> a criterion that has been 'invented' in the sense that it is projected
> onto the retentional screens forming the machinery of its time.
> (Stiegler, 2011b: 175)

Contributory economies are defined principally and precisely by what is valorised: the creation of positive externalities, namely activities which generate 'benefits' for those outside of any particular exchange in the milieu in question. When the concept of 'externalities' is introduced in economics textbooks, the example of national education (whether pri-mary, secondary, or tertiary) is often cited as an industry that generates positive externalities, such as higher levels of literacy, increased social cohesion, and so forth (Stiglitz, 2000: 426–427). The valorisation of pos-itive externalities flows from a valorisation of *care*, and the judgement that caring milieus are ones in which the contribution of each is made possible and cared for: social sculpture. In this sense, economies of con-tribution are ones in which what exceeds the immediacy of any particular exchange – namely, the externalities exchanges produce, and which are in contemporary capitalistic milieus subject either to commodification, accumulation, and paranoiac control (derivatives, futures, the attempt to control risk) or externalised (such as atmospheric pollution, or arrhyth-mic effects in the mental environment) – becomes integrated into the milieu through the valorisation of care and the creation of long-term cir-cuits of participatory exchange. In terms of rhythmically dramatising new modes of exchange beyond our contemporary debt-credit ecology, we could instead imagine new economies that valorised (invariably qualita-tive) modes of care, participation, experimentation, joy, and the extension of access to the means to cultivate singularising existential refrains.

Although we make no claims on the possibility of coming to a stable or static conclusion on how these new modes of exchange may be invented and what forms they could take, one of the key points being drawn from Massumi, Raunig, and Stiegler here is the virtual abundances of alternatives, an abundance which can only be worked through and worked out through experimentation, collaboration, and care. Processes of invention are themselves crucial ('Invention is a plug-in to the impossible. It is only by plumbing that connection that anything truly new can arise' (Massumi, 2002: 96–97)).

Importantly, and as we already mentioned, many of these projects would not be possible if they did not, temporarily, operate within contemporary capitalistic milieus: insofar as the map immanently participates in the territory, one cannot experiment from the outside, and thereby one must always confront the conditions of the present. Attracting virtual and actual money, and developing systems of mutual aid, would thus be crucial initial steps in creating the spacetime for these projects to acquire their own stable rhythmic parameters of ontological security. In Stiegler's terms, such processes would additionally confront the questions of *subsistence* (the collaborative organisation and distribution of the 'means of reproduction' – i.e., food, shelter, healthcare, and so forth); *existence* (social relations, sensibilities, affects), constituted by practices free from the worry of subsistence (2011a: 65); and *consistence* (which he identifies with the mind or spirit, theory, deliberation, and decisions on the to-come) (2016a: 31). The point, in other words, is not to foundationally seek to dissociate from contemporary capitalistic milieus, but rather to invent new practices and rhythms that would in time abolish the axioms of capitalist milieus, developing practices of mutual aid in order to sustain the experimental process. At what point, in a gradual abolition of the creditor-debtor distinction (both through practices of striking debt and through the attempt to harness financial investment into new modes of exchange), would we have abolished the hierarchy as such? At what point could there be said to be a post-capitalist milieu? Such a question cannot be answered without experimentation. Rather than positioning this as symptomatic of a process of capitalist co-option, we suggest instead that this could form part of a strategy of rhythmic dramatisation as such, gradually 'sucking' capital investment into these collaborative processes for the purposes of co-creating modes of exchange irreducible to any general equivalent. That is, the 'return' on capital investment into these processes would not be surplus value or capital accumulation, but, rather, as contributions to the ontological insecurity of the capitalist milieu in question. The proliferative invention of ever-new matrices of emergence for our milieus-to-come. Massumi usefully describes such a strategy as one of *camouflage* or of *processual duplicity*: 'To succeed at the reform side of the coin, to work within the existing order to ensure the survival of oneself and one's group, requires the ability to "pass" on the "inside"' (Massumi, 1992: 105); 'An anti-capitalist counter-ontopower is one that connects to and prolongs emergent tendencies which, if they were to follow their arc to its logical conclusion, would ultimately lead to the abolition of property as we know it' (Massumi, 2017a: 32).

Furthermore, it is important to connect this discussion with the *decolonising* element we have folded into scaping. We have already mentioned on several occasions in this chapter the differentially skewed manner in which debt is distributed, as well as the global political economy and history of the ways in which indebtedness forms a crucial part of macroeconomic governance: it is not possible to separate the creditor-debtor ecology in contemporary capitalistic milieus from the history of imperialism, nor with the question of the mental environment. Ngũgĩ wa Thiong'o highlights this clearly:

> Imperialism is the rule of consolidated finance capital and since 1884 this monopolistic parasitic capital has affected and continues to affect the lives even of the peasants in the remotest corners of our countries. If you are in doubt, just count how many African countries have now been mortgaged to IMF – the new International Ministry of Finance as Juliuis Nyerere once called it [. . .] Imperialism is total: it has economic, political, military, cultural and psychological consequences for the people of the world today. (Thiong'o, 2005: 2)

Credit-based debt is fluid and deterritorialising, and, as such, no practices of *striking debt* nor of the *sculpting of new modes of exchange* could remain within a geographic-territorial milieu. The dissolution of the creditor-debtor hierarchy cannot occur in *this* or *that* milieu, insofar as credit-based indebtedness is global in scope. While such macropolitical questions are beyond the immediate scope of our scaping of the mental environment, passing through the question of how to *decolonise debt* would confront the question of the political economies of memory that could be created in our milieus-to-come: how to remember the histories (and present) of colonialism, settler colonialism, slavery, debt bondage, and so forth? This would, of necessity, be in part and initially another question of *listening*: the results of what would emerge from a process of social sculpture confronting this question cannot be foretold. Nonetheless, the process of abolishing the creditor-debtor ecology would *expand* the range and scope of existential refrains for those in our milieus-to-come, and as such would contribute to the decolonisation of the rhythms of everyday life in contemporary capitalistic milieus. Jason Thomas Wozniak, for example, explicitly connects the decolonial project to one that confronts the question of credit-based indebtedness (for reasons we have noted: the racialised distribution of indebtedness in the present, the entangled history of debt and history of colonialism, and the manner in which debt colonises everyday life). Countering, amongst other things, the temporality of debt is for him thereby a crucial element of the decolonial, and we would add revolutionary, process (Wozniak, 2017: 349–351; also see Mignolo, 2011: 176–180).

The abolition of the creditor-debtor hierarchy could not stand alone in a process of decolonising debt, however. As we have mentioned a number of times already, debt is a *technology of remembering*. But it is also, in another sense, a *technology of forgetting*. How so? In order to respond to this, let us briefly take an example outside of finance: that of national curricula. National curricula (including university curricula) serve, in part, to *generationally transfer* memory, which, in the UK at least, has historically tended to *efface* colonial histories, serving to reproduce new colonial mentalities in the present.[4] In this sense, the disciplinary passage through education systems – as a vital node in processes of acculturation through its contribution to and sustenance of the surrounding framework of habits and expectations (that is, *rhythmic parameters of ontological security*) that are generationally transferred – is a *technology of forgetting* through this process of effacement. Insofar as national curricula, today, are technologies of forgetting, they not only constitute a mechanism of epistemic violence or exploitation, but they are also technologies of acculturation that inscribe very few and limited 'lessons of the past' into the *milieu*. These 'lessons' cannot be inscribed into the history of the milieu by the very elite who guard these technologies presently: this pertains *precisely* to the creditor-debtor ecology, too. Debt functions as an imperial machine not just in terms of the material impoverishment and exploitation it enacts, but also in how it *constitutively forgets* these things, instead reversing it through producing *indebted colonial subjects*, who owe material and existential debt to creditors-colonisers for progress (access to History), science (access to Truth), culture (access to Logos and Being), and so forth.[5] *Decolonising debt* would necessitate abolishing imperial and technologies of forgetting and creating new *technologies of remembrance* which inscribed the 'lessons of the past' into the milieu, helping to create the spacetime for *reparative work* and rhythmic dramatisation, rather than the perpetual production of colonial mentalities: decolonisation 'brings a new rhythm into existence' (Fanon, 2001: 28).

Let us draw some of these threads together before concluding this section. We suggested above that a combination of our *minority experiment* of striking debt, with the collaborative sculpture of new modes of exchange which, in turn, sucked capital investment into these collaborative processes, constitutes a triple strategy for pushing capitalistic milieus to their region of ontological insecurity as it pertains to the creditor-debtor ecology. We noted that, confronting the conditions of the present, our collaborative processes pursuing the sculpting of new modes of exchange would *extend* access to the technologies of exchange, as well as *extending* the access to the transformation of these technologies. This generates a certain 'fluidity' to the modes of exchange sculpted, but a fluidity, importantly, not *reducible* to any general equivalent (which itself is a manifestation of paranoiac control and symptomatic of the *destruction of trust* and solidaristic possibilities); rather, this fluidity is generated as part of the *constitutively open* process of social sculpture engaging with new virtual ecologies of value and new modes of valorisation, flowing from a *common investment* in the future and an attentive collaborative focus on creating the conditions for singularising existential refrains. Such fluidity is processual, and, once again, as Guattari reminds us: '*revolution is either processual or it isn't revolution*' (Guattari, in Guattari and Rolnik, 2007: 260).

d. Conclusion

The debtor-creditor hierarchy, and the debt-credit ecology to which it pertains in the mental environment, has a complex, variegated, and differential history, and is teeming with pressure points to be hacked in the service of its eventual abolition in our creation of new worlds. Credit-based indebtedness is not homogeneously distributed: lines of race, class, and so forth are continuously reproduced through hierarchies of indebtedness. These differential elements cannot be effaced in any revolutionary process which *itself* is concerned with working towards, as we have noted previously with Guattari, 'complexification', 'processual enrichment', and 'ontological heterogeneity' (2006: 61). Nonetheless, the creditor-debtor hierarchy can function as a shared object of experience and revolutionary attack: helping in the process of creating new solidarities (new inclusive disjunctions) in the mental environment, and towards milieus-to-come which *listen*, embed the 'lessons of the past', and collaboratively sculpt modes of exchange towards mutual empowerment.

e. Chapter 6 reprise

[92] Systems of indebtification are libidinally pulsed with machines of guiltification and responsibilisation, producing the interiorisation of these affective dynamics: the creditor–debtor distinction being produced through the social function of the *promise*, a promise inscribed in *memory*, and which must be fulfilled through new habits in everyday life. Blocks of debt in contemporary capitalistic milieus are 'parcels of destiny' which 'render debt infinite' and permeate the rhythms of everyday life of the indebted subject.

[93] The creditor–debtor distinction in contemporary capitalistic milieus is a hierarchical and asymmetric distinction through which debt becomes an inexpiable, unpayable, and fundamental component to contemporary capitalism, a distinction which pedals continuous indebtedness, and, as such, functions as oil to processes of capital accumulation.

[94] The granting of access to credit is immediately a process through which debt is privatised, isolated, and reduced to the *I*, where the *I* becomes rhythmically subjected, or rather produced in the process of subjection, to machines of libidinal and material culpabilisation through mechanisms of surveillance.

[95] Those who only have access to money in the sense of a *flow* are those whose exchange partakes only in the *actual*: commodity-money is actual money, exchange within pre-defined zones, within the closed elements of an open financial system. Money as financing, credit money, or simply *Capital*, is money operating between the virtual and the actual, inscribing particular memories and deploying it to control the field of possible futures; that is, money operating at the borders of the system of indebtedness as such, seeking to direct the expansive process: finance.

[96] As with the digital divide, there are milieus in which *access* to financial technologies in the first place (i.e., the ability to even *acquire* debt, the ability to be *granted* credit) is a privilege, and, indeed, one of the perks of being a 'creditor' is the ability to acquire vast amounts of debt for the purposes of capital accumulation.

[97] *Debt functions as a mechanism of rhythmic subjection through (1) continually reproducing the creditor-debtor hierarchy; and (2) the temporal squeezing it effectuates on debtors' rhythms of everyday life, having a contractive effect on possible existential refrains.*

[98] Through every credit card transaction, the creditor–debtor distinction is further instantiated and reproduced. Whether the debtor is utilising her transactions for purposes of production or consumption is beside the point, insofar as *subjection* to the creditor–debtor hierarchy

is the *condition* of engaging in such economic activity in the first place, and a state of personal or individualised indebtedness is the *consequence:* indebtedness becoming the rule of the game. *Since* the creditor-debtor distinction is indissociable from the perpetuation of contemporary capitalistic milieus, that *in principle*, credit-based-debt functions as a process of *perpetual rhythmic subjection of debtors to creditors*, and as a continuous reproduction of the creditor-debtor hierarchy.

[99] As continuously solicited to *accrue* and *repay*, the *rhythms of everyday life* for the contemporary indebted subject are ones surrounded by debt-based injunctions. The indebted subject's rhythms of everyday life are ones through which mechanisms are responsibilisation and guiltification – which themselves are mechanisms of identity filtration in processes of rhythmic subjection – are continuously solicited and demanded. Under such a continuous process, the indebted subject is incentivised to internalise such responsibility and such guilt, that is, incentivised to internalise and reproduce the creditor-debtor hierarchy through the filtering of the affective components of responsibility and guilt into his rhythms of everyday life; a libidinal and rhythmic contraction. One *feels* one's indebtedness in the mental environment: psychic pain, anxiety, guilt, resentment. The debtor's responsibility is to *fulfil* the promise he made to the creditor, and the affective component of guilt enters primarily as a *libidinal* and *motivational* mechanism to spur repayment activity and psychic disempowerment, and also when such a fulfilment appears unlikely or difficult.

[100] When the *rhythms of debt repayment and debt accrual* come to dominate the rhythms of everyday life, anxiety, stress, desperation, responsibility, guilt, fear, and permanent insecurity are the predictable effects which manifest in the mental environment. Given the necessity of operating within the realm of actual money, and increasingly needing to access indebtedness to *invest in one's human capital*, the indebted subject's self-investment – his pursuit of happiness – becomes bound within a tight grid of moral and economic accountability. Credit-based debt promises only the freedom of the capitalist *I*.

[101] Perpetual indebted rhythmic subjection functions as an *effacement* of the structural economic mechanisms that render the ability to *escape* the creditor-debtor hierarchy itself an impossibility within contemporary capitalistic milieus. Debt is *essential* oil to the cogs of capitalistic production and consumption machines, and therefore essential for the perpetuation of the ontological security of capitalistic milieus themselves, though nonetheless indebtedness is positioned as that which the indebted subject must *feel guilty for.*

[102] *Debt functions as a mechanism of rhythmic containment: the subject in contemporary capitalistic milieus is increasingly required to submit to pre- and supra-personal intervention, and compulsory indebtedness, in order to pursue their own existential refrain.*

[103] Debt is inseparable from tertiary retentions (increasingly digital), which store the *memory* of debt. Indebtedness is a system of (selected) memory. Such memory is utilised to submit debtors to particular rhythms of repayment and in the calculation of the debtor's 'worth' in relation to previous financial records ('credit ratings') to decide what type of debt the debtor is 'worthy' of, in a dividualised and machinic process of rhythmic containment.

[104] This (necessary) *submission* to one's financial data being stored and deployed in and through tertiary retentions is a submission process of pre-personal intervention in the material-economic sense of an intervention that enables the contraction or enhancement of possible existential refrains. Further, in the sense in which systems of moral-economic accounting come to play a role in a subject's rhythmic processes of individuation towards their individual interiorisation of responsibility for this moral-economic balance sheet and a felt guilt in the face of the continuous surveillance of capital. These processes of inscription, in other words, function as an *automatic confessional process.* Such data are centrally also utilised by creditors, through financial technologies, as a process of supra-personal intervention insofar as access to these tertiary retentions enables creditors to *control the future* through financial, legal, and economic mechanisms, but, also, through tactics of securitisation, for further capital accumulation. *Securitisation as rhythmic containment: foreclosing the future of the debtor and enhancing the future of the creditor.*

[105] For the debtor, these tertiary retentions function in an *ontologically contractive* sense. For the creditor, these tertiary retentions function in an *ontologically expansive* sense. The creditor, in this sense, *relies* upon the debtor to expand the field of capital.

[106] Debt works on the *deterritorialised* components of subjectivity through these processes of automatic confession (moral-economic accounting) and continual incentive-structure rebalancing, towards the production of an embrained body that works 'for the machines', part of the general tendency we have been noting *towards the automatisation of practices which tend to securitise capitalistic milieus.*

[107] *Debt forecloses the future for debtors, and opens the future for creditors, and, so, for the continuous transference of privileged access to the means to control and transform financial technologies.*

[108] The inscription and recording in of creditor-debtor hierarchies functions contemporary capitalistic milieus to, precisely, *retain* and

transmit these asymmetries into a perpetual future. Debt is a retentional apparatus – or perhaps more clearly: a set a tertiary retentions and financial technologies – through which this historical privilege is *transferred* or *conferred* to future creditors. While these technologies are constantly undergoing mutations and transformations depending on social, historical, political, and economic contexts, what is maintained is *the privileged access to the control and transformation* of these financial technologies *in the future: arrhythmic closing of the future.*

[109] Insofar as the creditor-debtor ecology is based upon hugely inaccessible financial technologies that debtors have no access to control or transform, this status as a 'debtor' is *perpetually transferred into future generations.* The position of 'creditor', as a privileged position through which the scale and scope of one's existential refrains are enhanced, is a position through which creditors *perpetually hold debtors to account* and, further, through their privileged access to financial technologies, creditors *perpetually transfer this privilege onto future generations.* The continuing ontological security of capitalistic milieus is perpetually enhanced and expanded through all transactions between creditors and debtors in everyday life.

[110] For our purposes, the minority experiment of *striking debt* would function as an *extemporaneous counter-actualisation* in the creditor-debtor ecology in at least two senses: (i) through the collective participation and creation of *new* supra-personal imaginaries on debt, and, through this, the transformation of the rhythmically subjected and enslaved indebted subject (once again, such collective participation has the potential for the co-production of *solidarity*); (ii) through the epistemological-technical proliferation on how debt functions (as a predominantly digital tertiary retention) in contemporary capitalistic milieus.

[111] The counter-actualisation of the creditor-debtor ecology would constitute the *breaking* of the automatic circuits through which debt functions to economically (the automatic confessional function made possible thorough rhythmic containment) and morally (through processes of rhythmic subjection) subject the becomings of bodies in contemporary capitalistic milieus and through which we have acquired arrhythmic habits of thought and practice *as if* such indebtedness were necessary.

[112] Our debt-credit ecology, today, consists of a political war on memory and the future leveraged through privileged abilities to access, control, and transform the mnemotechnical milieu, but which is always already a war on the present insofar as it actualised through the indebted subject's contracted rhythms of everyday life. A revolutionary politics of the debt-credit ecology must, in this sense, concern itself crucially with the mnemotechnics through which our becomings are oriented.

[113] Collaborative sculpting processes of alternative modes of exchange (involving the *investment* of participants, but, also, insofar as these strategies confront contemporary capitalistic milieus, may indeed require *capital* investment) with various forms of experimental tactics we discussed above in terms of *debt strikes* conducted periodically.

[114] The *collaborative sculpting of alternative modes of exchange* would centralise the creation and operation of modes of exchange collaboratively and deliberatively decided within and across milieus. What we suggest here is that the process of co-operatively inventing and practising new modes of exchange could mobilise around the three temporally oriented strategic points we have been focusing on. In this specific ecology, this could take practical shape through: first, confronting the conditions of the present in the debtor-creditor ecology we scaped in section 6a (requiring, at least initially, operating at the edge of the parameters of contemporary capitalistic milieus); second, through the co-creation of *sustainable*, long-term circuits of exchange *irreducible to any putative general equivalent*; third, through a collaborative and solidaristic *investment* in creating the conditions for singularising existential refrains.

[115] Credit-based debt is fluid and deterritorialising, and, as such, no practices of *striking debt* nor of the *sculpting of new modes of exchange* could remain within a geographic-territorial milieu. The dissolution of the creditor-debtor hierarchy cannot occur in *this* or *that* milieu, insofar as credit-based indebtedness is global in scope.

Notes

1. For an interesting analysis of the arrhythmic nature (in Lefebvre's sense which is close to but distinct from our own) of contemporary work in the 'creative economy', see Jones and Warren (2016).

2. For example, we will not discuss in any detail here the function of debt as it pertains to international financial institutions and their relationships to economies in the Global South, and the expansive debt regime that crystallised especially from the early 1980s. This involved, for example, the tripling of Latin American debt in the 1980s and the increasing 'liberalization' of 'debtor economies' through Structural Adjustment Programmes (Moore, 2015: 256–264; Schaeffer, 2003: 96; Lensink, 1996).

3. As Sune Sandbeck and Etienne Schneider note: 'More than simply constituting a technical "financial facility", the EFSF [European Financial Stability Facility] has been turned into an important political vehicle for the implementation of austerity packages designed under the aegis of the Troika [constituted by the European Commission, the European Central Bank, and the International Monetary Fund] and imposed on crisis-ridden member states. In a similar way, the granting of loans by the permanent ESM [European

Stability Mechanism] will be conditional upon agreeing on the austerity demands of the FC [Fiscal Compact] and will thus, as the European Council bluntly puts it, provide a "new framework of reinforced economic governance, aiming at an effective and rigorous economic surveillance"' (Sandbeck and Schneider, 2014: 852; also see European Council, 2010: 8).

4. See, for example, Deana Heath's (2016) article entitled 'School Curriculum Continues to Whitewash Britain's Imperial Past'.

5. Fanon discusses the psychological *splitedness* resulting from colonisation, considering 'the native' who is ascribed *guilt* but permanently refuses it: 'the native's guilt is never a guilt which he accepts; it is rather a kind of curse, a sort of sword of Damocles, for, in his innermost spirit, the native admits no accusation' (2001: 41).

Conclusion: The Rhythmanalytical Project and the Way of Rhythm (Endtroduction)

The Way of Rhythm pervades all life, and indeed all physical exist-ence. This common principle of Rhythm is one of the reasons for believing that the root principles of life are, in some lowly form, exemplified in all types of physical existence. In the Way of Rhythm a round of experiences, forming a determinate sequence of con-trasts attainable within a definite method, are codified so that the end of one such cycle is the proper antecedent stage for the beginning of another such cycle. The cycle is such that its own completion provides the conditions for its own mere repetition. It eliminates the fatigue attendant upon the repetition of any one of its parts. Only some strength of physical memory can aggregate fatigue arising from the cycle as a whole. Provided that each cycle in itself is self-repairing, the fatigue from repetition requires a high level of coordi-nation of stretches of past experience [. . .] the Rhythm of life is not merely to be sought in simple cyclical recurrence. The cycle element is driven into the foundation, and variations of cycles, and of cycles of cycles, are elaborated. We find here the most obvious example of the adoption of a method. (Whitehead, 1929: 22–23)

This book has been an experimental attempt to construct a new method or mode of rhythmanalysis, attuned towards the rhythms of everyday life and their relationship to our mental environment that traverses con-temporary capitalistic milieus. I have attempted to develop this mode of rhythmanalysis, scaping (or mindscaping in this particular iteration), through an analysis of time and desire across the levels through which our everyday lives are constituted, and have positioned it alongside work in the fields of naturalism, cybernetics, critique, decoloniality, seeking to develop a mode of revolutionary rhythmanalysis. Scaping is, to repeat, about immanent participation in the territory; that is, it does not attempt to stand elsewhere to judge the territory. Scaping is the only 'place' it can be – in the middle. Intersecting this analysis with work concerned with our contemporary attention economy, with the relationship between capitalism and depression, and with our debtor-creditor premised political economy, an overarching thematic has been a politicisation of the mental environment, and an argument that our shared psychic ecology can become an object of revolutionary struggle towards the creation of our worlds-to-come, towards the creation of milieus of shared participation and the collaborative sculpting of the social, with shared control over technics, and with a shared participation in the determination of our rhythms. A further element that has been important to the arguments developed here is that of a processual conceptualisation of revolution. These attempts have been tentative, speculative, and partial, and the completion of this process of rhythmanalysis seeks to move towards new ones: not the continual repetition of this cycle, but the opening towards new cycles to come.

As I indicated at the beginning of this book, a key inspiration of this work is Guattari's *Three Ecologies* (2014), which distinguished between mental, social, and environmental ecologies. These latter two ecologies will thus become the objects of future rhythmanalysis, and the future development of scaping as it (differently) repeats across these distinct domains. The termination of this rhythm, in other words, functions to open the way for ones yet to be actualised.

Postscript by Conor Heaney and Iain MacKenzie

IM: From within our contemporary capitalist milieu, there is a reassuring nostalgia for those disciplinary institutions that moulded us into the subject positions that once defined our life course and even for those corrective institutions that put us back on track should we transgress. As transgression itself increasingly becomes the norm of a smoothly lived life within control societies, we are no longer faced with the consequences of being forced into subject positions, rather we are having to live with the paradoxical demand that only we can define our subjectivity: paradoxical because 'who am I to say who I am', and demanding because we must answer this question again and again, constantly transgressing every answer we come up with. The consequences of this neoliberal embrace of the collapse of disciplinary norms with respect to our experience of the world, ourselves, and our exchanges with each other are profoundly explored in your work. You have taught us that we need a new critique of everyday life, in the lineage of Lefebvre but never beholden to him, that will revolutionise critically oriented therapeutics. The rhythms of the world and the mind are so deeply intertwined that we can only change one by changing the other; that is, by forging new milieus of self-care and exchange.

CH: It is true that subject positions are less defined by the mould, and instead by incessant modulation. But modulations still have rhythms and still operate with parameters: so instead of fitting the mould, we have targets, protocols, and key performance indicators for optimisation. 'Mental illness' therefore becomes less about fitting or not fitting a template, it is rather evidence that you have (temporarily) not optimised for mental-emotional health, providing the subject with information to integrate and modulate in relation to. Too much time scrolling social media is on the one hand incentivised, but on the other hand is a failure to optimise your dopaminergic rhythms (and who else could be responsible for them?). The question is whether it is possible, and if so how, to practise critique in such a milieu, and what critique might mean today. Is critique lapsing into arrhythmia? Which is to say: Are we finding that the practice of critique, today, is following the same old gestures, habits, and routines? Or is it that this very tendency of thinking, in that it always seeks the comfort of repetition, means that this is *precisely* what critique must always relate to?

IM: There is no doubt that after decades of 'critical turns' we are now witnessing a turn away from critique. We have become uninterested in yet another critical turn, the same old habits played out in (apparently) new domains. Criticism has become part of the sedimented rhythm of social reproduction, operating increasingly through the hyper-discursive realms of social media. I see this problem front and centre in your work. Deleuze said of Foucault, 'you taught us the indignity of speaking on behalf of others' whereas you show us what happens when we think that we must only speak on our own behalf. It is disastrous for thought when 'speaking only for myself . . .' or 'speaking only from my experience . . .' and other such refrains are the necessary preamble to every critical intervention and the implacable defence against every response. Of course, let us not hark back to an image of rational critique, the very one that built the walls of the disciplinary institutions we sought to transgress. And that's why I see you offering a new critique: one for our times, ready to grasp the potential for how we might know the world we have created by making it differently.

CH: While critique is already creative *to the extent* that it executes a distinct compositional style, both rationalist and empiricist critique (in their puritanical senses) are full of tropes and snares. Their sedimentation means they risk scripting or choreographing thought; and if philosophy (and critique) are at all about the ordering and sequencing of thought patterns, then these scripts seem to protocol *critique with a minimum of creativity*. Beginning from the middle (where else?), I wonder whether it's possible to dance between and beyond the two, and to both discover and invent the new thereby. It's not that one cannot or should not speak from experience, but it is that experience is always a product, with a particular genesis, emerging from its milieu. Our singularity emerges from this shared mental environment. This is what I wanted to try and play with – I hope sufficiently carefully and cautiously – with the notion of *mindscaping* and a rhythmanalytical critique of everyday life.

IM: It's all in the grammar, isn't it? Landscapes imply a spectator, a point of view that surveys, whereas landscaping brings us to the construction of those perspectives. And so it is with mindscaping: a compositional method that critiques established views of what constitutes our inner life by bringing forth new arrangements of the rhythms of our mental milieus. Mindscaping invites us to think of ideas as vibrating and resonating within us and through us in ways that unsettle the arrhythmical, the settled habits of thought. It also invites us to practise, to experiment with the everyday rhythms of our existence so that we may, for once, think. Changing our mind, that everyday expression that seems so banal, becomes a question about how we change the world, not in some wholescale once and for all sense but in the manner of finding out what it is that we must do to even to begin to think within and yet beyond our established perspectives. We are invited to divest ourselves of our tendency to spectate on our own lives and, instead, to get actively involved. Mindscaping may have the mental as its object, but it has activity in the world as its method, and revolutionary activity at that. It may be that certain forms of critical thought are deemed complicit in the neoliberal excesses of our current conjuncture, but there is, it seems to me, always the need to return to one of the questions that emerged from within the critical tradition: What is to be done? How do you find your rhythm in an arrhythmic society?

CH: Complicitly can have multiple senses: when concerned with the attribution of moral and legal accountability, to be complicit is to be discretely identified as within the ambit of wrongdoing as it pertains to some transgression committed. But we can also consider the issue of *systemic* or *ecological* complicity: com-*pli*-city's etymology bearing the mark of the *fold [pli]* which speaks to the ways in which we are ecologically enmeshed, to the unquantifiable ways in which we are in this sense complicit with each other and with the world (just as Deleuze wrote of Foucault that he was ultimately researching the problem of the fold, of the relation between the inside and the outside). This brings us back, I think, to the question of *mapping* and to what I take to be Korzybski's experimental injunction: test the usefulness of your maps! How are we mapping our rhythms of everyday life? I'm less interested in the ascription of past complicity in this sense than in the creation of new forms of complicity: new maps will require new complicities – which is also to say new solidarities – the collaborative creation of new projects where our mutual incalculable indebtedness is elaborated again and again. For me this will of necessity requires patience and care: the openness to begin again and again. The ultimate source of this – this ceaseless energy of difference and repetition – and perhaps the literal incarnation of rhythm thereby (at least in our cosmic locality), is undoubtedly the Sun. Sunlight teaches us this folding of repetition and difference. Wavelengths folded together, refracting through the atmosphere, being organically synthesised into vitamin D, photosynthesised into glucose, activating neural pathways to alert circadian rhythms. Contemporary capital-ist milieus are tendentially arrhythmic, but it is not hard to begin to unlock the power of rhythm when one begins to pay attention (which, as we said, is itself a kind of care), to mobilise it, and begin to map out your own rhythms. My approach to method is rhythmic. A method lays down, or maps, a rhythm . . .

References

Abraham, Nicolas, *Rhythms: On the Work, Translation, and Psychoanalysis*, trans. by Benjamin Thigpen and Nicholas T. Rand (Stanford, CA: Stanford University Press, 1995).

Abrams, Jerrold J., 'Peirce, Kant, and Apel on Transcendental Semiotics: The Unity of Apperception and the Deduction of the Categories of Signs', *Transactions of the Charles S. Peirce Society*, 40, 4 (2004), 627–677.

Adams, David, 'Joseph Beuys: Pioneer of a Radical Ecology', *Art Journal*, 51, 2 (1992), 26–34.

Ahmed, Sara, 'The Happiness Turn', *New Formations*, 63 (2008), 7–14.

Ahmed, Sara, *The Promise of Happiness* (London: Duke University Press, 2010).

Akmut, Camille, 'Notes on the Freedom Tower. Current issues in Networking (mesh)' (2019). https://doi.org/10.31219/osf.io/m8g4s

Al-Saji, Alia, 'The Memory of Another Past: Bergson, Deleuze and a New Theory of Time', *Continental Philosophy Review*, 37 (2004), 203–239.

Alleyne, Aileen, 'Black Identity and Workplace Oppression', *Counselling and Psychotherapy Research*, 4, 1 (2004), 4–8.

Alliez, Éric, *Capital Times: Tales from the Conquest of Time*, trans. by Georges Van Der Abbeele (Minneapolis: University of Minnesota Press, 1996).

Althusser, Louis, *Essays in Self-Criticism* (London: NLB, 1976).

Anderson, Benedict, *Imagined Communities* (London: Verso, 2006).

Ansell Pearson, Keith, 'Viroid Life: On Machines, Technics and Evolution', in *Deleuze and Philosophy: The Difference Engineer*, ed. by Keith Ansell Pearson (London: Routledge, 1997), pp. 180–210.

Anzaldúa, Gloria, *Borderlands/La Frontera: The New Mestiza* (San Francisco, CA: Aunt Lute Book Company, 1987).

Appadurai, Arjun, *Banking on Words: The Failure of Language in the Age of Derivative Finance* (Chicago, IL: University of Chicago Press, 2016).

Argys, Laura M., Friedson, Andrew, and Pitts, M. Melinda, 'Killer Debt: The Impact of Debt on Mortality'. *FRB Atlanta Working Paper No. 2016–14*. https://ssrn.com/abstract-2879277 (accessed 19 June 2018).

Austin, John Langshaw, *How To Do Things With Words* (Oxford: Oxford University Press, 1976).

Bachelard, Gaston, *The Dialectic of Duration*, trans. by Mary McAllester Jones (London: Rowman & Littlefield, 2016).

Baker, Andrew, and Underhill, Geoffrey R. D., 'Economic Ideas and the Political Construction of the Financial Crash of 2008', *The British Journal of Politics and International Relations*, 17 (2015), 381–390.

Barad, Karen, *Meeting the Universe Halfway: Quantum Physics and the Entanglement of Matter and Meaning* (London: Duke University Press, 2007).

Barad, Karen, 'Interview with Karen Barad', in *New Materialism: Interviews and Cartographies*, ed. by Rick Dolphijn and Iris van der Tuin (Ann Arbor, MI: Open Humanities Press, 2012), pp. 48–70.

Barcelo, Jaume, Bellalta, Boris, Baig, Roger, Roca, Ramon, Domingo, Albert, Sanabria, Luis, Cano, Cristina, and Oliver, Miquel, 'Bottom-up Broadband Initiatives in the Commons for Europe Project' (2012). arXiv:1207.1031v1

Bateson, Gregory, *Steps to an Ecology of Mind* (London: University of Chicago Press, 2000).

Baudrillard, Jean, *The Impossible Exchange*, trans. by Chris Turner (London: Verso, 2001).

Baugh, Bruce, 'Transcendental Empiricism: Deleuze's Response to Hegel', *Man and World*, 25 (1992), 133–148.

Becker, Gary, *The Economic Approach to Human Behavior* (Chicago, IL: University of Chicago Press, 1990).

Becker, Gary, *Human Capital: A Theoretical and Empirical Analysis with Special Reference to Education* (London: University of Chicago Press, 1993a).

Becker, Gary, *A Treatise on the Family* (Cambridge, MA: Harvard University Press, 1993b).

Beckmann, Lukas, 'The Causes Lie in the Future', in *Joseph Beuys: Mapping the Legacy*, ed. by Gene Ray (New York: Distributed Art Publishers, 2008), pp. 91–111.

Beistegui, Miguel de, *Immanence: Deleuze and Philosophy* (Edinburgh: Edinburgh University Press, 2010).

Belli, Luca (ed.), *The Community Network Manual: How to Build the Internet Yourself* (2018). https://comconnectivity.org/wp-content/

uploads/2020/05/The-community-network-manual-how-to-build-the-internet-yourself.pdf

Benveniste, Emile, *Problems in General Linguistics*, trans. by Mary Elizabeth Meek (Coral Gables, FL: University of Miami Press, 1971).

Berardi, Franco 'Bifo', 'What does Cognitariat Mean? Work, Desire and Depression', *Cultural Studies Review*, 11, 2 (2005), 57–63.

Berardi, Franco 'Bifo', *Félix Guattari: Thought, Friendship and Visionary Cartography*, trans. by Giuseppina Mecchia and Charles J. Stivale (Basingstoke: Palgrave Macmillan, 2008).

Berardi, Franco 'Bifo', *And. Phenomenology of the End: Sensibility and Connective Mutation* (South Pasadena, CA: Semiotext(e), 2015).

Bergsma, Ad, 'Transhumanism and the Wisdom of Old Genes: Is Neurotechnology a Source of Future Happiness?', *Journal of Happiness Studies*, 1 (2000), 401–417.

Bergson, Henri, *Time and Free Will*, trans. by F. L. Pogson (Edinburgh: George Allen and Unwin Ltd, 1910).

Bergson, Henri, *Matter and Memory*, trans. by Nancy Margaret Paul and W. Scott Palmer (Mansfield Center, CT: Martino Publishing, 2011).

Bergson, Henri, *Creative Evolution*, trans. by Arthur Mitchell (Createspace Independent Publishing Platform, 2014).

Beuys, Joseph, 'Introduction', in *Energy Plan for the Western Man: Joseph Beuys in America: Writings by and Interviews with the Artist*, ed. by Carin Kuoni (New York: Four Walls Eight Windows, 1990).

Beuys, Joseph, *Par le présente, je n'appartiens plus à l'art*, trans. by Fr O. Mannoni and P. Borassa (Paris: L'Arche, 1994).

Beuys, Joseph, *What is Art?: Conversation with Joseph Beuys*, ed. by Volker Harlan, trans. by Matthew Barton and Shelley Sacks (West Hoathly: Clairview Books, 2004).

Beuys, Joseph and Schwarze, Dirk, 'Report on a Day's Proceedings', Documenta 5, Kassel, 1972, translated in Adriani Götz et al., *Joseph Beuys, Life and Work* (New York: Barron's, 1979), pp. 244–249.

Bidima, Jean-Godefroy, 'Music and the Socio-Historical Real: Rhythm, Series and Critique in Deleuze and O. Revault d'Allones', in *Deleuze and Music*, ed. by Ian Buchanan and Marcel Swiboda (Edinburgh: Edinburgh University Press, 2004), pp. 176–195.

Bindewald, Leander and Steed, Susan, 'Money With a Purpose: Community Currencies Achieving Social, Environmental and Economic Impact', *New Economics Foundation*, May 2015. https://neweconomics.org/2015/05/money-with-a-purpose (accessed 26 June 2018)

Bispham, John, 'Rhythm in Music: What Is It? Who Has It? And Why?', *Music Perception*, 24, 2 (2006), 125–134.

Bleiker, Roland, 'The Aesthetic Turn in International Political Theory', *Millennium: Journal of International Studies*, 30, 3 (2001), 509–533.

Bogue, Ronald, 'Violence in Three Shades of Metal: Death, Doom and Black', in *Deleuze and Music*, ed. by Ian Buchanan and Marcel Swiboda (Edinburgh: Edinburgh University Press, 2004), pp. 95–117.

Borch, Christian, 'Urban Imitations: Tarde's Sociology Revisited', *Theory, Culture & Society*, 22, 3 (2005), 81–100.

Borch, Christian, Hansen, Kristian Bondo, and Lange, Ann-Christina, 'Markets, Bodies, and Rhythms: A Rhythmanalysis of Financial Markets from Open-outcry Trading to High-frequency Trading', *Environment and Planning D: Society and Space*, 33, 6 (2015), 1080–1097.

Bösel, Bernd, 'Affective Synchronization, Rhythmanalysis and the Polyphonic Qualities of the Present Moment', in *Timing of Affect: Epistemologies, Aesthetics, Politics*, ed. by Marie-Luise Angerer, Bernd Bösel, and Michaela Ott (Zurich/Berlin: Diaphanes, 2014), pp. 87–102.

Bourdieu, Pierre, and Wacquant, Loïc J. D., *An Invitation to Reflexive Sociology* (Chicago, IL: University of Chicago Press, 1992).

Brefczynski-Lewis, J. A., Lutz, A., Schaefer, H. S., Levinson, D. B., and Davidson, R. J., 'Neural Correlates of Attentional Expertise in Long-term Meditation Practitioners', *Proceedings of the National Academy of Sciences*, 104, 27 (July 2007), 11483–11488.

Brown, Tony N., Williams, David R., Neighbors, Harold W., Torres, Myriam, Sellers, Sherrill L., and Brown, Kendrick T., '"Being Black and Feeling Blue": The Mental Health Consequences of Racial Discrimination', *Race & Society*, 2, 2 (2000), 117–131.

Bryant, Levi, *Difference and Givenness: Deleuze's Transcendental Empiricism and the Ontology of Immanence* (Evanston, IL: Northwestern University Press, 2008).

Buchanan, Ian, 'Schizoanalysis: An Incomplete Project', in *The Edinburgh Companion to Poststructuralism*, ed. by Benoît Dillet, Iain MacKenzie, and Robert Porter (Edinburgh: Edinburgh University Press, 2013), pp. 163–188.

Bueno, Claudio Celis, *The Attention Economy: Labor, Time and Power in Cognitive Capitalism* (London: Rowman & Littlefield, 2016).

Burton, James, 'Metafiction and General Ecology: Making Worlds with Worlds', in *General Ecology: The New Ecological Paradigm*, ed. by Erich Hörl with James Burton (London: Bloomsbury Academic, 2017), pp. 253–283.

Butler, Judith, 'Performative Acts and Gender Constitution: An Essay in Phenomenology and Feminist Theory', *Theatre Journal*, 40, 4 (1988), 519–531.

Butler, Judith, *Gender Trouble: Feminism and the Subversion of Identity* (New York: Routledge Classics, 2006).

Caliandro, Rocco, Streng, Astrid A., van Kerkhof, Linda W. M., van der Horst, Gijsbertus T. J., and Chaves, Inês, 'Social Jetlag and Related Risks for Human Health: A Timely Review', *Nutrients*, 13 (2021), 4543.

Canguilhem, Georges, *The Normal and the Pathological*, trans. by Carolyn R Fawcett in collaboration with Robert S. Cohen (New York: Zone Books, 1991).

Canguilhem, Georges, *Knowledge of Life*, trans. by Stefanos Geroulanos and Daniela Ginsburg (New York: Fordham University Press, 2008).

Carr, Nicholas, *The Shallows: How the Internet is Changing the Way We Think, Read and Remember* (London: Atlantic Books, 2010).

Certeau, Michel de, *The Practice of Everyday Life*, trans. by Steven Rendall (London: University of California Press, 1988).

Chen, Yi, *Practising Rhythmanalysis: Theories and Methodologies* (London: Rowman & Littlefield, 2018).

Chernoff, John Miller, *African Rhythm, African Sensibility* (Chicago, IL: Chicago University Press, 1981).

Citton, Yves, *The Ecology of Attention*, trans. by Barnaby Norman (Cambridge: Polity Press, 2017).

Clark, Andy and Chalmers, David, 'The Extended Mind', *Analysis*, 58, 1 (1998), 7–19.

Clisby, Dale, 'Deleuze's Secret Dualism? Competing Accounts of the Relationship between the Virtual and the Actual', *Parrhesia*, 24 (2015), 127–149.

Colwell, Chris, 'Deleuze and Foucault: Series, Event, Genealogy', *Theory and Event*, 1, 2 (1997).

Connolly, William E., *Neuropolitics: Thinking, Culture, Speed* (Minneapolis: University of Minnesota Press, 2002).

Connolly, William E., 'White Noise (2005)', *William E. Connolly: Democracy, Pluralism and Political Theory*, ed. by Samuel A. Chambers and Terrell Carver (Oxon: Routledge, 2008), pp. 303–311.

Connolly, William E., *The Fragility of Things: Self-Organizing Processes, Neoliberal Fantasies, and Democratic Activism* (London: Duke University Press, 2013).

Cramer, Kenneth M., Gallant, Melanie D., and Langlois, Michelle W., 'Self-silencing and Depression in Women and Men: Comparative Structural Equation Models', *Personality and Individual Differences*, 39, 3 (2005), 581–592.

Crary, Jonathan, *24/7: Capitalism and the Ends of Sleep* (London: Verso, 2014).

Crenshaw, Kimberlé, 'Demarginalizing the Intersection of Race and Sex: A Black Feminist Critique of Antidiscrimination Doctrine, Feminist Theory and Antiracist Politics', *University of Chicago Legal Forum* (1989), 139–167.

Crenshaw, Kimberlé, 'Mapping the Margins: Intersectionality, Identity Politics, and Violence Against Women of Color', in *Critical Race Theory: The Key Writings That Formed the Movement,* ed. by Kimberlé Crenshaw, Neil Gotanda, Gary Peller, and Kendal Thomas (New York: The New Press, 1995), pp. 357–384.

Crockett, Clayton, *Deleuze Beyond Badiou: Ontology, Multiplicity, Event* (New York: Columbia University Press, 2013).

Crowley, Martin, 'Bernard Stiegler Goes Seal-Hunting with Joseph Beuys', *Forum for Modern Language Studies*, 49 (1), 2012, 45–59.

Davies, William, *The Happiness Industry: How the Government and Big Business Sold Us Well-Being* (London: Verso, 2015).

Davis, Erik, 'Roots and Wires'. https://techgnosis.com/roots-and-wir es-2/ (accessed 27 May 2017).

Debaise, Didier, 'The Dramatic Power of Events: The Function of Method in Deleuze's Philosophy', *Deleuze Studies*, 10, 1 (2016), 5–18.

Debord, Guy, *The Society of the Spectacle*, trans. by Ken Knabb (Canberra: Hobgoblin Press, 2002).

Debord, Guy, 'Perspectives for Conscious Changes in Everyday Life', in *Situationist International Anthology*, ed. and trans. by Ken Knabb (Berkeley, CA: Bureau of Public Secrets, 2006), pp. 186–206.

Debt Collective, 'The Potential of Debtors' Unions', *ROAR Magazine*, 3 (2016), 82–95.

Deleuze, Gilles, *Différence et répétition* (Paris: Presses Universitaires de France, 1968).

Deleuze, Gilles, *Bergsonism*, trans. by Hugh Tomlinson and Barbara Habberiam (New York: Zone Books, 1988a).

Deleuze, Gilles, *Spinoza: Practical Philosophy*, trans. by Robert Hurley (San Francisco, CA: City Lights Books, 1988b).

Deleuze, Gilles, *Empiricism and Subjectivity: An Essay on Hume's Theory of Human Nature*, trans. by Constantin V. Boundas (New York: Columbia University Press, 1991).

Deleuze, Gilles, 'Postscript on the Societies of Control', *October*, 59 (Winter, 1992), 3–7.

Deleuze, Gilles, *Negotiations 1972–1990*, trans. by Martin Joughin (New York: Columbia University Press, 1995).

Deleuze, Gilles, *The Logic of Sense*, trans. by Mark Lester and Charles Stivale (London: Bloomsbury Academic, 2004a).

Deleuze, Gilles, 'The Method of Dramatisation', in *Desert Islands and Other Texts, 1953–1974*, trans. by Michael Taormina (Los Angeles, CA: Semiotext(e), 2004b).

Deleuze, Gilles, *Nietzsche and Philosophy*, trans. by Hugh Tomlinson (New York: Columbia University Press, 2006).

Deleuze, Gilles, *Kant's Critical Philosophy: The Doctrine of the Faculties*, trans. by Hugh Tomlinson and Barbara Habberjam (London: Continuum, 2008).

Deleuze, Gilles, *Difference and Repetition*, trans. by Paul Patton (London: Bloomsbury Academic, 2014).

Deleuze, Gilles, *Francis Bacon: The Logic of Sensation*, trans. by Daniel W. Smith (London: Bloomsbury Academic, 2016).

Deleuze, Gilles and Guattari, Félix, *Anti-Oedipus: Capitalism and Schizophrenia*, trans. by Robert Hurley, Mark Seem, and Helen R. Lane (Minneapolis: University of Minnesota Press, 1983a).

Deleuze, Gilles and Guattari, Félix, *On the Line*, trans. by John Johnstone (New York: Semiotext(e), 1983b).

Deleuze, Gilles and Guattari, Félix, *A Thousand Plateaus: Capitalism and Schizophrenia*, trans. by Brian Massumi (London: Bloomsbury Academic, 2013a).

Deleuze, Gilles and Guattari, Félix, *What is Philosophy?*, trans. by Hugh Tomlinsin and Graham Burchill (London: Verso, 2013b).

Derrida, Jacques, *Of Grammatology* (Baltimore, MD: Johns Hopkins University Press, 1974).

Dijksterhuis, Ap, 'Think Different: The Merits of Unconscious Thought in Preference Development and Decision Making', *Journal of Personality and Social Psychology*, 87, 5 (2004), 586–598.

Donovan, Shaun, 'Promoting the American Dream of Homeownership' (August 2013). https://obamawhitehouse.archives.gov/blog/2013/08/06/promoting-american-dream-homeownership (accessed 23 September 2018).

Dudouet, Veronique, Fischer, Martina, and Schmelzle Beatrix, 'Dealing with the Past in Israel-Palestine and in the Western Balkans: Story-telling in Conflict: Developing Practice and Research'. *Berghof Working Paper No. 5* (2008). http://www.berghof-foundation.org/fileadmin/redaktion/Publications/Other_Resources/wp5e_workshop_report_bar_on.pdf (accessed 1 August 2016).

Easwaran, Eknath (trans.), *The Dhammapada* (Tomales, CA: Blue Mountain Centre of Meditation, 2007).

Ehrenreich, Barbara, *Smile or Die: How Positive Thinking Fooled America and the World* (London: Granta Books, 2010).

Elden, Stuart, *Understanding Henri Lefebvre: Theory and the Possible* (London: Continuum, 2004).

Esposito, Elena, 'An Ecology of Differences: Communication, the Web, and the Question of Borders', in *General Ecology: The New Ecological Paradigm*, ed. by Erich Hörl with James Burton (London: Bloomsbury Academic, 2017), pp. 285–301.

European Council, *Conclusions – 16–17 December 2010, EUCO 30/1/10 REV 1* (Brussels: European Council, 2010). http://www.consilium. europa.eu/uedocs/cms_data/docs/pressdata/en/ec/118578.pdf (accessed 22 July 2016).

Fanon, Frantz, *The Wretched of the Earth*, trans. by Constance Farrington (London: Penguin Books, 2001).

Federal Reserve Bank of New York, 'Total Household Debt Reaches $17.05 trillion in Q1 2023; Mortgage Loan Growth Slows'. https:// www.newyorkfed.org/newsevents/news/research/2023/20230515 (accessed 26 July 2023).

Finlayson, Alan, 'Nationalism as Ideological Interpellation: The Case of Ulster Loyalism', *Ethnic and Racial Studies*, 19, 1 (1996), 88–112.

Fisher, Mark, *Capitalist Realism: Is There No Alternative?* (Winchester: O Books, 2009).

Fitzgerald, Paul B., Laird, Angela R., Maller, Jerome, and Daskalakis, Zafiris J., 'A Meta-analytic Study of Changes in Brain Activation in Depression', *Human Brain Mapping*, 29 (2008), 683–695.

Fitzpatrick, Noel, 'Symbolic Misery and Aesthetics – Bernard Stiegler', *Proceedings of the European Society for Aesthetics*, 6 (2014), pp. 114–128.

Flett, Gordon, L., Besser, Avi, Hewitt, Paul L., and Davis, Richard A., 'Perfectionism, Silencing the Self, and Depression', *Personality and Individual Differences*, 43, 5 (2007), 1211–1222.

Foucault, Michel, *Discipline and Punish: The Birth of the Prison*, trans. by Alan Sheridan (London: Penguin Books, 1991).

Foucault, Michel, 'What is Critique?', in *The Politics of Truth* (Los Angeles, CA: Semiotext(e), 1997), pp. 41–81.

Foucault, Michel, *The Order of Things: An Archaeology of the Human Sciences* (London: Routledge Classics, 2002).

Free Network Foundation, FAQ. https://thefnf.org/faq/ (accessed 4 August 2016).

Freer, Alexander, 'Rhythm as Coping', *New Literary History*, 46, 3 (2015), 549–568.

Freud, Sigmund, 'Mourning and Melancholia', in *The Standard Edition of the Complete Psychological Works of Sigmund Freud, Vol. 14: 1914–1916: On the History of the Psycho-analytic Movement, Papers on Metapsychology, and Other Works*, ed. and trans. by James Strachey

(London: The Hogarth Press and the Institute of Psychoanalysis, 1957), pp. 237–258.

Freud, Sigmund, 'A Note Upon the "Mystic Writing Pad"', in *The Standard Edition of the Complete Psychological Works of Sigmund Freud, Vol. 19: 1923–1925: The Ego and the Id and Other Works*, ed. and trans. by James Strachey (London: The Hogarth Press and the Institute of Psychoanalysis, 1961), pp. 227–232.

Frieling, Rudolf, 'Toward Participation in Art', in *The Art of Participation: 1950 to Now*, ed. by R. Frieling (London: Thames & Hudson, 2008), pp. 32–49.

Gallagher, Shaun, 'The Socially Extended Mind', *Cognitive Systems Research* (2013). http://dx.doi.org/10.1016/j.cogsys.2013.03.008

Gallope, Michael, *Deep Refrains: Music, Philosophy, and the Ineffable* (Chicago, IL: University of Chicago Press, 2017).

Genosko, Gary, *The Party Without Bosses: Lessons on Anti-Capitalism from Félix Guattari and Luís Inácio 'Lula' da Silva* (Winnipeg: Arbeiter Ring Publishing, 2003).

Genosko, Gary, 'A-signifying Semiotics', *The Public Journal of Semiotics*, II, 1 (2008), 11–21.

Genosko, Gary, *Critical Semiotics: Theory, from Information to Affect* (London: Bloomsbury Academic, 2016).

Genosko, Gary, *The Reinvention of Social Practices: Essays on Félix Guattari* (London: Rowman & Littlefield International, 2018).

Geoghegan, Bernard Dionysius, *Code: From Information Theory to French Theory* (Durham, NC: Duke University Press, 2023).

Gilbert-Walsh, James, 'Revisiting the Concept of Time: Archaic Perplexity in Bergson and Heidegger', *Human Studies*, 33, 2 (2010), 173–190.

Gille, Bertrand, *The History of Techniques, Volume 1: Techniques and Civilizations*, trans. by P. Southgate and T. Williamson (London: Gordon and Breach Science Publishers, 1986).

Gilroy, Paul, *The Black Atlantic: Modernity and Double Consciousness* (Cambridge, MA: Harvard University Press, 1993).

Gilroy-Ware, Marcus, *Filling the Void: Emotion, Capitalism and Social Media* (London: Repeater Books, 2017).

Goleman, Daniel and Davidson, Richard J., *Altered Traits: Science Reveals How Meditation Changes Your Mind, Brain, and Body* (New York: Avery, 2017).

Goodman, Steve, *Sonic Warfare: Sound, Affect, and the Ecology of Fear* (London: The MIT Press, 2012).

Goodwin, Brian, 'Biology Is Just a Dance', in *The Third Culture*, ed. by John Brockman (New York: Touchstone, 1996), pp. 96–110.

Graeber, David, *Debt: The First 5,000 Years* (New York: Melville House, 2012).

Gratch, Linda Valden, Bassett, Margaret E., and Attra, Sharon L., 'The Relationship of Gender and Ethnicity to Self-Silencing and Depression Among College Students', *Psychology of Women Quarterly*, 19 (1995), 509–515.

Guattari, Félix, *Molecular Revolution: Psychiatry and Politics*, trans. by Rosemary Sheed (Middlesex: Penguin Books, 1984).

Guattari, Félix, *Chaosmose* (Paris: Éditions Galilée, 1992).

Guattari, Félix, *Chaosmosis: An Ethico-Aesthetic Paradigm*, trans. by Paul Bains and Julian Pefanis (Sydney: Power Publications, 2006).

Guattari, Félix, *The Three Ecologies*, trans. by Ian Pindar and Paul Sutton (London: Bloomsbury, 2014).

Guattari, Félix, *Lines of Flight: For Another World of Possibilities*, trans. by Andrew Goffey (London: Bloomsbury, 2016).

Guattari, Félix and Negri, Antonio, *Communists Like Us: New Spaces of Liberty, New Lines of Alliance*, trans. by Michael Ryan (New York: Semiotext(e), 1990).

Guattari, Félix and Rolnik, Suely, *Molecular Revolution in Brazil*, trans. by Karel Clapshow and Brain Holmes (Los Angeles, CA: Semiotext(e), 2007).

Habermas, Jürgen, *The Theory of Communicative Action, Volume 2: Lifeworld and System: A Critique of Functionalist Reason*, trans. by Thomas McCarthy (Boston, MA: Beacon Press, 1987).

Hall, Gary, *Pirate Philosophy: For a Digital Posthumanities* (Cambridge, MA: The MIT Press, 2016).

Han, Byung-Chul, *The Burnout Society*, trans. by Erik Butler (Stanford, CA: Stanford University Press, 2015).

Han, Byung-Chul, *Psychopolitics: Neoliberalism and New Technologies of Power*, trans. by Erik Butler (London: Verso, 2017).

Harcourt, Bernard E., 'Political Disobedience', *Critical Inquiry*, 39, 1 (2012), 33–55.

Harlan, Volker, 'A Note on the Text', in *What is Art?: Conversation with Joseph Beuys*, ed. by Volker Harlan, trans. by Matthew Barton and Shelley Sacks (West Hoathly: Clairview Books, 2004).

Harman, Graham, *Bruno Latour: Reassembling the Political* (London: Pluto Press, 2014).

Harney, Stefano and Moten, Fred, *The Undercommons: Fugitive Planning and Black Study* (Brooklyn, NY: Autonomedia, 2013).

Harris, Sam, *Waking Up: A Guide to Spirituality Without Religion* (London: Black Swan, 2015).

Harris, S., Kaplan, J. T., Curiel, A., Bookheimer, S. Y., Iacoboni, M., and Cohen, M. S., 'The Neural Correlates of Religious and Nonreligious Belief', *PLOS ONE*, 4, 10 (2009), e7272.

Haworth, Michael, 'Bernard Stiegler on Transgenerational Memory and the Dual Origin of the Human', *Theory, Culture & Society*, 33, 3 (2016), 151–173.

Heaney, Conor, 'What is the University Today?', *Journal for Critical Education Policy Studies*, 13, 2 (2015), 287–314.

Heaney, Conor, 'The Academic, Ethics and Power', in *Engaging Foucault: Volume I*, ed. by Adriana Zaharijevic, Igor Cvejić, and Mark Losoncz (Belgrade: Institute for Philosophy and Social Theory, 2016), pp. 185–201.

Heaney, Conor, 'Stupidity and Study in the Contemporary University', *La Deleuziana*, 5 (2017), 5–31.

Heaney, Conor, 'Pursuing Joy with Deleuze: Transcendental Empiricism and Affirmative Naturalism as Worldly Practice', *Deleuze and Guattari Studies*, 12, 3 (2018), 374–401.

Heaney, Conor, 'The Disparity Between Culture & Technics', *Culture, Theory and Critique*, 60, 3–4 (2019), 193–204.

Heaney, Conor, 'Rhythmic Nootechnics: Stiegler, Whitehead, and Noetic Life', *Educational Philosophy and Theory*, 52 (4), 2020, 397–408.

Heaney, Conor, *Rhythm: New Trajectories in Law* (Oxon: Routledge, 2023).

Heaney, Conor, 'On the Clock: *Uber* and the Chronopolitics of Control', in *The Routledge Handbook of the Lived Experience of Ideology*, ed. by Başak Ertür, Naveed Mansoori, James Martel, and Connal Parsley (forthcoming).

Heaney, Conor and Mackenzie, Hollie, 'The Teaching Excellence Framework: Perpetual Pedagogical Control in Postwelfare Capitalism', *Compass: A Journal of Learning and Teaching*, 10, 2 (2017).

Heath, Deana, 'School Curriculum Continues to Whitewash Britain's Imperial Past', *The Conversation* (January 2016). http://theconversa tion.com/school-curriculum-continues-to-whitewash-britains-im perial-past-53577 (accessed 3 August 2016).

Heidegger, Martin, *Being and Time*, trans. by John Macquarrie and Edward Robinson (Oxford: Blackwell Publishing Ltd, 2013).

Heroux, Erick, 'Guattari's Triplex Discourses of Ecology', in *An [Un] Likely Alliance: Thinking Environment[s] with Deleuze|Guattari*, ed. by Bernd Herzogenrath (Newcastle upon Tyne: Cambridge Scholars Publishing, 2008), pp. 176–195.

Holland, Eugene W., *Deleuze and Guattari's Anti-Oedipus: An Introduction to Schizoanalysis* (London: Routledge, 1999).

Holland, Eugene W., 'Studies in Applied Nomadology: Jazz Improvisation and Post-Capitalist Markets', in *Deleuze and Music*, ed. by Ian Buchanan and Marcel Swiboda (Edinburgh: Edinburgh University Press, 2004), pp. 20–35.

Hörl, Erich, 'A Thousand Ecologies: The Process of Cyberneticization and General Ecology', trans. by Jeffrey Kirkwood, James Burton, and Maria Vlotides, in *The Whole Earth: California and the Disappearance of the Outside*, ed. by Diedrich Diederichsen and Anselm Franke (Berlin: Sternberg Press, 2013), pp. 121–130.

HR Leadership Forum to Target Depression in the Workplace, *Depression in the Workplace in Europe: A Report Featuring New Insights from Business Leaders* (2014). http://targetdepression.com/wp-content/uploads/2014/04/TARGET_Report_Final.pdf (accessed 18 November 2015).

Hui, Yuk, *On the Existence of Digital Objects* (Minneapolis: University of Minnesota Press, 2016a).

Hui, Yuk, *The Question Concerning Technology in China: An Essay in Cosmotechnics* (Falmouth: Urbanomic, 2016b).

Hui, Yuk, 'Archives of the Future – Remarks on the Concept of Tertiary – Protention', *Inscription* (2018), 129–151.

Hume, David, *An Enquiry Concerning Human Understanding* (New York: Oxford University Press, 2007).

Husserl, Edmund, *Analyses Concerning Passive and Active Syntheses: Lectures on Transcendental Logic*, trans. by Anthony J. Steinbock (Dordrecht: Kluwer, 2001).

Hyppolite, Jean, *Logic and Existence*, trans. by Leonard Lawlor and Amit Sen (New York: State University of New York, 1997).

Ikoniadou, Eleni, 'A Rhythmic Time for the Digital', *The Senses and Society*, 7, 3 (2012), 261–275.

Ikoniadou, Eleni, 'Abstract Time and Affective Perception in the Sonic Work of Art', *Body & Society*, 20, 3–4 (2014a), 140–161.

Ikoniadou, Eleni, *The Rhythmic Event: Art, Media, and the Sonic* (Cambridge, MA: The MIT Press, 2014b).

Iliadis, Andrew, 'Informational Ontology: The Meaning of Gilbert Simondon's Concept of Individuation', *communication +1*, 2 (2013).

Jack, Dana C., *Silencing the Self: Women and Depression* (New York: HarperPerennial, 1993).

Jack, Dana C. and Ali, Alisha (eds), *Silencing the Self Across Cultures: Depression and Gender in the Social World* (Oxford: Oxford University Press, 2010).

Jacobs, B. L., Praag, H. van, and Gage, F. H., 'Adult Brain Neurogenesis and Psychiatry: A Novel Theory of Depression', *Molecular Psychiatry*, 5 (2000), 262–269.

Jones, Phil and Warren, Saskia, 'Time, Rhythm and the Creative Economy', *Transactions of the Institute of British Geographers*, 41 (2016), 286–296.

Kandel, Eric R., 'The Biology of Memory: A Forty-Year Perspective', *Journal of Neuroscience*, 29, 41 (2009), 12748–12756.

Kant, Immanuel, *The Conflict of the Faculties*, trans. by Mary J. Gregor (Lincoln: University of Nebraska Press, 1979).

Kant, Immanuel, *The Critique of Judgement*, trans. by J. H. Bernard (New York: Prometheus Books, 2000).

Kelly, Gráinne, '"Storytelling" Audit: An Audit of Personal Story, Narrative and Testimony Initiatives Related to the Conflict in and About Northern Ireland', *Healing Through Remembering* (2005). http://cain.ulst.ac.uk/issues/victims/docs/kelly0905storytelling.pdf (accessed 1 August 2016).

Kelso, J. A. Scott, *Dynamic Patterns: The Self-Organization of Brain and Behavior* (Cambridge, MA: The MIT Press, 1995).

Killingsworth, Matthew A. and Gilbert, Daniel T., 'A Wandering Mind is an Unhappy Mind', *Science*, 330, 6006 (2010), 932.

Kittler, Friedrich, *Gramophone, Film, Typewriter*, trans. by G. Winthrop-Young and M. Wutz (Stanford, CA: Stanford University Press, 1999).

Kleiner, Dmytri, *The Telekommunist Manifesto* (Amsterdam: Institute of Network Cultures, 2010).

Konings, Martijn, 'Financial Affect', *Distinktion: Scandinavian Journal of Social Theory*, 15, 1 (2014), 37–53.

Korzybski, Alfred, *Science and Sanity: An Introduction to Non-Aristotelian Systems and General Semantics* (Brooklyn, NY: Institute of General Semantics, 1994).

Kramer, Adam D. I., Guillory, Jamie E., and Hancock, Jeffrey T., 'Experimental Evidence of Massive-scale Emotional Contagion Through Social Networks', *Proceedings of the National Academy of Sciences of the United States of America*, 111, 24 (2014), 8788–8790.

Krieger, Janice L., 'Shared Mindfulness in Cockpit Crisis Situations: An Exploratory Analysis', *Journal of Business Communication*, 42, 2 (2005), 135–167.

Kurzweil, Ray, *The Singularity is Near: When Humans Transcend Biology* (New York: Viking Books, 2005).

Kymlicka, Will, 'Liberal Equality', in Will Kymlicka, *Contemporary Political Philosophy: An Introduction* (Oxford: Oxford University Press, 2002), pp. 53–75.

Laasonen-Balk, T., Viinamäki, H., Kuikka, J. T., Husso-Saastamoinen, M., Lehtonen, J., and Tiihonen, J, '1231-beta-CIT Binding and Recovery from Depression: A Six-month Follow-up Study', *European Archives of Psychiatry and Clinical Neurosciences*, 254 (2004), 152–155.

The Lancet, 'Neuromarketing: Beyond Branding', *Lancet Neurology*, 3, 2 (2004), 71.

Lanier, Jaron, *Who Owns the Future?* (London: Penguin Books, 2013).

Lasn, Kalle, *Meme Wars: The Creative Destruction of Neoclassical Economics* (New York: Seven Stories Press, 2012).

Latour, Bruno, *We Have Never Been Modern*, trans. by Catherine Porter (Cambridge, MA: Harvard University Press, 1991).

Latour, Bruno, 'On Interobjectivity', *Mind, Culture, and Activity: An International Journal*, 3 (1996), 228–245.

Lazenby, J. F., *The Spartan Army* (Chicago, IL: Bolchazy-Carducci, 1985).

Lazzarato, Maurizio, 'Immaterial Labour', in *Radical Thought in Italy: A Potential Politics*, ed. by Paolo Virno and Michael Hardt (Minneapolis: University of Minnesota Press, 1996), pp. 133–147.

Lazzarato, Maurizio, *The Making of the Indebted Man: An Essay on the Neoliberal Condition*, trans. by Joshua David Jordon (Los Angeles, CA: Semiotext(e), 2012).

Lazzarato, Maurizio, *Signs and Machines: Capitalism and the Production of Subjectivity*, trans. by Joshua David Jordan (Los Angeles, CA: Semiotext(e), 2014).

Lazzarato, Maurizio, *Governing by Debt*, trans. by Joshua David Jordon (South Pasadena, CA: Semiotext(e), 2015).

Lazzarato, Maurizio, *Experimental Politics: Work, Welfare, and Creativity in the Neoliberal Age*, trans. by Arianna Bove, Jeremy Gilbert, Andrew Goffey, Mark Hayward, Jason Read, and Alberto Toscano (Cambridge, MA: The MIT Press, 2017).

Lechte, John, 'Eleven Theses on Sculpture', *Art & Design*, 55 (1997), 18–21.

Lefebvre, Henri, *The Survival of Capitalism: Reproduction of the Relations of Production*, trans. by Frank Bryant (New York: St. Martin's Press, 1976).

Lefebvre, Henri, *Dialectical Materialism*, trans. by John Sturrock (Minneapolis: University of Minnesota Press, 2009).

Lefebvre, Henri, *Rhythmanalysis: Space, Time and Everyday Life*, trans. by Stuart Elden and Gerald Moore (London: Bloomsbury, 2015).

Lefebvre, Henri, 'Critique of Everyday Life, Volume I: Introduction', trans. by John Moore, in *Critique of Everyday Life: The One Volume Edition* (London: Verso, 2014a), pp. 1–272.

Lefebvre, Henri, 'Critique of Everyday Life, Volume II: Foundations for a Sociology of the Everyday', trans. by John Moore, in *Critique of Everyday Life: The One Volume Edition* (London: Verso, 2014b), pp. 273–652.

Lefebvre, Henri, 'Critique of Everyday Life, Volume III: From Modernity to Modernism (Towards a Metaphilosophy of Daily Life)', trans. by Gregory Elliot, in *Critique of Everyday Life: The One Volume Edition* (London: Verso, 2014c), pp. 653–842.

Leibniz, Gottfried Wilhelm, *Discourse on Metaphysics and Other Essays*, trans. by Daniel Garber and Roger Ariew (Cambridge, MA: Hackett Publishing Company, 1991).

Lensink, Robert, *Structural Adjustment in Sub-Saharan Africa* (New York: Longman, 1996).

Leroi-Gourhan, André, *L'homme et la Matière* (Paris: Albin Michel, 1943).

Leroi-Gourhan, André, *Gesture and Speech*, trans. by Anna Bostock Berger (London: The MIT Press, 1993).

Leuchter, Andrew, Cook, Ian, Uijtdehaage, Sebastian, Dunkin, Jennifer, B. Lufkin, R., Anderson-Hanley, Cay, Abrams, M., Rosenberg-Thompson, S., O'Hara, Ruth, Simon, Sara, Osato, S., and Babaie, A., 'Brain Structure and Function and the Outcomes of Treatment for Depression', *The Journal of Clinical Psychiatry*, 58, Supplement 16 (1997), 22–31.

Lewis, Marc, *The Biology of Desire: Why Addiction is Not a Disease* (London: Scribe Publications, 2016).

Lordon, Frédéric, *Willing Slaves of Capital: Spinoza and Marx on Desire*, trans. by Gabriel Ash (London: Verso, 2014).

Lukács, Georg, *History and Class Consciousness*, trans. by Rodney Livingstone (London: The Merlin Press Ltd, 1971).

Lünen, Alexander von, 'Beuys Don't Cry: From Social Sculptures to Social Media', in *The Digital Arts and Humanities: Neogeography, Social Media and Big Data Integrations and Applications*, ed. by Charles Travis and Alexander von Lünen (Switzerland: Springer Geography, 2016), pp. 23–45.

Lutz, A., Brefczynski-Lewis, J., Johnstone, T., and Davidson, R. J., 'Regulation of the Neural Circuitry of Emotion by Compassion Meditation: Effects of Meditative Expertise', *PLOS ONE*, 3, 3 (2008a), e1897.

Lutz, Antoine, Slagter, Heleen A., Dunne, John D., and Davidson, Richard J., 'Attention Regulation and Monitoring in Meditation', *Trends in Cognitive Sciences*, 12, 4 (2008b), 163–169.

Lutz, Antoine, Greischar, Lawrence L., Rawlings, Nancy B., Ricard, Matthieu, and Davidson, Richard J., 'Long-term Meditators

Self-induce High-amplitude Gamma Synchrony During Mental Practice', *Proceedings of the National Academy of Sciences*, 101, 46 (November 2004), 16369–16373.

Lyon, Dawn and Coleman, Rebecca, 'Rupture, Repetition, and New Rhythms for Pandemic Times: Mass Observation, Everyday Life, and COVID-19', *History of the Human Sciences*, 36, 2 (2023), 26–48.

McCracken, Lance M. and Vowles, Kevin E., 'Acceptance and Commitment Therapy and Mindfulness for Chronic Pain: Model, Process, and Progress', *American Psychologist*, 69, 2 (February-March 2014), 178–187.

McDaid, David and Park, A.-La et al., *The Economic Case for Investing in the Prevention of Mental Health Conditions in the UK*. 2022. https://www.mentalhealth.org.uk/sites/default/files/2022-06/MHF-Investing-in-Prevention-Full-Report.pdf (accessed 26 June 2023).

MacKenzie, Iain, *The Idea of Pure Critique* (London: Continuum, 2004).

MacKenzie, Iain and Porter, Rob, 'Dramatization as Method in Political Theory', *Contemporary Political Theory*, 10 (2011), 482–501.

McNeill, William, *Keeping it Together in Time: Dance and Drill in Human History* (Cambridge, MA: Harvard University Press, 1995).

Malaspina, Cécile, 'Epistemic Noise', *Systema*, 2, 1 (2014), 48–58.

Malaspina, Cécile, *An Epistemology of Noise* (London: Bloomsbury Academic, 2018).

Malinen, Fanny, 'The "Golden Noose" of Global Finance', *ROAR Magazine*, 3 (2016), 72–81.

Manning, Erin and Massumi, Brain, *Thought in the Act: Passages in the Ecology of Experience* (Minneapolis: University of Minnesota Press, 2014).

Marx, Karl, 'Comments on James Mill, *Eléments d'Economie Politique*', in *Karl Marx, Frederick Engels: Collected Works, Volume 3, Marx and Engels: 1843–1844*, trans. by Clemens Dutt (London: Lawrence & Wishart, 1975), pp. 211–228.

Marx, Karl and Engels, Frederick, *The German Ideology: Part One*, ed. by C. J. Arthur (London: Lawrence and Wishart, 2007).

Marx, Karl and Engels, Frederick, 'The German Ideology', in *Karl Marx, Frederick Engels: Collected Works, Volume 5, Marx and Engels: 1845–1847*, trans. by Clemens Dutt, W. Lough, and C. P. Magill (London: Lawrence & Wishart, 2010), pp. 15–452.

Massumi, Brian, *A User's Guide to Capitalism and Schizophrenia: Deviations from Deleuze and Guattari* (Cambridge, MA: The MIT Press, 1992).

Massumi, Brian, *Parables for the Virtual: Movement, Affect, Sensation* (London: Duke University Press, 2002).

Massumi, Brian, *Ontopower: War, Powers, and the State of Perception* (London: Duke University Press, 2015a).

Massumi, Brian, *Power at the End of the Economy* (London: Duke University Press, 2015b).

Massumi, Brian, *The Principle of Unrest: Activist Philosophy in the Expanded Field* (London: Open Humanities Press, 2017a).

Massumi, Brian, 'Virtual Ecology and the Question of Value', in *General Ecology: The New Ecological Paradigm*, ed. by Erich Hörl with James Burton (London: Bloomsbury Academic, 2017b), pp. 345–373.

Mazzilli-Daechsel, Stefano, 'Simondon and the Maker Movement', *Culture, Theory and Critique*, 60, 3–4 (2019), 237–249.

Merriman, Peter, 'Molar and Molecular Mobilities: The Politics of Perceptible and Imperceptible Movements', *Environment and Planning D: Society and Space* (2018).

Messiaen, Olivier, *Music and Color: Conversations with Claude Samuel*, trans. by E. Thomas Glasgow (Oregon: Amadeus Press, 1994).

Michon, Pascal, *Elements of Rhythmology: 1. Antiquity* (Paris: Rhuthmos, 2018).

Mignolo, Walter D., *The Darker Side of Western Modernity: Global Futures, Decolonial Options* (London: Duke University Press, 2011).

Mill, John Stuart, *Utilitarianism* (Chicago, IL: University of Chicago Press, 1906).

Mitchell, W. J. T., 'Image, Space, Revolution: The Arts of Occupation', *Critical Inquiry*, 39, 1 (2012), 8–32.

Monk, Ellis P., 'The Cost of Color: Skin Color, Discrimination, and Health among African-Americans', *American Journal of Sociology*, 121, 2 (2015), 396–444.

Moore, Gerald, '*Adapt and Smile or Die!* Stiegler Among the Darwinists', in *Stiegler and Technics*, ed. by Christina Howells and Gerard Moore (Edinburgh: Edinburgh University Press, 2013), pp. 17–33.

Moore, Jason W., *Capitalism in the Web of Life: Ecology and the Accumulation of Capital* (London: Verso, 2015).

Motta, Sara C., 'Decolonising Critique: From Prophetic Negation to Prefigurative Affirmation', in *Social Sciences for an Other Politics: Women Theorizing Without Parachutes*, ed. by A. C. Dinerstein (Basingstoke: Palgrave Macmillan, 2016), pp. 33–48.

Nakagawa, Atsuo, Mitsuda, Dai, Sado, Mitsuhiro, Abe, Takayuki, Fujisawa, Daisuke, Kikuchi, Toshiaki, Iwashita, Satoru, Mimura, Masaru, and Ono, Yutaka, 'Effectiveness of Supplementary Cognitive-Behavioral Therapy for Pharmacotherapy-Resistant Depression: A Randomized Controlled Trial', *Journal of Clinical Psychiatry*, 78, 8 (September/October 2017), 1126–1135.

Nakagawa, Atsuo, Sado, Mitsuhiro, Mitsuda, Dai, Fujisawa, Daisuke, Kikuchi, Toshiaki, Abe, Takayuki, Sato, Yuji, Iwashita, Satoru, Mimura, Masaru, and Ono, Yutaka, 'Effectiveness of Cognitive Behavioural Therapy Augmentation in Major Depression Treatment (ECAM Study): Study Protocol for a Randomised Clinical Trial', *BMJ Open*, 4, 10 (2014), e006359.

Nancy, Jean-Luc, *Listening*, trans. by Charlotte Mandell (New York: Fordham University Press, 2007).

Nash, Louise and Lyon, Dawn, 'Work, Boredom and Rhythm in the Time of COVID-19', *The Sociological Review*, 71, 3 (2023), 642–659.

Nestler, Eric J., Barrot, Michel, DiLeone, Ralph J., Eisch, Amelia J. Gold, Stephen J., and Monteggia, Lisa M., 'Neurobiology of Depression', *Neuron*, 34, 1 (2002), 13–25.

Nietzsche, Friedrich, *The Twilight of the Idols*, trans. by R. J. Hollingdale (New York: Penguin, 1968).

Nietzsche, Friedrich, *Thus Spoke Zarathustra: A Book for Everyone and No One*, trans. by R. J. Hollingdale (London: Penguin Books, 2003).

Nietzsche, Friedrich, *'On the Genealogy of Morality' and Other Writings*, ed. by Keith Ansell-Pearson, trans. by Carol Diethe (Cambridge: Cambridge University Press, 2017).

Norris, Pippa, *Digital Divide: Civic Engagement, Information Poverty, and the Internet Worldwide* (Cambridge: Cambridge University Press, 2001).

O'Donnell, Aislinn, 'Shame is Already a Revolution: The Politics of Affect in the Thought of Gilles Deleuze', *Deleuze Studies*, 11 (1), 2017, 1–24.

Otter, Chris, *The Victorian Eye: A Political History of Light and Vision in Britain, 1800–1900* (Chicago, IL: Chicago University Press, 2008).

Pettman, Dominic, *Infinite Distraction: Paying Attention to Social Media* (Cambridge: Polity Press, 2016).

Pickett, Kate and Wilkinson, Richard, *The Spirit Level: Why More Equal Societies Almost Always Do Better* (London: Allen Lane, 2009).

Pickett, Kate and Wilkinson, Richard, *The Inner Level: How More Equal Societies Reduce Stress, Restore Sanity and Improve Everyone's Wellbeing* (London: Allen Lane, 2018).

Pickert, Kate, 'The Art of Being Mindful. Finding Peace in a Stressed-Out, Digitally Dependent Culture Might Just Be a Matter of Thinking Differently', *Time*, 3 (2014), 40–46.

Piketty, Thomas, *Capital in the Twenty-First Century*, trans. by Arthur Goldhammer (London: The Belknap Press of Harvard University Press, 2014).

Plutarch, *Plutarch's Lives*, trans. by Bernadotte Perrin (London: William Heinemann Ltd, 1914).

Prigogine, Ilya and Stengers, Isabelle, *Order Out of Chaos: Man's New Dialogue with Nature* (London: Bantam Books, 1984).

Protevi, John, *Political Affect: Connecting the Social and the Somatic* (Minneapolis: University of Minnesota Press, 2009).

Protevi, John, *Life, War, Earth: Deleuze and the Sciences* (Minneapolis: University of Minnesota Press, 2013).

Railton, Peter, 'Nietzsche's Normative Theory? The Art and Skill of Living Well', in *Nietzsche, Naturalism and Normativity*, ed. by Christopher Janaway and Simon Robertson (Oxford: Oxford University Press, 2012), pp. 20–51.

Rancière, Jacques, *The Nights of Labour: The Workers' Dream in Nineteenth-Century France*, trans. by John Drury (Philadelphia, PA: Temple University Press, 1989).

Rancière, Jacques, *The Politics of Aesthetics: The Distribution of the Sensible*, trans. by Gabriel Rockhill (London: Continuum, 2004).

Rancière, Jacques, *The Future of the Image*, trans. by Gregory Elliott (London: Verso, 2009).

Raunig, Gerald, *Dividuum: Machinic Capitalism and Molecular Revolution Vol. 1*, trans. by Aileen Derieg (South Pasadena, CA: Semiotext(e), 2016).

Ravaisson, Félix, *Of Habit*, trans. by Clare Carlisle and Mark Sinclair (London: Continuum, 2008).

Rawls, John, *A Theory of Justice* (Oxford: Oxford University Press, 1999).

Reid-Musson, Emily, 'Intersectional Rhythmanalysis: Power, Rhythm, and Everyday Life', *Progress in Human Geography*, 42, 6 (2018), 881–897.

Reigeluth, Tyler Butler, 'Why Data is Not Enough: Digital Traces as Control of Self and Self-control', *Surveillance & Society*, 12, 2 (2014), 243–254.

Renvoisé, Patrick and Morin, Christophe, *Neuromarketing: Understanding the 'Buy Button' in Your Customer's Brain* (Nashville, TN: T. Nelson, 2007).

Risk, Mysoon, 'Fields in Flux: At the Threshold of Becoming-Animal Through Social Sculpture', *Angelaki*, 11, 1 (2006), 137–146.

Ritter, Maria, 'Silence as the Voice of Trauma', *The American Journal of Psychoanalysis*, 74, 2 (2014), 176–194.

Rölli, Marc, *Gilles Deleuze's Transcendental Empiricism: From Tradition to Difference*, trans. by Peter Hertz-Ohmes (Edinburgh: Edinburgh University Press, 2016).

Romero-Canyas, Rainer, Reddy, Kavita S., Rodriguez, Sylvia, and Downey, Geraldine, 'After All I Have Done For You: Self-Silencing Accommodations Fuel Women's Post-Rejection Hostility', *Journal of Experimental Social Psychology*, 49, 4 (2013), 732–740.

Rose, Nikolas and Abi-Rached, Joelle, *Neuro: The New Brain Sciences and the Management of the Mind* (Princeton, NJ: Princeton University Press, 2013).

Rose, Nikolas and Abi-Rached, Joelle, 'Governing through the Brain: Neuropolitics, Neuroscience and Subjectivity', *Cambridge Anthropology*, 32, 1 (2014), 3–23.

Ross, Andrew, *Creditocracy: And the Case for Debt Refusal* (London: OR Books, 2013).

Rouvroy, Antoinette, 'The End(s) of Critique: Data-behaviourism vs. Due-process', in *Privacy, Due Process and the Computational Turn: Philosophers of Law Meet Philosophers of Technology*, ed. by Mireille Hildebrandt and Ekatarin De Vries (London: Routledge, 2013), pp. 143–167.

Saarinen, P. L., Lehtonen, J., Joensuu, M., Tolmunen, T., Ahola, P., Vannin- en, R., Kuikka, J., and Tiihonen, J. 'An Outcome of Psychodynamic Psychotherapy: A Case Study of the Change in Serotonin Transporter Binding and the Activation of the Dream Screen', *American Journal of Psychotherapy*, 59 (2005), 61–73.

Sampson, Tony D., *The Assemblage Brain: Sense Making in Neuroculture* (Minneapolis: University of Minnesota Press, 2017).

Sandbeck, Sune and Schneider, Etienne, 'From the Sovereign Debt Crisis to Authoritarian Statism: Contradictions of the European State Project', *New Political Economy*, 19, 6 (2014), 847–871.

Sanín-Restrepo, Ricardo, *Decolonizing Democracy: Power in a Solid State* (London: Rowman & Littlefield, 2016).

Savulescu, Julia and Persson, Ingmar, 'The Perils of Cognitive Enhancement and the Urgent Imperative to Enhance the Moral Character of Humanity', *Journal of Applied Philosophy*, 25, 3 (2008), 162–167.

Savulescu, Julia and Persson, Ingmar, *Unfit for the Future: The Need for Moral Enhancement* (Oxford: Oxford University Press, 2012).

Savulescu, Julia and Persson, Ingmar, 'Getting Moral Enhancement Right: The Desirability of Moral Bioenhancement', *Bioethics*, 27, 3 (2013), 124–131.

Sayers, Sean, 'Marxism and the Dialectical Method: A Critique of G. A. Cohen', in *Socialism, Feminism and Philosophy: A Radical Philosophy Reader*, ed. by Sean Sayers and Peter Osborne (London: Routledge, 1990), pp. 140–169.

Sayers, Sean, 'Contradiction and Dialectic', *Science & Society*, 55, 1 (1991), 84–91.

Sayers, Sean, 'Progress and Social Criticism', *The European Legacy*, 2, 3 (1997), 544–549.

Schaeffer, Robert K., *Understanding Globalization* (Lanham, MD: Rowman & Littlefield, 2003).

Schaff, Adam, 'Marxist Theory on Revolution and Violence', *Journal of the History of Ideas*, 34, 2 (1973), 263–270.

Schmidt, Vivien A., 'Speaking to the Markets or to the People? A Discursive Institutionalist Analysis of the EU's Sovereign Debt Crisis', *The British Journal of Politics and International Relations*, 16, 1 (2014), 188–209.

Schultz, Theodore W., 'Capital Formation by Education', *Journal of Political Economy*, 68, 6 (1960), 571–583.

Schultz, Theodore W., *Investment in Human Capital: The Role of Education and Research* (London: Collier-Macmillan Limited, 1971).

Serres, Michel, *Genesis*, trans. by Geneviève James and James Nielson (Ann Arbor: University of Michigan Press, 1995).

Shannon, Claude E., 'The Mathematical Theory of Communication', in *The Mathematical Theory of Communication*, ed. by Claude E. Shannon and Warren Weaver (Chicago, IL: University of Illinois Press, 1998), pp. 29–115.

Shāntideva, *The Way of the Bodhisattva*, trans. by The Padmakara Translation Group (Boulder, CO: Shambhala, 2006).

Shapiro, S. L., Oman, D., Thoresen, C. E., Plante, T. G., and Flinders, T., 'Cultivating Mindfulness: Effects on Well-Being', *Journal for Clinical Psychology*, 64, 7 (2008), 840–862.

Shaw, Robert, 'Bringing Deleuze and Guattari Down to Earth through Gregory Bateson: Plateaus, Rhizomes and Ecosophical Subjectivity', *Theory, Culture & Society*, 32, 7–8 (2015), 151–171.

Simondon, Gilbert, 'Technical Mentality', trans. by Arne De Boever, *Parrhesia*, 7 (2009a), 17–27.

Simondon, Gilbert, 'The Position of the Problem of Ontogenesis', trans. by G. Flanders, *Parrhesia*, 7 (2009b), 4–16.

Simondon, Gilbert, 'Culture and Technics', trans. by O. L. Fraser, revised by G. Menegalle, *Radical Philosophy*, 189 (2015), 17–23.

Simondon, Gilbert, *On the Mode of Existence of Technical Objects*, trans. by Cécile Malaspina and John Rogove (Minneapolis, MN: Univocal, 2017).

Smith, Linda Tuhiwai, *Decolonizing Methodologies: Research and Indigenous Peoples* (London: Zed Books, 2012).

Spencer-Oatey, Helen, 'Mindfulness for Intercultural Interaction. A Compilation of Quotations', *GlobalPAD Core Concepts*, 2013. https://www2.warwick.ac.uk/fac/soc/al/globalpad/openhouse/intercultur alskills/mindfulness.pdf (accessed 20 July 2016).

Spinoza, Benedict de, *Ethics*, trans. by Edwin Curley (London: Penguin Books, 1996).

Stahl, Titus, 'Habermas and the Project of Immanent Critique', *Constellations*, 20, 4 (2013), 533–552.

Stiegler, Bernard, *Technics and Time, 1: The Fault of Epimetheus*, trans. by Richard Beardsworth and George Collins (Stanford, CA: Stanford University Press, 1998).

Stiegler, Bernard, *Technics and Time, 2: Disorientation*, trans. by Stephen Barker (Stanford, CA: Stanford University Press, 2009).

Stiegler, Bernard, *For a New Critique of Political Economy*, trans. by Daniel Ross (Cambridge: Polity Press, 2010a).

Stiegler, Bernard, *Taking Care of Youth and the Generations*, trans. by Steven Barker (California, CA: Stanford University Press, 2010b).

Stiegler, Bernard, *The Decadence of Industrial Democracies: Disbelief and Discredit, Volume I*, trans. by Daniel Ross and Suzanne Arnold (Cambridge: Polity Press, 2011a).

Stiegler, Bernard, *Technics and Time, 3: Cinematic Time and the Question of Malaise*, trans. by Stephen Barker (Stanford, CA: Stanford University Press, 2011b).

Stiegler, Bernard, 'Relational Ecology and the Digital *Pharmakon*', *Culture Machine*, 13 (2012), 1–19.

Stiegler, Bernard, *The Re-Enchantment of the World: The Value of Spirit Against Industrial Populism*, trans. by Trevor Arthur (London: Bloomsbury, 2014a).

Stiegler, Bernard, *Symbolic Misery Volume 1: The Hyper-industrial Epoch*, trans. by Barnaby Norman (Cambridge: Polity Press, 2014b).

Stiegler, Bernard, *Symbolic Misery Volume 2: The Katastrophē of the Sensible*, trans. by Barnaby Norman (Cambridge: Polity Press, 2015).

Stiegler, Bernard, *Automatic Society: Volume 1, The Future of Work*, trans. by Daniel Ross (Cambridge: Polity Press, 2016a).

Stiegler, Bernard, '*Ars* and Organological Inventions in Societies of Hyper-Control', ed. by Colette Tron, trans. by Daniel Ross, *Leonardo*, 49, 5 (2016b), 480–484.

Stiegler, Bernard, 'General Ecology, Economy, and Organology', trans. by Daniel Ross, in *General Ecology: The New Ecological Paradigm*, ed. by Erich Hörl with James Burton (London: Bloomsbury Academic, 2017a), pp. 129–150.

Stiegler, Bernard, 'The New Conflict of the Faculties and Functions: Quasi-Causality and Serendipity in the Anthropocene', trans. by Daniel Ross, *Qui Parle*, 26, 1 (2017b), 79–99.

Stiegler, Bernard, *The Negathropocene*, ed. and trans. by Daniel Ross (London: Open Humanities Press, 2018).

Stiglitz, Joseph E., *Economics of the Public Sector* (London: W. W. Norton & Company, 2000).

Strike Debt, *The Debt Resisters' Operations Manual* (Oakland, CA: PM Press, 2014a).

Strike Debt, 'Principles of Solidarity' (March 2014b). http://strikedebt. org/principles/ (accessed 2 August 2016).

Suquet, Annie, 'Archaic Thought and Ritual in the Work of Joseph Beuys', *RES: Anthropology and Aesthetics*, 28 (1995), 148–162.

Sutter, de, Laurent, *Narcocapitalism: Life in the Age of Anaesthesia*, trans. by Barnaby Norman (Cambridge: Polity Press, 2018).

Swim, Janet K., Eyssell, Kristen M., Murdoch, Erin Quinlivan, and Ferguson, Melissa J., 'Self-Silencing to Sexism', *Journal of Social Issues*, 66 (2010), 493–507.

Tan, Josephine and Carfagnini, Brooke, 'Self-silencing, Anger and Depressive Symptoms in Women: Implications for Prevention and Intervention', *Journal of Prevention & Intervention in the Community*, 35, 2 (2008), 5–18.

Taylor, Astra, *The People's Platform: Taking Back Power and Culture in the Digital Age* (London: Fourth Estate, 2014).

Thiong'o, Ngũgĩ wa, *Decolonising the Mind: The Politics of Language in African Literature* (Oxford: James Curry, 2005).

Thornton, Cassie and Haiven, Max, 'The Debts of the American Empire', *ROAR Magazine*, 3 (2016), 58–71.

Tiebout, Charles Mills, 'A Pure Theory of Local Expenditures', *Journal of Political Economy*, 64 (1956), 416–424.

Tisdall, Caroline, *Joseph Beuys* (London: Thames & Hudson, 1979).

Toffler, Alvin, *Future Shock* (London: The Bodley Head, 1970).

Trebitsch, Michel, 'Preface: The Moment of Radical Critique', in Henri Lefebvre, 'Critique of Everyday Life, Volume II: Foundations for a Sociology of the Everyday', trans. by John Moore, in *Critique of Everyday Life: The One Volume Edition* (London: Verso, 2014b), pp. 277–293.

Trost, Wiebke, 'Time Flow and Musical Emotions: The Role of Rhythmic Entrainment', in *Timing of Affect: Epistemologies, Aesthetics, Politics*, ed. by Marie-Luise Angerer, Bernd Bösel, and Michaela Ott (Zurich/Berlin: Diaphanes, 2014), pp. 207–223.

Turetsky, Phil, 'Rhythm: Assemblage and Event', in *Deleuze and Music*, ed. by Ian Buchanan and Marcel Swiboda (Edinburgh: Edinburgh University Press, 2004), pp. 140–158.

Turner, Ben, *Returning to Judgment: Bernard Stiegler and Continental Political Theory* (New York: State University of New York Press, 2023).

Valéry, Paul, *Cahiers*, vol. 2, ed. by Judith Robertson (Paris: Gallimard, 'La Pléiade', 1974).

Vaneigem, Raoul, *The Revolution of Everyday Life*, trans. by Donald Nicholson-Smith (Oakland, CA: PM Press, 2012).

Varela, Francisco J., Thompson, Evan, and Rosch, Eleanor, *The Embodied Mind: Cognitive Science and Human Experience, Revised Edition* (Cambridge, MA: The MIT Press, 2016).

Verwoert, Jan, 'The Boss: On the Unresolved Question of Authority in Joseph Beuys Oeuvre and Public Image', *e-flux journal 1* (December 2008). http://www.e-flux.com/journal/01/68485/the-boss-on-the-unresolved-question-of-authority-in-joseph-beuys-oeuvre-and-public-image/ (accessed 22 June 2017).

Vignola, Paolo, 'Symptoms and Speed of νοῦς: Toward a Critical Invention of the Future', *London Journal of Critical Thought*, 1 (2016), 38–48.

Virilio, Paul, *The Administration of Fear*, trans. by Ames Hodges (Los Angeles, CA: Semiotext(e), 2012).

Volkan, Vamik D., 'Not Letting Go: From Individual Perennial Mourners to Societies with Entitlement Ideologies', in *On Freud's 'Mourning and Melancholia'*, ed. by Leticia Glocer Fiorini, Thierry Bokanowski, and Sergio Lewkowicz (London: Karnac Books, 2009), pp. 90–109.

Waddell, Gordon and Burton, A. Kim, *Is Work Good for Your Health and Well-Being?* (London: The Stationary Office, 2006). https://assets.publishing.service.gov.uk/government/uploads/system/uploads/attachment_data/file/214326/hwwb-is-work-good-for-you.pdf (accessed 14 June 2018).

Weber, Max, *The Protestant Ethic and the Spirit of Capitalism*, trans. by Talcott Parsons (London: Routledge Classics, 2001).

West-Eberhard, Mary Jane, *Developmental Plasticity and Evolution* (New York: Oxford University Press, 2003).

Whitehead, Alfred North, *The Function of Reason* (Princeton, NJ: Princeton University Press, 1929).

Whitehead, Alfred North, *Symbolism: Its Meaning and Effect* (New York: Fordham University Press, 1985).

Wiener, Norbert, *Cybernetics: Or Control and Communication in the Animal and the Machine* (Cambridge, MA: The MIT Press, 1961).

Wiles, Nicola, Thomas, Laura, Abel, Anna, Ridgway, Nicola, Turner, Nicholas, Campbell, John, Garland, Anne, Hollinghurst, Sandra, Jerrom, Bill, Kessler, David, Kuyken, Willem, Morrison, Jill, Turner, Katrina, Williams, Chris, Peters, Tim, and Lewis, Glyn, 'Cognitive Behavioural Therapy as an Adjunct to Pharmacotherapy for Primary Care Based Patients With Treatment Resistant Depression: Results of the CoBalT Randomised Controlled Trial', *The Lancet*, 381, 9864 (2012), 375–384.

Wiles, Nicola, Thomas, Laura, Abel, Anna, Barnes, Maria, Carroll, Fran, Ridgway, Nicola, Sherlock, Sofie, Turner, Nicholas, Button,

Katherine, Odondi, Lang'o, Metcalfe, Chris, Owen-Smith, Amanda, Campbell, John, Garland, Anne, Hollinghurst, Sandra, Jerrom, Bill, Kessler, David, Kuyken, Willem, Morrison, Jill, Turner, Katrina, Williams, Chris, Peters, Tim, and Lewis, Glyn, 'Clinical Effectiveness and Cost-effectiveness of Cognitive Behavioural Therapy as an Adjunct to Pharmacotherapy for Treatment-resistant Depression in Primary Care: The CoBalT Randomised Controlled Trial', *Health Technology Assessment*, 18, 31 (2014).

Williams, David R. and Williams-Morris, Ruth, 'Racism and Mental Health: The African American Experience', *Ethnicity & Health*, 5, 3–4 (2000), 243–268.

Williams, James, *A Process Philosophy of Signs* (Edinburgh: Edinburgh University Press, 2016).

Wilson, Elizabeth A., *Gut Feminism* (London: Duke University Press, 2015).

Winnubst, Shannon, 'The Queer Thing about Neoliberal Pleasure: A Foucauldian Warning', *Foucault Studies*, 14 (2012), 79–97.

Witte, Tricia and Sherman, Martin, 'Silencing the Self and Feminist Identity Development', *Psychological Reports*, 90 (2002), 1075–1083.

Wittgenstein, Ludwig, *Tractatus Logico-Philosophicus*, trans. by D. F. Pears and B. F. McGuinness (London: Routledge Classics, 2001).

Wozniak, Jason Thomas, 'Debt, Education, and Decolonization', in *Encyclopedia of Educational Philosophy and Theory*, ed. by M. A. Peters (Singapore: Springer Science+Business Media, 2017), pp. 345–352.

Zepke, Stephen, 'The Readymade: Art as the Refrain of Life', in *Deleuze, Guattari and the Production of the New*, ed. by Simon O'Sullivan and Stephen Zepke (London: Continuum, 2008), pp. 33–44.

Zepke, Stephen, 'Eco-Aesthetics: Beyond Structure in the Work of Robert Smithson, Gilles Deleuze and Félix Guattari', in *Deleuze | Guattari & Ecology*, ed. by Bernd Herzogenrath (Basingstoke: Palgrave Macmillan, 2009), pp. 200–215.

Žižek, Slavoj, 'Cyberspace, or the Virtuality of the Real', *Journal for the Centre for Freudian Analysis & Research*, 7 (1996).

Žižek, Slavoj, 'From History and Class Consciousness to Dialectic of Enlightenment . . . and Back', *New German Critique*, 81 (2000), 107–123.

Žižek, Slavoj, *Did Somebody Say 'Totalitarianism'?* (London: Verso, 2001).

Žižek, Slavoj, *The Year of Dreaming Dangerously* (London: Verso, 2012).

Filmography

'eps1.0_hellofriend.mov', Mr. Robot. Written by Sam Esmail. Directed by Niels Arden Oplev. USA Network. 24 June 2015. Television.

Free the Network: Hackers Take Back the Web, Motherboard. March 2012. https://www.youtube.com/watch?v=Fx93WJPCCGs (accessed 4 August 2016).

'Gilbert Simondon – The Technical Object as Such'. Eidos84. November 2012. https://www.youtube.com/watch?v=eXDtG74hCL4 (accessed 23 September 2018).

'The Racial Politics of Time', Brittney Cooper, TED. TEDWomen. October 2016. https://www.ted.com/talks/brittney_cooper_the_racial_politics_of_time (accessed 6 March 2017).

Last Week Tonight with John Oliver, 'Season 3, Episode 14'. Directed by Paul Pennolino. Home Box Office (HBO). 5 June 2016. Television.

Index

EU representative:
Easy Access System Europe
Mustamäe tee 50, 10621 Tallinn, Estonia
Gpsr.requests@easproject.com